Praise for *Welcome to the Re*

"This book is joyfully jammed with the wisdom, experience, tools, vation to overcome the ravages of the corporate state. On page after page, the theme is about building democratic initiatives and institutions for the common good—and the good life of justice, peace, and freedom. So gripping and personal is *Welcome to the Revolution*, you can scarcely put this book down without putting yourself down. Read, digest, reflect, and join with others for a functioning democracy."

—**Ralph Nader**, consumer advocate and author of *Unstoppable: The Emerging Left/Right Alliance to Dismantle the Corporate State* and *Breaking Through Power: It's Easier Than You Think*

"*Welcome to the Revolution* could not have come at a better moment. With the election of Donald Trump, millions of Americans suddenly found themselves attending women's rallies, supporting sanctuary cities, protesting Islamophobia, confronting their elected officials—even doing civil disobedience or running for local office. But activists, and the movements they are part of, need strategy, they need direction, they need to know not just what they are resisting but what transformations they aim for. Charles Derber's brilliant and inspiring new book provides the glue that will help us craft a revolutionary movement that can resist, transform, and prevail. Read it!"

—**Medea Benjamin**, co-founder of CODEPINK and of Global Exchange, and author of *Kingdom of the Unjust* and *Drone Warfare*

"Charlie Derber's new book calls us all both to work harder on our particular issues and to get out of our silos to make common cause with others to change the system as a whole. This is the right message for the Trump era, and it is presented in powerful, moral, and practical terms. A must read for anyone serious about building a meaningful and positive future!"

—**Gar Alperovitz**, co-founder of the Next System Project and author of *What Then Must We Do? Straight Talk About the Next American Revolution*

"Derber has written the theoretical and practical manifesto for this historical moment, reminding us of the tremendous possibilities at hand. *Welcome to the Revolution* explains how extractive capitalism has led to expanding systemic social, economic, and ecological system disruptions. Yet these same forces have seeded 'universalizing resistance' movements that, if they succeed, will push us back from the brink and toward a next system that is more democratic, equal, and peaceful and lives in harmony with the earth's ecological limits. To find out how you can 'universalize' and make a difference, read this book."

—**Chuck Collins**, Senior Fellow at the Institute for Policy Studies and author of *Born on Third Base*

"Activists the world over are connecting the dots: our struggles are linked, our liberation is collective, and our best hope is each other. *Welcome to the Revolution* shows us why 'universalizing resistance' is so important and so necessary, and offers a clear and compelling road map for how to do it. Essential and inspiring reading for these dark times."

—**Dave Oswald Mitchell**, co-editor of *Beautiful Trouble* and of *Beautiful Rising*

"*Welcome to the Revolution* is critically important and a timely call to action—a compelling book about universalizing resistance. Through persuasion and example, Derber demonstrates how single-issue or siloed activists can forge alliances both locally and transnationally towards transforming militarized capitalism. Personal stories from a broad range of activists and lucid political analysis welcome readers to the revolution, demonstrating that many have begun to live the alternative world we want to see. This is a must read for seasoned activists as well as newcomers to organizing for transformative change."

—**M. Brinton Lykes**, co-director of the Center for Human Rights and International Justice, Boston College, and winner of the American Psychological Association's International Humanitarian Award

"Thought-provoking and necessary, Charles Derber's *Welcome to the Revolution* is a timely assessment of how capitalism and partisan movements have led to our current political environment. Covering a range of movements and policies, *Welcome to the Revolution* provides a rich and deeply fascinating take on the rise of Trump and the failures of the Right and Left along the way. A must read."

—**Marcus Hunter**, Professor of Sociology and African-American Studies, UCLA, and author of *Black Citymakers: How The Philadelphia Negro Changed Urban America*

"This book by preeminent scholar Charles Derber helps us to understand the deep significance of this historical moment and that we only have one choice—to confidently and assuredly join the growing protest as we articulate alternatives that are just and fair. Teachers of various course topics who want their students to understand how we arrived at this scary moment—and what they can actually do to help save democracy—will want this wise and learned 'guide book' for their students. All citizens awakening to the frightening politics of the Trump era will find here an inspiring account about what they're facing and what to do."

—**Judith Blau**, author of *Human Rights: A Primer* and founder of Sociologists without Borders

"How can people and communities forge unity and solidarity within a 'socio-pathic' global capitalist system built on division, exploitation, and conquest? Drawing from a wealth of scholarly and activist sources, Charles Derber provides a clear and accessible analysis of the systemic forces that have produced today's multiple crises and that reinforce 'silo activism.' This systemic perspective informs the roadmap he offers, which builds upon the collective wisdom of past struggles for social justice, to guide movements for '*progressive universalism*.' This book will be invaluable to everyone—including both newly engaged and experienced activists and teachers—hoping to help realize the necessary and '*Greatest Transformation of all time*.'"

—**Jackie Smith**, Professor at the University of Pittsburgh and author of *Social Movements for Global Democracy*

"The unexpected electoral victories of Brexit and Trump have temporarily overshadowed a wave of mobilization by progressive grass-roots movements, which has been growing and spreading since the turn of the Millennium all over the globe. This thought provoking book reminds us however that, even if fragile and repressed by powerful elites, a convergence of struggles can be triggered by the very threats that these perilous times bring about for democracy and social justice. The challenge, in the US as elsewhere, is in universalizing the resistance through convergence, a not easy, but definitively needed shift."

—**Donatella della Porta**, Director of Centre of Social Movements Studies Scuola Normale Superiore, Italy

Other books (selected) by Charles Derber:

PEOPLE BEFORE PROFIT: THE NEW GLOBALIZATION IN THE AGE OF TERROR, BIG MONEY AND ECONOMIC CRISIS
"Charles Derber helps vault the globalization debates to the next level . . . it will help kick-start a much-needed debate on the principles that should unite our world." —NAOMI KLEIN

REGIME CHANGE BEGINS AT HOME: FREEING AMERICAN FROM CORPORATE RULE
"Charles Derber is one of our most astute and eloquent social critics . . . His political analysis is persuasive and is enlivened by graceful prose, all aimed with perfect timing . . ." —HOWARD ZINN

SOCIOPATHIC SOCIETY: A PEOPLE'S SOCIOLOGY OF THE UNITED STATES
"Shows that there remains real hope that mass mobilization by currently fragmented social movements can reverse the sociopathic impetus." —NOAM CHOMSKY

BULLY NATION: HOW THE AMERICAN ESTABLISHMENT IS CREATING A BULLYING SOCIETY
"A canny and sobering look at bully behavior and how it permeates our nation's major institutions." —OLIVER STONE

CORPORATION NATION: HOW CORPORATIONS ARE TAKING OVER OUR LIVES AND WHAT WE CAN DO ABOUT IT
"A work of generous imagination that looks wisely to the future and lays out a sober plan of action for Americans committed to a truly just and equitable social order." —JONATHAN KOZOL

GREED TO GREEN: SOLVING CLIMATE CHANGE AND REMAKING THE ECONOMY
"This is the right book at the right—and crucial—moment." —BILL MCKIBBEN

WELCOME TO
THE REVOLUTION

Universalizing Resistance for Social Justice and Democracy in Perilous Times

Charles Derber

A Revolutionary Progressive Strategy for the Trump Era and Beyond

Routledge
Taylor & Francis Group
NEW YORK AND LONDON

First published 2017
by Routledge
711 Third Avenue, New York, NY 10017

and by Routledge
2 Park Square, Milton Park, Abingdon, Oxon, OX14 4RN

Routledge is an imprint of the Taylor & Francis Group, an informa business

© 2017 Taylor & Francis

Library of Congress Cataloging-in-Publication Data
A catalog record for this book has been requested

ISBN: 978-1-138-64819-7 (hbk)
ISBN: 978-1-138-64820-3 (pbk)
ISBN: 978-1-315-62656-7 (ebk)

Typeset in Avenir LT Std
by Apex CoVantage, LLC

Printed and bound in the United States of America by Sheridan

With Love and Gratitude to my Amazing Sister,
Clara Bloomfield

Acknowledgments

This book is an act of solidarity, created by a community of people working to create social justice and save the world. I am grateful to everyone who has helped me and devoted overburdened time to support this project.

In one of our many improvisational conversations, Randall Wallace not only helped inspire the idea of "universalizing resistance" but made the book possible by supporting it with a generous grant from the Wallace Action Fund. Randall's devotion to books, critical thinking and visionary activism continuously inspires me.

I also want to thank Randall's wife, Janet, who has inspired me with her own universalizing activism to defend indigenous rights, protect nature, and bring justice to women and children everywhere. I am grateful for the brilliant original essay she contributed on the resistance at Standing Rock.

Dean Birkenkamp, my editor at Routledge, has been indispensible to me as friend, critical thinker, activist colleague, and extraordinary editor. This book could not have been accomplished without him. He worked tirelessly on every aspect of the book, and devoted more of his time and creativity than any author has a right to expect. In many ways, this is our joint book.

I want to thank my friends and colleagues on my Advisory Council, who include Chuck Collins, Suren Moodliar, Paul Shannon, Jonathan White, and Shelley White. They contributed enormously to the vision of the project and the evolving drafts of the book. Their support and help made it clear that writing is a collective enterprise, and that inspiration comes best in a loving community.

I also deeply thank the wider circle of inspiring thinkers and activists who contributed original short essays to the book. Many helped bring the book to the attention of their own organizations and colleagues—building the Universalizing Resistance Network. These include Juman Abujbara, Gar Alperovitz, Katherine Asuncion, Medea Benjamin, Andrew Boyd, Noam Chomsky, Chuck Collins, Bill Fletcher, Jr., Corrie Grosse, Janet MacGillivray Wallace, Ben Manski, Dave Mitchell, Suren Moodliar, Ralph Nader, Matt Nelson, Jodeen Olguin-Tayler, Alana Yu-lan Price, Mike Prokosch, Fred Redmond, Jamala Rogers, Maya Schenwar, Juliet B. Schor, Paul Shannon,

Mark Solomon, Marcel Taminato, John Trumpbour, Jonathan White, Shelley White, and Sofia Wolman. No author could have a more brilliant contributing community of scholars and activists. Whatever merits this book has is due in large part to their generosity of time and the originality and importance of their own essays. They have made this book a collective "living voice" of our movements, and a "master class" in creating social change from some our greatest change-makers.

I want to thank, in particular, Ralph Nader and Noam Chomsky, who have so deeply inspired my own thinking and took precious time to contribute important essays to the book.

Suren Moodliar, whom I mentioned earlier, has not only written a wonderful essay but helped me at every stage of the project. Suren has taken many extra hours consulting with me on ideas, activist strategies, groups to reach out to, and ways that the book can reach and catalyze new waves of activism. I want to thank Suren for all his brilliant intellectual feedback, insights and generous support.

I thank Joseph Gerson at the American Friends Service Committee who offered support and helped arrange feedback from local thinkers and activists. I also thank Paul Shannon again for the feedback on the book that he offered along with astute commentary from Mark Solomon, Weimin Gobeil-Tchen, and Cole Harrison during meetings of the Majority Agenda Project.

And I want to thank Matt Nelson for his many helpful insights and for suggesting the book's title.

I have received wonderful support from all the people at Routledge, involved with different aspects of the book—a big thank you to all of them.

I want to thank many colleagues, students and friends at Boston College, and especially David Karp and John Williamson, who offered support and affirmation that is precious to any writer.

And, finally, I want to thank Elena Kolesnikova, whose love and support kept me going from start to finish. Without her, none of my work would be possible.

Contents

Interludes

A Personal Prelude

Dear Reader,

I don't think I was born to be an activist.

I don't like confrontation. I don't like anger.

I don't like asking for things or demanding things.

And I've always been very busy, in my career, and with my friends and personal life. I don't have a lot of time to be an activist.

I've often been unsure if activism will produce results. Activism is a gamble. It may or may not create the democracy and social justice that I feel passionate about.

The 1% may beat the rest of us. They seem to have the cards and the jokers.

Despite all these doubts, I have been an activist all my life.

When I was 6 years old, my mother took me to the doctor, who wanted to prick my finger for a routine blood test. I ran out of his exam office, climbed up on a chair in the waiting room and gave a passionate speech about my rights.

This activism ended badly. The doctor and nurse picked me up, unceremoniously carried me back into the exam room, and drew the blood they wanted.

But it didn't end my activism.

In the 1960s, I went to Mississippi to join the civil rights movement. I almost got shot when I drove on back roads in the South with Black friends. I spent some time in Mississippi jails, as I tried to help to overcome the Jim Crow laws and register people to vote.

And then I went to graduate school and spent my time eating too many baloney sandwiches on thin white bread with spoiled mayonnaise in crowded prisons in Washington DC, when I was arrested multiple times for trying to levitate the Pentagon, or at least shut it down. I tried to stop traffic crossing from Washington DC over the bridge into Virginia toward the Pentagon. I protested against military companies making napalm and other chemical weapons for Vietnam. I helped to start a national student strike against the war and participated in one of the first campus occupations protesting the draft.

My activism never quite ended, though it waxed and waned over the years. Activism became part of my writing, my teaching, and my life on campus and in the media and the community. I continued it partly because it was so fulfilling and meaningful, connecting me to causes larger than myself and to some of the most wonderful people I ever met.

When the movements seemed to fade, I kept making the case for them, joining protests supporting living wages for janitors; trying to prevent my university from giving an honorary degree to Condoleezza Rice for her role in starting the war in Iraq, arguing with Bill O'Reilly on his show, *The O'Reilly Factor*, about why our protests were justified; and giving hundreds of radio interviews and writing scores of op eds and books about why we needed to act to create a less violent and fairer world.

After Donald Trump came to power in the 2016 Republican sweep, leading toward an ever more authoritarian society, I saw the stirring of another activist wave, that reminds me a little of the 1960s. It crested on the streets of scores of US cities for weeks before and after Trump's election. The day after the Inauguration, the gigantic Women's March brought a record number of hundreds of thousands of protestors to Washington DC and to cities in all 50 states, saying "Trump is not my President." January 21, 2017 may have witnessed the biggest number of protesters on the street in any day of history, with an estimated 3 million protesters on seven continents. It evoked memories of the huge anti-war and civil rights demonstrations of the turbulent 1960s and the global protests against President George W. Bush's 2003 invasion of Iraq.

Many protesters—backed up by large organizations, unions, and social movements—spoke over and over about solidarity and unity. They were hopeful and non-violent and loving. They would build a new movement and run for office, and protest every day of Trump's Presidency until he was gone.

But this rising movement actually began in the years before Trump—against the Establishment that he too claimed to fight. It surfaced on campuses, in a new civil rights movement led by African-American students, in Black Lives Matter activists protesting police violence, in protests against walling off or banning immigrants led by Hispanic and Muslim-American communities, movements against US drone wars around the world, in student and community fights to divest from oil and gas companies and block their pipelines, in labor struggles for worker rights and a higher minimum wage, in Occupy Wall Street, targeting the big financial institutions where the 1% of the 1% makes its billions and erodes democracy with big money, and in "democracy movements" challenging an ever more oligarchic and authoritarian capitalism.

Protesters at Women's March, January 21, 2017

Photo Credit: Janet MacGillivray Wallace

And just beneath the surface of this progressive activist wave, even before Trump's election, was the fear of apocalypse. In an age of climate change, weapons of mass destruction, and militarized capitalism, there is the painful recognition that our very survival is at stake. All these rising movements are somehow interconnected by the realization that failure dooms all future generations as well as thousands of other living species.

It is this terrifying reality—of growing authoritarianism, symbolized and intensified by Trump, and of looming extinction that arises from the militarized corporate system preceding and creating him—that animates the new activism and leads me to write this book.

Of course, the new progressive grass-roots movement wave is fragile, and Trumpism may appear to make it irrelevant, perhaps by crushing it with police and Big Brother repression.

But the rise of Trump and Republican dominance make the progressive activism that I focus on in this book even more important. It is the last best hope not only for social justice and human survival, but for stopping the rise of an American police state or neo-fascism. Trump's Presidency may actually help to "universalize" the new progressive grass-roots movements by helping them mobilize far more members and bringing them together in a far larger and more unified life-and-death struggle, against Trumpism and the larger authoritarian and bullying corporate system that assisted in creating him. The aim is to bring an end to that system and create a revolution for a new society that will enshrine ideals of democracy, equality, peace, and sustainability.

The system has always had the potential to create the universalizing resistance that will overcome it. Its economic crises have now become so widespread, its injustice so painful, and its violence and looming catastrophes so omnipresent that much of the public has lost faith in the system itself. While this helped to elect Trump, it has opened the door wide to activists of all political stripes, including the progressive activists on the ground—and their potential allies in Washington DC and around the world—who are the focus of this book and the pioneers of the political and social revolution we need.

I think we can survive—and resist both US authoritarianism and corporatism while creating a democratic revolution—only if the majority of Americans either become the kind of activist I describe in this book—or support those who do. Economic, cultural, and demographic shifts, along with the outrages of Trumpism, will likely create more of the activists I describe—and increase their long-term prospects for progressive revolution.

Might you be one of the following three main audiences I hope to reach in this book?

1) *Are you an activist or advocate for democracy and social justice?*
   If so, you are one of my heroes—and part of a crucial community I want to reach and engage. Transformative change comes from the bottom, through grass-roots advocacy and social movements. This book is an effort to help you think through the great challenges of our current struggles.

   I believe there are serious problems in the way that we have organized our progressive movements since the 1960s. We need to change dramatically the culture and structure of our activism. We need a new wave of progressive grass-roots movements that mobilize neighbors in their communities and also work closely together nationally and globally—with broad parts of the Democratic Party and the general public. We must "universalize" our resistance rather than fight alone, or simply resign ourselves to doing nothing.

   The changes we need in our progressive movements are beginning, but they are difficult. For example, the identity movements focusing on rights for people of color, women, the Muslim-American community, and the LGBT (lesbian, gay, bisexual, and transgender) community have achieved heroic gains. These are the groups most vulnerable to terrible repression, symbolized in the first week of the Trump Administration by the banning through executive order on January 28, 2017, of 134 million people in seven Muslim-majority countries, including Green Card holders, from entering the United States. But to protect their populations, identity groups need to help lead the struggle for a new democratic economy and politics, and work with the white working class whose rage at being left behind fueled Trump's rise to power. Likewise, activists fighting economic injustice and the class system need to fight racism and sexism which underpin and bolster the US economic order. And activists in the climate, peace, and labor movements must come together to ensure our very survival.

2) *Are you a student or teacher?*

As a professor, I am also one of you. In a period of great crises, with the future of democracy and human survival at stake, the possibilities of transformation depend on our education. We desperately need a student population and scholarly community committed to critical thinking and passionate citizen action.

Unfortunately, big corporations, conservative Republican politicians, and Far Right social movements have long been trying to take control of the educational system for their own aims. They seek to "dumb down" education, teach to the test, and eliminate critical thinking in the name of vocational training. They discourage questioning of free market dogma and seek to suppress the passion to pursue any kind of free thinking that might challenge ruling elites and the corporate system.

But there is great hope for the younger generation. I see them in my classes every day, and I know how eagerly they respond to new ways of thinking.

Saving the world requires that a new kind of education—linking deep critical thinking with social action—grows rapidly. It's already begun to happen. The support by millions of college students for a socialist activist such as Bernie Sanders for President makes it clear that young people are hungry for deep social change and receptive to a new activism.

In this book, I try to suggest how students and their teachers—and the whole millennial generation—can help to mobilize a revolution in education and our larger society. We need millions of younger and older students and teachers to become more engaged in the struggle to understand our sociopathic, money-driven society and commit to creating a new society.

3) *Are you somebody who may not be an activist but is interested in politics and social change?*

I am also writing for the general public, my third big audience. If you are part of the public, especially if you are interested in politics and social change, this book is for you. Even if you are not an activist, your role as a witness and possible participant in social change is crucial to whether we end inequalities and poverty, successfully resist an anti-democratic regime change led by Trump, or, in the long run, even survive as a species.

No sane person can be indifferent to the apocalyptic crises of climate change, war in an age of nuclear and biological weapons, or a global economy fueling extreme inequality, wage stagnation, vast poverty, and a disinvestment in health, education, and the infrastructure that we all depend on.

All these problems will get worse faster if Far Right movements continue to take ever more power under the guise of Trumpism and a more reactionary and bigoted Republican Party.

The US public is being enclosed in a proverbial bubble. The short-term corporate and authoritarian threats to democracy as well as the longer-term threats to humanity and the survival of other life species are treated too often as non-existent or marginal. And the collective actions that the general public must take to ensure survival itself are themselves largely ignored.

This is a form of collective insanity, something like a cancer patient ignoring or denying his or her own potentially terminal condition. "Establishment" Republican elites and Far Right populists have helped to create this insanity. Trump himself wants to spread nuclear weapons to other countries and famously dismissed climate change as a hoax invented by the Chinese, a madness shared by many of his followers. This disaster can only be un-done by the new educational and political movements I describe in this book.

So I am writing to break through our new collective insanity. It requires simply an openness to new ideas and the courage to recognize the greatest threats we have ever faced—as well as the new societal possibilities that I discuss. And I believe the public will regain its sanity when it recognizes that there are ideas and action that have a real chance of creating economic and social democracy and saving all of us.

The only way we can create justice and survive is by uniting together in new communities and common struggles supported by the majority of the population. We already have many people working for social justice and a new society, but they are scattered in many different small groups and movements, and we haven't figured out how to bring them together—with each other and with the larger public—in what I call universal resistance for social justice, equal rights, and democracy. I believe it is the most important thing we can do to save ourselves and the world. How to do this is what this book is all about.

You may be part of the larger public that has not been—and may never be—activist. Even if you never become an activist, your role is incredibly important. Activists are always a small percentage of the population. What determines our future is not just what activists themselves do, but how the broader public thinks about and responds to what they are doing. Ultimately, the future of the world rests on you: how you understand activism and what different groups of activists are trying to do; whether you decide to support certain social movements on the Left or Right, and how you engage with the struggles that activists are leading.

The entire public can only act responsibly if they have an understanding of social movements and those championing social change. That is why I hope people who are not activists will read this book, recognizing that being a citizen, especially in a world of existential crises, requires, at a minimum, an understanding of the activists and social movements seeking to protect all of us from a world of injustice, violence, and even collective extinction. What could be more important?

Moreover, you may surprise yourself and become more of an activist than you ever imagined. I became an activist because of values I am sure most of you share: a concern for others, a desire to help those in need, a belief in justice, a lack of faith in "the Establishment" and the rich people in power, and a desire to make a difference. I also knew that the United States didn't live up to its high ideals of equality and democracy, and I really believed I had an obligation to help put those ideals into practice.

I also knew that people with power don't give it away. You have to join with others and fight to make your voice heard and to make a difference. Joining together to fight for justice is what social movements are all about—and the United States has had a long history of wonderful social movements: from abolitionism and civil rights, to feminism, to the peace movement, to the labor movement, to immigrant rights, to populist "democracy movements." All these movements have had success but their work is far from done. The most important struggles lie still ahead of us.

I know that taking the time and making the effort to change the world is very difficult. We have our own personal lives—and they are hard. You may feel you just don't have the strength, time, or dedication to work beyond your own personal goals of making your family and career work. I have experienced all these concerns—everybody does, including all activists. This gives everyone the right to make their own choices about when and how to be involved in changing the world.

But even if you are not an activist, at some stages of your life you may become one. Half the millions of people in the anti-Trump Women's March world-wide on January 21, 2017 had never protested before. Unexpected adverse circumstances that affect you politically or personally may make you an activist—and you will want to know what I have written about here. And even should you never become an activist, you are still a citizen and a human being who will help determine—by action or inaction—the success of movements and the future of the world. Is there anything more important than this—and is it not reason enough to read and understand more about how to make change and how to relate to those trying to do so?

There are some limitations I must acknowledge in helping you. One is that I focus primarily on the United States, although my own analysis suggests that we need increasingly to focus on the world system as a whole—since the fate of the entire planet is threatened. Indeed, the long-term goal of universal resistance is creating a globally democratic system and progressive internationalism: a global system ensuring universal human rights and justice around the world. But I know the American scene best and can't survey global activism in one short volume, though I draw on global voices and survey the new corporate globalization and global resistance to it.

As a white male, I also am limited in my ability to express the views of people of color and women. Again, my own analysis suggests this is a serious drawback. I do my best to remedy this by bringing in many important voices of writers and activists who are people of color and female.

I don't just quote these diverse and brilliant activists, but include short "interludes" they have written about universalizing resistance, as well as some "activist autobiographies." These are interspersed through my book, creating a symphony of voices other than my own. You, the reader, can find them in almost every chapter, and can choose to read them after finishing my chapter or in the middle of the chapter where they appear.

Likewise, I have added photos, so that the spirit of activism and universalized resistance jumps out at you not just in words, but in vivid and graphic images.

There are no definitive answers to how change will unfold. While this book was mostly written before Trump's election, and completed during his first 100 days in office, it is intended to further progressive change in any era, certainly beyond Trump and even during more liberal presidential administrations. I am old enough to know that when you ask the big questions, you should always be prepared for surprises. Moreover, despite the best analysis, the answers ultimately come in the doing. That doing has already begun— maybe by you. But I hope that this book gets you more engaged in the conversation and movements to change the world.

There is no time to waste.

Introduction: A Call to Action

"What good is having the right to sit at a lunch counter if you can't afford to buy a hamburger?"

Martin Luther King

"Let us imagine the prospect . . . of a population united for fundamental change . . . It would be a new kind of revolution, the only kind that could happen . . ."

Howard Zinn

"The people united cannot be defeated"

Protest slogan

Stephen Colbert tickles our funny bone with his take on our current plight:

> This is a crucial time in the fight for corporate civil rights. Just look at the hateful signs at Occupy Wall Street: "Corporations Are Not People!" Wow, I thought we were past the point in this country where some people aren't people just because they have different color skin or different religion or were born in a lawyer's office, only exist on paper, have no soul and can never die.[1]

Of course, Colbert is hinting that we may be seeing a long-awaited revolutionary counter-reaction to a corporate system—now headed by President Trump and the many billionaire CEOs in his cabinet—reaching too far into the public till and creating multiple threats to our very survival.

The United States has created some advances in human rights and wellbeing, arising largely from social movements that won reforms. But we have core values and institutions—the "system" Colbert is referencing—whose main aim is to generate profit at a brutal and unsustainable cost.

The system is subversive of the democratic ideals it espouses. It is increasingly authoritarian, with entrenched features of a police state that appear particularly alarming after the election of President Trump. I call this system "militarized corporate capitalism."

While in earlier centuries, it freed millions from ancient forms of bondage and want, today's capitalism helps to create and perpetuate isolation and insecurity, joblessness and extreme inequality, militarism, rule by billionaires, authoritarianism, climate change, racism, xenophobia, and sexism, which are all intertwined and collectively threaten the survival of life on the planet.

A new anti-establishmentarianism—a surprising challenge to the whole system and a passionate fight for a new order—coming both from Left and Right, is growing stronger, symbolized on the Right by President Trump and on the Left by Bernie Sanders. Anti-establishment politics is fueled by ten ways in which the system is spreading or "universalizing":

1. Universalizing Extreme Inequality
2. Universalizing Global Control
3. Universalizing the Corporation and Corporate Power
4. Universalizing Authoritarianism, Militarism, Surveillance, and Repression
5. Universalizing Ideological Control
6. Universalizing Western Ways of Knowing
7. Universalizing Trans-Species Violence and Destruction of Nature
8. Universalizing "Kochamamie" Corporatized Democracy
9. Universalizing Existential Threats to All Life
10. *Universalizing the Death Culture.*

These ten types of system universalizing are creating together a new "stage" of capitalism, which is terrifying, but is also creating new resistance because:

- systemic power is greater than ever before—one might say it is "supersized"—and universalized into all spheres of life and society;
- it is concentrated in a smaller and more tightly connected group of global corporate and financial elites, creating an anti-democratic corporate globalization that is impoverishing and leaving behind millions of workers in the United States and abroad as well as killing the American Dream for millennials and younger generations to follow;
- it is enforced by more extreme violence and repression in an increasingly authoritarian system, laced with bigotry, racism, and xenophobia;
- it is atomizing us and breaking down loving, life-affirming communities.

The power and violence of the system is spreading across the planet, into space, into the earth-based habitats of all living species, into all economic, political, and cultural sectors of society, and deep into our own internal psyches.

This new stage of capitalism is the first to bring the very real prospect of the end of civilized life—indeed all life.

As the system universalizes, we need a new universalizing approach to social change. As the power and violence of the system intensify and spread, and the existential threats to our very survival rise, the resistance against it—and the popular passion for transformation to a truly democratic system—must take on a new form to have any chance of success. The scale of intensifying capitalism and the specter of fascism means we must coalesce in universalizing movements that reinvent resistance itself.

The universalizing system is thus concentrating power, but also watching its control of and legitimacy among the public unravel. We are entering a new period in which the economic and cultural and demographic foundations of the system and its "Establishment" are losing popular support, opening up surprising space for the movements I describe in this book. This became visible—to many for the first time—in the mass outpouring of millions of protesters in the streets during and after President Trump's inauguration.

Contrary to popular wisdom in the age of Trump and Republican dominance, progressive or Left grass-roots activism has not waned or disappeared in the United States. Quite the contrary! Such movements were rising even before Trump—and since his election have been mushrooming into a major movement.

They have become ever more important as Far Right activism has grown and gained new political power. The Republican Party, most notably under President Trump, is increasingly a marriage of corporate elites with Far Right authoritarian movements. Progressive and Left movements discussed in this book are essential to defeating the corporate and Far Right matrix. And, as noted earlier, they have the potential to unite not only with each other and a more progressive Democratic Party, but also with a growing number of disenchanted working-class populists who voted for Trump and have lost faith in the system.

But the progressive and Left movements have a serious problem. For several decades, they have been operating largely in old historical patterns. They are dedicated and inspiring, but they have been largely committed to their own particular causes and issues—and to fighting the new universalized system in the old way. This produces a kind of *"silo activism"* that plays an important role in identifying and fighting specific forms of injustice, but has serious limits. It fails to identify and challenge the overall system that is fueling almost all of the evils we are fighting. It has failed thus far to bring us together in a sustained way in the universalizing resistance we need to build a democratic system-changing revolution.

In a super-universalizing system, we have been de-universalizing our resistance. We have not seen how all our struggles are ever more deeply intertwined; in some ways, we have fragmented progressive movements—at least until Trump's election—more than in earlier periods of mass resistance, such as the 1890s, the 1930s, and the 1960s. We have stayed, as the great African-American writer on mass incarceration, Michelle Alexander, has said, in "our own lanes."[2] She says she will never do so again; in her writing and activism, she is going to cross over into all the other lanes.

This is the right metaphor for progressive universalized resistance. That resistance brings all of our movements and activists and our many unidentified and de-mobilized potential allies in the public—who make up many millions of people—together in a common struggle against the system that threatens harm to everyone, and in favor of a new one that ends those universalizing harms.

What does this resistance look like and how do we build it and a new system? That is the main question of this book. It's a wave of grass-roots democracy and justice movements of unified Black, brown, other people of color, and white people, including many white workers, building a shared vision and infrastructure of popular power to move beyond isolation, joblessness and extreme inequality, militarism, and planetary peril and create a new democratic economy and society. It's ordinary people working together in their neighborhoods and workplaces and local governments—and moving forward in larger organizations and movements—to stop our growing police state and create a new loving and inclusive society. We are seeing the seeds of this universalizing resistance in the Trump era.

Progressive universalizing resistance is non-violent and loving, but it refuses to let the system continue business as usual. Its activists refuse to be a cog in the machine; universalizers use their own bodies to slow the system down and prevent it from spreading more poison and harm.

It aims to create a new system that can sustain a just democratic order and the environment we all depend on. And, as a non-violent democracy movement, it aims for a new society that moves beyond corporate oligarchy, authoritarianism, militarism, racism, sexism, homophobia, and inequality in all forms.

It aims to engage the universal spirit for freedom and justice and survival in all of us. And it aims to bring us together in new life-affirming communities, as part of a new economic and social democracy, one building on the vision that Bernie Sanders called "democratic socialism"—and that, ironically, also may be able to get some traction from the populist economics that Trump campaigned on, even though his version will not benefit the American worker, but rather consolidate the power of his billionaire friends.

There are ten new "rules of the road" for the new movements. Each is a way of responding to universalized system power with new unifying forms of popular power:

1. *Fight the Power, A.K.A. the System*
2. *Win the Majority*
3. *Converge!*
4. *Democratize the World*
5. *Protect Mother Earth*
6. *Say Yes to Alternatives*
7. *Create Media of, by, and for the People*
8. *Let's Get Political*
9. *Think, Learn, and Teach*
10. *Choose Life and Love.*

Major change cannot occur without embracing these ten new rules of the road, and we all need to come together and act on them.

The smarter and faster we build our new movements, the faster we can achieve a great systemic transformation. And time is short; we can no longer dream of an endless time frame to succeed.

Can we expect to witness and participate in a new era of progressive resistance and revolution—particularly in an era of scary right-wing revival and a general public despair about politics and the prospects of progressivist activism? For many, it seems a starry-eyed dream.

And for a good reason. Universalizing resistance today faces formidable hurdles. Right-wing universalizing movements—with millions of white workers represented in their base and funded by activist billionaires such as the Koch brothers—are very potent in the United States and other nations. As noted, the Republican Party has been evolving for several decades as a right-wing universalizing movement. With the election of President Donald Trump, right-wing universalizers won a major triumph. Trump himself calls his Presidency a "movement"—and he is not entirely wrong. Many progressive activists went into deep mourning after his election, fearing he would wipe out their own movements.

But progressive universalizing organizations and movements, while at risk, have been growing for decades and are mushrooming in size since Trump's election. They are building a vision of a new democratic society that counters corporate power with people power; ends hierarchies and inequalities based on class, race, and gender; and creates peace, inclusiveness, and environmental sustainability. Think, just in the United States, of recent big economic and anti-racist movements such as Occupy Wall Street and Black Lives Matter; peace groups such as the American Friends Service Committee, National Peace Action, ANSWER, United for Peace and Justice, and CODEPINK; mass climate movements such as 350.org, Blockadia, and People's Climate Movement; political groups such as MoveOn.org, the Democratic Socialists of America, the Green Party, the Working Families Party, Progressive Democrats of America, the Liberty Tree Foundation for the Democratic Revolution, and Indivisible; labor and anti-corporate groups such as Corporate Accountability International, Moral Monday, minimum-wage movements such as Fight for $15, student debt movements, UNITE HERE, the Service Employees International Union (SEIU), the United Steelworkers, and National Nurses United. There are also activist Unitarian, Quaker, Catholic, Jewish, Muslim, and Protestant religious groups working for equality, immigrant rights, and economic justice; community-based organizations such as National People's Action, City Life, Evergreen Cooperatives, and the People's Assemblies; and indie and movement media such as Democracy Now!, Truthout.org, Presente.org, and the entire Pacifica Network. Think also of the mass outpouring of anger by millions of Americans against the Supreme Court decision "Citizens United" that gave corporations the right to give candidates as much money as they wanted as well as other plutocratic plagues on the constitution, and the new orange, green, jasmine, and velvet "democracy movements" around the world.

These movements helped to bring millions of people out into the streets for days and weeks after Trump's election. *Ironically, Trumpism—the nightmare culmination of the universalizing capitalist system—has begun to catalyze the universalizing resistance that might overthrow the system itself and lead us toward a new one.*

The stability and legitimacy of the Establishment in the United States have severely cracked. This helped to elect Trump and opens the door for new mass resistance on both the Left and the Right. If progressive universalizers do not mobilize for mass movements to counter both the Far Right and the Establishment, the anti-democratic forces will win; thus the rise of Trump and the "Alt-Right" movements makes it more important than ever to build counter-movements of Left activists and liberal Democrats, while also reaching out to disenchanted populist working-class Trumpists.

This book shows why and how this very, very hard work is desirable and do-able.

"Imagine the impossible" has been the slogan of many revolutions. But I suggest here that the creation of the "impossible" is already underway. *Activists—on both Left and Right—are increasingly dissatisfied with the limits of silo activism and are already beginning to universalize.* It is past time

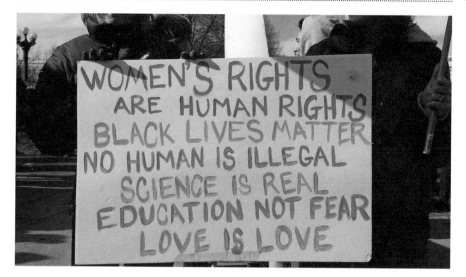

Women's March protest in Denver, Colorado, January 21, 2017

Photo credit: Dean Birkenkamp

for progressive and Left movements—and their millions of supporters in the public who turned out in the streets to protest Trump's inauguration—to urgently and immediately universalize resistance to build a revolutionary new economic and social democracy. It's hard work and there's no guarantee of success. But it is the most meaningful—and often pleasurable—thing you can do. It connects you with others—whether in your neighborhood, workplace, campus, political party, or social movement—and it's a matter of individual dignity, social justice, and collective life or death.

It's always helpful to have a map or guide to a book. So here's your map. I hope it will help you navigate and keep track of where you are on the path.

The book has three Parts.

Part I, with two chapters, is about the system under which we are living and suffering.

Chapter 1 describes the system. It offers a new way of thinking about the intertwining of class, race, and gender in militarized capitalism. Before you change something, you have to understand what it is—and we see it only through a glass darkly. We need light.

Chapter 2 describes how the system is universalizing. This creates a new stage of capitalism and therefore requires a new kind of revolution. Chapter 2 is essential reading because the universalizing of the system creates the need for the new universal resistance that this book is about.

Many of you will want to rush to Part II, which is about how to *change* the system by universalizing resistance. But you wonderful change-makers should be patient and at least glance at Part I, since it provides the reason why we need a new progressive anti-establishment and anti-systemic movement leading toward a democratic revolution.

Part II is the heart of the book. While discussing right-wing movements, it focuses on the fierce and urgent new progressive movement we need. We are trapped in old struggles and we need a new one if we are to survive.

Chapter 3 is a history of the earlier waves of universal resistance—on both Left and Right—that give us guidance for the future. Some of you may have been parts of these waves—and they will bring nostalgia as well as a sense of how the future always draws from the past.

Chapter 4 is a very brief introduction to the key ideas behind universal resistance.

Chapters 5 through to 14 lay out the ten new rules of the road of the new progressive movement we need. They comprise a manifesto for transformative change and the activists and movements that must make it. These are the wake-up calls that most of you are probably looking for—and will want to ponder and see whether you agree. They include stories by activists and thinkers who are beginning to create the vision and carry out the practice of new movement. And they include some lists of possible concrete action items. Do you believe they will work?

Part III is an effort to help you to digest the earlier material and lead you toward your own summary and conclusion.

Chapter 15 raises five major questions about Grand Strategy that emerge from the discussion of the new rules in Part II.

Chapter 16 goes to Nuts and Bolts. It tries to get as concrete as possible about what specific steps we need to take. But as in the whole book, it is less a list of formulaic steps than queries, reminders, and provocations that will help you to decide your next actions.

PART I

THE UNIVERSALIZING SYSTEM: MILITARIZED CORPORATE CAPITALISM AND THE APOCALYPSE

1

The System and Its Discontents: The Militarized Matrix versus Us

"What the main drift of the twentieth century has revealed is that the economy has become concentrated and incorporated in the great hierarchies, the military has become enlarged and decisive to the shape of the entire economic structure; and moreover the economic and the military have become structurally and deeply interrelated, as the economy has become a seemingly permanent war economy; and military men and policies have increasingly penetrated the corporate economy."

C. Wright Mills, 1957

"This country has socialism for the rich and rugged individualism for everyone else."

Martin Luther King

"The prisoners of the system will continue to rebel, as before . . . The new fact of our era is the chance that they may be joined by the guards. We readers and writers of books have been, for the most part, among the guards."

Howard Zinn

DEFINING THE SYSTEM

America's second richest man, Warren Buffett, is becoming an unexpected multi-billionaire populist, saying famously that it's outrageous that his secretary pays a higher tax rate than he does: "My friends and I have been coddled long enough by a billionaire-friendly Congress."[1]

The majority of Americans seem to agree with the oracle from Omaha, telling pollsters for years that something is deeply awry in the United States: that the nation is moving in the wrong direction, that big money is trumping democracy, that inequalities of class, race, and gender are mushrooming while bigotry, xenophobia, violence, and social decay are spiraling out of control. According to progressive movement archivist, Paul Hawken, there are now "tens of millions of people working toward restoration and social justice."[2] Millions of other right-wing activists oppose Hawken's left-leaning activists, but share a hatred of "the Establishment" or what their hero, Donald Trump, called "a rigged system."

What many have not fully grasped is the depth of the systemic crisis and why popular malaise against "the system" is destined to grow. The 99%, whether on Right or Left, are mad as hell and not ready to take it anymore. In 2016, some of the same voters supporting Donald Trump also supported Bernie Sanders. After Trump's election, Left and labor movements such as Fight for $15—to raise the minimum wage to $15—waged massive new protests aimed at building alliances with working-class Trump voters. Resistance to the Establishment is spreading and potentially uniting very strange bedfellows.

Camille Paglia, the literary critic, asks "Are we like late Rome, infatuated with past glories, ruled by a complacent, greedy elite, and hopelessly powerless to respond to changing conditions?"[3] Well, yes to the Rome example, but no to the hopelessly powerless! While it enshrines democratic procedures such as voting, the system has long been run of, by, and for an oligarchic "power elite" of political leaders, military commanders, and corporate executives. Sociologist C. Wright Mills documented this more than half a century ago in his masterpiece, *The Power Elite*. The system wraps itself around ideals of democracy, but it undermines rule by ordinary citizens who dimly sense that corporations are the real "people" in power.

The system incorporates important forms of progress, rights, and creature comforts that help to sustain it even through deep destabilizing crises. To dismiss the technological, material, social, and political advances of capitalism—which Karl Marx himself celebrated as major progress beyond the feudal order it replaced—would be foolhardy. Yet the system prioritizes profit over people; as Marx wrote, capitalism "has left remaining no other nexus between man and man than naked self-interest, callous 'cash payment'."[4] Pope Francis writes that "In this system, which tends to devour everything which stands in the way of increased profits, whatever is fragile, like the environment, is defenseless before the interests of a deified market, which become the only rule."[5]

Occupy Wall Street movement protest, New York City
© Michael Rubin/Dreamstime.com

The Establishment running this system is losing public faith as it breeds ever more crises and inequalities. This opens entirely new horizons for universalizing movements. But the global corporate system—while facing anti-establishment activism and now contending with the uncertainties and dangers of its rogue populist President, Donald Trump—remains the governing system.

That is why we must shine a bright spotlight on the system, even as it simultaneously universalizes and begins to unravel, confronted by universalizing movements from Left and Right hoping to build a revolutionary new order.

INTERSECTIONALITY: HOW RACE, CLASS, AND GENDER HIERARCHIES MAKE UP THE SYSTEM AND SHAPE THE ACTIVIST AGENDA

Militarized capitalism is what social scientists now call an "intersectional" system. Intersectionality is what makes universalized resistance both necessary and possible.

Black feminist scholars, including Patricia Hill Collins, Audre Lorde, and bell hooks introduced the idea of intersectionality to help explain the relations between class, race, and gender. All structures of power are intertwined in what Collins calls "a matrix of dominations,"[6] and constitute pillars of the larger system of militarized capitalism. *Each pillar, an anti-social form of power, has its own roots, some preceding the contemporary system. But all are partially caused and intensified by the system, and are integral to it—and all create intertwined oppressions that must together be overcome in a new order.* As writer and intersectional activist, Shiri Eisner, puts it, "It means understanding that different kinds of oppression are interlinked, and that one can't liberate only one group without the others,"[7] an insight at the heart of universalizing resistance.

Movements today are increasingly recognizing the intersectional nature of the system. Alicia Garza, a founding activist of Black Lives Matter, says

> [W]e've been having a lot of conversations about state violence against Black domestic workers . . . People say "what's the connection?" Well, we are three dimensional beings and black women who are working in other people's homes have families and are afraid for their children. These are women who are living in communities that have really high levels of unemployment . . . over sixty percent of black domestic workers that we talked to said that they didn't have food in the last month.[8]

Garza is making clear that Black Lives Matter sees police violence against Blacks as part of a much bigger systemic issue intertwining race, class, plutocratic economics, and survival.

Garza, a democratic socialist, is explicit about the need to challenge capitalism to end racism:

> [W]e are living in a political moment where for the first time in a long time we are talking about alternatives to capitalism. . . . It is a political moment that's opening opportunities to envision a world where people can actually live in dignity. So whether that's abolishing a criminal justice that feeds off the labor and the lives of black and brown people, whether that's abolishing an economic system that thrives on exploitation, poverty and misery: this is the time for us to not just dream about what could be, but also start to build alternatives that we want to see.[9]

This is a manifesto for resistance against an intersectional system, where Black Lives Matter is connecting the dots and recognizing the threat to individual and collective survival, while envisaging a revolutionary new system.

Despite its democratic ideals, the system is a structure rooted in intersecting caste and class hierarchies, as well as militarism and violence toward the environment, thus melding economic (class) and caste (race, gender, sexual orientation) power and inequalities. Caste refers to statuses in which people are born and which they cannot change: caste systems are based on "blood" or "essence," whether perceived as God-given or built into one's genes. Aristocratic noble "blood" or serf inferior "essence" were central in the polarized castes of the Middle Ages. We think of caste systems surviving today in faraway countries like India, where Brahmins have been seen as an innately superior group and the "Untouchables" so inferior that they should not ever be touched or given rights.

But many modern societies, including that of the United States, have their own caste groups, including those based on gender, skin color, sexual orientation, and ethnicity. The American system claims to overcome caste as a basis of social discrimination, but it never did (except in legal form); it involves a profit-driven system based on inequalities of capital, divisions of wealth ownership, and race and gender hierarchies wrapped tightly around each other like so many intersecting strands of system DNA.

Intersectionality is in the DNA of capitalism—and as the system universalizes, we desperately need a new intersectional resistance in the United States and the world, that can build a new democratic order free of classism, sexism, and racism. Sadly, this new resistance, while beginning to surface and grow, remains maddeningly elusive, with class movements torn asunder from race and gender movements, as well as from anti-war and environmental struggles. The only antidote: new rainbows of resistance uniting classes, castes, colors, and causes around the world in the ultimate service of a revolutionary project of democracy, social justice, and survival. As the feminist poet, Audre Lorde, writes, "There is no such thing as a single-issue struggle because there is no such thing as a single-issue life."[10]

Activists increasingly recognize the "intersectionality" of the system. NTanya Lee and Steve Williams, brilliant and seasoned activists themselves who interviewed 157 activists in 2011 and 2012, report that their interviewees

> offered a sharp intersectional analysis of the issues that they are working on. Teachers are grappling with climate change; domestic workers are taking on immigration reform; unemployed people are confronting banks; transgenders are talking about the need for healthy and sustainable food choices; and the organizations in each of these sectors are struggling to connect the dots.[11]

At the same time, intersectional theorists recognize that some issues sometimes must take personal precedence, as in this story from the great African-American writer, bell hooks:

> I was teasing my brother that he was penniless, homeless, jobless. Right now in his life, racism isn't the central highlighting force: it's the world of work and economics. It doesn't mean that he isn't influenced by racism, but when he wakes up in the morning the thing that's driving his world is really issues of class, economics and power as they articulate themselves.[12]

The system has defined itself from its late Medieval origins as "beyond caste." The existing system is, in fact, an order that moves toward eliminating legal privileges based on race and gender or other inherited caste identities, a very important form of progress. There are now African-American, Hispanic, and female leaders in every field, as well as middle classes comprised of women and people of color. Nonetheless, the system, which has never truly acknowledged the role of race in forming and sustaining the capitalism system, makes certain racial legal and social reforms while deepening the economic exploitation of both poor African-American and white working-class groups.

As Cornel West has noted, racial domination, while totally intertwined with economic injustice, is not "identical" to it; race and gender exploitation are not simply residuals of economic income or class. Racism and sexism existed long before capitalism. West writes that

> Cultural practices, including racist discourses and actions, have multiple power functions (such as domination over non-Europeans) that are neither reducible to nor intelligible in terms of class exploitation alone. In short these practices have a reality of their own and cannot simply be reduced to an economic base.[13]

But racism has always been central to keeping white workers bonded emotionally with their corporate bosses and sustaining capitalism. White supremacy, long a central feature of US Southern culture, is also a disguised prop of capitalism throughout America; it gives white workers the feelings of respect, belonging, and superiority in a system that increasingly impoverishes them. Donald Trump's America First politics is part of what Samuel Huntington might call a "civilizational war" against people of color, while also offering poor "white trash" and declining working-class whites a reason to identify with Trump's billionaire-run capitalism. President Trump campaigned and won as a civilizational as well as class warrior, as a dog-whistle white nationalist as well as a capitalist profiteer.

Racism is intimately tied to class exploitation. Even in the wake of a Black President and cracking of the glass ceiling for women, militarized capitalism cannot operate without racism and sexism. Wealth gaps between Black and white families exploded under a Black President. It is still the case that two-thirds of those in poverty are female.

"Leaning in" to the system, as Sheryl Sandberg, a top corporate executive at Facebook describes it in her best-selling book, can pay off for privileged female managers like Sandberg.[14] But what about poor and working women? Their "leaning in" leads to persistent insecurity and failed dreams, as they compare their fate with Sandberg's. Working-class women voted for Trump in 2016 rather than Hillary Clinton, signaling that economic populism has to be part of feminism. Sandberg illustrates a "silo" feminism that hurts women by ignoring the very different realities of affluent white females, white working-class women, and minority women of color. *Ms Sandberg: stop ignoring the class realities of the corporate system that pays you so well!*

In fact, it is to be hoped that Sandberg listened to the hundreds of thousands of women who flocked the streets the day after Trump's inauguration. Leaders such as Senator Kamala Harris of California, when asked about the women's issues at stake, talked immediately about economic inequality, jobs, social welfare, racism, and climate change; these are all, she made clear, "women's issues." That historical Women's March opening the Trump era made clear that feminism was no longer just about justice for women, but for all people. The Women's March opened a new feminist wave that is militantly intersectional: that does not separate women's rights from the rights of all people and all species.

And so too must be a new wave of anti-racist movements, as shown by Black Lives Matter and the thought of people such as Michelle Alexander and Alicia Garza. The slave trade and slavery itself were a rich source of profit in early Western and American capitalism. We have eliminated the legal basis of slavery, but not the profitability of institutional racism and sexism. On top of such economic violence is police violence against African Americans and a war against Hispanic immigrants that is applauded by many white male workers (and some female workers too)—those who love Donald Trump, or other Republicans. The system helps these workers identify with the corporate system that bends in their racial favor and turns them against African-American workers, even as it undermines their wages and job security and threatens their survival. African-American socialist and labor leader, Bill Fletcher, Jr., calls this "solidarity divided," in his book of the same name,[15] a key way that racism and capitalism are structurally intertwined and must be resisted together.

Republican Presidential nominee in 2012, Mitt Romney, famously argued that 47% of people in the United States are "takers." His veiled reference, especially, to racial minorities illustrates use of race and gender to legitimate the system's extreme inequality of wealth and power. Donald Trump rose to power with less veiled racist, sexist, and homophobic insults and attacks. Resistance to the system, thus, is blind without resistance to race and gender caste hierarchies and cultural stereotypes. Convergence of race, gender, and class movements—coalescing also with labor, peace, and environmental movements—is the key to universal resistance.

In an intersectional capitalism, transformative movements unite a visionary economic agenda for what Bernie Sanders calls "democratic socialism" with a relentless fight against racism, sexism, and homophobia, protecting the rights, dignity, and respect of all groups. The way to make a revolution is not to choose between class politics and identity politics, but to intertwine them

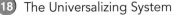

so that identity politics advances economic justice for all and class politics advances the rights and self-worth of all identity groups.

THE SOCIOPATHY OF THE SYSTEM

Despite very real advances in freedom and material wellbeing, allowing American elites to call it "exceptionalist," the system is sociopathic. Profit trumps social, human, and environmental basic needs. It requires exploitation of labor and the commons, poisoning our air, water, and all of the earth.

As Noam Chomsky suggests, sociopathy is built into our culture and psyche, partly to preserve the power of the system and its sociopathic elites:

> [I]f you care about other people that's now a very dangerous idea. If you care about other people you might try to organize or to undermine power and authority. That's not going to happen if you care only about yourself. Maybe you can become rich, you don't care whether other people's kids can go to school or afford food to eat or things like that. In the United States that's called libertarian for some wild reason. I mean it's actually highly authoritarian but that doctrine is extremely important for power systems as a way of atomizing and undermining the public.[16]

Pope Francis writes that:

> Once capital becomes an idol and guides people's decisions, once greed for money presides over the entire socioeconomic system, it ruins society, it condemns and enslaves men and women, it destroys human fraternity, it sets people against one another and, as we clearly see, it even puts at risk our common home.[17]

The Pope is making it clear in the strongest language that the system is sociopathic. Famed economist John Maynard Keynes puts it a different way: "Capitalism is the astounding belief that the most wickedest of men will do the most wickedest of things for the greater good of everyone."[18]

While many Americans enjoy important forms of freedom, too many are un-free, including not just 2 million prisoners, but millions of other "surplus people" whom the system has triaged through outsourcing, robots, racism, and rank exploitation of workers. Increasingly, their wages don't bring them out of poverty and their jobs are permanently temporary. In 2016, these workers supported Trump or Sanders or both—anything to register their hatred of the system and the Establishment and their hunger for transformation and system change.

Extreme individualism is the cultural nucleus of the system, breeding an epidemic of "me, me, me." The American Dream, that enshrines self-interest above all, is the master script of the capitalist system. Marx captures the sociopathic psychology of capitalism: "It has drowned the most heavenly ecstasies of religious fervor, of chivalrous enthusiasm, of philistine sentimen-talism, in the icy water of egotistical calculation."[19] Gordon Gekko, the Donald Trump-like investor in the Oliver Stone film, *Wall Street*, puts it simply: "Greed is good." However phrased, hyper-individualism erodes social movements by weakening the impulse for people to identify with others sharing burdens imposed by the system. Individuals see their difficulties caused by the system as their own fault and the solutions their own responsibilities. This mind-set makes it hard to define their private problems as a public or collective issue—which requires what C. Wright Mills famously calls "the sociological imagination."[20] When that imagination dies, so does the formation of the collective identity of the aggrieved or exploited, which is the solidarity around which all social movements form and build a new society.

THE SYSTEM'S ECONOMIC CONTRADICTIONS

The system is chronically vulnerable to many forms of crisis, stemming from multiple internal contradictions. Eminent Marxist David Harvey has identi-fied no less than 17 contradictions today that could bring down the system. Marxists have often been wildly premature in their predictions of capitalist collapse and the system is remarkably resilient. But the crises are remarkably persistent too—and may bring the system crashing down from the weight of its own contradictions.

Henry Ford paid his workers an astounding $5 a day in the 1920s because he realized the system's fatal flaw: the "wage paradox." Capitalists want to maximize profits, but to do so they must push down labor costs, the result being that Ford and his fellow capitalists don't have workers who are paid enough to buy Ford's cars and other goods. As Marx wrote, we have crises of overproduction: to produce profit, you have to reduce wages, which reduces purchasing power, which creates overproduction that reduces profit. Eco-nomic crises are seen as financial meltdowns (think of the 1929 market crash or the 2008 Wall Street meltdown), but they are rooted in deeper economic crises of overproduction and stagnation. There is no easy way out.

John Bellamy Foster and Fred Magdoff, in their book, *The Great Financial Crisis*, note that capitalists try to solve this problem by "financializing" the system, giving under-paid workers more credit to buy things. It's a short-term fix, leading to the bubbles and financial collapses that almost brought down the whole US economy in 2008. The increasingly financialized system—dominated more and more by huge Wall Street global banks, hedge funds, and private equity funds—spins like a wobbly top bound to topple because of multiple problems associated with massive financial speculation and underlying stagnation tendencies in the system.

Economist Thomas Piketty has shown that capitalism is an inequality engine that concentrates wealth in a tiny elite while workers find it very hard to make ends meet. In his master work, *Capital in the Twenty-First Century*, Piketty writes that "capitalism automatically generates arbitrary and unsustainable inequalities that radically undermine the meritocratic values on which democratic societies are based."[21] The greater the inequality, the less the social mobility and thus the more the economy becomes a caste system. As the system universalizes, tendencies increase in the 21st century for inherited wealth (or the lack of it) to permanently determine one's life station at birth, moving us toward an economic caste system. More and more, we are "anchor babies," tethered for life to the economic class where we began. Working people in all income brackets are declining in income relative to their parents, a relatively new development that threatens faith in the American Dream.

All these dynamics have created rage against the system among the working classes, leading to the populist explosions fueling both Bernie Sanders and Donald Trump in the election of 2016. The system's own self-destructive contradictions are food for universalizers who see the openings for revolution in the system's own tendencies to unravel, as they deny workers of all colors and genders and political leanings what they value and want: the opportunity for hard work in good jobs, as well as respect and a voice that people hear.

THE SYSTEM VERSUS HUMAN SURVIVAL: WHY ACTIVISTS MUST CONNECT THE DOTS OF CAPITALISM, CLIMATE CHANGE, AND MILITARISM

Systemic universalizing increases the threat of military and environmental crises that create authoritarianism in the name of democracy and jeopardize human survival itself. These horrific crises are fertile seeds of universalizing resistance on both Left and Right, but they paradoxically increase the difficulty as well as increase the probability of universalizing resistance, mobilizing much of the public with righteous anger and passion for solutions, but paralyzing millions of others with pessimism, resignation, and hopelessness. The job of the universalizers is to ensure that mobilization triumphs over resignation.

SYSTEMIC MILITARISM AND AUTHORITARIANISM

The system is inherently militaristic. The great revolutionary, Emma Goldman, wrote 100 years ago that "the greatest bulwark of capitalism is militarism."[22] Since the system privileges private wealth over the public good, it depends on violence to weaken or prevent popular anti-interventionist movements in nations across the world for self-determination and justice. Militarism and vast military spending are profitable, not just for the military–industrial complex, but to expand profitable production and markets abroad and at home; profit maximization depends on military enforcement by the US hegemon of "corporate-friendly regimes" around the world. Militarism also provides a key vehicle for expanding demand through military Keynsianism (spending to solve demand-side depressions or recessions); Nobel Prize-winning economist Joseph Stiglitz calls the Iraq invasion the $3 trillion war. Activists increasingly realize that violence drains money that could be used for rebuilding our society and has become an ultimate threat to personal and collective survival, giving rise to universalizing movements to bring the money and troops home on both Left and Right.

Nationalism and jingoism—essential corollaries of militarism—are also systemic imperatives because they divide the global working classes, and bind them to the elites oppressing them through the visceral cultural power of patriotism and nationalism. Patriotism becomes the only glue that unites a thoroughly atomized population, one hungry for real connection with others. Chief executives and workers, Blacks and whites, men and women, put their hand on their hearts and sing "The Star-Spangled Banner" or say the Pledge of Allegiance together at football and basketball games, university ceremonies, and other solemn occasions, affirming their primal nationalistic unity over their class, race, and gender differences. In 2015, the military and heads of big corporations, including sports franchises, paid big money to event sponsors to make sure that "The Star-Spangled Banner" and Pledge of Allegiance were built into major athletic and other public gatherings. But this begins early in life, when children learn to salute the flag and must pledge allegiance even in kindergarten. United States elites work hard on people of all ages to unite the 99% with the 1% in nationalistic wars against terrorists and Communists. But in 2016, when the pro football star, Colin Kaepernick went down on one knee in the field in protest during the National Anthem before his game, he sent a shock wave through the system. He was engaging in resistance that could universalize among millions of football fans and ordinary people who hate the system's violent racism and militarism.

Noam Chomsky observes that during the Cold War, US leaders "presented a frightening portrayal of the Communist threat, in order to overcome [US domestic] dissent."[23] The same is now true of the war on terrorism, intensified after 9/11 and then the 2015 ISIS attack on France and other nations: what is a more potent strategy to divert the attention of insecure workers from the greed of the corporations that exploit them than to blare on our own tele-screens the terrible brutalities of ISIS and Al-Qaeda—and the threat posed by Iran, China, and Russia?

Without resistance to militarism, universalizing resistance cannot succeed. But, as George Orwell has shown in *Nineteen Eighty-Four*, the system makes resisting militarism agonizingly hard—an affront to patriotism—with its 24/7 propaganda:

> The hate had started. . . . The face of . . . the Enemy of the People had flashed on the screen . . . Before the hate had proceeded for thirty seconds, uncontrollable exclamations of rage were breaking out from half the

people in the room . . . the horrible thing about the hate was not that one was obliged to act a part but that it was impossible not to join in.[24]

Islamic jihadists help to sustain an Orwellian world, shrouding US militarism in a fight against the awful violence of ISIS, Al-Qaeda, and other terrorist groups, while disguising the brutal state terrorism—whether perpetrated by dictators in the Middle East (think of Saudi Arabia today) or Central America (think of El Salvador in the 1980s)—that the United States has long helped to create and prop up. Universalizing resistance requires a universalizing anti-war movement shattering the system's Orwellian premise that War is Peace (another name for the "war on terrorism").

Militarism becomes increasingly linked to authoritarianism, with tendencies toward Big Brother masked by democratic speeches and endless rhetoric about protecting freedom at home through Orwellian steps to stop foreign enemies and domestic fifth columns. The system is not yet fully or overtly Orwellian, but the rise of Trumpism and other expressions of authoritarian right-wing movements are simply expressions of tendencies long embedded in militarized capitalism. Trump and the "Alt-Right" sometimes evoke cries of outrage among traditional Establishment elites, but the Establishment and the contradictions of its system create ever more authoritarianism and con-centration of power and violence. Trump appears to attack the system, but is actually a product of its own authoritarian and bullying tendencies. Trump is simply exposing the hidden hypocrisy of democratic rhetoric disguising the authoritarianism—long part of the system that universalizing resisters can put on full and open display to mobilize millions against Trump and build support for an anti-authoritarian revolution.

Systemic Climate Change

Karl Marx and Friedrich Engels wrote more than 150 years ago that exploita-tion of workers "yields nothing in immorality to the subsequent huckster-ing of the earth."[25] Degradation of soil, water, and air escalates with system universalizing, culminating in climate change. Because the system requires endless growth—driven through extraction of scarce resources and mass consumerism—it overwhelms the carrying capacity of the planet.

The system's core commitment to private property ensures private control over air, water, and all forms of the commons. Its commitment to a human-centric, profit philosophy means that the system is incompatible with a sustainable environment. Why did Anderson Cooper, Wolf Blitzer, Judy Woodruff, Megyn Kelly, and other mainstream moderators never once ask a question about climate change in the 2016 primary Republican and Democratic debates for President? President Trump has called climate change a hoax invented by the Chinese—and most Republican Party leaders and officials deny man-made climate change or call it unsubstantiated. Climate change denial is insane.

So is the failure to link it to capitalism. This alone makes universal resistance utterly essential to maintain our sanity, let alone our survival.

While the system claims that its own technological innovations are the only way to save the environment, it uses technology—as it uses all other instruments under its control—to perpetuate profit at the expense of both human survival and environmental protection. True, certain forms of technology offer many public goods and real environmental protections. But contrary to the fantasies of mainstream writers, like Thomas Friedman, who sees capitalist technological innovation as the solution, technology itself is far from adequate to save the environment or stop climate change. Note to Mr. Friedman: technology itself will never solve the environmental crises created by a mass consumer society that keeps expanding extraction, production, and consumption to create ever more profit. *Resistance to environmental degradation is thus central to system resistance, and all other movements must embrace the aim of building a revolutionary new order sustaining the natural world.*

SYSTEMIC INTERSECTIONALITY, EXTINCTION, AND THE CULTURE OF DEATH

"Intersectionality" was a term coined by Black feminists to describe the intertwined "identity" crises of race, gender, and class. Here is another way to frame intersectionality:

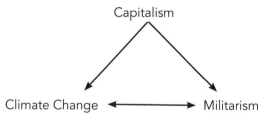

The intersectionality of issues

This causal matrix shows a different type of intersectionality from that normally described, showing the intertwining of structural capitalist crises such as climate and war. These are just as important as the intersectionality of identity tied to race, class, and gender. This new picture demonstrates the need for uniting anti-corporate movements with peace and environmental movements. The environmental movement must renounce silo activism and reconstruct itself as an environmental justice and peace movement.

The sociopathy, exploitation, violence, insecurity, atomization, and degradation of life for millions of citizens in the system leads toward a culture of death. Any system of conquest and domination, as famed educator Paulo Freire writes, reflects a veiled passion for death: "From the first, the act of conquest, which reduces persons to the status of things, is necrophilia."[26] Despite the relative abundance of magical technological gadgets and creature comforts, and the real liberties that Americans enjoy, the system puts enormous stress on millions of individuals whose will to live is undercut by the systemic barriers against a cooperative, meaningful, democratic, and safe life. Even many affluent people are vulnerable to the culture of death when they find that money does not feed the life impulse. Pope Francis writes in his 2015 Encyclical: "The joy of living frequently fades, lack of respect for others and violence are on the rise, and inequality is increasingly evident."[27]

Many millions of Americans retain a strong will to live and love. Millions are generous, even selfless. This reflects the system's delivery of important rights and material benefits advanced by earlier social movements. But the culture of death is manifest in an epidemic of psychological and spiritual malaise, expressing itself in atomization and social disconnection, pervasive psychological depression, anxiety, drug abuse, domestic abuse, rage, gun violence, bullying, illness, alienation, sense of meaninglessness, narcissism, competitiveness, and suicidal or homicidal impulses. The system defines these as personal, psychological, or biological disorders, to be treated by psychiatrists, therapists, and pharmaceutical pill-popping. The roots in the system are rendered invisible by the intensity of the therapeutic discourse resonating in an individualizing culture that doesn't recognize the very idea of a system. The decline of a will to live and love—a subliminal capitulation to the apocalyptic systemic threats to collective survival—is psychologized and medicalized. The task of universalizers is to bring back the will to live, not through Prozac or Celexa, but through civic and political revolutionary resistance giving people purpose and hope.

AN UNLIKELY ACTIVIST
Paul Shannon

When I graduated from Holy Cross College and entered the Jesuit seminary in 1969, I was one of the most unlikely people on earth to become an activist. Like many other Catholic baby boomers whose families headed out of Boston for outlying towns (not really suburbs yet) in the 1950s and 1960s, my life was completely enveloped by two powerful religions: Irish Catholicism and the all-pervasive religion of the American Empire.

Like most Catholic enclaves in Greater Boston, my home town was a place where the fear of Communism was only exceeded by the fear of sex. We had to live in the 14th and 20th centuries at the same time. Getting to heaven was all that mattered. And everything you did on earth was measured by whether it would get you there—or send you to hell if you got hit by a truck that day.

Hard as it may be to believe, I would not exchange this bizarre upbringing with that of anyone else I know. All the adults I knew were good to me. There were dozens of kind priests. My parents brokered no overt racism. We learned that everyone was our brother (not sister yet) and worthy of respect. Wealth was suspect if not sinful, and we knew that God was partial to those who were kicked to the side of the road.

One day in the supermarket, I read the newspaper headline: "Roncalli is Pope." Pope John XXIII was cut from the same cloth as Pope Francis of our time and he called a huge meeting of Bishops called "Vatican 2." And the Church started to change, giving us the permission to embrace the world and the duty to change it.

It was in college that many of us Catholics got caught up in these new ideas and where I changed from a conservative to a liberal. We now believed in the "Social Apostolate," going out into the world where there was loneliness or suffering or poverty, and making the world a better place. But note: all this activity was done within the "American system of empire" which was considered basically good and just.

It was the mid-1960s, a time of great optimism. The music, the new ideas. Our pre-digital radios were on all the time. Even someone living on the sidelines of this cultural upheaval, like myself, could not help getting caught up in it.

In truth, we lived in a bubble, oblivious to the crimes of empire as Washington DC overthrew elected governments, invaded countries, crushed popular movements, put despots in seats of power, financed death squads, and trained torturers, all as normal operating procedure. But that bubble was about to burst. For hanging over this optimism and well-intentioned naïvety about the roots of our problems was a virulent anti-Communism that was about to lead us into disaster.

It was the war that finally did it. It would take something as big as the Vietnam war to flush me out of my hiding place where I could avoid both seeing the dark truth about the machinery of empire and feeling the edgy hope of personal and social liberation.

Up until 1968, I passively supported the war. When Robert Kennedy turned against the war in 1968, so did I. But I still refused to sign a petition to stop the bombing of North Vietnam. Then in 1970, the upheaval over Nixon's invasion of Cambodia and the killing of unarmed students at Kent State and Jackson State universities pulled me out of my own personal crisis in seminary. I just felt I could not sit on the sidelines any longer.

I could feel my life changing—and not just about Vietnam.

Theologically, the non-violence theory of Gandhi and Martin Luther King and the Berrigan brothers provided a bridge for me to move from liberal Catholicism to a more radical theology and view of Jesus as a proponent of love and radical non-violent social and personal change. I was thrilled with my new-found freedom. My Christianity compelled me to be a social activist. Finally I was free of deeply rooted religious ideas that had crushed my spirit in seminary. My depression began to lift.

But how does one become an activist? I guess you start doing things. So I volunteered for the United Farm Workers' grape and lettuce boycotts led by an heroic proponent of non-violent social change, Cesar Chavez. Confronting produce truck drivers, supermarket managers, and fruit stand owners was uncomfortable. I also found it difficult to step over the line, leave my old self behind, and attend my first anti-war demonstrations. But I did.

Things started to move very fast now. Viewing faces and bodies of Vietnamese burned and bloated by napalm horrified me. As an American, I was a part of this killing machine. I just couldn't continue with business as usual. I decided I had to leave my theology studies and join the peace movement full-time.

There was no manual. So I started making it up as I went along, calling people from lists that some church gave me, asking them if they wanted to start a peace group. Eventually I found my community of resistance. We protested and blocked factories of bomb-making companies. We formed a political music group. We made and wore giant puppets of Nixon and Kissinger, mocking them for the lies that they told. We got arrested regularly for civil disobedience.

At first these constant actions were motivated by the simple human desire to stop the suffering of the war and to pay my dues for having gone along with this destruction for so long. I was furious that I had allowed myself to be lied to, allowing napalming of children and carpet bombing and torture of prisoners and burning of villages to be done in my name.

Our strategy was resistance. Throwing whatever we could at the war machine, trying to gum it up so it couldn't continue the killing and torturing. Vietnam veterans provided the leadership for the anti-war movement. They spoke from personal experience of the terrible crimes we committed, the terrible waste of the lives of their brothers,

and the need to immediately get out of Vietnam.

As the war continued, I started to wonder about the Vietnamese, this people that refused to give up. Studying the long history of the Vietnamese revolution, my image of the enemy was transformed. More and more, my opposition to the war was based on solidarity with their cause: independence, respect, and a social revolution against poverty.

By 1974 I had left the seminary and rented an apartment with other activists. I read books on history and political economy voraciously and devoured leftist literature. Now the connections between the war and all these other issues started to make sense to me: racism, prisons, welfare rights, labor unions, saving low-income housing, rent control. We believed we could be on the verge of wonderful changes if we just tried hard enough and did enough things.

We were in emergency mode—all the time.

After the war we organized a huge environmental movement against the dangers of nuclear power: 1,200 people were arrested trying to stop the construction of the Seabrook nuclear power plant in New Hampshire. We put 1 million people on the streets of New York to slow down the nuclear arms race. One of the broadest social movements I joined was the vast anti-war movement of the 1980s to oppose Reagan's war of terror against Nicaragua and US support for death squad governments in El Salvador, Guatemala, and Honduras.

The scariest thing I did was to visit Haiti in 1993 after military officers on the US payroll overthrew the popularly elected government of President Aristide. We interviewed underground leaders to bring their stories and struggles back to the United States. We could hear gunfire all night long. In the 1990s we did not grasp early enough the reality of the globalization of the world economy and its significance for issues of war, peace, and social justice. But eventually a new wave of activists brought together peace forces, environmentalists, and unions into a large and effective movement against corporate globalization, culminating in the 1999 "Battle of Seattle" against the World Trade Organization and its lethal threat to democracy.

If we had succeeded and turned back corporate globalization—which we may very well have been on the verge of doing—Donald Trump would never have been elected President almost 20 years later.

It didn't happen because the attacks on the World Trade Center and the Pentagon on September 11, 2001 dealt a major blow to our growing movement, turning everyone's attention away from increasing inequality and corporate control over society toward what they called the "war on terror." At least for a while Americans lost their minds, ignoring the historical background to the attacks, reveling in apocalyptic fear, and giving up their civil liberties, begging the military to kill all the bad guys and make them safe.

Once again, though, we dug in and, led by military families, created yet another powerful anti-war movement that helped to turn popular opinion against the Iraq war and made it possible for the anti-war candidate, Barack Obama, to defeat Hillary Clinton in the 2008 democratic primaries. But instead of taking bold measures to reverse inequality and take back the country from the rule of the banks and Big Pharma and the war companies, Obama yielded to them in far too many ways. And the modest positive initiatives that he did offer were all blocked by a group, including many rabid sociopaths, called the Republican Party. Inequality increased,

corporate domination expanded, and weapons sales skyrocketed while wages stagnated, tuition fees soared, and anger spread through the land stoked by a relentless hate-mongering media machine led by Fox News.

Today we face a unique crisis the likes of which I have never seen. This may well be the most dangerous moment in history since the Cuban Missile Crisis. Climate catastrophe, crippling social inequality, never-ending war, extremist mobilizations, attacks on vulnerable populations, and a new nuclear arms race stare us in the face all at the same time. And all are being waved on by our new leader.

But no one said it would be easy. For the planet needs us now, all of us, each with our own gifts, working together in intertwined movements to hold the world together and make it sane. Is there anything more worth our lives, even in such difficult times, than to keep fighting for a society in which we can be truly human?

For me, I never expected so many good things would come my way when I was young. I got to become friends and colleagues with some of the best people on earth. I got to help stop a war or two. Despite long periods of very difficult personal and political times, I must say that I never imagined that I would have such a great life.

Paul Shannon is an activist, writer, and speaker in various peace, union, prison reform, human rights, and social justice movements (particularly the United Farm Workers' union drives, the Vietnam anti-war and solidarity movements, the movement to end apartheid in South Africa, the 1980s Central American and Cambodian solidarity movements, the Haitian solidarity movement, the Afghanistan and Iraqi anti-war movements, and efforts to end the US permanent war state). He has been teaching social science courses at a number of colleges for 39 years and is a member of the program staff of the Northeast Region of the American Friends Service Committee.

2

The PAC-MAN System:
Universalizing and Extinction

"I can't breathe"

Eric Garner, choked to death by police in 2014

"The liberty of a democracy is not safe if the people tolerate the growth of private power to a point where it becomes stronger than their democratic state itself. That, in its essence, is fascism—ownership of government by an individual, by a group, or by any other controlling private power."

Franklin Delano Roosevelt, 1938

"Capitalism is out of control, thanks in no small part to Citizens United, the Supreme Court decision which said that a corporation is a person, even though it doesn't eat, drink, make love, sing, raise children or take care of aging parents. You can't have a people's democracy as long as corporations are considered people."

Bill Moyers, 2013

"Today, there is only free market vanilla or North Korea."

Thomas Friedman, 2000

WHAT I MEAN BY THE UNIVERSALIZING OF THE SYSTEM

The system grows like a cancer into every institutional and cultural sector across the world and across species, spreading certain liberating technologies and rights while also spreading its violent power and spilling its sociopathic poisons into institutions and, quite literally, into the air, water, and the commons supporting all life. It is like the monstrous plant in the film, *The Little Shop of Horrors*, which just keeps growing until it sucks the oxygen from all other life.

Capitalism must universalize in every historical era to maximize profits and expand growth and markets. So universalizing is not at all new, nor even are many of its current forms described below. But while the system has long been universalizing, it is happening at a pace and with consequences for human survival that are unprecedented. Quantitative change gives rise to qualitative change. This is creating a new stage of "super-universalized" capitalism which, fortunately, also lays the ground for universalized resistance and revolution.

Super-universalized capitalism can be understood, in a popular sense, as a super-sized system. It is the biggest system of power we have ever seen. It occupies nearly all space and time. All of us are forced to live under its massive influence and to digest it and surrender to it. And the consequences are something like getting super-sized by eating massive amounts of Big Macs every day. We get fat and unhealthy, but we also are addicted. We think we want more sometimes, but the more we eat, the unhappier we get. As we eat more, we may kill ourselves, but we may also choose life by universalizing and shifting toward a revolutionary diet of resistance.

WHAT CAUSES THE SYSTEM TO UNIVERSALIZE?

Universalizing is essential to maximize profits and control by elites. It is in the nature of capitalist development to expand and concentrate power and wealth. The pace and scale have quickened and expanded as part of what the Marxist theorist David Harvey has called the compression of time and space. Everything is happening more quickly and at a new scale—in trillions of dollars of global market transactions, especially of finance capital, in expansion of markets themselves, in concentration of wealth, in the scale and destructiveness of war, in the disruption of natural ecology, in the penetration and control of the human psyche, and electronic control of thinking, eating, and believing.

Technology plays a major role. The computer and the Internet are speeding up and spreading all aspects of corporate power, market transactions, social communications, political control, and military operation. High-tech compresses time by making all transactions nearly instantaneous. It compresses space by permitting profit-making market operations and military strategies to be carried out simultaneously across the entire earth, throughout the global economy, across all nation states, into all spheres of social, economic, and political life, as well as into the micro subconscious worlds of individual psyches. No earlier stage of capitalism has so quickly and deeply penetrated all levels of human experience, or spread it so deeply into the environment.

Technology is only one universalizing instrument of the system's elites. Global corporate chiefs are increasingly organizing on a global scale to maximize profits and control. This partly reflects greater money, organizational reach, military power, media sophistication, and political capacities to expand and universalize corporate power while undermining countervailing power by labor and communities.

But there is also a contradictory cause: a fear of systemic decline and loss of elite power caused by the system's own contradictions. Economic overproduction and decline, as well as political instability and delegitimated states, are leading Western corporate and political elites to desperately seek ways to maintain the system itself. Universalizing thus is driven not only by desire for more power, but fear of loss of the power already concentrated in the system.

This is a crucial point in understanding both Left and Right universalizing resistance. The universalizing system is increasingly unstable, with its great economic and social problems leading to a crisis of faith in the system itself. This is the cause of the revolt against the "Establishment" that led to the surprising election of Donald Trump—who savaged the "rigged system" he calls crony capitalism—and the equally unexpected popularity of Bernie Sanders. A popular Democratic candidate self-identified as "democratic socialist" won the hearts and minds of millions of ordinary citizens, including especially young people facing the reality of high student debts, shrinking jobs, Wall Street rule, and a climate change catastrophe. An authoritarian won the Presidency, but only by condemning the "rigged system" as too expansive and corrupt to deny—and promising to transform it.

The universalizing system is thus highly contradictory. It concentrates more power than any system in history. It has extended its tentacles more deeply into all spheres of economic, political, social, and personal life. But this super-sized system is also eroding under the weight of the crises it is producing. And the public is losing faith in the Establishment which runs this system. Universalization of the system thus contradictorily leads to the rise of universalizing movements—both on the Right and the Left—aiming to create a new world.

There are at least ten dimensions of system universalizing today. Each is a historical process and proceeds non-linearly and not necessarily in conjunction with other dimensions. There are real benefits to some forms of universalizing, but the process fuels plutocracy, inequality, exploitation, and sociopathy leading toward extinction of life.

System universalizing has reached an unprecedented scale with catastrophic impact, but it reflects the culmination of a long historical process unfolding over centuries. The ten systemic changes most relevant to activists are something like the ten plagues recited in the Jewish Passover Seder service; I summarize them below.

UNIVERSALIZING EXTREME INEQUALITY

In 2016, eight people, including six American billionaires—Bill Gates, Warren Buffett, Jeff Bezos, Mark Zuckerberg, Larry Ellison, and Michael Bloomberg, all CEOs of major corporations—owned more wealth than half of the world's population. Their net wealth was $426 billion. The eight super-tycoons own more wealth than the bottom 3.6 billion people in the world, the poor global half.[1]

The corporate monopolization of power and finance is growing, concentrated in JPMorgan Chase, Goldman Sachs, and a small number of other huge global banks and massive energy and pharmaceutical companies. The

Anti-austerity protest against big banks, London
© 1000words/Dreamstime.com

corporate chiefs are creaming off most of the wealth of global growth, with middle classes shrinking and falling into working poor or abject poverty, and the poor locked into even greater poverty. A 2015 Pew Research study shows that the "middle classes" have become, for the first time in decades, a minority of the population, as society polarizes between rich and poor.

As economist Thomas Piketty demonstrates in *Capital in the Twenty-First Century*, this process reflects a fundamental force in capitalism. The return on capital exceeds return on labor, and super-wages enrich corporate executives. The richest 64 Americans, all billionaires, now have more wealth than half the US population. Piketty writes that the explosion of CEO super-salaries and golden parachutes—along with the decline of the middle classes and the poor—have led income inequality in the United States to be the greatest of any nation in history. Workers losing ground are living less long than previous generations for the first time in US history. There is a dramatic shrinkage in the life expectancy of less educated white workers in their prime mid-life years—and also of younger white workers in their late twenties and thirties. More are killing themselves. Many voted for Trump, believing that he would bring a revolution against the "rigged system's" destruction of their jobs, wages, and American Dream—but such a revolution against the 1% also drives the work of progressive universalizers.

Piketty shows that the top executives' salaries "are set by the executives themselves . . . It may be excessive to accuse senior executives of having their hand 'in the till' but the metaphor is probably more apt than Adam Smith's metaphor of the market's 'invisible hand'."[2] As the same self-dealing CEOs reduce workers' wages, extreme inequality mushrooms and reduces social mobility. Nonetheless, the American Dream, symbolized by the small minority that rises from rags to riches, as well as the spread of cool new gadgets and creature comforts, shrouds the collapse of social mobility. New generations can no longer expect to live better than their parents. Millennials can look forward to working long hours into their older age as meeters and greeters at Wal-Mart, trying to collect wage pittances to feed their families and pay for their medications.

The system's extreme inequality has become a recipe for universalizing resistance on both Left and Right—*based on the system's own widely shared ideals of hard work, well-paid jobs, and the American Dream for all*. Trump rose to power by playing to white working-class despair about their economic decline and being left behind in an economic wasteland. For progressive universalizers, the vision is an egalitarian society leveling the playing field and delivering good jobs and fair rewards across class, race, and gender. In a surprising twist, Trump's economic populism—"keep jobs at home"—is structured as gifts to the corporations he challenges, but his rhetoric of attacking corporate outsourcers may actually increase the appeal of Left and

Sanders' universalizers, who have real solutions to the corporate exploiters that Trump campaigned against.

UNIVERSALIZING GLOBAL CONTROL

This is a historical process that unfolded with the rise of the capitalist world system and the rise of European colonial empires. Despite historical protectionism and President Trump's economic nationalism, the system is globalizing its own economic and political power. Marx and Engels, 150 years ago, saw global universalizing as integral to the system's DNA: "The need of a constantly expanding market for its products chases the bourgeoisie over the whole surface of the globe. It must nestle everywhere, settle everywhere, establish connections everywhere."[3] Marx proved prescient. Global corporations now dominate the world, chasing resources, cheap labor, low taxes, no environmental regulation, and the ability to threaten workers and governments in any country by using "exit power," the power to leave. Percy Barnevik, the President of the ABB Industrial Group, unashamedly confirms this predatory corporate view today: "I would define globalization as the freedom for my group of companies to invest where it wants when it wants, to produce what it wants, to buy and sell where it wants, and support the fewest restrictions possible coming from labour laws and social conventions."[4]

The global system has been universalizing for several decades through a) expansive neoliberal trade agreements such as the North American Free Trade Agreement (NAFTA); b) more integrated financial markets that crashed together world-wide in the US 2008 Wall Street meltdown; c) expanding global governance institutions such as the corporate-dominated World Trade Organization and the International Monetary Fund; and d) increasing state violence. This systemic global universalizing based on "neoliberal" corporate-built trade architecture, has created such extreme harm to workers in all nations that it has finally created a global universalizing resistance on both Left and Right, the latter helping to propel Donald Trump into the Presidency in 2016.

New forms of surveillance and policing reinforce the global universalizing of the system—carried out in the name of the war on terror and in the United States itself through militarized policing. Racial minorities and a huge flood of global immigrants drown as they flee or are hit by drones. Global control thus expands and intensifies along with national control. Nonetheless, localized factions, neocolonial and religious wars, and "states' rights" rhetoric create real barriers to total globalization, disguising the degree of growing global control. As journalist Thomas Friedman has put it, "the historical debate is over. The answer is free market capitalism."[5] There is now only the capitalist world and North Korea, and the former is seeking to starve and destroy—or assimilate—the outposts not yet fully assimilated or conquered (think also Russia, Venezuela, Cuba).

Donald Trump, sensing the working-class fury at the globalizing corporate Establishment, ran in 2016 on an anti-globalizing "America First" agenda. Trump realized that tapping into anti-globalization rage could propel him into the White House. But in doing so, he enshrined a commitment to resist corporate globalization that will fuel new universalizing resistance to the system's trade agreements and corporate architecture, while opening the door to a revolutionary new vision of internationalism and localism, feeding populist anti-corporate globalization movements on both the Left and Right in the service of good jobs and economic and social wellbeing.

UNIVERSALIZING THE CORPORATION

All major institutions are being turned into corporations—or modeled after them—throughout the United States and the world. Having taken form in the late 19th-century US Gilded Age, we see now this sort of "corporatization" of all sectors of society. This includes the corporatization of education, especially higher education, the corporatization of media, the corporatization of prisons. There's also the corporatization of religion and mega-churches, the corporatization of medical care, and even of governments, which act much like big businesses. The corporation becomes the dominant and defining model of social institutions, enshrining hierarchy, exploitation, profit-seeking, and money over people. One dollar, one vote trumps one person, one vote. The preservation of one-person, one-vote elections hides the erosion of democracy, supplanted by corpocracy.

The universalizing of corporations changes the configuration of power globally. Not only are society's major public and private institutions becoming corporations or acting like them, but they are increasingly working together through trade associations, mergers, and political lobbies to expand their power even as they compete for global market share and higher profits. Moreover, as markets expand and universalize globally, corporations and financial institutions grow ever larger. The bottom line is that the corporatization of everything and the universalizing of the markets create a vast expansion of corporate power in the United States, over the world, and deep into every sphere of social and political life.

To justify their vast power growth, corporations talk much about "corporate social responsibility" and corporate philanthropy (much of which reduces corporate tax liability). But while there have been some encouraging reforms, this has not reversed the rise in corporate power, deep inequalities, shrinking wages, curtailed benefits, and general erosion of the American Dream. This reflects the hard reality that corporations are tyrannies in their

DNA, whatever degree of personhood they have or social responsibility they preach, or however magical their product. Noam Chomsky writes that "a corporation or an industry is, if we were to think of it in political terms, fascist: that is, it has tight control at the top and strict obedience has to be established at every level . . ."[6]

Corporate universalizing is creating universalizing resistance to build a post-corporate world in which people, rather than corporations, rule the world. Left universalizers have long proclaimed that "Corporations are not people," and that Citizens United is a fraud. They fight for a society where corporations will have none of the constitutional rights of flesh-and-blood people—in fact, they will be turned into worker coops or "mom and pop" stores or community-owned businesses.

Left movements have long challenged corporations. But now Trump has, rhetorically, also campaigned against corporate outsourcing and trade agreements. This could open space up for progressive universalizers to engage the public in a far more serious conversation about corporations as predators.

UNIVERSALIZING AUTHORITARIANISM, MILITARISM, SURVEILLANCE, AND REPRESSION

The system is increasingly authoritarian, moving faster toward a police state. The election of Donald Trump as President made the new authoritarian dangers obvious—with frightening threats to free speech, a free press, and the right to protest. When he campaigned for President, Trump openly threatened newspapers and individual reporters who wrote critical stories. He warned that *The New York Times*, *The Washington Post*, and other major papers could be subject to new libel laws and that his government could retaliate against unfriendly news corporations with tax policies and prosecution. Meanwhile, he repeatedly lied about everything from President Obama's birth certificate, to whether Russia hacked the election, to the scientific consensus on climate change, and helped openly inaugurate what one of his campaign aides called a political world that did not believe in "facts." The only clear truth, as Trump defined it, was in what the President himself declared.

But these threats to civil liberties and free speech and truth, while more explicit and dangerous, began before him, and Trump simply accelerated police-state tendencies long brewing within the system. Trump's authoritarianism was perfectly in synch with the militaristic, surveillance, and repressive direction of the universalizing system—as well as the hierarchical exercise of power over ideas and action that capitalism embeds in its DNA. But it would give new life to the universalizing resistance that takes seriously the system's own rhetorical ideals of democracy and peace.

As the system universalizes, it brings frightening forms of violence and extreme militarism: intensifying surveillance and violence by military strikes abroad, militarization of space, militarization of immigration control, militarization of police, militarization of control of minorities, of the poor, and resisters of all stripes. New technology, including satellites, drones, and surveillance through government cooperation with telephone companies, computer firms, search engines, and Internet monitoring create an Orwellian model of a surveillance society, integrated with a militarized global order organized around permanent war—abroad and at home—in the name of fighting terrorism. Drones now permit the United States to strike anywhere on earth in the name of fighting preventive or pre-emptive wars against ISIS or its look-alikes. As Stephen Colbert has quipped: "If we're going to win our never-ending war against terror, there are bound to be casualties, and one of them just happens to be the Constitution."[7]

In the 2016 Presidential elections, a candidate such as Donald Trump, who argued for banning Muslims from the country and bombing ISIS into smithereens, was only the most bombastic, with "respectable" Republican primary candidates such as Marco Rubio calling for war in the Middle East to destroy jihad, even though it might lead to nuclear war with Russia as well as massive war and killing throughout the Muslim world. The fact that this universalized militarism is nuclear-tipped, with potential use of nuclear, chemical, or biological weapons, shows the apocalyptic threat of extinction brought by the system's universalization.

Democrats Hillary Clinton and Barack Obama used more restrained language, but also escalated the global "war on terrorism." Obama used executive power to ratchet up bombing of Syria and Iraq, while building up special operations not only in the fight against ISIS and Al-Qaeda in the Middle East, but to deploy more than 7,500 special operations forces fighting in 85 countries by January 2016. The spread of the ISIS and Al-Qaeda franchises into Africa, Asia, and Latin America led both Clinton and Obama to embrace persisting US interventionism and militarism that would bring violence in a new type of war across the planet, without Declarations of War.

The United States is building hundreds of new permanent sites for launching ground operations, especially across Africa, the greater Middle East, and Southern Asia. The Pentagon has spawned new small operational bases, sometimes disguised by the term "lily-pads," in which a relatively small US military presence can be made permanent. These sites permit immediate deployment of US troops into special operations and other campaigns anywhere in the world. It also facilitates launching of US drones from any country, which makes American universalized surveillance and warfare easier.

Meanwhile the system looks toward space; the Pentagon has said, "With regard to space dominance, we have it; we like it and we're going to keep it . . . We're going to fight *from* space and we're going to fight *into* space."[8] Universalizing repression at home, on earth, through militarism, mass incarceration, and surveillance, is just as ambitious. As journalist Glenn Greenwald, who helped to bring Edward Snowden's revelations to the world's attention, writes:

> Taken in its entirety, the Snowden archive led to an ultimately simple conclusion: the US government had built a system that has as its goal the complete elimination of electronic privacy worldwide. Far from hyperbole, that is the literal, explicitly stated aim of the surveillance state: to collect, store, monitor, and analyze all electronic communication by all people around the globe.[9]

Snowden explains the universalizing surveillance police state in his own words:

> If we do nothing, we sort of sleepwalk into a total surveillance state where we have both a super-state that has unlimited capacity to apply force with an unlimited ability to know (about the people it is targeting)—and that's a very dangerous combination. That's the dark future. The fact that they know everything about us and we know nothing about them—because they are secret, they are privileged, and they are a separate class . . . the elite class, the political class, the resource class—we don't know where they live, we don't know what they do, we don't know who their friends are. They have the ability to know all that about us. This is the direction of the future, but I think there are changing possibilities in this.[10]

Daniel Ellsberg, the United States' most famous whistleblower who revealed the Pentagon Papers in 1971, projects the universalizing surveillance and repression in similar terms, speaking, before the rise of Trump, about what Trumpism is bringing:

> We are not in a police state now, not yet. I'm talking about what may come. . . . White, middle-class, educated people like myself are not living in a police state . . . Black, poor people are living in a police state. The repression starts with the semi-white, the Middle Easterners, including anybody who is allied with them, and goes on from there . . . One more 9/11, and then I believe we will have hundreds of thousands of detentions. Middle Easterners and Muslims will be put in detention camps or deported. After 9/11, we had thousands of people arrested without charges . . . But I'm talking about the future. . . . I'm talking of hundreds of thousands in camps or deported. I think the surveillance is very relevant to that. They will know who to put away—the data is already collected.[11]

Or, as Michelle Alexander writes in her blockbuster book on prison and mass incarceration, *The New Jim Crow*, "the nature of the criminal justice system has changed. It is no longer primarily concerned with the prevention and punishment of crime, but rather with the management and control of the dispossessed."[12] Increasing repression becomes shrouded in the formal liberties of controlled media and carefully cordoned protests on the streets, with enough protest permitted to give a credible illusion of free expression.

Resisting militarism, surveillance, and the police state—all bound up at this time of writing to resistance to the Big Brother Trump Presidency—has become central to the universalizing movements we need. Trump may well seek to crush universalizers with bloody repression, but he has already unleashed throughout America and the world a fear and hatred of militaristic authoritarianism that will fuel new waves of national and global peace and democracy movements. They fight for a new system free of authoritarianism, militarism, anti-immigrant passions, racism, and state violence.

Child activism for immigrants and human rights
© Rrodrickbeiler/Dreamstime.com

A DREAMER'S STORY IN THE IMMIGRANT RIGHTS MOVEMENT

Katherine Asuncion

I did not know I would be called a "dreamer" due to a lack of status. I would like to be called a "dreamer" because I have big aspirations. But being a dreamer is associated with being undocumented in the United States.

I'm undocumented because my native country, the Dominican Republic, forced my family into poverty and violence. My parents were losing their jobs, the neighborhood was dangerous, and the government was corrupt. So we chose to emigrate to the United States. My dad was granted a visa and he traveled first to find a job and an apartment for us. A year later, my mom, my older brother, my little sister, and I were finally granted tourist visas and we boarded a plane to reunite with my dad.

I was afraid of moving to a new place. Despite the violence and dangers we faced, I loved my country and I identified with the Dominican Republic down to my bones.

In the fall of 2003, my dad drove me to my first day of 6th Grade in the United States; I was 10 years old. There were three levels of English for new immigrant students: low, medium, and high. I was enrolled in the "low" level. During lunchtime, I stood confused in the middle of the cafeteria getting trampled by a stampede of hungry students. I've always been shy, but first days in school are particularly difficult, and I was trembling with fear.

The language barrier had added a new level of anxiety that I couldn't cope with, but I was hungry. I asked a girl who was in my class earlier to direct me to the food. When I asked her, she said, "I don't speak Spanish," and walked away.

After that experience, every situation caused me anxiety. I begged my mom to return to the Dominican Republic, but every time she'd tell me that we could not. A few weeks later, I was told that Immigration and Customs Enforcement (ICE) had raided the house of a family friend. That struck great fear into my family and gave me the ultimate—a clear understanding of what our status in the United States meant: they could find us. I had to blend in. I was afraid.

By the time I reached high school, I had learned English, and made friends and did really well in school. Sadly, my sense of belonging faded. In 2007, my brother graduated from high school and fell into depression. My father, paranoid that ICE was onto us, made us move to a different apartment to evade them. In school, my friends asked me why I did not apply for a driver's license, why I wasn't job hunting with them, and why I wasn't excited about college, etc. My anxiety returned.

By 2010, I was fed up with being silent. I was expected to be outstanding in school, but to be invisible everywhere else. Around this time, I learned about the DREAM [Development, Relief, and Education for Alien Minors] Act and about the "dreamers."

On International Workers' Day (May 1, 2010), I learned of a rally for the DREAM Act. I invited my best friend and we rushed to downtown Boston. As soon as we stepped out of the Red Line train station, we were greeted by three girls from the Student Immigrant

Movement (SIM) who directed me to the rally. There were hundreds of people and organizations marching the streets of Boston, fighting for better wages, for protection and dignity for all.

I joined the group of undocumented students chanting "EDUCATION NOT DEPORTATION!" The march ended at a platform at the Boston Common where students were given the speakerphone to share their immigration stories. One of the students had immigrated from the Dominican Republic on a tourist visa, like me. The similarities of her story with mine made me cry.

To be honest, I was taken aback by all these students chanting "undocumented and unafraid!" when I was undocumented and very afraid. After hearing the stories of other *undocu-youth*, I embarked on my journey to become unafraid.

Next thing I knew, I was in a car on the way to Maine where we hosted an action to save a dreamer from deportation. Traffic delayed us and when we arrived, one of the SIM members told me I was the next person to speak. I put on a graduation cap and gown and I shared my story for the first time in front of journalists, bystanders, and dreamers. My heart was racing, but the experience fueled me with hope. The more I shared my story, the more I healed. It helped me to deal with my depression and isolation. I became more involved in SIM by making recruitment calls, fundraising, distributing flyers, and stopping deportations.

When the DREAM Act failed by four votes in the Senate, I felt like the movement had failed me. I distanced myself from the movement to figure out my life. I enrolled in a small private college and worked in a restaurant. Some months later, a SIM member called me back into the organization. We joined national gatherings and actions led by the United We Dream network with the intention of holding President Obama accountable for deporting and tearing apart our immigrant families.

After 2 years of persistent national action, the President announced the Deferred Action for Childhood Arrivals (DACA) program: DACA granted eligible youth a 2-year work permit and protection from deportation. Yet the result was bitter-sweet. Our immigrant movement had just won the biggest victory in over 20 years, but it only granted limited status to some people, and it criminalized others more. The result was that our victory split our movement even more.

Thinking more broadly, the immigrant rights movement comprises many people of different ethnicities and identities. Despite all of us being under oppression, we are still attacking each other in painful ways. Anti-Blackness in our movement is real, as well as LGBTQ [lesbian, gay, bisexual, transgender, and queer] discrimination and sexism. There have been "divide and conquer" tactics from the capitalist elites to keep us from organizing a strong working-class movement.

We have used identity politics in our organizations because it has facilitated organizing different groups into a focus on issues that they can relate to. Unfortunately, we're stuck in identity politics without reaching a conclusion and unifying as a working class against capitalism. In the immigrant rights movement, we have some organizations for students, others for adults, others for preventing deportation, others for labor exploitation, others for empowering women, others for defending LGBTQ communities from legislative attacks, others for defending war refugees, etc. We need to work toward intersectionality.

In SIM, we believe that our undocumented status is a result of US imperialism. Our oppression in the United

States is connected to the oppression of all members of the working class. We have collaborated with Black Lives Matter, but we need to do more. We want to form more intentional alliances with BLM, LGBTQ, student debt, refugee, health care, and housing and labor groups, because their issues are also our issues. As we encourage youth to get a college education, it is also our job to teach them popular education as a tool to organize and as the glue to keep the working class united.

Katherine Asuncion, 23, born in the Dominican Republic, lives in Dorchester with her husband and two cats. She is Development Director at the Student Immigrant Movement, the largest and only undocumented youth-led organization in Massachusetts.

UNIVERSALIZING IDEOLOGICAL CONTROL

Despite President Trump's rhetorical challenge to globalism, neoliberalism is the reigning economic ideology—based on hatred of government and the view of private property, "free trade," and "free markets" as the foundations of freedom and prosperity. Of course, capitalism is all about big government: think of the military and corporate welfare. But corporate ideology is universalizing across all economic sectors and geographic regions. Corporatization of media, universities, and schools—the "ideological apparatus"—locks in capitalist values and ideology. They repress truth, dignity, and democracy.

Ideological control is organized around TINA ("There Is No Alternative"), the idea that whatever the evils of the system, there is nothing better to replace it. Thomas Friedman writes that, by 2000, the system "blew away all the major ideological alternatives to free-market capitalism. People can talk about alternatives to the free market and global integration . . . but none is apparent."[13] The idea of TINA is hegemonic in the United States, reinforced by ideologies of exceptionalism and manifest destiny; globalization is spreading it to much of the rest of the world, but it still remains contested in the Middle East, Latin America, and parts of Asia.

"There Is No Alternative" erodes the collective capacity to question and dissent, leading Noam Chomsky to write that "Citizens of the democratic societies should undertake a course of intellectual self defense to protect themselves from manipulation and control, and to lay the basis for meaningful democracy."[14] The need is made less apparent by the fact that the universalizing propaganda system is disguised by the persistence of formal "freedom of speech" and media distractions of partisan politics, which appear to make America the land where you can say and believe whatever you want. And, while this is a seductive myth, it survives because it is not entirely false. As Chomsky and Edward Herman have noted, the legal and ideological ideas of free expression carry just enough truth to disguise the universalizing Orwellian control of discourse. There is also just enough ideological partisan polarization to mask the hegemony of state and corporate propaganda, churned out by Fox, CNN, and in softer form, MSNBC and NPR.

Corporate ideology has captured the Establishments of both the Republican and Democratic parties. The corporate and Wall Street sympathies of the Clinton Democratic Party regime helps explain why Trump won the 2016 election. As the working class was impaled on corporate global neoliberal policy, the Clintons and the Democratic Establishment had no alternative ideology or vision to save the working classes. When Sanders failed to displace the Clinton machine in 2016, the working classes understandably saw the Democrats as offering them no solutions, leaving Trump as the only possibility for change.

But neoliberalism and austerity are also losing credibility throughout the population as jobs disappear, wages decline, and poverty increases. Universalizers, especially on the Left, will find a new opening for alternative ways of thinking, something that Trump has already unleashed on the Right as he scrambles classic "free market" Republican ideology. The weakening of neoliberalism is the beginning of the end of TINA, and is the key to the rise of universalizing resistance, which argues that revolution against the current system and its corporate ideologies will be undone in a new democratic economy and society offering everyone meaningful, secure, and well-paying jobs.

UNIVERSALIZING WESTERN WAYS OF KNOWING

The system is universalizing Western epistemology, science, and technology, while eroding other approaches, especially in the Global South. This includes a relentless assault, carried out by media, political leaders, and the education system, to hegemonize Western capitalist philosophy and capitalist commodification and markets, eroding indigenous and noncapitalist ways of knowing and living. As the Portugese scholar, Boaventura de Sousa Santos, has written in his brilliant book, *Epistemologies of the South*, the Western capitalism system reduces "our understanding of the world to the Western understanding, thus ignoring or trivializing other non-Western understandings of the world."[15] Santos notes that this has devastating effects for those in the West who seek to develop a vision of resistance, because it is the epistemologies of the South where the "movements or grammars of resistance . . . have been emerging against oppression, marginalization, and exclusion . . ."[16]

The destruction of non-Western ways of thinking goes unrecognized by most Westerners. Non-Western approaches to knowledge and living have long been either invisible to Westerners or viewed as hopelessly primitive or romanticized. European empires long ago colonized the mind, and bred epistemological imperialism that sought to eradicate indigenous cultures in the name of science, technology, and progress.

Progressive universalizers, steeped in the history of colonialism and cultural imperialism, are fighting for societies incorporating the revolutionary epistemologies of the South.

UNIVERSALIZING TRANS-SPECIES VIOLENCE AND DESTRUCTION OF NATURE

The system is extending its violence and oppression from humans to all life species, including animals and plants. The system is accelerating its long devastation of the environment to an extreme form, most terrifyingly by climate change. Climate change reflects the deepest imperative of the system: it must expand to privatize all of the earth's commons and turn them into arenas for extractive production and profit. This lies at the foundation of apocalyptic universalizing of the system.

The decimation of hundreds of animal and plant species every day remains largely hidden. Species extinction is buried in the news under such stories as the prosecution of Michael Vick for his murderous dog-fighting, or by popular efforts to preserve animals from the worst slaughter houses of industrialized agriculture and global capitalist poaching. Corporate reports of environmental responsibility and some companies' genuine reforms to limit some of the worst forms of animal suffering appear to validate the public perception that the system is embracing more sustainable production and greater protection of the environment. In the meantime, we are killing off other species at an alarming rate, while climate change threatens all of nature.

The Center for Biological Diversity reports that

> although extinction is a natural phenomenon, it occurs at a natural "background" rate of about one to five species per year. Scientists estimate we're now losing species at 1,000 to 10,000 times the background rate, with literally dozens going extinct every day.[17]

The Center reports a growing catastrophe caused by the universalizing system:

> In fact, 99 percent of currently threatened species are at risk from human activities, primarily those driving habitat loss, introduction of exotic species, and global warming. Because the rate of change in our biosphere is increasing, and because every species' extinction potentially leads to the extinction of others bound to that species in a complex ecological web, numbers of extinctions are likely to snowball in the coming decades as ecosystems unravel.[18]

The system's claim that its technology and markets will protect the environment is, in fact, the Big Lie and perhaps the most dangerous of all. The system is hell-bent on privatizing all land and nature, the source of the unfolding tragedy of the commons that began with the rise of the capitalist system itself and may end with life extinction.

As President Trump seeks to sell off public lands to coal, gas, and oil companies, progressive universalizers put their bodies in front of the bulldozers and pipelines, promising revolution to stop human extinction and enshrining the protection of nature as the sacred heart of their new society.

UNIVERSALIZING "KOCHAMAMIE" DEMOCRACY

As the system universalizes, democracy is in peril. Corporate money and the wealth of billionaires increasingly dictate the policies of the political elites. With the election of Donald Trump, a billionaire became President: he put several other billionaires in his cabinet, symbolizing the unity of the extremely rich and the government.

But this was evident long before Trump. Plutocratic control—the growing concentration of political power among the wealthiest of the wealthy—has long been emerging as an assault on popular democracy too blatant to hide—a kind of "Kochamamie" democracy.

The Koch brothers themselves committed hundreds of millions of dollars to Republicans in recent Presidential and Congressional elections. But their fellow billionaires and the biggest corporations upped the ante, with total corporate and Super-PAC giving expected to exceed $5 billion. This led 2016 populist Democratic candidate, Bernie Sanders, to proclaim: "Let us wage a moral and political war against the billionaires and corporate leaders, on Wall Street and elsewhere, whose policies and greed are destroying the middle class of America."[19] Beyond buying candidates, the state and political leaders are subject to lobbying, capital strikes, or threats (including exiting the United States for friendlier lands with lower taxes) and a captive regulatory system that leaves little room for serious countervailing power, let alone system change.

As journalist Bill Moyers writes, "We are this close—this close!—to losing our democracy to the mercenary class. So close it's as if we're leaning way over the rim of the Grand Canyon waiting for a swift kick in the pants."[20]

UNIVERSALIZING EXISTENTIAL THREATS

The system creates climate change; species extinction; extreme economic inequality, frequent deep financial crises, and system-wide depressions; permanent warfare that can lead to nuclear war and extinction; and racial/

religious polarization. As the system universalizes, the threats to economic and environmental life—and to personal security—intensify, creating the possibility of total extinction never imagined before. This engenders both fear and mobilization, as well as paralysis, in the public. Pope Francis says:

> *Doomsday predictions can no longer be met with irony or disdain. We may well be leaving to coming generations debris, desolation and filth. The pace of consumption, waste and environmental change has so stretched the planet's capacity that our contemporary lifestyle, unsustainable as it is, can only precipitate catastrophes . . .*[21]

As the crises become more threatening, there are three prospects: right-wing universalizing movements; left-wing universalizing movements; or a depoliticizing of much of the public based on isolation, fear, and despair. All three can occur simultaneously—and seem to be doing so. The system puts all of its muscle into, first, depoliticizing the public and, second, bucking up right-wing populist movements. Denial of its possible destruction of all life is central to the system's own effort to keep universalizing and maintain legitimacy. President Trump has gone further, madly seeking to undermine nuclear anti-proliferation and climate change strategies that are the first steps toward avoiding extinction of civilization. But in this Trumpist and broader Republican Party insanity, progressive universalizers find one of their greatest mobilizers for their revolution, since all people have a stake in survival and a society which is constitutionally committed to preserving life by preventing climate change and other environmental destruction.

UNIVERSALIZING THE DEATH CULTURE

The culture of death spreads throughout many parts of the United States and the world as the system itself spreads; it is the dark internalizing of the life-threatening system in the psyche. It breaks down communities of love and replaces them with communities of fear and anger. The death culture spreads unevenly, affecting certain nations, classes, races, and ethnicities more rapidly and deeply than others, with those caught in climate disasters or war zones and trapped in poor nations and neighborhoods the most widely and profoundly affected. Global mass media and Hollywood project images of wealth, celebrity, glamor, romance, and spectacle, creating the impression of happiness everywhere, which serves only to intensify the misery of millions suffering from real-world adversities. The pharmaceutical industry's antidote to the pervasive will to die is drugs treating mental and physical illness that saturate the electronic airways and global advertising. Drugs medicalize natural responses to a systemic catastrophe of looming collective death.

The system projects its death culture on its global enemies in the war on terror. Organizations like ISIS and Al-Qaeda and countries like Iran breed their own death cultures today, inflamed by US occupation, war, and conquest. These death cultures are treated by the system as proof of the life culture of the West, a message masking the reality that Islamic terrorism and its death culture have been midwifed partly by the West's own brutalizing militarism and death culture. Many Americans and other global citizens resist the death culture, which is far from universal. But violence, social isolation, mental illness, depression, anxiety, drug abuse, human trafficking, domestic abuse, bullying, gun violence, homicide, suicide, and other signs of the death culture cross national, class, racial, and gender borders and boundaries. The universalizing of the death culture has a paradoxical effect on resistance. On the one hand, it overwhelms an increasingly atomized population with fear, confusion, and psychological paralysis sapping the life energies necessary to participate in politics. At the same time, the death culture creates a desperate passion for life that can catalyze resistance movements, which in turn offer people the community, purpose, and will to live—and can mobilize citizens to transform the apocalyptic system that lies at the heart of the death culture.

Systemic universalizing creates contradictions that both strengthen the system and open it up to legitimation crises. Universalizing is a system imperative to expanding profit, crushing dissent, and maintaining legitimacy. It involves deeper and deeper elite deception and lies about the spreading of systemic sociopathy, creating almost unbearable inner tensions in the population: as Inga Muscio writes:

> What happens to people living in a society where everyone in power is lying, stealing, cheating and killing, and in our hearts we all know this, but the consequences of facing all these lies are so monstrous, we keep on hoping that maybe the corporate government administration and media are on the level with us this time.[22]

As the system universalizes, it offers more magical technology and creature comforts, but forces millions of poor, disenfranchised, and other "surplus people"—as well as affluent but still miserable people—to admit the sociopathic horrors in their own lives and the suicidal life-extinguishing impulses of the universalizing system itself. The stages of historical systemic universalizing are not determinate, however, and they do not create a one-to-one formulaic or inevitable relation to universalizing resistance. Systemic universalizing is only one of several forces creating both greater systemic power and greater systemic vulnerability, but it is a key driver of universalizing resistance.

CALLS TO ACTION

Sofia Wolman

Now 27 years old, I see that many intertwined experiences have shaped my worldview since I was a child, leading me toward activism even as I seek to know the type of work I am called to do.

When I was very young, my concern was with plants, animals, and the earth, and I had a strong sense of the pain I felt we humans inflicted on the natural world. I recycled furiously, wrote a (misguided) petition to the Massachusetts District Attorney asking for protection of endangered manatees, encouraged peers to refrain from peeling bark off live trees, and reacted in horror as my sister tossed a piece of chewing gum out of the car window. "The birds!," I cried, sure that the gum would be the death of one, at least.

I enjoyed a safe, stable, and loving upbringing in a suburb of Boston, sheltered from poverty, from wars like the one my grandfather had experienced—first as a child in Nazi-occupied Greece, then as a young man fighting for the United States in the Korean War—and from racism, as I'm white.

I was 12 when four planes were hijacked on September 11, 2001. Exploded, burning buildings felt close by. Eighteen months later, I watched on TV when the United States went to war in Iraq. I didn't know that millions of people were demonstrating against the start of another war, but I heard that white people were violently attacking brown people. I understood that the government and mainstream media were feeding off and stoking people's fear, and I was disturbed by the phrase "axis of evil."

Whatever remained of my idealization of or trust in the President, already shaken after the commander-in-chief had sex with a White House employee in her early twenties, was in tatters by the second Bush Presidency.

At that same time, some classmates and I were watching documentaries and sharing articles about the movement to stop gun violence. Our parents organized a trip down to Washington DC where we joined a demonstration protesting the looming expiration of the federal ban on assault weapons. Near mourning, I gained awareness of how much violence exists in the United States, and of the industry and people that fuel and profit from it.

As a freshman at a small Quaker college, I learned about Zionism, the Israeli apartheid and occupation of Palestine, and the way politics tends to work: how certain groups and people decide and enforce the terms of debate, and play to racism and violence unreconciled over the course of history. I also learned about the nuances and manipulation of words like "security" and "terrorism"—and the potential for ongoing violence where collective trauma exists. I realized my new friends knew far more about many grim realities in the world than I did. I cried a lot and let go of my belief in Jewish exceptionalism.

In 2010, I spent a semester in Northern Ireland, then traveled to Palestine/Israel with a delegation of "citizen diplomats." There I experienced visceral outrage, felt it in my body, when I saw soldiers young and old treat people with no respect for dignity. I heard the phrase "existence is resistance" and wondered how my own might become that.

Our hosts expected us to "do something" when we went home, so in my senior year, a small group of us developed a Boycott, Divestment and Sanctions campaign to get our college to divest from companies profiting from the Israeli occupation. I believed deeply in this campaign to hold our college accountable, and remain moved by the powerful universalizing potential of this tactic to uproot a system in which militarism and oppression are profitable.

By the time I graduated, the discipline of Political Theory was opening new ways to name, frame, and share ideas. Thinking about "moments of democracy" has made me consider more honestly what it means to be an activist when, too often, I don't activate my caring sufficiently to claim this identity. Recently, my pastor pointed out that God calls us not just to know, but to do.

After graduating, I was drawn to focus on international issues and began volunteering with a large Quaker organization. I took on paid projects collecting signatures for a state-level referendum calling on the federal government to Move the Money out of the military and toward meeting human needs. I handled logistics (including communication with remarkable activists from near and far!) for a counter-summit at the time of the NATO and G8 meetings in Chicago in 2012, and I also continued with Palestine solidarity organizing: this included a powerful experience organizing a conference with other young people who became close friends, and efforts to raise awareness through public media campaigns.

When I traveled to Hiroshima and Nagasaki in 2013, testimonies by Hibakusha (atomic bomb survivors) and the pursuit of a nuclear-free world

by the thousands in attendance raised deep questions about violence, grief, struggle, and compassion. Until then, the issue of nuclear weapons had felt impossibly distant for me, and my time in Japan allowed me to understand the impact of this advanced technology in spiritual and human terms.

The next summer I walked in the final 17 days of the Japan Peace March, which was, among other things, an intense exercise in focus on which I continue to draw to mitigate my tendency toward distraction. In many ways, this period of my activism culminated with an international mobilization in New York City at the time of a major conference on nuclear non-proliferation at the United Nations. I supported and contributed what I could, and particularly enjoyed coordinating a festival using skills that I'd developed through co-organizing a monthly youth open mic for a couple years prior to this.

Too often, I've had a deep sense that I have more to give. The era of slacktivism and clicktivism and near constant media barrage is mostly not, for me, life-giving or activating. I thrive in and thus must actively maintain loving and challenging friendships and community to keep always seeing beyond what my privileged identity first makes visible.

Further, I've come to believe that God has a plan for me, and I must be more careful to heed calls and develop and refine my skills, thinking, and action. For me, reading and writing are necessary tools that center my priorities and help me through process and presence. A friend at the Derry Women's Centre in Northern Ireland taught me that "the personal is political." This phrase colors my growing relationship with the divine as a source of unique authority.

The activists that I admire channel what is in their hearts, minds, souls, and bodies into their work with extraordinary discipline. I think this is what's required if we're not to be resigned to the awful ways of this world, so full of beautiful and imperiled life.

Each day I wake up is a new one to do better. I feel urgently the need to cultivate practices and relationships that serve and fortify the work I do for peace, justice, life, healing, and love—and letting go of the rest.

Sofia Wolman *is pursuing the Master of Divinity degree at Harvard Divinity School.*

PART

UNIVERSALIZING RESISTANCE: THE NEW RULES AND STRATEGY OF SOCIAL CHANGE

3

Irresistible Resistance: The Big Waves of Social Change

"It is more accurate to picture a movement of many movements—a coalition of coalitions. Thousands of groups today are all working today against a force whose common thread might be described as the privatization of every aspect of life and the transformation of every activity and value into a commodity."

Naomi Klein

"For years I have written about mass incarceration, while staying mute about drones and other injustices. It is time to connect the dots."

Michelle Alexander

"An injury to one is an injury to all"

Labor slogan

"Power without love is reckless and abusive, and love without power is sentimental and anemic. Power at its best is love implementing the demands of justice, and justice at its best is power correcting everything that stands against love."

Martin Luther King ("Where Do We Go from Here?" 1967)

THE IDEA OF UNIVERSALIZING RESISTANCE

Resistance is activism bred by social movements to reject existing power hierarchies. It mobilizes countervailing power to prevent assaults on human and environmental rights and wellbeing, uniting isolated, disempowered people into new bonds of solidarity and community. Resistance is "people power" in action, responding to loss of popular control over the economy, politics, and ways of living and thinking. Grass-roots movement resistance is the most important force for change in all capitalist societies, whatever historical stage of universalizing the system has achieved. It can come from both the Right and the Left; we discuss both forms here, recognizing that Right universalizing movements have become ascendant in Washington, DC, but focusing more on the Left universalizing that is our best chance to create a world based on social justice and democracy.

Universalizing resistance is a distinctive form of activism—a special form of resistance. It seeks to mobilize massive **unifying** *popular power against the apocalyptic power of the system itself—seeking to transform the system itself and bring a new just and democratic order.* It brings people together into intertwined movements focusing on issues such as economic insecurity, racism, climate change, or militarism. The aim is to find connections and purpose in struggling together for a new culture, economic democracy, real political democracy, and community. In the United States and most advanced countries, universalizing resistance is largely non-violent. But that doesn't mean timid or reformist; resistance in its highest form is transformative. It seeks to prevent the system from operating normally and to build a new society. It is a risky business. It requires courage because the stakes are so high for the system.

Universalizing resistance does not settle for reforms and it does not surrender to the justifications of ever more expansive, brutal system power. It focuses not only on opposition, but on creating new communities, economies, and societies, recognizing that people will not fight for change unless they see real alternatives.

Resistance movements are not necessarily universalizing; that is, they do not necessarily create unifying power to create a new system. But most resistance generates *tendencies* toward universalizing. For example, Blockadia (the movement to block oil and gas drilling, fracking, power plants, and pipelines) started as a local environmental response, but soon encountered corporate and police powers that led activists to reflect about the larger system.

Resistance and activism—though much of it does not rise to the level of what I call universalizing resistance—are widespread and highly active on both Left and Right, involving millions of activists in the United States and the world. Moreover, resistance that is non-universalizing—which I call "*silo activism"*—is not irrelevant or unproductive. It is often the precursor of universalizing resistance and it has many virtues (see the section called "The Virtues of Silo Activism" in Chapter 7). It can create local or particularistic or single-issue communities and campaigns that awaken consciousness and create agency, solidarity, and empowerment in large numbers of activists, organizations, and campaigns. Many of these single-issue campaigns—for example, the right to gay marriage—may not transform capitalism, but they are profoundly important in themselves, and they can build consciousness

Pink hat protesters in Washington, DC Women's March, January 21, 2017
Photo credit: Janet MacGillivray Wallace

of larger systemic issues. The early stages of the civil rights movement of the 1960s and the early anti-Vietnam war movement illustrate the power of non-universalizing movements that make history, bringing millions into critically important forms of resistance. They led toward more universalizing resistance when Martin Luther King proclaimed that he could no longer restrict his activism to civil rights and embraced the causes of fighting militarism and capitalism.

The focus here on universalizing resistance should thus not be taken as a rejection of non-universalizing resistance. Universalizing resisters are grateful for their sister silo movements which are laying the groundwork in their own way for broader transformation.

"Catalyzing movements," such as the 1960s civil rights movement, build a mass base and help to midwife converging movements of universalizing resistance in wave eras, where the atomization and individualization of people give way to mass interlinked communities of resistance. Universalizing resistance is like other resistance movements, but it helps them come together in coalitions that strengthen their own core issue struggles by linking them to intersecting struggles, and focusing ultimately on the system that gives rise to all of them. Universalizers can strategically pursue what Marxist visionary André Gorz calls *"radical reforms,"* rather than outright revolution, in historical eras in which conditions for revolution are not ripe, or dangerous because they will lead to massive right-wing reaction.[1] But they never abandon transformational change.

Massive expansion of system power and repression may appear to undermine possibilities for universalizing resistance. But this is wrong. First, as system power increases, harm is spread to broader sections of the population who mobilize countervailing power in their defense. Second, the harm done to certain groups becomes more visible in a universalizing system to others, who are often subjected to the same disempowering and destructive power, and thus are more inclined to join together to fight their common enemy. Third, universalizing is creating far more destructive impacts—ultimately the extinction of all life—that can motivate previously passive populations. Fourth, in certain eras or stages, including the super-universalizing system of today, universalizing is partly a response to the fragility and weakening of the system as it succumbs to its own contradictions, crises, and decline. System weakening leads people to lose faith in the "Establishment," and creates an opening for social movements to create a new society.

There are many strategies for change, which is a long game, but potentially is now foreshortened by the looming existential threats to the human experiment. Universalizers can be practical (but fiercely urgent) in their visionary aims, embracing strategies that move the public toward large change visions without scaring people off with hyper-revolutionary slogans. Universalizers use radical reform in a broader vision of rapid system change, something that distinguishes them from non-universalizers. Like other forms of resistance, universal resistance is non-violent and uses strategies of non-cooperation, including boycotts, civil disobedience, lock-outs, lock-ins, sit-ins, petitions, street protests, workplace blockages, strikes, divestments, and many other non-violent tactics.

WAVE ERAS AND THE HISTORY OF UNIVERSALIZING RESISTANCE

Universal resistance bursts out like prairie fires in "wave eras." These are periods marked by the eruption of many single- and multi-issue movements. Socialist leader, Eugene Debs, who cut his teeth in the populist wave era, said in 1897, "The issue is Socialism versus capitalism . . . the time has come to regenerate society . . . we are on the eve of a universal change."[2]

Debs foreshadowed the universalizing resistance catalyzed by Martin Luther King in the 1960s wave era. King came to believe in an economic revolution, launching a Poor People's campaign and a bill for economic and social rights, espousing "a national responsibility to provide work for all" in a "social-ist" system.[3] He also became a passionate opponent of the Vietnam war and broader US militarism, famously denouncing his own nation, the United States, as "the greatest purveyor of violence in the world."[4] King helped to catalyze a "movement of movements"—linking the civil rights and racial jus-tice movements with the peace movement and anti-capitalist movements, embodying perhaps better than any other US movement leader the practice of universalizing resistance.

The four wave eras to learn from in the United States are the 1890s Gilded Age; the 1930s New Deal; the 1960s; and the 1970s New Right and the Reagan Era dating from the 1980s, which includes the right-wing populism of the Tea Party and Donald Trump. While universalizing resistance on the Left has not risen to levels seen in some earlier wave eras, we are witness-ing a multiplicity of new progressive movements—from the environmen-tal and climate movements (350.org) to the African-American movement against mass incarceration (Black Lives Matter) to various labor and polit-ical "democracy movements" challenging inequality, corporate power, and billionaire politics (Occupy Wall Street). Some of these movements are beginning to universalize around intersectional clusters bridging labor and the environment, race and poverty/inequality, feminism and peace, democracy and race, anti-war protest and immigrant rights, and corporate power and democracy.

The rise of a self-avowed "socialist" Presidential candidate, such as Bernie Sanders in 2016 (or, much earlier, Socialist Party leader Eugene Debs in 1916 and progressive leader Henry Wallace in 1948) backed by large social move-ments, shows that there is a history of progressive and Left universalizing movements spilling into the electoral scene. The Republican Party since Reagan—and especially in the wake of Donald Trump's take-over of the party in 2016—clearly indicates how the Establishment in both parties is par-tially weakening and being forced to the door by universalizing movements, especially on the Right. If Left universalizing movements don't step up, on the ground and in the electoral political arena, they will be ground under by the Right "Trumpist" or other authoritarian movements.

Political parties can unify movements for transformative change. Political parties in the United States rarely carry out this crucial movement work, but this is one such potential moment. The prospect for success depends on the ability to persevere even when it seems hopeless. And, even if universal resistance breaks out, on either Left or Right, it does not ensure a successful outcome; system change may not happen or may even create a worse social order. Nonetheless, without universalizing, no system change is possible. The universalizing resister must have an element of Don Quixote, possessed with a passion to pursue revolution and justice against all odds. Or as an old movement slogan goes: "Be realistic: Demand the impossible." The impossible then becomes possible.

THE POPULIST WAVE: DEATH TO THE ROBBER BARONS!

The 1890s gave birth to the modern American corporation as the dominant institution in the United States—and catalyzed a wave of resistance against it. The 1890s created juicy targets: a 1% of "robber barons," who stole much of the nation's wealth as they beat into poverty a new generation of immigrant workers; a greedy group of Wall Street bankers led by J. P. Morgan, who created a credit system that sucked in the nation's farmers and put them into insurmountable debt. The result was a tidal wave of universalized resistance, led by the catalytic movement of Southern and Western agrarian resisters known as populists. They created farmers' groups like the Southern Alliance, the Colored Farmers' Alliance, the Grange, and the Greenbackers, some of whom formed independent political parties.

The populists were the "Occupy Movement" of the 19th century. They called for a systemic revolution against the first wolves of Wall Street and for public take-over of the big Morgan and Rockefeller banks. Populist orator Mary Lease proclaimed, "Wall Street owns the country. It is no longer a government of the people, by the people and for the people, but a government of Wall Street, by Wall Street and for Wall Street."[5] The only solution: "The corporation has absorbed the community. The community must now absorb the corporation,"[6] meaning abolishing the private banking system, breaking up the Rockefeller and Morgan trusts, and rebuilding the economy around producer cooperatives. In 1892, the populists created "the People's Party" which agitated for systemic change in Wall Street to bring down the robber baron regime. The populist movement's chronicler, historian Lawrence Goodwyn, calls it the "flowering of the largest democratic mass movement in American history."[7]

Some populists in the South tried to unite Black and white farmers in an ambitious universalizing resistance. Populist Tom Watson in Georgia saw that if the white and Black farmers' alliances could unite the populists, it would create a revolution. He said of Black and white farmers:

> [Y]ou are kept apart that you may be separately fleeced of your earnings. You are made to hate each other because upon that hatred is rested the keystone of the arch of financial despotism that enslaves you both. You

are deceived and blinded that you may not see how this race antagonism perpetuates a monetary system which beggars both.[8]

Unfortunately, many populists had tendencies toward xenophobia, racism, and anti-Semitism, and failed to bring industrial immigrant workers into their fold. But they did help to catalyze and sometimes ally with militant sister movements in the urban working class of the Eastern cities where the workers, many of them impoverished immigrants, lived.

The populist period was a "wave era" because farmers' groups helped to catalyze, and sometimes united with, radical labor unions, such as the Knights of Labor and the American Railway Union (ARU). Terence Powderly, an early leader of the Knights, called for replacing capitalism with a cooperative economy run by workers: "There is no good reason why labor cannot, through cooperation, own and operate mines, factories and railroads. We are the willing victims of an outrageous system."[9] The ARU, led by socialist Eugene Debs, a Presidential candidate for the Socialist Party in 1916, earlier supported the populists and called for nation-wide strikes and for populist victory. In 1897, he wrote that, "The issue is Socialism versus Capitalism. I am for Socialism because I am for humanity . . . Money constitutes no proper basis of civilization."[10] By the late 1890s, other labor unions, such as the Industrial Workers of the World or "Wobblies," took up the populist anti-capitalist cause, adopting as a slogan the universalizing phrase "An injury to one is an injury to all." The Wobblies called for "anarcho-syndicalism," or economic democracy organized by autonomous worker groups.

The populists helped to unleash a long wave of universalizing popular resistance that portended a system change. Tragically, they were destroyed when the Democratic Party in 1896 selected as their candidate William Jennings Bryan, who appeared to some populists as one of their own, but divided their ranks. Bryan, a blend of conservative, liberal, and radical, effectively killed the populists and the People's Party. Bryan watered down the revolutionary populist agenda for nationalizing the banks and returning land to the people. Instead, his Democratic Party program focused on mere reforms (elaborated in his famous "cross of gold" speech and his embrace of the "free silver movement," believed to ease the debt of farmers by expanding credit based on currency backed by silver). While Bryan effectively ended the populist revolution, the populist legacy lived on in early socialist labor movements and the progressive movements of the next few decades, which made important reforms, improving the lives of workers and farmers, but saving the system that the early populists tried to overthrow. The populist era was the first great modern wave era—with potent currents of universalizing resistance. The populist era suggests that we must not forget that convergent movements to occupy Wall Street and create economic democracy are likely to recur over and over again.

THE NEW DEAL WAVE: PEOPLE OVER PROFITS

The 1% called the wealthy President, Franklin Delano Roosevelt (FDR) a traitor to his class, and he said, "I welcome their hatred." He also said that the New Deal was "saving capitalism from itself." Early 20th-century globalizing led to wars for colonies and credit universalizing and stock market bubbles, then to the 1929 crash and Great Depression. Roosevelt wanted to reform the system and many New Deal programs and organizations, as Richard Cloward and Francis Piven argue, stifled the spontaneous universalizing among grass-roots workers starting wildcat strikes, and tenants rising to resist eviction by landlords and police. But despite the repression of grass-roots disruptive resistance, FDR opened up space for universalizing. The 1930s was one of the great wave eras, spawning movements for poor people, the homeless, the unemployed, social welfare, civil rights, feminism, peace, socialism, Communism, anarchism, and more.

Desperate for what the founder of industrial labor organizing, John L. Lewis, called "a crust of bread," millions of workers organized and formed unions. But while Lewis, like FDR, fought mainly for more bread within the system, many rank-and-file workers wanted bread and roses, not just a job, but a new social contract. The "bread and roses" slogan came originally from a speech supporting the 1912 Lawrence, Massachusetts textile strike, which helped to inspire an immortal poem saying, "Our lives shall not be sweated from birth until life closes; Hearts starve as well as bodies, give us bread, but give us roses!"[11] This was a symbol of the universalizing anti-systemic spirit. By the 1930s, it spread like wildfire not only among workers and the unemployed, but across the wave of socialists, Communists, and anarchists signing up to help organize a fired-up working class. These revolutionary activists became prime movers in the new universalizing labor movement, adding their own explicitly anti-capitalist vision to help create a sense of revolutionary possibilities.

The white labor movement sometimes joined forces with Black labor groups, universalizing resistance across racial lines in organizations such as the National Negro Congress, uniting Black and white workers. The universalizing movements highlighted how low pay and abuse of Black workers dragged down the wages and working conditions of white workers, using language of class solidarity rather than the discourse of "white privilege." Nate Shaw, Southern Black worker and a member of the Sharecroppers' Union partly organized by the Communist Party, said:

> O it's plain as your hand. The poor white man and the poor black man is sittin in the same saddle today—big dudes done banched em off that way . . . The controllin power is in the hands of the rich man. . . . That class is standin together and the poor white man is out there on the colored list.[12]

The New Deal holds powerful lessons for universalizing across racial lines. Class politics is central to overcoming the fragmentation around race that has long plagued progressive universalizing movements. It is widely known that New Deal benefits were denied to farm workers, domestic workers, and other mainly African-American labor, as a way to keep Southern whites committed to the New Deal. But the Communist Party, during the New Deal years, helped to bridge the race divide through a class-based resistance. It became a more important force in America than ever before (and ever after), and helped to midwife a new universalizing spirit in politics and the workplace, fueling the idea that FDR's New Deal was just the opening act in a new American revolution. The labor movement, and its anti-capitalist organizers, were the catalytic movement of the era, bringing major reforms to the workplace, including industrial unions, wage and benefit standards, and new limits to the work day—some of these unions worked hard to bring together Black and white workers in common struggle against corporate elites (a lesson of great importance in the Trump era). Beyond these struggles and New Deal reforms, the 1930s became a wave era because multiple movements converged to fight for system change, including anti-war activists seeking to prevent the drift toward another world war, African-American and civil rights activists seeking to end Jim Crow laws, and female labor and socialist organizers who wanted to consummate a new revolution of bread and roses. As in the populist wave era, capitalism survived, and the labor-led revolt created several decades of reform by business-oriented politicians in the Progressive Era that consolidated corporate rule. It also subjected that rule to new possibilities, opening the way for a new wave era in the 1960s.

THE SIXTIES WAVE: WE SHALL OVERCOME

The 1960s was a period of relative affluence, universalizing the ideals of mass prosperity and caste rights that the system claimed as its own. But its mythical ideals of class and caste liberation clashed with the realities of a white Western affluence built on poverty and the bodies of people of color in the United States and abroad. Caste realities at home led to the civil rights movement that catalyzed a new wave era in America. The African-American activists awakened Americans as a whole, millions sickened by the racist violence and unraveling hypocrisy in the nation and system they had idealized—and millions also inspired by Martin Luther King's iconic "I Have a Dream" speech, an early harbinger of his evolution toward universalizing resistance.

White college students in the North flocked South, while many more stayed put and became activists on their own campuses, confronting class and caste inequalities in their universities and communities. Student activist Tom

Hayden penned the Port Huron Statement in 1962, a manifesto calling for a revolution of participatory democracy—a universalizing vision—that would finally align the reality of America with its highest ideals. Hayden wrote that "the economy itself is of such social importance that its major resources and means of production should be open to democratic participation and subject to democratic social regulation."[13] The new student movement, influenced by Hayden's call for a new economic system, and led by Students for a Democratic Society (SDS), became one expression of the universalization of civil rights resistance. It extended the fight against racial hierarchy into a broader anti-hierarchical struggle against the capitalist system. Berkeley student activist leader, Mario Savio, called it the machine: as Savio proclaimed at a rally on the Berkeley, California campus:

> There is a time, when the operation of the machine becomes so odious, makes you so sick at heart, that you can't take part; you can't even passively take part, and you've got to put your bodies upon the gears and upon the wheels, upon the levers, upon all the apparatus, and you've got to make it stop."[14]

The students blended the civil rights activism into resistance against the Vietnam war and the larger US militarized capitalist regime. A big part of the generation of young people started to awaken, struggling to find peace and justice in a system designed for war and exploitation that could end in an apocalyptic nuclear war between the United States and the Soviet Union. As former SDS leader, Todd Gitlin, has written recently, of an SDS slogan: "The issues are interconnected. They arise together and need to be solved together."[15] Such universalizing thinking was "an article of faith."[16] Moreover, the current threat of global extermination was, for the first time, becoming part of universalizing movements, the threat almost too scary to contemplate and creating more activism and more paralysis.

The students' universalizing against the system was reinforced when Martin Luther King, in one of the great universalizing speeches in history, "Beyond Vietnam," announced against the will of many of his single-issue advisors, that he could not remain silent about the Vietnam war, linking the violence against Blacks at home with America's unrelenting violence against colonized peoples abroad. King went further, as he joined with class as well as caste struggles, marching with the garbage workers of Memphis to support their strike just before he was killed. King's murder in 1968 reflected the threat and the promise posed by universalizing, especially when led by America's greatest freedom fighter, who moved from civil rights champion to a universalizing leader against America's militarized corporate capitalism.

After King turned against the war and embraced class struggle and a mass movement for socialism universalizing resistance exploded. Despite King's death, the 1960s wave bred new forms of the peace movement, the gay movement, the feminist movement, the environmental movement, and a fervent anti-militarized capitalist agenda. These movements retrenched to separate identities, partially reflecting the white male leadership of Students for a Democratic Society (SDS) that failed to diversify its class membership and to walk its talk about overcoming class and caste hierarchies. The unexpected rebellions arising among so many different groups partially converged into one of the great universalizing resistance forces in modern US history. It didn't overturn the system, but it created many radical reforms that changed the country.

THE NEW RIGHT WAVE: RESTORE AUTHORITY
AND THE RIGHTS OF WHITES

An unfortunate consequence of the 1960s wave was the rise of the New Right, whose own universalizing trends began in the 1970s and now threaten a system transformation of a very different stripe, with President Donald Trump taking power. The same conditions leading to Left universalizing resistance also spur the Right wing, as seen in the case of Weimar Germany in the 1920s, a classic instance of right-wing universalizing when Left socialist and Communist movements failed to respond to the crises of the faltering German republic and its sinking working classes.

Right-wing universalizing movements and parties are a major historical force that have created fascism, Nazism, military dictatorships, and other enduring authoritarian regimes. In the United States, they have traditionally involved right-wing populism linked to religious and cultural warriors rooted in the South, who organized to protest the breakdown of traditional cultural values, the growth of immigration, and a demographic shift toward a non-white population and the decline of jobs and the American Dream for the white working class. The election of Donald Trump foreshadows the culmination of right-wing US populism that could lead to a new form of US authoritarianism, similar in many frightening ways to the rise of fascism in Weimar Germany.

Right-wing universalizing entails efforts to restore traditional aristocratic or authoritarian rule, typically by reconstructing steep hierarchies of class and caste (race and gender), and rebuilding war-making powers and strong corporate and police control over the state and population. Classic right-wing universalizing movements arose in 1920s Weimar Germany, with Hitler ultimately gaining power through the convergence of German right-wing populist movements and their ultimate coronation by the German aristocracy and military, who feared the German socialist and Communist Left more than they feared Hitler and his universalizing right-wing populism. In the United States, right-wing corporate movements, confronting the anti-corporate movements of the 1960s New Left, rallied to organize the biggest corporations in new alliances and federations, to take back the state, leading to the "Reagan Revolution" in 1980.

After Reagan, the Republican Party fell increasingly under the sway of universalizing right-wing populist movements appealing to a Southern authoritarian, racist, anti-immigrant, populist base involving millions of Americans. These turned increasingly against the old pre-Reagan Republican Establishment, and, over recent decades have moved further and further toward an authoritarian and white supremacist politics. This shift led in 2016 to the populist anti-establishment take-over of the Republican Party by Donald Trump, a classic authoritarian leader who became President and grabbed state power through powerful appeals to Far Right movements in the Republican base and across the US working classes. Trumpism is a universalizing movement building ties across corporate elites, white workers, the Republican Party, Tea Party activists, and Evangelical Christians, among others.

To succeed, the New Right movements, funded partly by billionaires and large corporations, mobilized a new Southern base uniting Evangelical Christians, family value moralists, militarists, anti-immigrant movements, and the old racist Jim Crow Southern political infrastructure. Nixon created the discourse for organizing this new "moral majority," and talented grass-roots organizers in the 1970s created a new grass-roots prairie fire, involving direct-mail political organizing by Richard Viguerie, Evangelical Christian movements led by Pat Robertson and Jerry Falwell, and America First campaigns led by Pat Buchanan. All responded to the growing sense of disorder and breakdown of traditional white privilege and values, catalyzing a new right-wing universalizing movement. It would not only seek to reverse the radical reforms of the 1960s' New Left, but to dismantle FDR's New Deal and re-establish a new version of Gilded Age capitalism and white supremacy, marked by monopolistic giant global corporations and a vast military establishment, all organized around hyper-nationalist, anti-immigrant, and coded racist and sexist ideology.

This right-wing universalizing, led today by the Tea Party, a Far Right Republican populist movement, (and a vast infrastructure of grass-roots religious, anti-immigrant, militaristic, and super-conservative billionaire elites, such as the Koch Brothers), became a defining political force of the last several decades. It has led to an unprecedented Republican take-over not only of Congress, but of state governorships, legislatures, and courts. In 2016, they took control of the Republican Party and elected Donald Trump as President, a watershed moment heightening the need for universalizing progressive movements mobilizing all-out to counter and defeat the newly powerful and authoritarian right-wing universalizing project.

Even before nominating and electing Trump, the Republican Party had become a swampland of Far Right universalizing movements, calling themselves Tea Party, Libertarian, white nationalist, and populist—and now often categorized under the umbrella of the "Alt-Right." Under Trump, they have universalized to Evangelical churches, white workers, corporate elites, small business, Libertarians, and many other groups. They have taken control of all major elements of the state, an unprecedented triumph of authoritarian right-wing populism in modern America.

While this represents the greatest threat to US democracy in modern times, it is worth noting, as Ralph Nader has written, that the right-wing populists who elected Trump share some of the key concerns of progressive and Left universalizing. They denounce the big banks, crony capitalism, corporate trade agreements, loss of working-class jobs and stagnant wages, big money in politics, and an "Establishment" that has captured the government. There may be ways, despite the overwhelming differences, that Right and Left universalizing movements can come together on some key issues to challenge corporate globalization and US "crony capitalism." Left populists should invite a conversation with many disenchanted working-class Trump voters, as already noted, to build bridges and invigorate a new class politics on the Left.

Far Right US movements—creating a more authoritarian regime and potentially moving toward an American-style fascism—are an overwhelming threat to the United States. Jihad attacks on the United States itself are the perfect fuel for right-wing universalizing movements. We can expect many repetitions of such events as the 2013 Jihadi attacks at the Boston Marathon and the December 2015 attack in San Bernardino, California. These will fuel the Rightist movements that today are making Ronald Reagan look liberal.

The experience of Weimar Germany shows that right-wing universalizing creates even greater urgency for left-wing universalizing. In Weimar, the Far Right gained traction when economic problems and national German decline de-legitimated the German Establishment and opened the door to a new era of xenophobic, militarist, racist, and ultimately genocidal right-wing movements, including fascism. More populous left-wing movements, including socialist and Communist parties, fought each other and failed to offer solutions to the economic crisis driving German workers to despair. They also failed to speak to the authoritarian cultural, family, and nationalist upbringing of the German workers—and they didn't seek to build on common values including the honoring of labor and community. A strong unity government on the Left might have prevented Hitler, but the Left parties failed to carry out the universalizing progressive politics that could have won the allegiance of the German majority.

The lesson has never been more salient in the United States since the Republican Party embraced Trump, one of the most dangerous authoritarian leaders of modern times. The rise of Far Right universalizing movements—taking over much of the Republican Party—is the strongest argument now for progressive and Left universalizing movements. They are our best hope for preventing the rise of American fascism and combating the massive inequalities and environmental catastrophes of corporate militarized capitalism.

NOAM CHOMSKY ON LEFT PROSPECTS: UNIVERSALIZING ACROSS BOUNDARIES

This discussion between Noam Chomsky and Charles Derber took place on October 21, 2016, and is excerpted from a forthcoming film to be released in 2017.

Charlie Derber: Noam, recently you gave a very powerful talk on the theme of extinction, the nightmare looming over us from climate change and nuclear war. As I listened and read the transcript, one gets the feeling that we're entering a new stage of history. It's not an easy stage to contemplate. What I want to focus on in this conversation is just what can everybody do, especially in the wake of Trump's election as President. Trump's agenda appears to be taking out the climate initiatives that gave a little hope on climate change. And foreign policy measures that would make nuclear conflict more likely deserve attention in our discussion of extinction.

Do you believe we have moved into this new era? Do you see the threat of extinction as fundamentally changing the way the Left movements have to think about what they're doing?

Noam Chomsky: It's very difficult to talk about the Left as an entity because it's a collection of very disparate movements involved in all sorts of endeavors, many of them quite valuable.

The Left needs to become unified and integrated because whatever particular issue you're working on, this crisis of potential extinction is overshadowing it. There must be international solidarity.

The situation for organizing here is not that bleak. If you take a look at the last election, Clinton won a majority of the votes. The outcome has to do with special features of the US electoral system, which is pretty regressive by world standards. Among younger people, Clinton did win a substantial majority. More important, Sanders won an overwhelming majority. That's the younger part of the population. You take a look at Trump supporters. Many of them voted for Obama.

In 2008, they were seduced by his slogan which was Hope and Change. They pretty quickly found out that they're not getting hope and they're not getting change. Now they voted for someone else who's preaching hope and change, different orientation. They want change. They're right. The situation that much of the workforce and lower middle class has lived in is, it's not starvation, but it's stagnation.

The system has been designed. It's not a matter of economic laws. It's policy and decisions, which have been quite harmful to a large mass of the population. In fact, a majority. It's also undermined democracy, both here and even more so in Europe. There's a natural and justified call for change. These are opportunities for the Left. Many of the people who voted for Trump could have voted for Sanders.

Charlie Derber: A lot of people are saying now, they're putting a lot of onus of responsibility on Obama and on Clinton.

The Left has been highly critical of neoliberalism. But it hasn't been seen broadly by the population. Particularly the working-class parts of the population that you're identifying as being really harmed by this, as that somehow neither the Left nor the Democratic Party is really speaking to them. It's speaking to coastal elites, it's speaking to educated people, speaking maybe to young educated people. It's not speaking to them.

Noam Chomsky: Not speaking to people who are really deprived.

The Left should be working with and for the African-American community, it should be working on civil rights, it should be working for gay rights, for women's rights, and so on. That's fine. What it has dropped pretty much is class issues.

Charlie Derber: Would you encourage the Left to rethink the class issue and economic opportunities—that maybe a Sanders-style development will help reconfigure the Left? Not that it abandons the most depressed people in the society, but it finds a way to deal with larger forces of inequality, as you say, as integrated within the larger capitalist systems.

Noam Chomsky: It's certainly a must. The so-called identity politics has led to great successes, but when they are designed and presented in such a way that they appear to be an attack on the lifestyle, values, commitments of a large part of the population, there's going to be reaction. That shouldn't be done.

Charlie Derber: For example, the progressive movement uses the language of white privilege. Some of the people who live in working-class areas, white working-class areas, they look at that and they say, "What are you talking about? We're not seeing this privilege." Does this require the Left to re-assess its vocabulary?

Noam Chomsky: It's not just about our vocabulary. It's about an understanding. Actually, Arlie Hochschild's book is very revealing in this respect.

Charlie Derber: *Strangers in Their Own Land.* Hochschild is a noted sociologist.

Noam Chomsky: We know the story. She's lived for many years in the bayou country in Louisiana and gave a very sympathetic understanding, conception of what the people are thinking and why, from a point of view of a Berkeley progressive, which she is. She was accepted into the community. It's very revealing. The images she uses, which they accepted as the correct ones, is that people . . . they see themselves as standing in a line. They've been working hard all their lives, their parents worked hard, they're doing all the right things. . . . They go to church, they read the Bible, they have traditional families, and so on. They've done everything the right way.

All of the sudden the line is stalled. Up ahead of them, there are people leaping forward, which doesn't bother them because according to the doctrine, that's the American way. You work hard and you have merit, strange kind of merit, you get rewards. What bothers them is that the people behind them in the line, as they see it, are being pushed ahead of them by the federal government.

Charlie Derber: By liberal elites and so forth.

Noam Chomsky: By liberal elites and the federal government. That they resent. The facts are different. There's no basis in fact, but you can understand the basis for the perception. That can be dealt with by serious activist organizing. Many of the people Hochschild was dealing with are committed environmentalists, but they hate the EPA. They want to destroy the Environment Protection Agency. The families are very interesting. Hochschild's working in an area which is sometimes called cancer alley. Everybody's dying from cancer from the chemical pollution plants. Nevertheless, they vote for a Congressman who wants to dismantle the EPA entirely.

There's a reason. Turns out, there's an internal rationality to this self-destructive position. Organizers and activists can go after that. The internal rationality is that what they see is some guy from the EPA wearing a suit and jacket coming down to tell them, "You can't fish in this river." Meanwhile, he does nothing about the chemical plants. Why do they want the EPA?

Charlie Derber: Do you see any examples of progressive Left organizing that really operate out of that Hochschild narrative and find a way to really connect with these communities in a credible way to these people?

Noam Chomsky: The core of this, I think, which you've mentioned several times, is revitalizing the labor movement. Reasons include scale, history, and so on, the ways people interact, gain understanding, and become committed to work together for common goals that will benefit all. Labor has always been and will continue to be pretty much in the forefront of any progressive activities, just as it has been in the past. It's been severely damaged by corporate and government programs going back to right after the Second World War, but escalating during the Reagan and Clinton period, the neoliberal period. It can be revitalized. These are not just people living in the bayous. They're living 2 miles away from us. There are things to be done.

Just to take one example, a couple of years ago in a Boston suburb, Taunton, Mass., some multi-national decided to close down a factory. It was a factory producing specialized parts for airplanes. The factory was reasonably profitable, but it wasn't making enough profit for the bankers that run the multi-national, so they decided to close it down. The union and the workforce offered to buy it and run it themselves. It could have been run and been profitable. If they had had popular support, community support, activist support, they might have been able to work that out.

Charlie Derber: That's been done. Gar Alperovitz has documented that in Ohio . . .

Noam Chomsky: It's done, but this is a case right here in Boston. The things that Gar Alperovitz is doing, that are going on right now, these are indications of what could be done much more broadly. It could be done right here. It could be done on a mass scale. Go back to the financial crisis, really a housing bubble that burst and led to the financial crisis. At one point, the government, federal government, had basically nationalized the auto industry. Almost. There were choices at that point. If there had been a Left functioning, it could have influenced those choices. There was not, so it didn't influence them.

Charlie Derber: You mean by a Left functioning, do you mean a more active labor, popular community-based . . .

Noam Chomsky: Popular activist movements. There were choices that could *have been* made. One choice, the one that was taken, was to pay off the owners and managers, reconstitute the industry and hand it back to the former owners or other people much like them and have it go back to its old activities. That's the course that was taken. An alternative course would have been to have handed the industry over to the stakeholders, the workforce and the community. They'd need some support but no more than . . . probably less than what was paid off to the companies. Instead of having them produce cars, have them own and run and manage it and produce what the country needs, which is not more cars. Drive through Boston and you see that's not what the country needs.

What we need is some reasonable system of mass transportation, which goes right to the environmental problem and many others. Even just the simple comfort of not sitting in a traffic jam all day in getting where you want to go. That would have been an alternative. Was it feasible? It would have been feasible if there were an organized activist Left, just as in the Taunton case nearby. Those are directions in which activism can go. They can have massive effect on the economy, on the society, on the nature of the workforce, on what they perceive as real hope and change. Things like that can happen almost every day.

Charlie Derber: When you talk about this organized Left community as a front that's . . . do you have a more concrete image of what that looks like? Does it mean environmental movements and anti-racist movements becoming part of a unified . . .

Noam Chomsky: All of that, but even more than that. It can also become a serious independent party. In the US system, which happens to be very regressive by comparative standards, it's very hard for an independent party to enter the political system, but it's not impossible. If an authentic independent political party would develop, it could become an electoral alternative. That means a party that doesn't just show up every 4 years and say, I have a candidate for the election. It means starting at the local levels. School boards, town meetings, state legislatures, House of Representatives, all the way up. In some of these House of Representatives districts, a very small amount of money is enough to win the election. Many of them run unopposed. State legislature is the same.

Charlie Derber: Ralph Nader has been making this argument, that you have, district by district, a small number of people whom could be elected. There's a lot of debate about whether this is an independent party or working with some of the Sanders people to align with progressive Democrats. What's your view of how to think about that?

Noam Chomsky: I don't think you have to make a decision on that. You can try both and see which one succeeds. They're not opposed.

I think it's worth trying everything you can. If the Democratic Party could be taken away from the party bosses, the huge funders, the Democratic machine and turned into a popular party, fine. If an independent party . . .

Charlie Derber: In your view, just in terms of your personal view, is that a realistic possibility? Could Sanders, Warren, some of these new people who tried to get Pelosi out and dig in with labor, is this worth doing in your view?

Noam Chomsky: It's worth doing and it's not an alternative to trying to develop an independent party. Both should be done. They could even cooperate.

This is only one stream. This should be going on alongside many other activist efforts. For example, the effort, say, to get to worker ownership in Taunton or at a large-scale level to shift the whole auto industry toward what it ought to be, which could have been done had there been some kind of activist Left like we're talking about. I think there's a basis for developing that.

Charlie Derber:	I think you're saying there's a very pluralistic set of possibilities for the communities we're talking about.
Noam Chomsky:	A healthy Left would be one in which individuals, of course, follow what they're good at, what makes sense to them, what fits into their life, and so on. You have to make choices. You can't do everything. Each of those individuals should recognize that the many other choices are parallel and mutually supportive, and we can get together and . . .
Charlie Derber:	You want to build connections among these different organizations and different communities.
Noam Chomsky:	In the past that has often been built around the labor movement. If the labor movement can be revitalized, that can happen again. It doesn't have to be just labor, but that should be a central part.
Charlie Derber:	You brought up Trump and the neo-fascist trend we're seeing across the world, across Europe, and so forth. You know a lot about fascism and the problems with popular fronts and so forth. Do you see unification emerging . . . extinction itself ought to be bringing people together because it's the biggest crisis ever faced. The rising of Trump and his contribution to all these threatening things might unify people as well.
Noam Chomsky:	Could happen. First of all, in Europe, there are progressive alternatives developing just as there are here. Yanis Varoufakis's DiEM25 initiative, Podemos in Spain. Corbyn in the UK . . .
Charlie Derber:	New party, more visionary party . . .
Noam Chomsky:	Some of it *is* parties, some organizations . . . seeking to reverse the undermining of democracy in Europe and build it. Not to destroy the European union like Brexit, but to try to rebuild a democratic European union, save what was good and important in it. That could become an important movement. There are many things developing. They should develop in an integrated fashion. In fact, there are other possible alliances. The Right wing in Europe, many elements of it, are opposed to the increasing confrontation with Russia, on the Russian border. That's fine. Trump is saying, let's reduce tensions. Fine. We should be working for that. All of these are alliances of human beings, whatever their politics, whatever their religious beliefs, whatever it may be, with the interest in preserving human life on earth. Those interactions should be pursued and can lead to other ones. They don't end there.
Charlie Derber:	Ralph Nader has made very strongly the case, that there are ways that these communities can find common ground.
Noam Chomsky:	They do.
Charlie Derber:	There are people like Thomas Frank who have argued the cultural differences are so profound, the religious differences are

so profound, that he finds this very problematic. Then there are other people like Hochschild and a lot of other writers, like Nader, people who are saying if we do this in a way that we bring people in direct contact with each other . . .

Noam Chomsky: With common interests.

For example, take the people that Hochschild was studying on the bayou, who are environmentalists, committed environmentalists, no reason why they can't work together with environmentalists who say, "Look, let's get regulations that really work. Not just against your fishing, but against your chemical companies." That's a common basis. It happens that many of them regard the Bible as a much more authentic source of information than science, but that's not graven in stone either. That can be changed.

In fact, in the Evangelical community, there have been very progressive elements. Take the Central America solidarity movements. They were very significant. This is probably the first time in history that *in* the country that was responsible for the atrocities, individuals were going to help the victims. I don't think that's ever happened before. Nobody ever dreamt of going to a Vietnamese village to live with the villagers, to help them, to provide a white face, which is a little protection. It just never occurred to anyone. This happened with tens of thousands of people during the Central America solidarity period. Many of them were Evangelical.

I remember talking in Evangelical churches in the Midwest where people not only had direct experience, but knew more about what was going on than academics did. They were directly involved. For example, after the election in Nicaragua, the right-wing election, many of them stayed. Others gave up and left, but they stayed. There's plenty of opportunities. These are also Evangelical Christians.

Organize in churches, organize in communities. How did the Central America solidarity movements develop? People totally secular and Left like me were perfectly capable of working together with Evangelical Christians on concrete things, like helping communities protect themselves from criminal atrocities, state crimes, and so on.

Charlie Derber: This would partly mean hooking up with people, say, like Jim Wallis, an Evangelical leader who is organizing young Evangelicals to do that. Also, you're thinking also . . . I went down to the South during the civil rights movements. Are you imagining that some of this might be environmentalists who are now in colleges in the North, but would go back to their native South and would work there?

Noam Chomsky: Civil rights movements are a good example. There was real interaction, very constructive interaction between Northern college students and deeply impoverished repressed Black areas in the rural South. Helped each other, worked together, created bonds.

Charlie Derber: I experienced that. It was powerful. I slept on the floor of a Black family and lived in Jackson, Mississippi. You're saying, that's in a way a metaphor for what has . . .

Noam Chomsky: It can be done. There's no point arguing that it can't be done because the cultural differences are too great. Press forward as far as you can. My guess is one will find that the cultural differences, though they'll remain (why shouldn't they?) can be overcome by common concerns and interests.

Charlie Derber: Trump may end up simply crushing with brute repression many of the Left forces.

Noam Chomsky: I don't see any reason to expect real neo-fascism. Could happen, but I don't think the indications are strong.
    We shouldn't be frightened of it. We should proceed with the opportunities we have which are considerable. Others can be brought in as well. The repressive forces themselves can be undermined. That's happened often. They have shared interests in many ways. If demonstrations and other activities are taken with an eye toward reaching out to those who are unsympathetic and bringing them in, I think a lot of progress can be made.

Charlie Derber: That's a hopeful. Nonetheless, given what Trump represents and particularly around climate issues and nuclear proliferation, do you feel there's an imperative that the progressive Left community, the public sensibility that you've described, needs to find some common ground to organize against Trump on these extinction issues?

Noam Chomsky: First of all, on climate, Trump is not all that different from the leadership of the Republican Party, or those in the primaries. Every single candidate either denied that climate change is happening or said we shouldn't do anything about it. Trump's position is maybe rhetorically more extreme, but not fundamentally different from the Party. That's a big educational and organizing opportunity for the Left. The United States is off the spectrum, global spectrum on this issue in some respects, which can be dealt with. Almost half the population thinks there can't be a climate change problem because of the Second Coming within a couple decades. That is not dealt with by demonstrations, but by sympathetic interactions.

Charlie Derber: I like the spirit of what you've been arguing, which is very invitational. I think what you're saying, contrary to Thomas Frank, for example, is that one can bridge a lot of these cultural differences. You don't want to go around labeling these people a cultural backwater.

Noam Chomsky: You don't come to people and say, "You're a cultural backwater." You deal with the fact that the beliefs that they have ought to be changed through their own recognition that these beliefs are not . . .

Charlie Derber:	You don't mean their cultural values in terms of religion and that . . .
Noam Chomsky:	Yes, I do.
Charlie Derber:	You do?
Noam Chomsky:	The belief, if the Bible and science conflict, that science is automatically wrong, people can come to see that's not true. Many people have. Much of the population has already passed through that change. Others can as well.
Charlie Derber:	That seems like a struggle because when you get to people who are deeply into Biblical studies and Biblical beliefs . . .
Noam Chomsky:	It's all of us, if we go back a couple generations, that's . . . If I go back to my grandfather, that was his belief. Things change.
Charlie Derber:	That's an optimistic flavor in the analysis, because you're saying the progressive community should not be deterred in the way that Thomas Frank suggests.
Noam Chomsky:	No. It should not be deterred and it shouldn't be contemptuous. It should be sympathetic, understanding, find common ground, things you can work on. Not put aside these questions of belief and understanding. They can be changed too.
	Incidentally, just look at other possible common grounds. One major area is Trump's proposal for infrastructure development. The country needs that. It's needed it all along. These are actually Obama proposals which were blocked by the Republican Congress. The Republicans were a wrecking machine. Don't allow anything to work. One of the good things about their having control of the government is they might actually implement the policies instead of killing them. Here there are possible grounds for serious organizing and activism with the Trump backers and the workforce. These are jobs for them if it's done properly. A big "if." The vague indications about how to proceed from the Trump team are not encouraging, to put it mildly.
Charlie Derber:	There are unions who worked their hearts out during this election. Michael Moore, he was writing a lot about this. They found their own members were voting for Trump for many of the reasons that we've talked about. What is your response to that?
Noam Chomsky:	Labor union activists generally work hard and have achieved a great deal for union members and the rest of us. They now have to go back to their own unions. There's every reason to work with their members. There's a reason, after all, why they voted for Trump. No alternative was being presented to them. Present an alternative to them. Even Sanders didn't manage really to bridge the class issue. It should be done.

Charlie Derber: You've offered a very realistic but hopeful view of how to invite conversation and dialog and build connections to the whole country.

Noam Chomsky: Pursue the opportunities that exist. There are many of them. We don't know how far they can reach. There's no point mourning the bad things that happen. Find the things that can be done. Many of them with international connections, because there are similar problems. Many of them integrating people who seem to be on opposite sides of the divide, but really have common interests. Those could be extricated and pursued.

Charlie Derber: Wonderful. I feel very much in sympathy with the spirit of invitation and dialog and connection and unity. I think it's the way . . . it's at the heart of the progressive Left agenda in some way. We haven't done it very well very often, but it's consistent with our core values.

Noam Chomsky: That's what we should be pursuing.

Charlie Derber: That's what we should be doing. Thank you very much, Noam.

Noam Chomsky, *Institute Professor Emeritus of Linguistics at MIT, is renowned globally as a critical public intellectual, political theorist, and activist. He is the leading critic of US foreign policy and has championed grass-roots movements against US militarized capitalism, American hegemony, corporate globalization, and authoritarian regimes around the world.*

4

Movement GPS: Ten Rules of the Road to Justice and Democracy

"Climate change is real, it is happening right now. It is the most urgent threat facing our entire species, and we need to work collectively together and stop procrastinating. We need to support leaders around the world who do not speak for the big polluters, but who speak for all of humanity, for the indigenous people of the world, for the billions and billions of underprivileged people out there who would be most affected by this. For our children's children, and for those people out there whose voices have been drowned out by the politics of greed . . . Let us not take this planet for granted."

Leonardo DiCaprio (2016 Oscars ceremony)

"Sacred cows make the tastiest hamburger."

Abbie Hoffman

Ten new rules for the road guide the development of the universalizing resistance we need. The ten rules constitute an anatomy of resistance needed to respond to current expanding and apocalyptic systemic power and to create what Bernie Sanders calls a "democratic revolution" for a new system. You can't fight universalizing power without universalizing countervailing "people power." Nor can you fight today's super-universalized capitalism—or the Far Right universalizing Trumpist movements now seeking to govern in uneasy conjunction with the corporate Establishment—with a strategy appropriate to an earlier stage.

There are ten new "rules of the road" for progressive anti-system movements. Not just a laundry list, they are analytically tied to the expansion and intertwining of multiple forms of power and apocalyptic violence in the super-universalizing system. They are approaches that resistance movements around the world will embrace in different degrees at different eras, but they are ultimately all central to any successful resistance movements against the super-universalizing system. They are the foundation of a new strategy of systemic change to create a new society based on social justice and democracy.

They reflect the reality that ordinary people are the only ultimate checks and balances—and the only force that can transform the system itself.

These ten new rules are mandates for successful universalizing on both Left and Right. In what follows in the rest of the book, I apply the principles mainly to the Left universalizing movements that we desperately need now. The principles are essential to success in both Right and Left universalizing activism. But in the discussion below, unless otherwise indicated, I focus the application of the ten new rules to the Left-oriented universalizers and movements that fight for social justice, democracy, and planetary survival.

When you follow the ten new road rules, you are embracing a progressive universalizing movement strategy very different from the current approach. It can be boiled down to and implemented through a few tangible steps of "what to do." First, through schools, media, think-tanks and movement educational conferences, workshops, and institutes, it must build a new activist knowledge base, which educates activists and the general public about the new super-universalized system. It must show in its educational work how silo activism, while valuable, does not understand the power of the system and the fight needed to succeed. Second, it builds the space and campaigns and coalitions that bring silo movements together—with each other and the larger public—in common struggle to save the world. Third, it enables a general and sustainable infrastructure of universalized movements that make possible a new system protecting all life. This is a strategy uniting current silo movements in a fight—both in and outside the electoral arena—to create a new just, sustainable, and democratic system.

What is the relationship between the ten new rules and the three strategic principles? They are essentially two intertwined ways of talking about and framing a new kind of struggle. The "rules of the road" are the new principles which movements must embrace in what is a new, apocalyptic stage of the system itself. Strategic principles and tactics—which I describe in Part III—summarize the changing balance of forces and power in the system, the organizational means of increasing popular power through universalizing resistance, and the nuts and bolts of enacting the new movement rules.

Each chapter below (from Chapter 5 to Chapter 14) discusses one of the new "rules of the road" that highlights how universalized resistance differs from silo resistance. For each new rule, I explore what is new and different about universalized resistance. I make a case for each of these new rules and explore the dilemmas and contradictions of embracing them. Creating a new social change strategy is hard work—and we need to acknowledge all the challenges.

My discussion of each new rule is followed by brief reflections and stories by prominent intellectuals and activists in the trenches. The ten new rules are both descriptive and prescriptive, with chapters looking at examples of emerging new universalizing movements and the principles that can guide them toward success.

FROM GRIEVANCE TO GOVERNANCE: EIGHT FEATURES OF TRANSFORMATIVE CAMPAIGNS

Jodeen Olguin-Tayler

One morning, in December 2015, I found myself at the Ford Foundation watching Anna Galland, Ai-jen Poo, and Heather McGhee share a stage at an event called The Future of Organizing: Contesting for Power in a Changing World. The event, co-convened by National People's Action, was designed to highlight alignment about a shared aspiration for the progressive movement. Watching these three women, *together*, left me beaming.

Over the last 8 years, I've been honored to serve as a Field or Campaign Director for MoveOn.org, the National Domestic Workers Alliance (NDWA), and Demos—the three organizations led by these brilliant women. The emerging alignment of these three organizations, from different sectors, and with very different capacities, inspired me to distill the lessons from working with them, and our allies, to lead Transformative Campaigns.

Transformative Campaigns are a means to create the operational alignment

our progressive infrastructure needs to build a new, and specific, type of power: the power to govern based on our values. The capacities to govern are very different from the capacities we've needed to successfully elevate grievances and lead protests. In order to govern, we need political power. To govern with progressive and social justice values requires independence from the two dominant US political parties. That's why a critical mass of progressive and social justice organizations is aligning around a strategic focus on building Independent Political Power (IPP). Many of our organizations define IPP as the scope of social change capacities that must be executed in order to shift who governs and for what purpose.

A focus on building IPP is relatively new for many of our organizations. Infrastructure designed to make grievances felt is different from infrastructure designed to build the power to govern. To get somewhere different, we need to take a different path—which is why many of our organizations are experimenting with Transformative Campaigns.

Transformative Campaigns require us to do things differently. The momentum and work of these campaigns have been vehicles for organizations from the community-organizing field to expand their focus and capacities beyond protesting and mobilizing people on single issues. These organizations and their members are not content with protesting, changing laws, or even transforming systems. Increasingly, they are working in complex networks and long-term partnerships to advance campaigns that change the narrative, put forward a political agenda, and elect their own members to political office.

Transformative Campaigns push us to expand the lens we use to measure success. Two years ago, I wrote an appeal to progressive institutions to think differently about what it means to "win." I drew on my experience as NDWA's Campaign Director and from work with affiliates and allies to capture some lessons from our Transformative Campaigns and how we measured our success. Allies' campaigns have echoed and expanded upon these lessons.

When "winning" means having the types of power and capacities needed to govern based on our values, success is not defined solely as policy change. Success must also be measured in the increased alignment, capacities, and infrastructure built in the process, together.

Governing and building Independent Political Power cannot, and should not, be done by one organization or institution alone. Many of the progressive organizations focused on building IPP are increasingly connected through national networks like People's Action and the Working Families Party, as well as the multi-network capacity and field-building initiatives of bodies like the Inclusive Democracy Project and the Partnership Fund. Building and running transformative organizing campaigns is essential to operationalize strategic and functional collaboration across our sectors, networks, and institutions.

As a reflection on the lessons I've learned from these organizations and our allies, I offer *Eight Features of Transformative Campaigns* to describe how campaigns can be transformational (versus transactional)—making them essential for building the alignment we need to move from grievance to governance.

1) Start with Values and Vision

Transformative Campaigns don't start with a policy goal, a person we want to elect, or an action we want to pull off. They start with deeper purpose that is rooted in values and connected to a vision. Reaching that vision will require a long-term, multi-issue political program. Starting with values and vision must be the first step in transformative campaigning.

2) Intentionally Sequence, and Plan to Implement, Structural Reforms

Structural reforms are reforms that:

1. Address root causes of inequality.
2. Restructure relations of power as a means and an end.
3. Increase participation in public life and democracy (e.g., facilitating public input, negotiation, approval, and oversight into subsequent decisions and governing structures).

In order to operationalize our vision, we need a political program made up of an intentionally sequenced agenda of structural reforms. Transformative Campaigns are not isolated one-off initiatives. They are part of an intentionally sequenced set of issue priorities, mobilization, policy change, and election campaigns that are pursuing structural reforms.

Too often, we've left the task of implementing and administering what we win up to those already in power. Structural reforms include mechanisms for us to be involved in the implementation and administration. They create ways for us to practice governance. When we plan for this, we include capacity building as one key measure of success for the campaign. For those concerned about promoting reformism at the expense of transformation: structural reforms aren't in tension with transformation or even revolutionary change. Structural reforms differ from reformist agendas because they don't "fix" systems that are designed to fail, exclude, or oppress us. Instead, structural reforms structurally change those systems toward inclusivity. Because they are part of a long-term agenda and are executed through transformative campaigning, they do not compromise the end goal or vision for the sake of an illusory step "forward."

3) Engage, Constantly, in the Battle of Ideas

Invite, engage, and ignite an examination of how we organize our economy, society, and democracy. This means our campaigns must center, not shy away from, ideas about the role of government and the purpose of public services and regulation, markets, and ownership. We must name and combat the elite's and Right wing's intentional use of dog-whistle politics, patriarchy, and white supremacy to advance policies that ultimately hurt all of us.

Transformative Campaigns look beyond what is "winnable" in the short term and often demand the hard choice to forgo a short-term "win," if it requires us to abandon the battle of ideas. We can have a "win" without a policy change if we know we're moving the dial on how people experience, think, and feel about government, race, gender, democracy, and equity. In Transformative Campaigns, we are willing to "lose forward"—to take a short-term loss on a policy or election, rather than taking a transactional "win" that perpetuates the underlying ideas of our opposition.

For example, we don't win voting reforms if we've framed them as "efficient" and "cost saving." If we achieve a policy using neoconservative and neoliberal ideas, then we've failed to establish the role of government and will end up spending the next year fighting the repeal of a law we just changed. A real win requires our campaigns to unabashedly put forward the idea that government has a *responsibility* to facilitate participation, to create regulations that level the playing field, and to promote social good and participatory governance.

4) Commit to Scale: Embrace Culture Work, Civic Engagement, Field-Building, and the Technologies and Partnerships to Achieve Them

Transformational change, at scale, requires changing behavior, beliefs, and practices. Social networking and civic-engagement technologies as well as partnerships with cultural institutions and high-road businesses have proven critical to achieving changes in behavior and beliefs. Several campaigns yielding large-scale impact—including Caring Across Generations and Color of Change's ALEC (American Legislative Exchange

Council) campaign—have succeeded because they engaged cultural institutions and used pop-culture strategies. Other organizations—including Demos and many affiliates of People's Action—have led innovative civic-engagement initiatives and developed partnerships with high-road businesses (often B-corps) to successfully change behavior and beliefs about the role of people and government in our electoral process. The #BlackLivesMatter Network demonstrated the scale of impact of social networking technologies. Transformative Campaigns are often built with a goal of expanding a field or sector, in order to increase our ability to execute at scale.

5) Trust in Leaderful Networks Taking Direct Action

Harnessing the power of social movements to create change requires a relationship between inside and outside strategies. When we default into models of leadership that are singular (command and control) or leader*less*, we limit our ability to coordinate complex strategies and distributed tactics.

- The #BlackLivesMatter network popularized an understanding of *leaderful* networks and beautifully demonstrates the power of encouraging leaders in various roles and styles.
- The #M4BL, #Not1More, and #NoXLPipeline campaigns have demonstrated how distributed campaigning—including tactical diversity, creative and direct actions—builds leadership and scales leadership development.

Leaderful networks are necessary for supporting popular uprisings, direct actions, mobilizations, and the rebirth of powerful progressive social movements that institutions don't, and shouldn't, be able to control. Uprisings and social movements need to flourish in order for progressive infrastructure to have the demand, will, credibility, and accountability to govern.

6) Shift Individualism to Interdependence

Individual, organizational, and structural transformation happens when seemingly independent (and often limiting) individual and group interests are put into an interdependent framework that actualizes multiple interests at once. Interdependence expands the circle of stakeholders for a desired change, generating what NDWA calls "Strategic Empathy"—the ability to make connections and see each other's full human dignity across difference.

Moving toward interdependence is part of NDWA's practice of "Organizing with Love," and has informed their work to win what onlookers have called "unlikely allies" in the Caring Across Generations and the We Belong Together campaigns. Elements of this type of work are visible in what MoveOn did to organize gun-owners to take on the gun lobby and support gun control. Many of their members would say that there are no unlikely allies—just human connections we haven't yet made. Organizing from interdependence is necessary to move people, issue areas, and institutions (or entire fields) from being siloed and isolated into connected, authentic relationships.

7) Create Solutions for All of Us through an Inclusive, Specific, and Targeted Approach

There is something uniquely powerful at the intersection of experiences, where those at that intersection are in a unique position to understand how the world, and how power, work. We need leadership that comes from that place of intersection. This means that our leadership and our demands must be inclusive and specific. When we find solutions that are based on equity and dignity for those of us most impacted by injustice, we create benefits and equity for all of us. The Movement for Black Lives has elevated the fact that valuing Black lives—in particular, the lives of Black cisgender and transgender women—improves the world for everyone. Valuing Black lives benefits Latinos (some of whom are Black), Asians, Muslims, and, yes, white people.

This principle, as applied to policy design, is exemplified in an approach called Targeted Universalism (a term coined by John Powell), in which solutions are designed to be universal in terms of their goals, yet targeted with respect to the populations they specifically serve. One example is how Demos crafted a policy model for "universal" or "automatic voter registration" to be sure that policy is targeted to address racialized disparities in registration rates. This approach represents a commitment to reduce injustice and inequity by focusing resources on addressing the challenges faced by peoples and communities who have been disadvantaged by structural inequalities (racism, patriarchy, class, etc.). Targeted solutions to eliminate disparities, coupled with inclusive and specific leadership, will lead to improvements for all of us.

8) Move Into a "Forward Stance" and Expand the Realm of What Is Possible

Transformative Campaigns put us on the offensive—not defensive—in moving toward our vision and the long-term (sequenced) agenda it will take

us to get there. Transformative Campaigns require us to be responsive to conditions, without being reactive. By being deliberately proactive, Transformative Campaigns are about the values and vision they move us toward, not just about moving away from something.

Taken together, these eight features illustrate how Transformative Campaigning achieves the dual purpose of advancing change in the near term, while also building the capacities needed for Independent Political Power—power that we need to move from grievance to governance.

With our planet, lives, and future at stake, we aren't just trying to change what we are doing. We must change where we are going. We must create the infrastructure we need to govern ourselves, rather than make grievances about how we are governed. Let's take a close look at the initiatives driving coordination and deep alignment across fields and sectors:

- What do we see when we measure our number and strength of alignments as our success?
- What infrastructure expands the realm of what is possible?
- What infrastructure do we need not just to survive or be better off, but to actually govern based on our values and vision?

Our work together has pried open a path from grievance to governance. Our potential is transforming in front of us.

Let's take our path, together.

Jodeen Olguin-Tayler serves as the Vice President for Policy and Strategic Partnerships for Demos. She drives a campaign-oriented approach to advocacy work and to expanding strategic partnerships. Prior to Demos, Jodeen was the Organizing and Digital Campaigns Director at Caring Across Generations, and the Campaigns Director for the National Domestic Workers Alliance.

5

Fight the Power, A.K.A. the System: Choose Democracy Over Authoritarianism

"[Americans must] move toward a democratic socialism."

Martin Luther King

"I would describe myself as a libertarian socialist—I'd love to see centralized power eliminated, whether it's the state or the economy, and it is diffused and ultimately under direct control of the participants."

Noam Chomsky

"Be Realistic: Demand the Impossible!"

Movement slogan

First Rule: Challenge and disrupt the existing system! Don't settle for piece-meal demands or reforms! Don't open yourself to be divided and conquered by dividing yourselves!

Big Questions: How do you create a credible critique of the entire system? How do you overcome the view that there is no better system, indeed no realistic alternative whatsoever? How do you persuade people that the language of democracy has become a cover for authoritarianism and American neo-facism?

Slogans: Think big! Don't settle! Don't focus on one leg of the elephant!

What's New Here? Non-universalizing resistance involves silo movements fighting for a particular cause (climate, peace, equality) or a particular identity (women, African-American, Latino). These are crucially important movements, but they strike at just one pillar of the system or one leg of the elephant. Universalizing resistance as the system universalizes creates greater unity of these movements and thereby changes their vision, objective, and strategy. The new movements work together to challenge the new super-universalized system—which lies at the root of each silo movement's oppression or cause and threatens the survival of humanity. Universalizers are systemic activists; they are ultimately revolutionaries because they target militarized capitalism itself, the only effective way in the long term to break down its sociopathic pillars of power and truly solve its increasingly intertwined existential crises of extreme inequality and economic insecurity, war, and climate change, as well as racism, sexism, and the authoritarian neofascist strains shrouded by the discourse of democracy.

BEYOND TINA AND SILO ACTIVISM: HOW UNIVERSALIZING MOVEMENTS CHALLENGE THE SYSTEM

Resistance always challenges elements in the system, but universalizing resistance (UR) is a direct challenge to the system itself. Universalizing resistance targets the universalizing system of global militarized capitalism, the class and caste hierarchies that comprise it, and the military and environmental crises linked to the DNA of the system. These crises are more intertwined and more violent as the system universalizes. Universalizing resistance is systemic resistance in its most robust form, militantly challenging but refusing to limit itself to component crises of the system (e.g., racism, joblessness, or climate change) and moving, in addition, to highlight the need to change the system itself.

The central premise is that in order to solve any of the system's urgent component oppressions or crises, largely treated as "silo" issues in our current movements, the system itself must be challenged and movements must present clear and compelling systemic alternatives to create democracy and justice, and sustain all living species.

President Donald Trump could catalyze all progressive movements to come together to fight him. The system is abstract, but the face of Trump is tangible. He could destroy the movements, but they now increasingly realize they live or die together.

Universalizing resistance faces the challenge of up-ending the hegemonic view that "There Is No Alternative (TINA)" which is the core of the system's ideological discourse, along with the view that the current capitalist order is the only and best, indeed "exceptionalist," social order in human history.

Women's March signs in New York on January 21, 2017

Photo credit: Janet MacGillivray Wallace

The idea of TINA is deeply entrenched in much of the population, and is the most profound ideological obstacle to resistance. Universalizing movements must show the obvious: that history does not end with militarized capitalism, which is destroying much of what we treasure and has become an authoritarian system legitimating itself in the language of democracy. No system is permanent or eternal. Belief in alternatives will come through the movements themselves, which must spell out the possibilities and embody them in their practices.

The thinking and practice of movements themselves—all over the world—show that societies are profoundly diverse. Alternatives are integral to history, survival, and to the very nature of politics and human behavior. Think only of the "orange," "velvet," "jasmine," and other popular democracy movements—as well as the Zapatistas in Mexico, the Arab Spring, and indigenous American movements. During the last few decades, these movements have openly challenged militarized Western capitalism as well as non-capitalist authoritarian regimes and dictatorships. In the United States, we have already noted (in Chapter 3) a history of universalizing resistance movements, from the Gilded Age populists, to the socialists and Communists of the New Deal movement, to the anti-war and anti-capitalist 1960s movements.

In very recent years, even before President Trump's election, we have seen the rise of new movements with progressive and anti-systemic universalizing potential: Occupy Wall Street challenges casino capitalism and the ruling power of the 1%; Blockadia involves protestors placing their bodies in the path of the oil and gas pipelines that are the infrastructure of the current system; Moral Monday, Fight for $15, and other labor movements challenge the system's economic insecurity, inequality, and poverty; Black Lives Matter challenges the criminal justice system that polices the system and its racist underpinnings; Greenpeace, 350.org, and other climate movements question the existence of the system as incompatible with survival. Anti-war, anti-drone, anti-US-hegemony movements challenge the system's militarism: women's and peace movements (CODEPINK) and immigrant rights movements all challenge the global violence of the system; democracy movements challenge the rising authoritarian police state that practices democracy mainly in rhetoric.

Since the election of President Trump, we have seen the rise of many progressive movements with universalizing potential. They include Our Revolution, an institutionalization of Sanders support mobilizing to elect "democratic socialists" at every level of government; Indivisible, a group of hundreds of thousands mobilizing also to mount an electoral change to Republican, Tea Party, and Trumpist elected officials across the land; and thousands of spontaneous grass-roots and online groups mounting mass protests such as the Women's March, the protest against Trump's Muslim ban and "war" on Muslim-Americans, and the protests against the Wall and Trump's "war" on Mexican immigrants. The new wave of activism against Trump led people to rename America "Protest Nation"—and appeared to signal a shift toward the Left reminiscent of the Tea Party's movement of the country toward the Right.

With President Donald Trump, the threats have become so frightening and tangible that all these movements—rising before Trump and after his election—will have to rise together or potentially be crushed, one by one.

Millions are involved in these movements. But they are in their early phases and have much work ahead, to realize their anti-systemic and universalizing potential. In this book, I'll present the unified actions needed by these and other similar groups. They must persuade activists that challenging the system is essential and realistic. At the same time, TINA (the doctrine that no alternatives to capitalism exist) means that universalizers will often carry the stigma of Cervantes' Don Quixote. They must be prepared to endure endless ridicule as tilters at windmills.

Challenging the system is also an essential component of right-wing universalizing movements. Trumpism gained resonance because it spoke to the mass grievances of working people who felt economically and politically disenfranchised by the "crony capitalist" system that Donald Trump called "rigged." Of course, it appealed also to dangerous cultural, demographic, racist, and hyper-nationalist values that are outgrowths of the system—and it has gained power because it speaks for the violent and authoritarian regime that the system is increasingly practicing in the name of democracy. But, with his populist rhetoric, whatever his policy, Trump is opening up some new space for critique of what he calls the "rigged system" of American capitalism. In what follows, I mainly focus on the anti-systemic vision of progressive universalizers, since Trumpism, while screaming against the rigged system, has increasingly united with that system, leaving the real work to progressive movements.

FROM VISIONARIES TO UNIVERSALIZING MOVEMENTS

The Pulitzer Prize-winning writer and activist, Chris Hedges, has said that the revolutionary individual must have a kind of "sublime madness," a willingness to see beyond the truths propagated by the powerful and debunk them. Hedges takes the term from the theologian Reinhold Niebuhr, who says that such madness "disregards immediate appearances and emphasizes profound and ultimate unities."[1] Hedges continues that such "madness" is the only sanity: "it shows us that there is no hope for correction or reversal by appealing to power . . . it is only by overthrowing traditional systems of power that we can be liberated."[2]

Any discussion of changing the capitalist system, especially in the United States, might require a very strong dose of Hedges' inspired insanity. In all eras, major change—and history has always produced revolutions—has been led by prophets with improbable visions accompanied by growing numbers of ordinary people who seek to tear off the elites' blinders and end their control.

Many progressive activists (and many in the Far Right too), particularly after the 2008 economic collapse in the United States and the rise of the Occupy movement, are demanding change in capitalism itself. One interviewee in the Ear to the Ground study says:

> As an elder shaped by my time in the Black Freedom struggle, I have to say . . . we need to deal with the lack of clarity and analysis around the role of capitalism. It's so often the big elephant in the room. People are organizing around labor, immigration and all kinds of stuff but they are not talking about capitalism enough. It shows up in the limits of what we come up with and what people can imagine. It's like driving with a GPS but not knowing where you are driving to. People are driving

in circles—around strategy, resources, etc—because they are not clear about their destination.[3]

Once the impulse of systemic transformation emerges, many forms of evidence and argument can lead people to believe in alternatives. Change once defined as impossible takes on new light. As Noam Chomsky has argued, one source of hope is that a system of domination is contrary to human nature: *"the fundamental human capacity is the need for creative self-expression, for free control of all aspects of one's life and thought."*[4] Chomsky's argument is central to the prospect of combating the authoritarian system of repression that the rhetoric of democracy conceals even as it crushes popular power.

Hope also, as Howard Zinn has written, arises simply by looking closely at US history, which is a story of transformative movements, some ultimately successful, including the abolitionist movement against slavery, the suffragettes' movement for women's rights, and populist and labor movements for expanding human rights to include "positive rights" for an array of real if limited social welfare. Yet more hope lies in the deep disenchantment with the existing system, and growing awareness of the 21st-century existential crises of climate change and war with weapons of mass destruction.

Historical first wave feminist activities for the female right to vote
© Everett Historical/Shutterstock

None of this is proof that transformation will be achieved, and, if it is, that it will be progressive rather than reactionary. Persevering in the face of uncertainty does require some of the "sublime madness" that Hedges views as the revolutionary's ultimate form of sanity—and success. But it also requires connecting with and persuading the majority of the population, showing the very real sanity that would lead any rational citizen to turn against the system. Universalizing ultimately requires turning prophetic madness into common sense embraced by the majority. It may arise quickly or, as Greenpeace suggests, too slowly: "Only when the last fish is gone, the last river poisoned, the last tree cut down . . . will mankind realize they cannot eat money."[5]

Activists, though, often are frustrated by the failure to target long-term systemic change. Activists NTanya Lee and Steve Williams write:

> Our movement does not act like we plan to win lasting and fundamental changes in our communities, workplaces and the world. As a result, we either obsess exclusively on our immediate campaign—willing to make long-term sacrifices for short-term gains—or we simply plod along content to "put up a good fight."[6]

This obsession with immediate and local or narrow campaigns can be a death knell for creating an anti-systemic movement—which is insanity when human survival is at stake.

Universalizing resistance movements can have varying degrees of universalizing—and can misdiagnose or incompletely analyze the system they critique. Historically, many Marxist and other socialist movements challenged capitalism, but failed to challenge militarism and de-emphasized racism and sexism. (This manifested itself in the 2015 Black Lives Matter challenge to Presidential candidate Bernie Sanders, with the activists arguing that his "socialist" critique failed to highlight the importance of race in the ruling system.) Yet many race and gender movements challenge systemic racism or patriarchy, while failing to confront the militarized capitalism of which racism and patriarchy are inextricable parts. This can lead to failures so serious that poor and working-class women and minorities become even worse off in identity movements led by white upper-income caste members, as I discussed in relation to the "capitalist feminism" of Sheryl Sandberg (Chapter 1). It has also led to progressive and Left parties and movements that do not engage strongly with class and economic politics, a disaster that helped to produce Trumpism.

IDENTITY POLITICS, CLASS POLITICS, AND HURDLES TO CHALLENGING THE SYSTEM

Identity politics without class consciousness, as sociologist Todd Gitlin argues in *The Twilight of Our Common Dreams*, can play cruel tricks on the fate of the minorities and women they claim to represent. One reviewer of Gitlin's book captures the anti-universalizing elements of much of identity politics:

> Instead of coming together as a whole, there is a large tendency to fragment into small groups and accuse each other of heresy. Thus the emergence of hyphenated Americans and separate agendas!! The elites love this because the focus is not on them. They enjoy watching those towards the bottom fighting amongst themselves while they continue to accumulate more wealth and power. We're killing ourselves here! We need to see the commonal[i]ties of all our "victimizations" and realize who the true enemy is. Only then is there a chance for social change.[7]

This is a critical universalizing insight: that only a strong class politics that universalizes progressive organizing to potentially receptive white workers can rescue us from the Right's ability to capture these same workers in white working-class solidarity—around racism, hyper-nationalism, and anti-immigrant politics—and in response to the blindness of race and gender movements stripped of class consciousness.

Similarly, class politics that marginalizes racism and patriarchy is blind to the system it is opposing, and will lose its appeal to the increasingly large racial and gender groups that make up the working class. There is a long history of class movements ignoring caste—and of identity politics that is clueless about class.

Universalizing is contentious in progressive and Left movements, in part because there is disagreement about the core nature of the system, whose intersectionality is seen in different ways by different resistance movements. This has been a core problem for the Left as many members of the progressive identity movements in the United States have tended to ignore or discount the significance of the capitalist system in their race or gender politics. Freeing affluent members at the expense of the less affluent—while socialists and economic progressives have often not integrated caste into the core of their systemic critique and politics—weakens their ability to mobilize today's classes around both economic and identity politics.

It is important to note that the rising US and European right-wing universalizing movements have their own emotionally powerful identity movements. They are coded white supremacist movements that wrap themselves around the grievances of economically stressed whites who feel displaced by demographic changes, immigration, and anti-racist and anti-sexist movements. At the heart of right-wing anti-systemic movements is the hyper-nationalist identity that Donald Trump branded as "America First." Trump's nationalist appeal was universalizing because it appeared to bring all Americans into a unifying identity of a common American exceptionalism. But it was also profoundly divisive, because Trump's nationalism was a coded appeal to the white supremacism of the Jim Crow years. Trumpism is a right-wing identity politics of whiteness or white nationalism—sometimes called the "Alt-Right," "alternative Right," or simple "racist Right" movements—aiming to put people of color and women back in their place. It appeals to traditional values going back to an earlier era steeped in religion, patriarchal families, and respect for authority, as well as respect for physical labor and physical force. It has mass appeal among working whites in economic crisis and it has universalistic appeal, explaining its mass support, but disguising its rejection of universal human rights for all peoples and its authoritarian rejection of democracy itself.

Looking at the rise of both Left and Right movements that are anti-systemic and "anti-establishment" in their electoral politics, it appears that Hedges' "sublime madness" is gaining traction on the ground. Prior to Trump, the mood of the country was negative and sour on the system and the elites running it. Trump's election, though seen as a rejection of the Establishment, is only creating the worst form of the crony militarized capitalism that his voters thought they were voting against. Trump is melding a populist right-wing universalizing movement with the system, but there will be even more extreme right-wing populists—self-acknowledged white supremacists and neo-Nazis—seeking their version of Hedges' "sublime madness." And there is now the anti-systemic legacy of Sanders on the Left—and many more deeply anti-systemic Left movements operating to Sanders' left—pledged to fight Trump and the system he rules until the bitter end.

This means that TINA is eroding as the system universalizes and breeds larger social movements and unaffiliated citizens who are losing faith and are receptive to a new system. Progressive universalizing movements must seize the moment in a united front against Trump and the crony capitalist system he claims to attack, but now represents; it is their only way to survive and retain their own "sublime madness."

TO UNIVERSALIZE OR NOT TO UNIVERSALIZE: INCREMENTALISM, RADICAL REFORM, AND REVOLUTION

Contradictory dynamics facilitate and impede universalizing within movements. Fighting any specific issue, such as environmentalists blocking pipelines, immediately brings resisters into confrontation with the corporate system, embodied in the Big Oil and Big Gas companies. Local environmentalists quickly begin to understand that countering environmental degradation requires limiting corporate sovereignty. Still, focusing on the larger corporate system appears to divert energy from the immediate needs of saving one's community from dangerous pipelines—or from bulldozers tearing apart the streets you bike or drive every day. Energy thus frequently returns to highly localized or issue-specific problems required to solve the immediate problems mobilizing communities.

This narrower focus is not necessarily destructive of anti-systemic struggles. As discussed earlier, changing the system often involves a strategy of incremental change that constitutes what the ecological theorist, André Gorz, calls "radical reforms." They do not directly challenge or call for overthrow of the system, but they open the window to broader challenges to the system. Gorz distinguishes "radical reforms" from "reformist reforms," the latter involving changes that consolidate the system's power rather than making it more vulnerable to new challenges.[8] Radical reforms, developed incrementally, may, in many historical eras, be the best approach to creating larger system change, far more likely to succeed than immediate revolution. We see such radical reforms in demands made by protest groups such as Black Lives Matter (ending police violence and poverty in poor neighborhoods) and Fight for $15 (raise the minimum wage for almost half of US workers) and 350.org's successful resistance to the Keystone XL Pipeline before the Paris 2015 climate conference. Incremental change is a legitimate and crucial dimension of universalizing resistance as long as it promotes radical, rather than reformist, reform, and is embedded in a long-term vision and strategy of system transformation consistent with the time constraints posed by climate change and other apocalyptic threats. Activists struggle between these two kinds of reformism and need to embrace the more radical form, which is a form of anti-systemic activism most appropriate when revolution is not immediately possible.

Universalizers struggle not only with incremental versus revolutionary strategies, but also with the recognition that the larger corporate system has the upper hand. Trump's election made success in Washington DC and national politics seem hopeless. This leads to the judgment and the feeling that their only immediate leverage is on the local regulatory level, and their only immediate allies are other activists committed to their single issue, such as blocking pipelines. Indeed, universalizing resistance calling for broad system change can potentially diffuse or undermine the goals and passions of single-issue activists, whose activism burns from the fire they attach to specific issues. This is another reason why universalization must be built carefully and grow organically. Forced universalization can kill universalization itself and thereby contribute to human extinction. But universalizing tends to emerge spontaneously as silo activists bump quickly into the limits of the larger system—and with the recognition of the terrible dangers now posed by Trumpism, it will be hard for activists at any level not to be aware of the need to universalize against President Trump himself—and the ruling, dangerous Republican Party that he joined forces with.

UNIVERSALIZE POWER: BUILD THE DEMOCRACY MOVEMENT

Ben Manski

If we want to universalize justice, we best begin with the recognition that social systems are systems of power. Different systems favor and subordinate different groups of people, creating systemic injustice.

Capitalism is a system that empowers those who own capital and that constrains the possibilities for those who don't own capital to govern themselves. It undermines the capacity for working and poor people to develop financial independence and maintains the unproductive financial supremacy of global capitalists.

How should we evaluate social change campaigns that demand justice for all—*something that the current system cannot provide*—and yet accept the continuation of that system? Some social change efforts do just that, ignoring the fact that in the end, one cannot universalize justice without also universalizing power. Yet others seek to universalize both justice and power.

Today we see mounting evidence of awareness of the need for disparate struggles for justice to join together in transforming the relations of power throughout society. Such movements to universalize and equalize power are more commonly known as democracy movements. Democracy movements are becoming one of the more widespread and vital social movement forms of the 21st century.

The United States is no exception. Almost anywhere one turns, there is evidence of a growing movement for democracy in the United States. This movement is engaged broadly in a series of constitutional reform campaigns, as well as within particular social sectors in a range of efforts to democratize the economy, elections, government, security, and education.

The day-to-day work of building democracy continues to move forward on these and other fronts, often submerged beneath the surface of media publicity, though plainly visible to any who pay attention. At times over the past 20 years, however, the US democracy movement has broken through and seized attention, forming in the millions of people in the streets of Seattle, Madison, New York, Oakland, Ferguson, Chicago, Los Angeles, and thousands of other communities, occupying public spaces, and chanting that "This Is What Democracy Looks Like!"

In the post-midnight hours following Election Day 2016, massive crowds filled US streets protesting the announcement that Donald Trump was to assume the Presidency. Again, the cry was "This Is What Democracy Looks Like!," signifying the gulf between the democracy movement in the streets and the official institutions of Republican government in the capitals. At that moment, afraid of Trump's promises to dismantle public education and the free press, deport millions, jail his opponents, and to ignore constitutional limitations on his power, millions of people came to understand their personal issues as part of the larger democracy struggle. In this way, Trump's ascendency compelled all progressive movements to realign themselves with the democracy movement, and to begin to transform that movement in the process.

The Democracy Crisis

If we want to get a clear sense of where today's democracy movement might take us, and what it might take to get there—even in the face of one-party rule and a Trump Presidency—we'd do well to understand where this movement is coming from. After all, like today's movement, the challenges we face today also have their origins in the 1990s and late 1980s. We are confronted by the same global economic, ecological, and political forces that began to reshape our lives back then. And many of the same individuals, institutions, and networks that arose then are still in play today. The essential mechanisms of our social struggles are the same. What has changed over the past several decades is the intensity of those struggles.

Many of the core conflicts of the 1990s involved resistance to corporations and to the things corporations were doing. The resistance was personal and stemmed from the inherently undemocratic structure of corporations and their vast material and political control.

Workers fought back against union busting and factory closures all across the so-called "Labor Warzone" of the industrial Midwest.

Students resisted the corporatization of their schools, colleges, and universities.

Farmers organized against corporate agribusiness and the biotech giants.

Mothers, fathers, and children tried to defend themselves against the dismantling of the welfare and social services they relied on.

Prisoners and their families mobilized against private prisons and mass incarceration.

Journalists faced media consolidation and began to create their own media.

Indigenous red, Black, yellow, brown, and other frontline communities took on the extraction and pollution industries that tried to put mines, dumps, and incinerators in their backyards.

All these and more came together through coalitions that combated NAFTA, GATT [General Agreement on Tariffs and Trade], MAI [Multilateral Agreement on Investments], FTAA [Free Trade Area of the Americas], and the WTO. A globally-oriented, anti-corporate, pro-democracy politics emerged organically out of these sectoral and social struggles. People harmed by transnational capital could often figure out for themselves that corporations are institutions that serve the interests of those who own and manage them, not those they employ or claim to serve. Or in other words, "that it is not the things that corporations *do* that is the problem, it is what corporations *are* that is the problem."

That last phrase was a commonly repeated lesson of the Program on Corporations, Law, and Democracy (POCLAD), an organization that throughout the 1990s brought together thousands of activists from different social sectors in weekend gatherings to "rethink the corporation, rethink democracy." Those gatherings influenced the growth of a wave of new national, sectoral, and local organizations dedicated to building a democracy movement in the United States, including the Democracy Teach-Ins and 180/Movement for Democracy and Education on college campuses; the community-based efforts of the Alliance for Democracy,

Reclaim Democracy, End Corporate Dominance, Community Environmental Legal Defense Fund, and Democracy Unlimited; the business sector's American Independent Business Alliance; and the electoral democratization efforts led by the Center for Voting and Democracy, Green Party, New Party, and Labor Party. In each of those efforts, individuals began to self-identify as "democracy activists" and to implement detailed strategies for replacing "corporate rule" with "real democracy."

All of those efforts began in the 1990s, as did others still relevant today, including the Black Radical Congress and the modern immigrant rights, equal rights, and labor movements. Very little *explicit* pro-democracy activism occurred in the previous decade. What changed?

What happened between the 1980s and the 1990s was the collapse of the Soviet Bloc, a set of events that deeply impacted life and politics in America. Around the world, new markets opened up to transnational capital. Major corporations pushed hard to establish a new global economic order. And every institution of American life—including its political, legal, educational, and media institutions—became subject to the neoliberal blackmail of offshoring and the race to the bottom. The capitalist message was clear: accept the corporate take-over of social welfare and public services or we'll take our capital elsewhere. For Americans, as for people everywhere around the globe, capitalist expansion created a generalized sense that democracy was in crisis.

This look back to the 1990s helps us to understand the logic of the democracy movement in the United States today. That logic includes the emergent reality that aggressive capitalism of this sort produces social movements that are aggressively democratic. One

hundred thousand people shutting down the World Trade Organization in Seattle in 1999, and chanting "This Is What Democracy Looks Like!" is an example of aggressive democracy. May Day 2006's Un Día Sin Inmigrantes [A Day Without Immigrants] was a case of aggressive democracy. And so too has democracy beaten in the pulse of the Wisconsin Uprising, Occupy Wall Street, and Black Lives Matter, each of them efforts to assertively universalize power.

Democracy Is Everywhere

Since the 1990s, democracy activists in the United States have worked both to deepen and to broaden the movement. Deepening the democracy movement has meant strengthening existing campaigns to democratize particular institutions and social sectors, as well as sometimes initiating new ones. Here are just a few examples:

- In the *education sector*, students, faculty, and staff across the United States have come together to demand full funding for public education and an end to college tuition fees and student debt. They have organized student–faculty–staff–parent coalitions, and in some cases have transformed those coalitions into lasting unions.
- In the *national security sector*, active-duty military, military families, and veterans have come together with community-based activists to organize for the democratization of the military, beginning with the National Guard, and for the honoring of existing international treaties that outlaw war.
- In the *community sector*, elected officials have worked with community activists and independent political parties to advance reforms that strengthen local government's home rule powers, make

local governments more participatory, use local governments to expand cooperatives and other democratic economic institutions, and implement community control over policing.

- In the *energy sector*, a new wave of energy democracy and climate democracy initiatives are using public power and participatory reforms to rush forward the transition to a renewable energy economy.
- In the *public sector*, reforms such as rank choice voting, proportional representation, public financing, and same-day voter registration are advancing in some areas of the United States even as efforts to defend voting rights continue everywhere.
- In the *core economic sectors* of manufacturing, retail, finance, and services, workers and community members are expanding cooperatives, community ownership, credit unions, and democratic currencies and exchange as they build the plural raft of democratic economic alternatives to capitalism.

In the same period that activists have worked to deepen democracy in these sectors (as well as others: media, law, art, faith, social movements, food, agriculture, family, and more), they have also succeeded in broadening and raising up the democracy movement at the level of society itself. That the slogan "This Is What Democracy Looks Like!" has for some of us become an overdone, tired chant, speaks to how far we have already succeeded in making audible a new popular unity. Everywhere that chant goes up to the sky is another self-declared front in the democracy struggle. And accompanying the Seattles, Wisconsins, Liberty Squares, Freedom Plazas, and Fergusons, furthermore, are a series of more institutional social movement efforts that have helped to broaden, integrate, and raise up the democracy movement in the United States.

The U.S. Social Forum and the Democracy Convention are two ongoing processes that have contributed mightily. The U.S. Social Forum, part of the World Social Forum process, has gathered thrice, first in Atlanta in 2007, then in Detroit in 2010, and most recently in San Jose and Philadelphia in 2015. The Democracy Conventions met in 2011 and 2013 in Madison, Wisconsin, with the next meeting planned for 2017 in Minneapolis. In these mass gatherings, people working on democracy campaigns in different social sectors have been able to come together to compare notes and develop common agendas. The Democracy Conventions, in particular, make an effort to help activists "get out of their silos" and to build synergies between their efforts.

Constitutional reform campaigns for adoption of the Right to Vote Amendment, the Equal Rights Amendment, and the We the People Amendment are also providing critical cohering functions for the US democracy movement. Through each of these campaigns, broad and often overlapping coalitions are forming to democratize the basic law of the United States. As an illustration: a farmer in Wisconsin, an unemployed worker in Massachusetts, a teacher in Texas, and a small businessperson in Idaho may believe themselves to share a common interest in amending the Constitution to overturn *Citizens United v. Federal Election Commission* (2010) and to help end corporate domination of politics and the economy. And in fact, such diverse constituencies have demonstrated that they do share common interests in constitutional democratization, passing resolutions supporting the language of the We the People Amendment in over 700 municipalities and states.

Trump's ascendency is a genuine threat to all of these democratic initiatives, as well as many others. Yet Trump came to power on the backs of voters furious at corporations, Wall Street, and corporate trade deals like NAFTA and the TPP [Trans-Pacific Partnership]. Millions of these Americans will become disenchanted with Trump's solutions, which will only increase corporate power, government corruption, and economic hardship. The democracy movement, born out of decades of resistance to corporate capitalism, rooted in the cultural soil produced by America's historic democracy struggles, provides working Americans with an alternative to both Trumpism and Clintonism that is both radical and familiar. The movement is as radical as the disempowerment that most of us feel; it is as familiar as our professed national identity as the land of democracy, freedom, and equality.

Not Just a Movement, a Revolution

The work of creating, deepening, broadening, and raising up the democracy movement in the United States has long begun. What must be done from here?

First, we must recognize that the US democracy movement does not move in isolation. When the movement first became visible in 1999, it did so at the meeting of the World Trade Organization in Seattle. When activists mobilized for voting rights in the Florida 2000 and Ohio 2004 Presidential recounts, they sought international election observers. When Wisconsinites were preparing for the Wisconsin Uprising of 2011, they invited activists from Europe, Latin America, and Southeast Asia into phone conferences for a briefing on their democracy struggles.

Moving forward, Americans need to find more ways to move beyond national borders in building the global democracy movement. It is not enough to seek democratization of the US Constitution and US institutions. We must also increasingly articulate and fight for a democratic global economy and polity that protects human rights, ecology, and local democracy at a global level. And just as we support democratic resistance against fascism and authoritarianism in other countries, we must actively seek solidarity from activists in other countries, recognizing that the struggle for democracy in the United States is a vital concern to people around the world.

Second, we should recognize that democracy activists have been doing something right. And because they've been doing something right, the language of democracy has become hot in some funding circles. One danger of such moments is that innovators become victims of their own success, and get left in the dust. Rather than launching new initiatives inside the Washington Beltway that use the language of the democracy movement without paying attention to where this new politics came from, major foundations and institutions should invest in the resource capacity of the same organizations that developed and raised up the democratic politics of the past 20 years.

For instance, in 2004, a number of us who'd been active in the 1990s movements started the Liberty Tree Foundation for the Democratic Revolution with the express purpose of building the democracy movement in the United States. Liberty Tree has been engaged in that work ever since, playing critical roles in much of the history described in this Interlude. Practical experience produces knowledge and plans for building the democratic leadership and organizations, and for taking advantage of the political opportunities and crises of the future, as well as serious thought about what it will take to not only win democratic reforms, but to secure them.

Furthermore, because of this history, Liberty Tree and its partners are better prepared than Washington DC-based organizations for the kind of progressive populist economic, cultural, and social struggle that the Trump ascendancy necessitates.

This leads me to my third conclusion: at some point in the next decade, democracy advocates in the United States will find themselves facing the problem of having succeeded beyond common expectation. Such success will certainly come in the form of mass uprisings such as that of Wisconsin. Success may even far exceed that, and come in the form of political power, as won by political parties of radical democracy and liberation most recently in Greece, Portugal, and Iceland, as well as earlier in South Africa, Haiti, Venezuela, Bolivia, Brazil, Uruguay, and elsewhere. And like most of those cases, the democracy movement in the United States now faces the double prospects of repression and mass mobilization: repression by an unpopular authoritarian ruler; mass mobilization in response to that ruler's illegitimate actions. Therefore, the democracy movement must become ready to succeed beyond expectations, and to not only consolidate its successes, but to continue to push forward.

The goal, after all, is to universalize power. And if the experience of the democracy movements of the past 20 years has shown anything, it is that societies dominated by capital are extremely resistant to genuine democratization. The existence of a democracy movement in the United States suggests the possibility of a democratic revolution in this country. The ecological and social alternatives to democratization are dire. It is in our best interests to make the most of that possibility.

Ben Manski studies social movements, law, and political sociology in order to better understand and strengthen democratization. Manski practiced public interest law for 8 years (JD University of Wisconsin-Madison, 2005) and having just completed his MA, is nearing completion of a PhD in Sociology at the University of California, Santa Barbara. He is the founder of the Liberty Tree Foundation for the Democratic Revolution, an Associate Fellow with the Institute for Policy Studies, and a Fellow with the Next System Project.

6

Win the Majority: It's Easier than You Think

"If once we shook off our lethargy and fatigue and began to act . . . The walls of indifference, inertia, and coldness that now isolate each of us from others, and all of us from the past and future generations, would melt, like snow in spring."

Jonathan Schell

"Revolution is not something fixed in ideology, nor is it something fashioned to a particular decade. It is a perpetual process embedded in the human spirit."

Abbie Hoffman

"Democracy means everyone."

Common Cause

"Screw us and we multiply"

Occupy street protestor's sign

Second New Rule: Create a mass base of resistance! Mobilize "majority movements" supported by vast sectors of the public! Don't create silo demands that appeal to small parts of the population and alienate others!

Big Questions: How do universalizing movements dramatically expand their base? How do we mobilize majority movements in a period of a largely apathetic, fearful, atomized, and depoliticized public, many terrified of jihad?

Slogans: Aim for a majority! Activate the (largely) silent progressive majority!

What's New Here: Non-universalizing movements fight for particular communities or causes, limiting their ability to recruit or build support from the entire population. Universalizing resistance does not try to weaken these struggles, but rather to strengthen them by encouraging collaboration, thereby creating a large base for each particular movement as well as a struggle for the rights of all people and communities. Since the universalizing system directs violence against all peoples, universalizers can more credibly appeal to majorities of the population and ultimately solve the problems targeted by current silo movements. President Trump, who campaigned against it, became a visible face of the system; progressives can appropriate some of his anti-system rhetoric to universalize in an authentic populist movement for a new society.

BUILDING THE BASE

Building a mass base in the public is central to UR. All resistance movements seek a large following. But non-universalizing silo movements often restrict their constituencies by limiting their issues. Because universalizing movements challenge the entire system, their potential base is everyone living and suffering in the system—and today, everyone in the world facing ultimate extinction from nuclear war or climate change.

Building a mass base means building majoritarian movements. But that does not mean turning a majority of the population into activists, a phenomenon that rarely occurs. As sociologist Richard Flacks has shown in *Making History*, most people will in most periods of history be involved in "making life"; that is, preoccupied with trying to survive and be happy in their personal life, rather than "making history," changing the world through participation in movements.[1] Ralph Nader argues that a small number of committed and well-organized civic activists in each US Congressional District can win majoritarian progressive campaigns and elect a progressive Congress that can overthrow the anti-democratic corporate regime now running the country. *Thus, a mass base for universalizing movements is a stratified public, consisting of full-time activists, part-time activists, and supporters who do not become activists, but support the cause and may vote locally or nationally in support of its demands.* The struggle of universalizing activists is to build the size of all three groups, and to solidify the connection between activists and non-activist supporters.

Global research suggests that it takes a relatively small base of activists (as little as 3.5% of the population) to win campaigns of non-cooperation with the system. Yet to achieve full regime or system change in powerful nations like the United States, support from much larger sectors of the population, who are never likely to be activists themselves, is crucial to universalizing movements. Movements that do not aim for the majority may win campaigns but will ultimately lose the war, since the majority, goaded by elites, may turn against the movements even if they partially or fully support their issues. In the 1960s, a public majority by the late 1960s had turned against the Vietnam war, but many in the majority hated the anti-war activists more than they hated the war. Elites could easily create what sociologist Jerry Lembcke, in his book, *The Spitting Image*, shows were largely false images of activists spitting on and "dissing" veterans, making the activists look anti-patriotic and thereby leading a majority to remain silent about the war.

The success of the elites in mobilizing what President Nixon called "the silent majority" into passivity or active hostility toward anti-war activists grew out of the failure of movements to reach deeply enough into the working classes—especially the white working classes—whose children were fighting and dying in the war. This is also true of many caste movements—movements for gender or African-American rights—that fail to reach into the majority populations and show how the oppression of women or Black workers holds down the wages and wellbeing of white workers, too. This is a crucial insight that movements such as Fight for $15 are beginning to teach the nation. Nearly half of all American workers—disproportionately people of color and women, but including millions of white males—make less than $15 an hour. In 2015, the Fight for $15 movement mobilized big multi-racial protests in over 250 US cities in one weekend. Universalizing progressive movements must reach deep into the majority and create emotional and political resonance with the larger population. As Paulo Freire writes,

> trusting the people is the indispensable precondition for revolutionary change. A real humanist can be identified more by his trust in the people, which engages him in their struggle, than by a thousand actions in their favor without that trust.[2]

If progressive movements don't engage the majority and fight for a majoritarian movement, history suggests they will pave the way for countermovements on the Right, seen most dramatically in 20th century fascist movements. Today, Right movements are attracting many white workers. We take up this theme later in this chapter in discussing the potential of progressive movements to universalize their struggle to include white workers under great economic stress and anxiety about their place and worth in society.

As shown in the next section, public opinion polling also shows the limits of Far Right cultural resonance—and hopes for majoritarian appeals by progressive universalizers.

Progressives can and must try to universalize deeply into the white working class—or risk losing the battle to the right-wing universalizing movements such as Trumpism. This is exceedingly difficult, but there are many ways to build connections. One is to show how US militarism and jingoism are stealing trillions of dollars that could be invested into working-class jobs in the United States, health care, and education for all, and clean energy infrastructure to protect workers' children and grandchildren. As long as a majority of the white working class identifies with US hyper-nationalism and militarism, the progressive universalizing strategy may not find its natural majoritarian base. Convergence of the peace movement, the labor movement, and the environmental movement lies at the heart of the progressive universalizing strategy to create a majority. It will require deep cultural sensibilities and awareness beyond what universalizing movements have mastered. But it has to be achieved, and there are possibilities based on a new class politics and finding unexpected cultural shared values that unite Left and Right working-class populists—including honor for hard work, community, and "people power" over the "Establishment."

Resistance appears limited today by the perceived prevalence of small movement bases, which fail to bring large numbers of people out in the streets in support of campaigns and marches. Community organizers knock on neighbors' doors and find it can be difficult to get others interested. Among the serious cultural obstacles to mobilizing ordinary citizens is pervasive individualism, which keeps people focused on "me, me, me" rather than the public good; the culture of immediacy that runs counter to the perseverance required by long-term successful movements; and fear that joining a movement might lead to loss of a job, career, or one's very freedom.

THE BASE IS ALREADY BIGGER THAN YOU THINK

While these constitute real barriers to mobilizing large-scale movements, they are too often used—by elites or the media—to obscure the involvement of millions of Americans in grass-roots activism, in addition to millions more who are receptive to them. The success of some massive protests, such as the 2014 People's Climate March in New York City, which brought 400,000 people into the streets of Manhattan, and hundreds of thousands more in other cities in the United States and world-wide, belies the idea that large or even majoritarian movements are impossible or even rare. There are hundreds of thousands of community-based and issue-specific resistance organizations—their vast numbers documented in archives created by researchers such as Paul Hawken (see his book, *Blessed Unrest*, and his Appendix and his online data archive that lists many thousands of resistance organizations). In his endeavor to count, Hawken writes:

> I soon realized that my initial estimate of 100,000 organizations was off by at least a factor of ten, and I now believe that there are over one—and maybe even two—million organizations working toward ecological sustainability and social justice. . . . What does meet the eye is compelling: coherent, organic, self-organizing congregations involving tens of millions of people dedicated to change.[3]

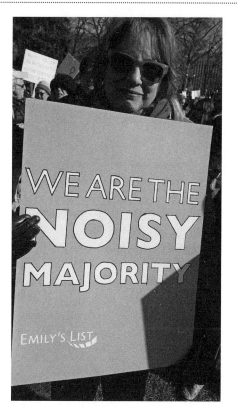

Women's March in Washington DC, January 21, 2017
Photo credit: Dean Birkenkamp

NTanya Lee and Steve Williams, the authors of the large Ear to the Ground study of activists, say that activists themselves agree:

> 50% of participants noted that thousands of local, grassroots organi-zations and trade unions are organizing key constituencies of working class and communities of color. This level of organization did not exist 15 years ago. These organizations identify and develop tens of thou-sands of grass roots community and worker leaders . . .[4]

Lee and Williams report that activists believe that they have the numbers to counter the Far Right and coalesce a popular majority, something that remains a possibility in the near future despite Trump's election.

Hawken believes that a huge progressive activist community already exists and that its views resonate with a majoritarian or near-majoritarian public in the United States and around the world, although he views the movements as autonomous, and he tends to embrace silo activism. Many of what he calls his "Blessed Unresters" recruit relatively small numbers of activists. But

Hawken is right that they have the support of millions of Americans who agree with them on the issues. The problem is very often not so much the absence of majoritarian support bases, but the difficulty in mobilizing them, especially under conditions of economic insecurity, political despair, and the failure to embrace a universalizing strategy to build a "movement of movements" that could challenge the system and avert its mad rush toward collective extinction.

It would be a serious mistake to deny the potential of mass base-building in the environment, anti-war, anti-racist, pro-immigrant, labor, and anti-capitalist movements. A universalizing movement, writes Howard Zinn, "that took hold in hundreds of thousands of places all over the country" would be difficult "to suppress because the very guards the system depends on to crush such a movement would be among the rebels. . . ."[5] Zinn notes that despite pervasive self-interest and atomization by design, spawned by the system, universalizing resistance would bring "the immediate satisfactions that people have always found in the affectionate ties of groups striving together for a common goal."[6] In the United States, millions are either activists already or supporters, a fact the ideological apparatus has successfully obliterated from public awareness.

PUBLIC OPINION AND THE PROGRESSIVE MAJORITY

The idea of a majority progressive base—that could support universalizing progressive movements—might seem preposterous in a country that has elected Trump as President. But remember that Trump got elected as a populist opposing, in his words, the "rigged system" of "crony capitalism." He ran on an economic agenda with many similarities to that of populist and "democratic socialist" Bernie Sanders.

In 2016, at the time of the Trump election, large percentages of the population, including Trump supporters, strongly opposed corporate globalization, big money in Washington DC, international trade agreements, and crony capitalism. They wanted Trump to purge Washington DC of big money and thousands of corporate lobbyists, which he promised he would do.

An Ipsos–Reuters poll taken on election day 2016, when Trump won the Presidency, is revealing. The poll showed that 72% agreed that "the American economy is rigged to advantage the rich and powerful." Many Trump supporters voted for him because they thought he could take down the "rigged system" created by corporate elites and Wall Street, also the goal of anti-Trump progressive populists.

This hints that Trump's election was not a sign of a conservative majority in the United States. Trump actually got elected with an economic populist appeal against the Establishment that has been at the heart of 1930s New Deal progressive politics and more visionary protest movements.

Many Far-Right and conservative people voted for Trump, but he was elected in a public whose majority has long been supportive of progressive core beliefs. And Hillary Clinton won the popular vote (i.e., the total number of people voting) by a huge margin of well over 2 million votes (but lost the Electoral College vote).

A quick look at opinion polls of US political attitudes over recent years offers clear proof of this entrenched majoritarian progressivism. Consider the chart below:

US PUBLIC OPINION ON MAJOR ISSUES*

84% believe money has too much influence on US politics (*The New York Times*/CBS, 2015)

84% say they worry about "Wall Street political influence" (CBS News, 2015)

79% want tougher Wall Street regulation (Lake Research, 2015)

60% believe "the economic system in this country unfairly favors the wealthy" (Pew Research Center, July 2014)

58% support breaking up "big banks like Citigroup" (Progressive Change Institute poll, 2015)

52% want heavy taxes on the rich to redistribute wealth (Gallup, 2015)

92% want a society with far less income inequality than exists in the United States (Harvard Business School poll, 2010)

92% favor a distribution of income existing in Sweden over that in the United States (Harvard Business School poll, 2010)

84% think money has too much influence on US politics (CBS News poll, 2015)

78% believe Citizens United should be overturned (Bloomberg, 2015)

63% believe the federal minimum wage should be raised to $15 (Hart Research Associates poll, 2015)

58% support a single-payer "Medicaid for All" (Kaiser Research Online poll, 2015)

71% support a "public option" for anyone seeking health insurance (Progressive Change Institute, 2015)

59% support free universal child care/pre-kindergarten programs (Gallup, 2016)

55% support free college tuition for all students (YouGov, 2015)

55% support gay marriage (Pew Research Center, 2016)

76% oppose US ground troops in the Middle East to fight ISIS (Gallup, 2015)

77% support nuclear weapons abolition (WorldPublicOpinion.org, 2008)

87% support funding more research into renewable energy sources (Yale Project on Climate Change, 2010)

83% support tax rebates for fuel-efficient vehicles and social panels (Yale Project on Climate Change, 2010)

77% support regulating carbon dioxide as a pollutant (Yale Project on Climate Change, 2010)

65% support US signing of a global treaty reducing US carbon emissions by 90% by 2050 (Yale Project on Climate Change, 2010)

59% believe the United States needs to continue to change to achieve racial equality (Pew Research Center poll, July 14–20, 2015)

50% say racism is a "big problem" in the United States (Pew Research Center poll, July 14–20, 2015)

67% say police violence against minorities is a serious problem (NORC, 2015)

75% of voters support equal pay for women as a major determinant of their vote (Gallup, 2014)

*All are percentages of Americans sampled in major polls.

On nearly every major issue, from anger at Wall Street and crony capitalism, support for a minimum wage and unions, preference for diplomacy over force, strong support for government to reduce carbon emissions and climate change, belief that big business is corrupting democracy, support for many major social programs including Social Security, Medicare, free college tuition for all students, the progressive position has been supported by an American majority and the support is growing. This suggests that a universalizing strategy—which moves beyond silo activism—is not utopian. Public opinion can resonate to a well-crafted progressive anti-systemic agenda that presents universal campaigns across issues appealing to large majorities of the population.

These liberal public opinion attitudes are obscured not only by Trump's election, but by the dominant Republican Party's successful denigration of "big government" and of concepts of "liberalism" and socialism. Majorities of the public support major government social programs and progressive policies on most specific issues while claiming to be against "big government." Persistent majoritarian support on the specific issues shown above suggests that the United States is a Center-Left country. But the ideological distrust of "liberalism" and "big government" suggests the need for a universalizing progressive politics sensitized to these contradictions.

Progressive majoritarian positions (on issues) have been obscured not just by Trump's election, but by media characterizations of the United States as a "Center-Right" nation rather than "Center-Left." The gap between elite opinions and popular opinions on most issues is vast, helping to explain the overwhelming public disapproval of the Establishment of both mainstream parties, which are correctly seen as handmaidens to big business.

Neither mainstream party looks attractive to an American public that is progressive on most specific issues. The public has contempt for big money in politics, sees big corporations as self-serving, is repulsed by the wolves of Wall Street, supports large-scale social entitlement programs, and believes in human rights, not to mention the need to save the human race from military or environmental catastrophe. Trump beat Clinton because he opposed the system, while Hillary Clinton seemed the embodiment of it. Trumpism, the Tea Party, and right-wing populism looked attractive because the public did not see a Democratic Party or even highly visible Left movements that seemed to be committed to strong economic populism; moreover, the progressive populists whom they did see seemed a part of coastal elites, and a social world and cosmopolitan culture worlds apart from the "traditionalist" mainstream middle of the country.

With Trump's election and Republican dominance, the United States thus looks far more conservative than it actually is. As Trump's election shows, this doesn't mean that there is not widespread conservative ideology or that right-wing populism cannot take power. Think also of the early 1930s in Weimar Germany, where extreme right-wing movements representing a small minority of Germans ultimately took power under Hitler, showing that minority Far Right populist movements can become ascendant—and horrifyingly dangerous.

A moderately Center-Left country such as the United States is, of course, not necessarily going to flock to universalizing Left movements; widespread liberalism on the issues documented above is something quite different from a majoritarian base acting and voting for system transformation. But previous wave eras such as the 1890s populist movements, the 1930s New Deal, and the 1960s show us that certain historical, economic, environmental, and political conditions can create universalizing resistance movements that become attractive to the liberal majority. If Trump and the right-wing populists can win in a public with the progressive views shown in the polls, surely Left-leaning parties and populist movements can do so as well. In fact, they can even win over many populist Trump voters who are likely to discover that Trump did not deliver the jobs or cultural values that he promised.

MASS SUPPORT FOR DEMOCRATIC SOCIALISM?

Majoritarian progressive populist and anti-systemic movements—essential foundations of Left-leaning universalizing resistance—look more promising in the wake of intriguing recent polls.[7] A series of polls by the Pew Research Center, YouGov, Rasmussen Reports, and Gallup asked the public about whether they viewed the words "capitalist" and "socialist" as positive or negative.[8] Only a bare majority of the public views "capitalism" as a positive term, and a growing minority endorse "socialism," with 47% in a Pew 2015 poll saying they could vote for a socialist.

The story gets more interesting when you look at two vital sub-groups. One is youth, particularly the "millennial generation" currently between the ages of 18 and 30. In a 2010 Pew poll, just 43% of Americans under 30 describe "capitalism" as positive.[9] Even more striking, the same percentage, 43%, describes "socialism" as positive. In 2013, a Pew poll found that 46% of people aged 18 to 29 have a positive view of capitalism, but 47% have a negative view. A 2015 YouGov poll also showed that the under-30 generation is equally divided between capitalism and socialism, with 49% having a positive view of socialism and only 43% a negative view. A 2016 Harvard poll showed that 51% of millennials nation-wide reject capitalism.[10] A 2015 Gallup poll showed that 58% of Democrats have a positive view of socialism. An even more striking 2016 poll by Republican Frank Luntz showed that 58% of young people chose socialism as the more compassionate system than capitalism; 66% said corporate America embodies "everything that is wrong with America." A 2015 Rasmussen poll also showed an equal split among all Democratic voters between a preference for socialism and a preference for capitalism. A majority of all adult Americans in 2016 say they would vote for a socialist candidate for President.

Because socialist leanings are rising among the young, it suggests that we might be moving toward an America that is either Center-Left or actually, by a plurality, democratic socialist, in its own self-definition. The enormous popularity, especially among young people, of the self-identified "democratic socialist" Bernie Sanders in the 2015/2016 Democratic primary race suggests that these poll numbers are not artifacts of the polling itself.

Yet what the public actually believes "capitalism" and "socialism" to mean remains largely unclarified by the polls. It certainly correlates with majoritarian issue positions against global neoliberalism, US oil-driven wars, billionaire politics, extreme inequality and the corporate plutocracy, and a surprising interest in or support for the social democracies of Sweden and Denmark. Bernie Sanders' social media support and funding grew after the first Democratic debate in 2015, when he said that he viewed Denmark as his model of democratic socialism, a system better described as social democracy. Just the use of the term "socialism" by a mainstream candidate has changed the conversation, giving more credibility to alternatives to capitalism or "the system" that can be discussed in "respectable" discourse. A universalizing movement against President Trump will be taken up by Sanders supporters on and off campus, and we show in Chapter 14 that student and community movements are popping up before and after Trump's election to support major system change for social justice and democracy.

These favorable trends in public opinion and the proliferation of activist communities against Trump do not ensure mass mobilization of young people or older folks into activism sweeping Trump and the Republicans quickly out of power. There are many factors inhibiting activism of any form. Economic insecurity keeps people with their nose to the grindstone. Individualism keeps people focused on just helping themselves. Time pressures keep people focused on their own personal problems rather than collective issues. The very magnitude of problems and power makes people feel powerless. In the face of problems such as war and climate change that don't seem immediate personal threats, people find ways of distancing or detaching themselves emotionally, making it easier to do nothing.

Both universalizing and non-universalizing progressive movements must find messages and mobilizing strategies to overcome these hurdles, which may become more possible as more of the population is turned off by Trump's authoritarianism, frightening bigotry toward people of color and immigrants, and his failure to deliver system change truly benefiting the working public. New social media provide powerful ways to present visceral images and calls to action to millions of people, as shown by organizations such as MoveOn. org, Truthout.org, and Presente.org. Political campaigns, as evidenced by the Sanders campaign that is seeking to mobilize a "political revolution" against Trump, can suddenly mobilize people into political action they have never been engaged in before. Universalizing movements can bring smaller activist groups into larger coalitions that attract the attention of much larger sectors of the public.

UNIVERSALIZING TO WHITE WORKERS: OVERCOMING RIGHT-WING UNIVERSALIZING MOVEMENTS AND BRIDGING LEFT AND RIGHT POPULIST MOVEMENTS

If progressive movements don't engage the working majority and fight for a majoritarian movement against both Trump and the capitalist system that created him, history suggests they will pave the way for the spread of counter-movements in the "Alt-Right," seen most dramatically in 20th-century fascist movements. Today, as Trump has made Steven Bannon, a leader of the Alt-Right, into his most important advisor in the White House, the Far Right is attracting even more white workers. The white working class since the Reagan Revolution in 1980 has increasingly been voting Republican, even as its fortunes under capitalism decline, reflecting cultural alienation, religious conservatism, white nationalism, and lack of social ties to, or trust in, members of progressive movements. A significant percentage of less educated white workers, watching their jobs vanish, wages decline, and their sense of self-worth and respect plummet, succumb to the dog-whistle racist messages and white nationalist or civilizational appeals of the Right, a nightmare successfully staged to win the Presidency by Trump. His white working-class supporters find their voice and sense of self-esteem in the bombastic appeals of Trump and other Far Right politicians about American exceptionalism and white nationalism, blaming their own decline on left-wing immigration policy, African Americans who live off welfare, liberals who hate America and undermine "traditional values" of family and religion, and Islamic terrorism. Climate change denial blinds them to the looming apocalypse we face under the current system.

Public opinion divides whites, and especially white males, from the progressive majorities growing among minorities, women, immigrants, and other identity groups. The progressive majority and many of the Left identity movements fighting against racism, sexism, homophobia, and even against economic inequality, are out of touch with a large swath of the less educated white workers who stand to benefit from progressive universalizing resistance to the system. But common economic interest and some shared underlying cultural and political values can help progressive populist movements universalize into the white working class. Building unions is a crucial part of making this possible, since unions, while drastically weakened, are more essential than ever in universalizing resistance across an increasingly diverse labor force.

White workers, especially in the South and Plains states, tend to identify ideologically as conservative, even though they are liberal on specific issues and policies. This has roots in the Right's success in demonizing "big government" and turning working-class whites against progressivism and the Left, defining them as nothing but advocates for big government and minorities. Republicans argue that liberals and progressives hate whites, pointing to things like affirmative action, and the identity politics that stereotypes white workers as recipients of "white privilege." The Right's success, as Trump has proved dramatically, is based on their own identity politics of hyper-nationalism and racism, which leads workers losing jobs and economic viability to recoup their sense of self-worth through identification with white nationalism and America, the "exceptionalist" nation.

The system has also nurtured psychological predispositions toward authoritarianism that are widespread in American society—and help to explain why progressive universalizing to white workers is a formidable challenge. Major survey studies over the last decade in the United States have shown an alarming authoritarianism among a wide swath of the American population. In 2011, in a preview of the possible rise of power of an authoritarian leader such as Donald Trump, the World Values Survey found that 34% of Americans supported "having a strong leader who doesn't have to bother with Congress or elections."[11] Among Americans with only high-school education, 42% agreed.

Political scientist Stanley Feldman asked Americans four questions: "Which is more important for a child to have: independence or respect for elders? Obedience or self-reliance? A tendency to be considerate or well-behaved? Curiosity or good manners?"[12] He argued that these child-rearing questions are a good measure of attitudes toward authority and political authoritarianism. And he found that 44% of white Americans presented as "authoritarian" and 19% as "highly authoritarian."[13] Feldman found that these tendencies often remain culturally submerged, but in periods of economic crisis or demographic change can surface in surprising ways. The level of support for Donald Trump in 2016 is one such manifestation of underlying values of authoritarianism in a significant part of the population. It points to how the system itself has culturally helped to immunize itself against the progressivism of the majoritarian views already documented in this chapter.

This means that winning and keeping the majority is possible for Trumpists and other universalizing Right movements, even after Trump is gone. After Hitler's rise to power, leading European social scientists, such as Theodor Adorno and the Frankfurt School, devoted their lives to explaining how a great nation like Germany could go fascist. They concluded that an authoritarian disposition in the German public and culture provided fertile soil for Far Right universalizing movements. This appears true in the United States as well, particularly among whites and particularly less educated white workers.

Militarized capitalism is, by its nature, a system based on power concentration and domination by elites of workers and ordinary citizens. The American system preaches freedom, but it intimidates and bullies workers, consumers, students, and other countries into submitting to its authority. There are important niches of freedom, and the authoritarian culture varies greatly by region, education, class, religion, and other factors. But winning the majority of white workers over the long term is a prospect that Right universalizing movements can realistically fight for. The fact that the Right is capable of winning such resonance makes it even more important that the Left goes all out to pre-empt that possibility.

Universalizing resistance thus means universalizing to many whites, especially white male workers facing declining class opportunities, and older white workers confronting the same challenges. Thomas Frank, in his riveting work, *What's the Matter with Kansas?*, Arlie Russell Hochschild in her equally powerful ethnography of Tea Party champions in Louisiana bayou country,[14] and other authors are certainly correct in pointing to the difficulties of progressives attracting culturally conservative white workers. But a reconfiguration of progressivism and populism that universalizes to whites, and rejects an identity politics stripped of class interests or separating itself from white workers, may make significant inroads in a key population that movements have despaired of reaching. Hochschild hints that shared values of hard work, community, and anti-establishment anger in the Tea Party Louisiana working classes offer hope that Left universalizers can reach out to them, a theme I already introduced and will return to repeatedly.

The success of Bernie Sanders shows that there is substantial promise in a universalizing Left which puts the economic crisis faced by workers of all races in a globalizing capitalism at the heart of all its intersectional demands. By running against the power of Wall Street, and highlighting the job insecurity, wage stagnation, and economic anxiety of lower-educated workers tossed aside by corporations moving abroad to find cheap labor, Sanders won the support of millions of white workers. He showed that if the Left and all progressive movements fought for a new economic global order, with public investment supporting millions of new infrastructure and green economy jobs, culturally conservative workers could join inter-racial movements for progressive transformation. The failure of the Democratic Party to create such a transformative economic solution for the working class explains much of the receptivity of white workers to Trumpism, and belies the idea that cultural conservatism makes it impossible to win over white workers in a cross-race, universalizing, progressive national and global movement against neoliberal global capitalism.

Uniting the resistance of minorities and whites in our increasingly diverse labor force is difficult. Whites of all classes have failed to fully understand and reject the racism that built the system and still allows it to function. Yet progressive universalizing across race and class has potential because it 1) speaks to the real economic interests of white as well as minority workers; and 2) is consistent with the issue positions of white workers on many central economic and political issues. Both the white working class and working-class people of color tend to be hostile to big corporations and corporate welfare, oppose bail-outs of the rich and Wall Street, and support unions and major entitlement programs on which they depend. They also worry about the survival of their children and future generations in the light of the system's impetus toward environmental and military catastrophe. They share values of hard work, community, and rage at a cruel, greedy Establishment.

Indeed, a 2016 careful survey of non-college white workers by economic analyst Guy Molyneux reveals that a significant sector of these workers are culturally moderate and are not racist.[15] They actually share progressive economic values that benefit them, including a higher minimum wage, higher taxes on the wealthy, strong Wall Street regulation, public infrastructure spending, and more spending for public health and public education. The problem is that they do not believe that the Democrats—or the government—will deliver these benefits, since they have been flooded by anti-government messages for decades. They see the government as benefiting the very rich or very poor, but not themselves. The progressive possibilities, as demonstrated by the appeal of Bernie Sanders to these workers, require working in communities and organizing an authentic, progressive, populist political agenda (both inside and outside the Democratic Party) to overcome their distrust of the government to support the progressive economic initiatives that they themselves strongly support. Molyneux says: "The stumbling block isn't cultural values. Few moderates (among the non-college white workers) believe the Democrats are even trying to improve their economic conditions."[16] If the Democrats and Leftists embrace a strong working-class populist economic program, it will be the beginning of a Left populism that begins to overcome the distrust of government and the entire political system, and moves millions of white workers to oppose Trumpism and move toward a Sanders-style democratic socialism.

Ralph Nader has argued that progressives have not seen or acted on the explosive ideological similarities between right-wing populist movements such as the Tea Party and Trumpists, on the one hand, and left-wing populist movements, such as the one Bernie Sanders has tried to build after his loss to Hillary Clinton in the 2016 Democratic primary. *As noted earlier, both Right and Left populism attract white working-class movements with fiery anti-establishment agendas.* Both target crony capitalism and the power of Wall Street and big companies that create trade agreements and other economic policies which fleece workers of all races on the shrine of corporate profits. Both want a "political revolution" that returns power to the people. Both culturally value jobs for all, and recognize the value and honor of work, community, and honesty (rather than corruption) that is central to workers across race and the political divide. Nader understands that, as currently structured, right- and left-wing populism takes workers in different political directions, but he argues that it is possible to build bridges that would unite white and Black and brown workers, whatever their earlier partisan alliances and whether or not they supported Trump, into a movement against a corporate-dominated America.

It's not easy and it won't win over anything remotely like all culturally conservative white workers. But a universalizing movement needs only to win some of them. Nader is right that winning the biggest sector possible of populist white workers is crucial.

LABOR MOVEMENTS AND UNIVERSALIZING RESISTANCE

John Trumpbour

Political scientist Joseph Luders in *The Civil Rights Movement and the Logic of Social Change* reflects in an obscure footnote that "Curiously, the labor movement is conventionally ignored by scholars of social movements." This stark observation is the starting point of environmental and labor organizer Jane F. McAlevey's new book on transforming the US labor movement, called *No Shortcuts: Organizing for Power in the New Gilded Age.*

It is often forgotten that the US labor movement, despite having many elements complicit with white supremacy and interventionist foreign policy, played a critical role in advancing the civil rights movement. The original push for a March on Washington came from A. Philip Randolph, the President of the Brotherhood of Sleeping Car Porters. The labor movement's involvement in so many civil rights struggles, including Martin Luther King's last fight in Memphis for the city's sanitation workers, has been largely erased from public memory.

In a speech to the AFL-CIO [American Federation of Labor and Congress of Industrial Organizations] in 1961, Martin Luther King saw the connection between the denial of labor rights and degrading conditions for African Americans and for all workers:

> In our glorious fight for civil rights, we must guard against being fooled by false slogans, such as "right to work." It is a law to rob us of our civil rights and job rights. Its purpose is to destroy labor unions and the freedom of collective bargaining by which unions have improved wages and working conditions of everyone . . . Wherever these laws have been passed, wages are lower, job opportunities are fewer and there are no civil rights. We do not intend to let them do this to us. We demand this fraud be stopped.

King observed in his AFL-CIO address that "the labor-hater and labor-baiter is virtually always a twin-headed creature, spewing anti-Negro epithets from one mouth and anti-labor propaganda from the other mouth."

There has been much written in recent decades about "the wages of whiteness," "how the Irish became white," and places where racism flourished in the US labor movement. Necessary exposure of white supremacy has led some people to miss where the labor movement pursued a more universalizing mission that brought progress for both white and African-American workers. These include alliances between Italian and African-American miners in early 20th-century West Virginia, as well as the shared struggles of Black and white timber workers in the Piney Woods of Texas–Louisiana.

It is well worth recovering these historical moments when so much of the political culture foments division and animosity, with white nationalism surging in certain quarters. Les Moonves, the CBS executive who took home $56 million in compensation during 2015, exclaimed in February 2016 about the meteoric rise of Donald Trump: "It may not be good for America, but it's damn good for CBS."

With so much media focus on seething eruptions of white nationalism among the Trump-infatuated segments of the working class in 2016, it might be valuable to explore those forces in the labor movement that have sought universalizing forms of resistance to economic and racial injustice.

In the aftermath of Hurricane Katrina, the Bush Administration allowed labor contractors to bring in welders, pipefitters, and many other workers from India, Peru, and Bolivia. Employers avoided hiring workers from the United States, with the Bush team suspending rules known as Davis–Bacon that normally require contractors to pay the prevailing wage: US workers denied opportunities for employment soon sought retaliation against the newcomers.

The Indian workers were confined in labor camps built for them in the borderlands of Mississippi and Texas. With 24 people to a trailer and under constant surveillance, the new arrivals saw their hopes for a piece of the American Dream die swiftly in these sweatshop stockades. Their long hours of labor were punctuated by a few brief moments of freedom from toil: heavily monitored visits to Wal-Mart and to an Evangelical church where they were encouraged to pray.

Saket Soni of the National Guestworker Alliance recalls how he was able to get the South Asian laborers to meet African-American building trades workers who had been denied the opportunity to rebuild New Orleans. They built solidarity and overcame the tendency of workers to turn on each other. Soni saw how the South Asian workers soon became inspired by the Memphis workers who received Martin Luther King's final speech before his assassination. "On one proud day in 2008," declared Soni, "250 Indian workers holding signs that said 'I Am a Man' escaped from the labor camps and then proceeded to walk from New Orleans to Washington where they went on a hunger strike." Singing "We Shall Overcome" in Hindi, they regularly invoked the words of Martin Luther King and Gandhi.

The National Guestworker Alliance now builds solidarity with workers throughout the United States. One of the most successful initiatives was the Justice at Hershey's campaign in which hundreds of students on J-1 cultural exchange visas from nations such as China, Turkey, and eight former countries of the Soviet Union fought back when they were compelled to work at the chocolate manufacturer or be deported from the United States. The National Guestworker Alliance connected the students with their heavily white working-class neighbors in Pennsylvania, and the students campaigned for these jobs to be restored as $18-an-hour positions for US workers.

The transformation of educational exchange programs into a labor supply chain for ravenous corporations may have been foreshadowed by the capture of many US public schools by politicians who hail business models as the cure for lackluster outcomes in the classroom. Out with music, theater, and the arts, and in with cramming for standardized tests and imposing discipline that will deliver a more docile, unquestioning pupil for the future workplace.

A labor union that has stoked the imagination of those seeking to universalize resistance is the Chicago Teachers Union (CTU). In 2012, they confronted the foul-mouthed, F-bomb-dropping Mayor of Chicago, Rahm Emanuel, who has fostered corporate models of education and routinely closes neighborhood schools. "These are our children, not corporate products!," exclaimed teachers and parents in the resistance. They noted that Emanuel sends his children to expensive schools offering arts and music. But among Emanuel's coterie, the creative arts became judged as luxurious frivolities unsuited for the children of Chicago's inner cities. The CTU won parental and community support when they went on strike fighting to keep neighborhood schools and maintaining music, theater, and the arts for students in poverty-stricken neighborhoods.

Back in 1995, the election of the New Voices slate for the leadership of the AFL-CIO heralded what many believed to be a turning point in the labor federation. The more inclusive leadership seemed prepared to deliver a new epoch of universalizing resistance. But the decision of the current leadership to support with gusto the construction of a pipeline through the sacred lands of the indigenous peoples of the Dakotas has shattered lingering faith that the AFL-CIO can rebuild alliances of Turtles and Teamsters, the environmentalists and workers who in 1999 fomented the Battle of Seattle against the economic and ecological depredations of corporate globalization. And yet, some unions such as National Nurses United and the Communications Workers of America have risen up to rebuke the labor leadership for their capitulation to the fossil fuel industry. This short-term bargain has alienated labor from allies in the environmental movement and among the indigenous peoples of the Americas.

Jane F. McAlevey's new work (*No Shortcuts*) on revitalizing the labor movement notes that activist organizations commonly come in three forms: 1) advocacy, 2) mobilizing, and 3) organizing. She argues that the advocacy and mobilizing models have dominated social movements and too often bring with them control by professionals: attorneys, researchers, pollsters, lobbyists, staffers, and lifelong activists. In contrast, the organizing model seeks to get ordinary workers to take charge of their union and ultimately their destiny. For McAlevey, the recent revitalization of the Chicago Teachers

Union is one of the best lessons. It demonstrates how labor organizations which are able to infuse ordinary members with a sense that the union belongs to them can go on to build powerful alliances with the community. This stands as a potent reminder of how universalizing resistance might give labor the audacity to overcome those forces plunging America into the new Gilded Age.

The organizing model thrived in the 1930s when labor leader John Lewis of the Congress of Industrial Organizations discovered that his most effective organizers came from Left-leaning backgrounds. The trouble for Lewis was that at heart he was a maverick Republican, and so he later sought to purge these rabble-rousers after they had triumphantly organized industrial workplaces. The ferocious Red Scares of the 1950s pushed many more of these successful organizers out of the labor movement.

In the 21st century, the 2016 Sanders campaign showed that young people could be turned on to politics The Pew Research Center surveyed the 18–29-year-old demographic in February 2011, and 58% had a favorable view of labor unions compared with only 37% of Americans aged 65 years and over. Sixty-two percent of African Americans judged labor unions as favorable to workers, in contrast to only 43% of whites. Forty-six percent of women regarded unions as favorable and 37% saw them as unfavorable, while men were deadlocked at 45% favorable and 45% unfavorable. The Pew data indicate that the organizing model will find a receptive response if the labor movement can reach out to young workers, African Americans, and women. Indeed, labor unions continue to gain in public support since the time of this in-depth survey (February 2011). For the new generation of organizers, the challenge is to connect with these labor-friendly communities, while showing disaffected white working-class males that solidarity trumps swashbuckling Trumpism when it comes to healing the wounds inflicted by capitalism in the Age of Goldman Sachs and the Fortune 500.

John Trumpbour is Research Director of the Labor and Worklife Program at Harvard Law School. He is the author of Selling Hollywood to the World: U.S. and European Struggles for Mastery of the Global Film Industry, 1920–1950 *(Cambridge University Press, 2007).*

7

Converge! Get Out of Your Silo

"(Activist) Groups are intertwingling. There are no exact words to describe the complexity of this web of relationships."

Paul Hawken

"Injustice anywhere is a threat to justice everywhere."

Martin Luther King

"I am still committed to building a movement to end mass incarceration, but I will not do it with blinders on . . . we should connect the dots between poverty, racism, militarism and materialism. I'm getting out of my lane. I hope you're already out of yours."

Michelle Alexander

Third New Rule: Overcome the existing fragmentation of movements! Rethink Silo Activism! Build a movement of movements!

Big Questions: How do movements "converge"? How do they learn to work in solidarity with other movements? How does passion for one cause create passion for other causes?

Slogans: Converge in strong solidarity! Movements of the world unite! Listen to the Pope!

What's New Here? Non-universalizing resistance is based on silo movements disconnected from movements that speak for other communities and causes. Universalizing resistance brings silo movements into what Naomi Klein calls a "movement of movements." It recognizes the growing inter-twining of different hierarchies of power, different oppressed communities, and different causes in a super-universalizing system. It leads silo movements to expand their boundaries and vision, and to build collaborative spaces and campaigns, working in coalitions with sister movements subjected to the same systemic power. The new universalizing movements converge to create a common movement infrastructure—a space and agenda for movements to meet, think, and act together in collaborative agendas and campaigns—to topple the super-universalizing system, while also more fully advancing their own particular struggles. At this time of writing, a President Trump offers a frightening face around which such convergence can crystallize—not only bringing together Left movements with each other, but with much of the Democratic Party and with disillusioned Trump supporters.

WHAT IS CONVERGENCE? VARIETIES AND VIRTUES

Convergence is a foundation of universalizing resistance. To change the system has always required convergence. Successful movement waves have always been composed of intertwined, exploited communities all threat-ened by converging crises. Today, they face together the prospect of a new authoritarianism and the end of humanity itself. But since the break-down of the converging civil rights and anti-Vietnam war movements of the 1960s, our movements have fragmented and de-universalized, even as the system itself has universalized. This is a movement crisis, recognized by a growing number of activists. In the Ear to the Ground interview study of activists, NTanya Lee and Steve Williams report that the majority of activists worry about it as a central issue: "50% said the movement is frag-mented."[1] Universalizing resistance is the only solution, with convergence its cutting edge.

You can only defeat a super-universalized system with convergent move-ments. No community can gain full rights, nor can a single issue be totally solved unless the larger system and elites running the world are exposed and successfully challenged by convergent thinking and resistance. Conver-gence creates the vision and infrastructure of an alternative system that will bring all our movements together to change a system that rules by dividing and conquering.

Convergence can take multiple forms. There are one-time or temporary coa-litions of single-issue movements in a specific protest or campaign. There are also enduring coalitions of diverse movements committed to multi-issue agendas. And there are new "people's parties," or in some parts of the world, revolutions, mobilizing much of the population under one conver-gent movement for system transformation of peace, equality, inclusion, and democracy.

The 2014 People's Climate March in New York City exemplified convergence on one of the great issues of our day. Peace, labor, feminist, and other single-issue organizations marched together with climate activists under their own "flags," in dramatic, if short-term, solidarity to stop climate change and save the earth. It was one of the largest protest events in US history. A temporary convergence also occurred at the 1999 Battle of Seattle anti-corporate globalization march, linking Teamsters (labor) and Turtles (environmentalists). Naomi Klein described the Battle of Seattle as the beginning of a "movement of movements," which brought together, as Klein says, "oppositional threads, taking form in many different campaigns, driven by the shared subliminal sense of looming catastrophe."[2]

The spirit that convergent, universalizing movements share is a radical democratic reclaiming of the commons. We depend on the commons to survive, even as corporations conquer and degrade them for profit. As our communal spaces—town squares, streets, schools, farms, plants—are displaced by the ballooning market-place, a shared spirit of resistance is taking hold around the world. People are reclaiming bits of nature and of culture, saying "this is going to be public space and we need it to survive and prosper." The Occupy movement, a more recent variant of the Battle of Seattle convergence, directly targeted Wall Street, the financial heart of the system, and drew together anti-corporate, student, urban, social welfare, housing, environmental, labor, and other grass-roots movements. Occupiers waved signs saying "we are all in the same boat."[3] In the same universalizing spirit, major labor unions, including the AFL-CIO, issued sympathetic "Demands for and by the 99%." Unions, the unemployed, low-income housing activists, students, professors, anarchists all jumped on the boat, and general public support was expressed in about 3 million people "liking" the 680 Occupy Facebook pages.

Union support was especially important to Occupy, and reflected a general universalizing, converging spirit that had been rebuilding for some time in the labor movement. The BlueGreen Alliance, formed more than a decade earlier by major unions and environmental groups, was an example of a labor convergence linking economic and environmental agendas as workers began to recognize that, not just jobs, but their future survival was at stake. The same convergent agenda was reflected in the early work of African-American writer and activist Van Jones' organizations, such as Green for All and Rebuild the Dream, that were designed as coalitional organizations melding race, economic, and environmental issues. The "People's Party" formed by US populists in 1892, calling for national take-over of Wall Street banks and a shift from America's first plutocracy to a populist democracy was the Gilded Age's catalytic Occupy movement, beginning to bring systemic convergent resistance of the era under one movement "roof." As noted earlier (see Chapter 3), this fell apart, but led to progressive reforms a decade later, indicating some of the strengths and weaknesses of America's historical models of anti-systemic universalizing.

With President Trump's election, the convergence against Wall Street and the rule of the 1% has gained new momentum because of the urgent need to resist authoritarianism and bigotry, as well as save the human race from extinction. All progressive movements face Trumpist repression and the loss of earlier gains they have accomplished. The silver lining of Trump is that he will mobilize a new universalizing spirit, bringing together all progressive movements to protect people of color, immigrants, and the environment, as well as rein in the wealthy 1%, and build a new democratic economy and society.

Convergence may be catalyzed by Trump, but it is an enduring imperative for movements long after Trump to build a new democracy. It highlights the need to bring down different sociopathic pillars of the system. If you focus on only one pillar—whether race, economy, or war—you see only one leg of the elephantine beast and not its overall structure. If you don't see and fight to dissolve the systemic glue tying together the different issues, whether race, war, or corporate power, you condemn yourself to an incomplete understanding of your issue, and a blindness to the larger system. You not only limit the numbers you can turn out for your campaigns in rallies, protests, and public persuasion, but you lose the ability to create enduring wins for your own community or cause, let alone to change the system.

Without convergence, you lack the infrastructure—the shared movement space, campaigns, and institutional networks and financing—that is the clearest way of exposing the system itself. Convergence, in other words, is the structural underpinning of any anti-systemic universalizing vision, since full-scale convergent movements are the only way to expose and challenge a super-universalizing system. Convergence builds into activists' DNA a unifying agenda of transformation.

No one has said this more clearly than Michelle Alexander, the leading writer on mass incarceration:

> For the past several years, I have spent virtually all my working hours writing about or speaking about the immorality, cruelty, racism and insanity of our nation's latest caste system: mass incarceration. . . . I have not been talking publicly about the connections between the corrupt capitalism that bails out Wall Street bankers, moves jobs overseas and forecloses on homes with zeal, all while unemployment rates reach record levels and private prisons yield high returns as they expand operations into a new market: jailing immigrants. . . . But no more.[4]

Alexander conveys the key message of Martin Luther King's legacy:

> [H]e connected the dots and committed himself to building a movement that would shake the foundations of our economic and social order, so that the dream he preached in 1963 might one day be a reality everywhere in the country.[5]

Universalizing labor struggle protest in Atlanta, Georgia
© Redwood8/Dreamstime.com

"Dr. King said that nothing less than 'a radical restructuring of society' could possibly ensure justice and dignity and security for all. And he was right. . . ."[6] Alexander tells us about her new universalizing aspiration:

> I am still committed to building a movement to end mass incarceration, but I will not do it with blinders on. If all we do is end mass incarceration, this movement will not have gone nearly far enough. A new system of racial and social control will simply be erected in its place, all because we did not do what Dr. King demanded we should: connect the dots between poverty, racism, militarism and materialism.[7]

Alexander has become a prophet of convergence, telling us she is "connecting the dots," and hopes we will too.

THE DANGERS AND LIMITS OF CONVERGENCE

Convergence has dangers. In earlier wave eras, some convergent organizations—or a totalistic convergence involving the creation of one central party or umbrella organization—have led to authoritarian power-grabs. Or they have privileged one movement or issue over others, or created doctrinal purity that restricts the holistic spontaneity and diversity essential to the life of all forms of resistance movements. Excessive or coerced convergence—where all resistance is shoehorned into one doctrine and one organization—can create movement authoritarianism and hierarchy mirroring the very system it is confronting.

Examples include the movement hegemony of the Communist Party in the 1930s that led much of the resistance of the era down the rabbit hole of one politically correct transformational economic agenda, linked to Soviet Communism, blinding progressives to the false gods of Stalinism. In a different way, the rise of Students for a Democratic Society (SDS) as a unifying and hegemonic resistance force of the 1960s led to a white-male-dominated movement with its own pathologies of blind convergence. By the end of the 1960s, some of the larger system's own worst elements, including authoritarianism and doctrinal purity, began to tear SDS apart. Internal wars for control of the movement by splinter groups—and alienation of women, minorities, and other marginalized groups and issues—led to the convergent movement's self-destruction.

This is not an argument against convergence, but a recognition that convergence must be built carefully, respecting the democratic will and interests of the different movements seeking to cooperate in democratic coalitions and anti-systemic politics.

A major obstacle to convergence is the powerful resistance of some activists themselves who are constrained by limited time, resources, and their own single-issue strategies. Many believe that grass-roots resistance can only be sustained by an "ecology" of relatively autonomous movements that will succeed best by focusing mainly on single-issue campaigns. Implicit here is belief in the "invisible hand" of silo movements which, by focusing on their own issues, will solve all problems and sustain the future of humanity.

In this view, convergence can actually hamper systemic change. Some believe instead that hundreds of thousands of self-regulating non-convergent organizations will tend to inevitably highlight systemic issues, both because of the way the system hampers their own struggles, and the ways in which the autonomy (some would say anarchy) of so many movements unleashes a political bombshell that will move toward systemic transformation in its own fashion. This is the view of environmental activist, Paul Hawken, who celebrates the movement as "non-ideological" and anarchic, free of political dogmatisms: "The key contribution of this movement is its rejection of one big idea in order to offer in its place thousands of practical and useful ones. Instead of isms, it offers processes, concerns and compassion."[8]

Sociologist Richard Flacks, in his masterful history of the US Left, *Making History*, also sees virtue in "letting a thousand flowers bloom,"[9] fearing the dogmatized centralism that killed the Left during its Stalinist period in the 1930s.

This caution about the dangers of centralized political parties and dogmas is very important. But it does not settle the argument in favor of non-convergence. We have lived through several decades (since the Reagan Revolution) where thousands of progressive, but fragmented, single-issue organizations and movements have not propelled a systemic transformation—and their failure to unite played a role in the election of Trump.

The best convergence will support many coalitions without browbeating each partner into abandoning its own cause or embracing a single blueprint or doctrine. Moreover, successful convergence can only occur if activists engaged in non-universalized movements decide it is the best strategy, and recognize that their own issues are organically connected with those of other movements. Coerced convergence is bound to fail, but failure to converge is also a recipe for disaster, since ultimately humanity will survive only if all movements converge around system change to save us.

THE VIRTUES OF SILO ACTIVISM

Convergence is critically important, but must be genuinely inclusive, truly democratic, and anti-authoritarian in its organizational structure and vision. It must be driven by the will of activists who passionately want it. Many of the dysfunctions of historical Left movements have flowed from non-inclusive authoritarian convergence led by a self-appointed "vanguard" with a rigid vision of the system and its alternative.

Convergence must be consistent with resistance driven from the bottom, fiercely protective of diversity of visions, respectful of the vital importance of many different issues, and resistant to any privileging of a single issue or doctrine. It must create diverse and fully accountable leadership structures that ensure non-hierarchical movement development, while enabling and empowering activists at every level of the movement to take leadership of their own campaigns and issues. Convergence, in other words, must be a kind of "organized autonomy" or "diverse unity" that melds movements and fuels anti-systemic visions with the spontaneous passion and grass-roots self-direction that cannot be subjugated to top-down control.

Silo (or non-convergent) activism will always play an important role in the rise of transformational movements. Most activists are motivated by injustices of personal or moral importance to them—and these are their greatest passion. That life-long passion remains, for some activists, a compelling argument for always focusing on their particular "single issues" and remaining "in their silos."

But many of these and other activists will ultimately choose to converge, as they see the limits of the silos in winning on even their single issues. One key reason is that "single issues"—such as racism, sexism, climate change, militarism, class oppression—are never divorced from each other or from the intersectional system that gives rise to all of them.

Because of intersectionality, silo activists inevitably butt their heads against broader systemic power, and begin to experience the connections between their "single issue" and other movements. Climate activists seeking to block oil pipelines may be motivated by environmental passions, but will soon inevitably discover the power of the big fossil fuel corporations that they need to challenge to stop the pipelines. This is an "Aha!" moment that gets people to jump out of their silos—in this case, causing climate activists to universalize by becoming anti-corporate activists as well. In the Trump era, they also have to work in coalition with liberals in the Democratic Party and disenchanted Trump voters who have "buyers' remorse."

In fact, the virtue of silo activism is that it engages so many different activists who might never have become active without the passion taking them into their silo. While initially a limited activism, it leads many activists in their own particularistic struggles to grasp the nature of the larger system—and its role in creating their own narrower crisis.

In other words, silo activism is often the first step into resistance and social movements. It is a great birther of activists and social change champions.

A second virtue is that silo activists often make major progress on their own single issues. They can stop particular horrific wars, even if they don't end systemic militarism. They can reduce racist police violence, even if they don't end racism. They can shut down coal plants or gas pipelines, even if they don't end climate change.

A third virtue is that silo activists often evolve into universalizers. Universalizing activists are most often "graduates" of silo activism, when they learn that they cannot solve their own issues without changing the larger system. Universalizing movements depend on silo activism as the "watering holes" from which their own members are born.

Silo activism often melds seamlessly with universalizing resistance. Michael Moore has suggested that every neighborhood create a "Rapid Response Team" of ten people to go to their local Congressperson's office and lobby hard every time Trump proposes another hateful or dangerous policy. Would thousands of such local Rapid Response Teams, each perhaps made up of ten people, constitute silo or universalizing resistance? Probably both, depending a bit on the extent to which they coordinate and work together.

As usual, Michael Moore is on to something. Local and universalized resistance can be intertwined, informally or formally. Even when localized community-based activism of the kind Moore suggests is not highly coordinated with that of other communities, it invisibly aligns you with resisters across the country with the same concerns. So such forms of neighborhood "silo activism" have a universalizing quality and may be particularly important in the Trump era for the reasons Moore suggests.

Silo activism and universalizing movements are thus interdependent. The overall ecology of resistance may prosper from the co-existence and simultaneous growth of convergent and non-convergent movements—or movements that have qualities of both silo and universalizing resistance.

Moreover, universalized resistance does not necessarily mean that all movements must converge or even universalize. Activists are the "experts" in resistance, and will ultimately decide how much universalizing to do, keeping in mind that some form of major convergence must occur to achieve our shared goal of creating justice and saving humanity.

There is no scientific formula for the correct or best balance of convergent and non-convergent movements that can ultimately create systemic change. Yet without many strong universalizing convergent movements, it is highly improbable that the system will change in time to ward off the worst effects of climate change, wars of mass destruction, or economic deep recession or collapse. Convergence remains the heart of anti-systemic resistance—and to oust Trump and build a new democratic society, movements will have to embrace universalizing politics wholesale.

CONVERGING IN BLACK AND WHITE

Of all the vital nodes of convergence today, among the most important—and most difficult—are those connecting class and caste (especially race) movements. It's hard to look at movements today without noticing how many of them are either all-white or all-Black. This is senseless because neither class nor caste issues can be won without the convergence of Black and white movements, Black and white activists, Black and white anti-systemic agendas. Moreover, Trump would not have been elected had there been strong universalizing movements uniting large sectors of the white working class with anti-racist movements seeking to unite the races in the workplace and community.

Yet the racial segregating of many otherwise universalizing movements reflects entrenched and powerful hurdles in bringing whites and Blacks together, hurdles that have resurfaced in all the wave eras we have already considered. The populist movements of the Gilded Age were virtually all white and had racist elements, paying little attention to issues of racial justice. The New Deal excluded Blacks from many of its most important labor and welfare protections. And, with the exception of some civil rights organizations, white male leaders dominated the movements of the 1960s, especially on campuses and within SDS.

Nonetheless, in all these eras, forms of Black–white coalescence and convergence of class and caste movements emerged. The most important example is the civil rights movement, led by Blacks, but supported by thousands of white activists. Relations among white and Black movement participants were often tense and hostile, with Black SNCC (Student Nonviolent Coordinating Committee) leaders sometimes telling white civil rights volunteers coming South (including myself) to go home. Nonetheless, working coalitions across race did emerge in powerful ways in the civil rights era. The success was due to several reasons. Blacks spawned the movement (Rosa Parks and the Montgomery bus boycott, and Black young SNCC activists). Black leadership was pivotal in inter-racial movements (Stokely Carmichael, Martin Luther King). And the leadership fought for Black liberation goals as part of a larger struggle for social justice.

The civil rights movement aimed to end Jim Crow laws and all forms of racial segregation. But it also universalized the agenda. Over time, Martin Luther King reframed civil rights as not just overcoming racial discrimination, but working against the Vietnam war and US foreign policy, as well as aligning with the class struggles of both Black and white workers (symbolized in the Memphis trash workers' strike in which he marched just before his assassination). King is arguably the most important universalizer in American history, promoting a unique convergence of race, economic, and peace movements. King ultimately preached an economic revolution, launching a Poor People's Campaign and a bill for economic and social rights, espousing "a national responsibility to provide work for all" in a "socialist" system.[10] Following the lead of some of the young Black civil rights workers who were among the first draft resisters, King also became a passionate opponent of the Vietnam war, claiming that American involvement in Vietnam "has torn up the Geneva Accord" and "strengthened the military-industrial complex."[11]

Elites have succeeded in erasing mass public awareness of King's embrace of the anti-war movement, along with his deep critique of capitalism, treating him as a champion of the system and its own ideals. Universalizers must set the record straight. King was, by the end of his life, an authentic revolutionary seeking justice and the survival of all humanity. But his heroism as a universalizer did not produce an enduring legacy that overcame all the problems of convergence, including melding class and caste.

Each generation has to find its own approach and consensus. No coerced convergence of Black and white activists—or of movements which do not want to work together—will produce good results. Many efforts to bring the races together into common organizations today face continuing opposition from many—in both white and Black movements and activists. The prognosis is not necessarily pessimistic, because while historic barriers remain, many white activists feel urgency about the importance of working with and for racial justice agendas. Many Black movements and leaders are promoting convergence on class and caste agendas and building organizations uniting Black and white participants. These include temporary working alliances between the NAACP (National Association for the Advancement of Colored

People) and major unions, such as SEIU (Service Employees International Union), leading to mass rallies such as One Nation in 2014 in Washington DC. It spoke up for economic and racial justice, a harbinger of more enduring labor, race, and gender convergences as the labor force increasingly becomes populated by people of color and women.

We are also seeing Black socialists and prophetic Black figures speaking for total system transformation (Cornel West); Black activists and authors working on convergence of economic, environmental, and racial movements (Bill Fletcher, Jr. and Van Jones); and Black writers on mass incarceration and police violence (Michelle Alexander and Jamala Rogers). Black Lives Matter is quietly engaging with whites and the relation of racism to capitalism in their movement, beginning their own process of universalizing among a group often seen, incorrectly, as single-issue. Alicia Garza, a founder of Black Lives Matter, says, "Even though Black Lives Matter gets talked about as being primarily focused on transforming law enforcement, Black Lives Matter has always been an intersectional organizing approach and intersectional organizing project."[12] Garza connects issues of police violence with poverty, housing, jobs, and capitalism as a whole. Moreover, there is an obvious connection between the militarization of the police and the militarization of US foreign policy. As Martin Luther King made clear, waging violence abroad leads to militarization and violence at home, leading some poor African-American and multi-racial communities to begin converging struggles against police violence with movements against US global militarism.

FERGUSON IS AMERICA: THE ROOTS AND RISE OF UNIVERSAL RESISTANCE

Jamala Rogers

When all hell broke loose in Ferguson, Missouri, after the murder of a Black, unarmed teen, it was not clear, to the untrained eye, all of the intersecting forces that had collided. In the weeks—and months—following the murder of Mike Brown by Ferguson cop Darren Wilson, those forces became more visible.

Political disenfranchisement. A majority African-American city (nearly 70%) was being ruled by a minority white city council, school board, and police department.

Segregated housing. As Black residents from the City of St. Louis were pushed north of the city limits, municipalities like Ferguson steered them into particular neighborhoods and wards.

Failing schools. Mike Brown made it to graduation, but unbeknownst to most people outside of St. Louis, his high school was part of an unaccredited Black school district. His diploma was worthless in the real world.

Militarization of the police. St. Louis County police were trained by the Israeli military in counter-terrorism tactics. During the Ferguson Uprising, police departments unveiled their arsenal of military weaponry made possible with the support of the 1033 Program that donates billions of dollars in surplus military equipment to mainly urban police departments.

Labor solidarity. It was difficult to ignore the role of labor, especially once it was revealed that Mike Brown's mother, Lesley McSpadden, was a member of the United Food and Commercial Workers International Union (UFCW). In the aftermath of the Ferguson Uprising, AFL-CIO President Richard Trumka met with key leaders on the ground, and proclaimed that racial justice would be central to his labor organization. This gutsy proclamation has resulted in tensions inside the labor movement, tensions that will have to get resolved as the demographics of workers become more Black and brown, and more female.

International solidarity. In a matter of days after unbridled anger manifested on the streets of Ferguson, messages of unity from other parts of the world, in struggling against capitalism and globalism, took social media by storm. Most notable were words of advice and solidarity from Palestinians who instantly recognized the military tactics used on them daily. There were lots of hashtags connecting Ferguson and Gaza, and soon #BlackLivesMatter protests were happening in major cities around the world, from London to Tokyo.

If the above forces—and how they crush working-class communities of color—weren't clear enough, I felt it was important to write about them in a historical context. In *Ferguson Is America: Roots of Rebellion*, I went back some 40 years so that readers could see that what is happening in our urban centers is planned and insidious. That Ferguson blew up is no accident, but it also could've been any number of municipalities surrounding the City of St. Louis, which had similar issues simmering just beneath the surface.

In a post-Ferguson era, there have been genuine efforts by the social justice movements to deepen their understanding of this period and to construct a protracted, organized response that leads to victories for our people. This process is made more challenging due to the high levels of individualism and confusion that consume our movement spaces. In spite of this, what I see emerging is the collective will to forge a disciplined, highly-organized resistance to a sophisticated, well-financed assault (literally and figuratively) on the US working class.

A Black boy's body lying on the hot asphalt of a sweltering summer day for nearly 5 hours should matter to everyone. Black Lives Matter has never been just a hashtag. It has come to echo the accumulated Black screams of suffering from hundreds of years of enslavement, lynchings, Jim Crow segregation, institutional racism, corporate profiteering, and state violence. Until all Black lives matter, the work of racial justice remains unfinished.

We are in the bastion of white supremacy, so racial justice must be front and center in US movements. To build a true anti-racist movement means that the struggle against racism is happening simultaneously inside and outside our organizations/movements.

When I was asked to give remarks at the opening of the Netroots Nation Conference held in St. Louis, I tackled the reality of any social justice group still being predominantly white in 2016. Unacceptable, I said.

There were several conference participants who later came to me with true confessions: theirs was one of those majority white groups, either in governance or membership—or worse, both. Unacceptable!

First and foremost, we are building an anti-racist, anti-patriarchy, anti-homophobic, anti-Islamophobic movement. Yes, we're big on lots of "antis" and often come up short on articulating what kind of society we are trying to build. We chant, "This Is What Democracy Looks Like!," but what exactly *does* that look like?

In 1980, I helped to found the Organization for Black Struggle (OBS). One of its pillars of work is exposing and dismantling the prison–industrial complex, a lucrative profit center of American capitalism in recent decades. The tentacles of this system are long and tough. Over the years, the OBS has been relentless in educating people about the real role of the police. You can't have a bloated prison system (2 million strong) without the active participation of a racist police department. If you're dealing with the death penalty or wrongful convictions, all roads lead to corrupt policing. If your community is burdened by a court system that uses citizens—in the words of former U.S. Attorney General Eric Holder—as "ATM machines," you will see the vile conspiracy between police, prosecuting attorneys, and courts.

The OBS, through its coalition partners, led a courageous and lengthy fight for a civilian oversight board that was put in place last year. The Coalition Against Police Crimes and Repression (CAPCR) facilitated a robust democratic process which understood that such a board is not a panacea, but that education and citizen engagement are critical. And while there's still work to be done in perfecting our model, and in staying vigilant to protect what we fought for and won, there are now citizen groups in other cities looking to the St. Louis experience to revamp or to resuscitate their own existing but ineffective review boards.

Most recently, CAPCR partners have engaged in an exciting campaign to "Re-envision Public Safety." This is primarily a campaign to engage citizens and to help them understand that they have the power to determine the character and destiny of their neighborhoods.

In St. Louis, the arrest and incarceration model sucks up a whopping 56% of the city budget. We have the seventh highest police per capita rate in the country. The Lou is right up there with Detroit's police force, only with half its population. Yet there is still legitimate fear about personal and public safety, especially in the predominantly Black and poor sections of the city. The stale response of city officials to these concerns is what? More police, of course.

Through a series of town hall meetings, we have been taking neighbors through a process of looking at where their hard-earned tax dollars are currently going and how to harness their power. We explore how we could redirect a substantial percentage of dollars from the police and courts budgets to address some of the root causes of crime and economic instability. Meeting basic human needs—now that's a radical concept!

The town hall meetings have unlocked the practical but creative ideas of citizens in looking at public safety in a different, more humane way. The narrative that public safety equals more law enforcement is slowly changing and empowering citizens along the way.

As some political and military observers have accurately noted, we are on a slippery slope to a police state. Because the dangers of state violence are real, this is an area where all social movements need to be fully engaged. Whether you are active in environmental justice, reproductive rights, workers' rights, or the peace movement, you have experienced—or will experience—state violence at the hands of the police for standing up for your beliefs. This is the nexus where movements can develop a domestic strategy rooted in a global political analysis. This is where the work can happen to build enduring relationships that value trust and practice accountability.

I believe that the US social movements have a reservoir of summed-up experiences and creative juices that can successfully inform our strategy and tactics for a 21st-century struggle for human liberation. We also have a lot of baggage that must be unpacked. Our organizations must step up our struggles against those -isms (racism, sexism, etc.) that undermine democracy in our organizations, as well as in the broader society, and prevent us from being a serious, lean fighting machine.

If we truly believe another world is possible, we must work to create it. Not to do our part is a betrayal of the working class in the United States and abroad.

*This year, **Jamala Rogers** celebrates 50 years of commitment to racial justice and human rights. She is a long-time community organizer in St. Louis and a freelance writer.*

TEAMSTERS AND TURTLES: CONVERGING ECONOMY AND ENVIRONMENT

Two other central nodes of convergence today are the economy and the environment; and the economy and war. Starting with the economy and the environment, labor unions and environmental groups have traditionally been at odds. Labor sees environmentalists as undermining jobs. Environmentalists see labor as indifferent or hostile to environmental protection. This remains a major problem—and President Trump is seeking to exploit it. He is creating infrastructure agendas based on "Drill, baby, drill!" to persuade us that he can create new jobs only by ignoring the "hoax" of climate change and the mamby-pamby attitude of environmentalists and their job-reducing regulations. This finds resonance among many workers and some unions.

Yet a paradigm shift in the labor–environment political and movement nexus is emerging. Labor groups increasingly see their agenda as intertwined with the construction of a new green economy that will create millions of new jobs. Building new solar, wind, and geothermal energy sources, creating new clean public infrastructure and transportation systems, retrofitting factories, offices, and homes for greater energy efficiency—all will add many new jobs. Environmental groups are moving toward an environmental justice vision that links environmental aims to social justice, including a more equal, full-employment economy that internalizes the externalities of capitalist production and resists the neoliberal agenda to privatize everything—especially the commons, on which human survival depends.

Unitarian Minister Fred Small speaks for the environmental justice movement when he says:

> *Global warming is a justice issue. It's a justice issue because global warming is theft—theft from our own children and grand children, of their right to a livable future. It's a justice issue, because its victims are, and will be, disproportionately poor and of color, those least able to contend with or to flee, the storms, droughts, famines, and rising tides of global warming.*[13]

A host of movement organizations, such as Green for All and the Blue-Green Alliance, tied to big labor unions, including the AFL-CIO, and to big environmental groups, are coming together to fight climate change. Together they are remaking the foundations of extractive capitalism and moving toward a post-fossil-fuel economy that will create millions of new jobs while saving the environment and humanity itself. In the United States, we saw the beginning of this paradigm shift at the 1999 Battle of Seattle, marked by the first major coming together of labor and environmental groups combating neoliberal corporate globalization, a major focus for both movements. The crisis of 9/11 temporarily broke this convergence apart, as militarism and patriotism eclipsed public focus on the economy and the environment.

More recently, the new paradigm is bringing together labor groups and environmentalists on a much larger scale, all seeing the future of jobs, and the future of the environment and of the human race as linked to the end of neoliberal globalization, the end of the fossil-fuel energy system, and the end of militarized capitalism. Naomi Klein has been the prophet of this convergence in her blockbuster book, *This Changes Everything*. Klein argues that capitalism causes climate change; therefore the environmental movement must converge with labor and openly anti-capitalist movements to stop climate change. Klein writes,

> I am convinced that climate change represents a historic opportunity . . . As part of the project of getting our emissions down to the levels many scientists recommend, we once again have the chance to advance policies that dramatically improve lives, close the gap between rich and poor, create huge numbers of good jobs, and reinvigorate democracy from the ground up.[14]

This is also the central theme in Pope Francis' universalizing 2015 Encyclical on climate and inequality. Success in building this critically important node of convergence could determine the fate of universalizing movements, as well as the fate of the planet.

A JUST TRANSITION: THE UNIVERSALIZING MOVEMENT FOR A SUSTAINABLE ECONOMY AND PLANET

Chuck Collins

A global movement is universalizing resistance to the fossil fuel industry, a sector that includes some of the most powerful corporations on the planet. While big coal, oil, and gas industries have systematically embedded their interests into our energy, political, and economic structures, climate change and labor activists are finding ways to push back.

Together, they are building a universalizing movement for a "just transition" away from fossil fuels to a green economy that can save our planet.

In the United States, the movement to shift away from coal consumption has been successful. Since 2002, hundreds of coal plants have closed, thanks to both the declining economics of coal and increasing environmental regulation. In 2015, 94 coal plants closed and another 41 were scheduled to be shuttered in 2016.

In the port city of Richmond, California, a newly elected progressive city council and Mayor pushed back against Chevron refineries located in Richmond that have both contaminated the community and provided high-paying jobs for decades. The city sued Chevron over a 2012 refinery fire that sent 15,000 residents seeking medical attention. Chevron responded in 2014 by pouring $3.1 million into municipal elections to elect a more company-friendly city council and regain their "company-town" dominance. But voters rejected Chevron's candidates, and a progressive majority now holds Chevron accountable for local health and safety.

Meanwhile, a Protestant congregation in Bedford, Massachusetts, passed a resolution stating that their community has a "right to a livable climate, and that right trumps laws legitimizing the continued extraction and consumption of fossil fuels." They dispatched dozens of protesters to join a resistance movement in the Boston neighborhood of West Roxbury, Massachusetts, where Spectra Energy hopes to pump fracked gas from Pennsylvania to export terminals and local communities. Locals have organized non-violent blockades of the gas pipeline construction project. Over a year, more than 200 neighbors and religious leaders were arrested, often blocking construction equipment for hours.

These resistance movements recognize that the extraction and continued burning of carbon and methane materials is propelling us toward catastrophic climate change. Naomi Klein calls this international pattern of localized actions "Blockadia," as communities adopt tactics of non-violent resistance, taking matters into their own hands when governments fail to protect their local safety and prevent climate change. From First Nations tribes in the United States and Canada blocking pipeline projects on traditional lands, to villagers in India resisting the construction of coal plants, these movements are truly globalized and local.

Blockadia is bolstered by a powerful movement to divest from fossil fuel corporations. As of June 2016, managers of over $3.4 trillion in investment capital have pledged to move assets out of major fossil fuel companies and into the new energy economy. This includes individuals, foundations (such as the Rockefeller Family Foundation), religious congregations and denominations, educational institutions, and the sovereign wealth fund of Norway. Divestment aims to revoke the social license of the private oil, gas, and coal industries to destroy the habitability of the planet, and to weaken their political power to influence rules governing energy policy.

In all of these cases, social movements are pressing to weaken the considerable power of the fossil fuel sector and to stop new fossil fuel infrastructure from being built. But these actions have tremendous consequences for workers and communities whose livelihoods have historically been tied to coal, gas, and oil extraction, processing, burning, and disposal.

In the Kentucky and West Virginia coalfields, coal miners are facing job losses as energy and climate policy makes the transition away from fossil fuels to renewable energy. Since 2012, coal-mining employment has dropped 38%, from 89,800 to 55,500 workers. No wonder that many workers oppose these transition efforts.

As the United States shifts to a renewable energy future, no individual community or sector should have to disproportionately shoulder the economic costs of job losses and community economic decline. A central component to building broad coalitions is committing to a "just transition" for workers and communities that have disproportionately shouldered the burden of fossil fuel extraction.

In contrast to the United States, the German labor movement has embraced a rapid transition to decentralized renewable energy, especially in the aftermath of the 2011 Fukushima

Daiichi nuclear power plant disaster in Japan. Thanks to strong social safety nets in most European countries, labor unions and workers are full partners in the energy transition.

"German workers have less to fear," observes Joe Uehlein, co-founder of the Labor Network for Sustainability. "They already have a just transition in the form of a social safety net. These German workers are not afraid that they will lose their health care, pension, vacation with pay, and educating their kids."

"Environmentalists need to understand the centrality of a job in the U.S.—and that in a society with deep social insecurity, your job is everything," says Uehlein. "We have everything to fear from an environmental movement that is silent about workers."

Activists like Joe Uehlein, who come out of the labor movement, believe that the environmental movement needs to become a vocal advocate of a "just transition" program for workers, especially when the results of their advocacy would eliminate jobs.

One component of this program would be creation of a Just Transition Fund, an idea first proposed by labor organizer Tony Mazzocchi of the Oil, Chemical and Atomic Workers. Mazzocchi believed that there should be a "Superfund" for workers displaced by environmental regulations.

Most proposed transition plans are woefully insufficient to reassure workers and communities. The Obama Administration's Power Plus Plan included $75 million for job retraining and economic diversification. Candidate Hillary Clinton proposed a $30 billion fund to revitalize communities threatened by coal's decline. Until a fully funded just transition program is put in place, our transition efforts will fail to win the level of worker and community support required.

Another component of a just transition plan is to create good jobs through massive investment in green infrastructure, including renewable energy-generating facilities, retrofits to existing infrastructure, and expanded mass transit. People's Action and Green for All are working on state campaigns to ensure that federal plans to reduce power plant emissions create economic opportunities for displaced workers and low-income communities. The Climate Justice Alliance has launched an "Our Power" campaign that aims to create 10 million good, green, and family-supporting jobs for the un- and underemployed as well as former workers in dirty-energy industries.

The concept of an equitable and "just transition" has been embraced by the environmental justice movement. Organizations such as the Climate Justice Alliance have lifted up communities like Richmond, California, the coalfields of Kentucky, and the Black Mesa reservation in Arizona, as communities that have been exploited by the fossil fuel industry. They are pressing for just transition policies and programs at the community level.

The movement against fossil fuel dominance and climate change will succeed when the environmental movement becomes more of a new economy movement that advocates for full employment, a just transition for workers, and job-boosting public investment in education, infrastructure, and research. This is currently happening in ways that break across traditional silos of constituency and issue, in part because of the urgency of the climate crisis.

Several streams of activity flow into the universalizing resistance river moving us toward a just transition. They include campaign work addressing climate change, including 350.org, DivestInvest, the Climate Justice Coalition, the Grassroots Global Justice Alliance, the anti-fracking movement, and hundreds of citizen groups popping up to resist fossil-fuel infrastructure projects. These overlap with local community efforts to build just and resilient communities as part of the global transition movement.

These organizational efforts are heavily shaped and led by resistance leaders in the movement for Black Lives Matter and other racial justice networks. The just transition also includes movements within organized labor such as the Labor Network for Sustainability and the BlueGreen Alliance that bring a jobs and livelihood program as solutions. The just transition movement includes coalitions and researchers charting new economic frameworks, such as the New Economy Coalition, the Next System Project, and the Institute for Policy Studies.

These movements may not appear as coordinated campaigns or as centralized institutional forms. Some are more "swarms" than formalized organizations, with their professional staff, boards, and tax-exempt donation status. But these threads of resistance will converge at times to facilitate surges of social change energy with the potential to alter political power relationships.

These movements have the potential to aid in a political re-alignment in electoral politics. In the 2016 Presidential contest, the insurgent campaign of candidate Bernie Sanders tapped into outside social movement energy to bring issues such as student debt, wealth inequality, climate change, and anti-fracking into the center of Democratic Party debate and primaries. These movements, along with Sanders-inspired political formations such as "Our Revolution," have the potential to elect progressive candidates at state, local, and national levels, independent of the fossil fuel industry, and to enact a just transition program.

As climate change threatens the habitability of our planet alongside our food systems, livelihoods, and health, powerful resistance to the fossil fuel industry and its political agenda is expanding and universalizing. A deeper analysis of the drivers of inequality and ecological destruction is bringing movements to understanding of the structure of extractive capitalism, with its rapacious desire to extract, burn, and dump fossil fuel by-products, and exploit human labor. In the seeds of this understanding is the possibility for our transition to a just and sustainable future.

Chuck Collins *is a senior scholar at the Institute for Policy Studies where he directs the Program on Inequality and the Common Good and co-edits Inequality.org. His most recent book is* Born on Third Base: A One Percenter Makes the Case for Tackling Inequality, Bringing Wealth Home, and Committing to the Common Good *(Chelsea Green Publishing, 2016).*

PEACE AND JUSTICE: THE CONVERGENCE OF LABOR AND ANTI-WAR MOVEMENTS

The convergence of labor and peace movements is another key node of universalizing resistance in the 21st century. Through much of the 20th century, the system constructed the fear of Communism as its core legitimating principle. It intimidated major labor groups from aligning with peace movements because they feared being labeled as "Communists." System elites routinely used such scare tactics. Labor leaders in the AFL-CIO willingly embraced this twisted discourse, collaborating with the CIA, and swimming in the jingoism of the Cold War era, fearful that criticizing US foreign policy would prove that they were unpatriotic allies of the Soviet Union.

Earlier labor leader, Eugene Debs, resisted this cant when he opposed the First World War. Later socialist and Communist labor leaders during the New Deal resisted it, as did Vice President Henry Wallace (1941–1944) who had argued forcefully against this reactionary view in favor of labor and broader US solidarity with its Soviet ally. Subsequently, however, the Cold War era of nationalistic war-mongering prevented any genuine labor universalizing and set back universalizing resistance for a century, with the "war on terrorism" threatening to do the same.

Labor largely supported the Cold War, fearful of being targeted as anti-American. This has been the trump card of right-wing universalizing: persuading white workers that their true loyalties lie with their corporations and bosses in a unified struggle to preserve the nation against terrible foreign and domestic enemies. Workers who were losing their jobs or seeing their wages stagnate could recover their self-worth by their pride in being an American. Even if you were falling out of the middle class, being an American made you an exceptional person. The universalizing project on the Left has always bumped hard into this right-wing cultural and militaristic Orwellian project. All through the Cold War, the unions were afraid to show that workers' economic interests required rejecting hyper-nationalism and wars draining billions of dollars from investment in jobs and social welfare in the United States, as well as even threatening human survival, as during the 1962 Cuban Missile Crisis.

After the collapse of the Soviet Union, and especially after costly militarization and economic decline under President George W. Bush, a new era began. Labor leaders began to catch up with broader sentiment in a public disenchanted with Bush's Middle East wars. The wars diverted funds from economic development and job creation at home. They facilitated outsourcing of jobs. They contributed heavily to a rise in unemployment, decline of wages and benefits, and the rise of extreme inequality. With the 2003 invasion of Iraq, massive peace movements in the United States and abroad turned against US militarism, and some labor leaders and unions joined with peace campaigns, arguing for a diversion of state funding from wars that hurt all US workers, to rebuilding the economy in the United States. Even candidate Donald Trump embraced this argument, calling for fewer "silly wars" for regime change abroad by US forces. He said that US money was better spent on jobs at home, even though he advocated increases in US military spending that would create a kind of military Keynesian stimulus.

The convergence of labor and peace movements remains an incomplete and tenuous project. But it is growing and may prove to be one of the key forces powering 21st-century universalizing resistance. If and when labor and peace movements converge, the system of militarized capitalism inevitably comes into public scrutiny as a regime counter to the interests of American workers and the nation itself, not to mention those of the larger world and human survival.

With militarist, hegemonic ideology dominating the Establishment of both parties in Washington DC, fueled and legitimated by the "war on terrorism," the question of how to build labor–peace convergence is absolutely crucial to the future of universalizing resistance. Fear-mongering arising in the wake of ISIS and other terrorist groups could become as great an obstacle as the Communist threat was to changing the system, and particularly to the convergence of labor and peace movements. Yet there are aspects of Trumpism, as noted above, that could help to bring down traditional US militarism and interventionism around the world.

A paradigm shift has begun to emerge as the labor movement itself becomes more dominated by minority and female workers and immigrants, all groups with histories of resistance and the strongest need for an economic revolution. As demographic change turns the labor movement into a rainbow of diverse people of color, with labor and peace movements working alongside race and gender movements, there is the prospect of emancipating labor from its 20th-century militarist shackles. A new 21st-century diverse anti-war labor movement can seek to end US militarism, cut the massive military budget, and shift priorities to domestic reconstruction based on social justice. We have not yet reached a decisive demographic tipping point, but we will. This will be a body blow to the militarized capitalist system—one of the great triumphs of convergence.

BRINGING THE ANTI-WAR MOVEMENT HOME

Mike Prokosch

Many peace activists wonder why it's so hard to bring new people into their movement. It's worth trying a different strategy: merging with other movements and constituencies. African Americans, for example, are more anti-war than any other segment of the US population. For 50 years they have led efforts to move money from the Pentagon's budget to domestic social needs.

That was true in Boston, Massachusetts, 10 years ago when Roxbury's district city councilor called for a 90% cut in military spending. Just 10% should be used for defense, Councilor Chuck Turner said, and the rest of the military budget should be redirected to jobs and anti-poverty programs. Quoting Dr. King's 1967 "Beyond Vietnam" speech, Turner worked with peace activists and tried to form a Fund the Dream coalition during the Iraq war.

Turner's call resonated strongly with a peace group that was trying to bridge the Black–white, global–local divide. In 2002, white and Black activists founded a new peace group in Dorchester, Boston's most diverse neighborhood. To succeed, they had to try something new. Dorchester People for Peace would have to work against the war at home: racism, violence, budget cuts, political repression. It would have to work with local groups to build a multi-racial peace movement. It would have to connect Washington DC's

neglect of human needs with its drive toward a permanent war. And people of color would have to be in the leadership, setting the agenda and representing the organization.

The new organization recruited people of color into its member and leader ranks. In 2003, it launched a campaign targeting No Child Left Behind. This federal law required high schools to send their student contact lists to the Pentagon so that military recruiters could call them. But there was an out: students or their parents could tell the school department to take their names off the list. Dorchester People for Peace (DPP) printed leaflets in four languages, with "opt-out" postcards you could send to your Principal. "What?," the front-desk person at the local health center or the Y would exclaim when they saw the leaflet. "I didn't know that. Give me more of those!"

The campaign took off because:

- Interests overlapped. There was a single solution for peace activists' issues and the interests of Dorchester's communities of color.
- Activists with race and class privilege built trust with people of color who were focusing on their children's survival. Dorchester People for Peace built relationships with over 70 community-based organizations.

- Youth projects in Boston picked up the campaign as a way to develop their constituency's organizing skills by systematically collecting opt-out cards and turning them in. Eventually the school department added opt-out information to its annual student handbook, and they asked DPP's youth allies to tell them how to write it up.

Dorchester People for Peace also conducted sign-holding and leafleting actions and public table campaigns. It joined marches against street violence and held forums on the war's impact in its neighborhood. The movement also conducted internal anti-racism training, promoted the leadership of people of color, and sponsored community forums with Cape Verdean, Haitian, and Vietnamese organizations in Dorchester. Taking leadership from organizations led by people of color, DPP joined campaigns to reform state criminal record laws; block a dangerous biological warfare research lab in Roxbury; block subprime mortgage evictions; respond to the 2010 earthquake in Haiti and expand the capacity of the Association of Haitian Women in Boston; construct a mosque in Roxbury, send humanitarian relief to Gaza, and support the US Campaign to End the Israeli Occupation.

Dorchester People for Peace saw the opportunity for a larger cross-movement-building initiative when Wall Street nosedived in 2008. More people needed unemployment benefits, government support, jobs—but the recession was strangling city, state, and federal budgets. Where to find the money? Why not the Pentagon?

"[I]f we do not make reductions approximating 25 percent of the military budget starting fairly soon, it will be impossible to continue to fund an adequate level of domestic activity," Barney Frank wrote in *The Nation*.

Here was the unthinkable—a Congressman saying we should cut a quarter of the Pentagon's budget! In July 2009, DPP and 12 community allies kicked off the Coalition to Fund Our Communities—Cut Military Spending 25%. Eighty-five people representing 40 organizations attended the initial meeting. Its purpose was to mobilize Boston's communities of color— the people who most needed social programs—to demand them, funded by Pentagon cuts.

Clearly, this would be a long-term effort, a 5-year commitment for starts. The new 25% Coalition began to grow. It met with members of Congress and their staffs. (One Congressman listened very differently to Black 25% activists than he did to peace people.) It sent them thousands of signatures on petitions calling for a 25% cut in Pentagon funding. It organized visibility and leafleting actions. In 2011, it helped to build a large community forum to reform the state's income tax system and restore essential public services. It protested public transit fare hikes, but increasingly focused on funding jobs and youth programs.

Throughout, DPP's role was not to lead, but to support people-of-color leadership by staffing the Coalition, doing outreach, getting food for meetings, and writing up the notes. White activists used their privilege— skills, access to resources, time to volunteer—to strengthen the Coalition. Dorchester People for Peace was becoming a movement-building organization.

The Coalition's growth leveled off. For 2 years, a dozen people from six organizations attended its monthly meetings. They weren't leaders with decision-making power. They were people who wanted to get together and talk. When the Coalition started, it didn't ask organizations to commit staff time.

That wasn't realistic, especially with the recession squeezing their funding.

Still, those groups could mobilize for the right 25% Coalition effort, and that came in 2012 when peace activists organized a non-binding state referendum campaign. The Budget for All referendum had four demands: create jobs, save services, tax the rich, and cut the Pentagon. The demands caught the attention of Right to the City Boston, whose members were Boston's strongest base-building community organizations of color. The demands spoke to their members' needs and would help turn people out for the fall election. Members of the 25% Coalition coordinated Dorchester signature-gathering, and the referendum was won three-to-one.

The 25% Coalition disbanded in 2015, but its accomplishments included:

- building relationships among activists of color;
- raising awareness in communities of color that taxpayer money was being diverted from neighborhood survival to fund war and those who get rich off it;
- adding anti-war thinking to the worldviews and narratives of community organizations in neighborhoods of color;
- creating a space where white people weren't running the discussion. (Many white activists wanted to get into that space, and DPP members chased them away.)

- providing a powerful anti-racist, cross-constituency model for coalition-building that can orient and inspire peace and justice activists in other cities.

What are some of the Coalition's lessons?

- It's not realistic to think that oppressed people will put time and leadership into an issue that they haven't decided is crucial to their communities. It's unlikely that a dominant-culture group like DPP could start an effort like this, and then see it thrive.
- To survive long-term, the 25% Coalition either had to find more activists of color who'd take charge of the whole effort, or become a non-profit.
- Still, systematic organizing—and DPP's years of trust- and relationship-building—allowed the 25% Coalition to pull off successful initiatives and change community consciousness.
- The 25% Coalition's model is probably too place-specific to be replicable. This is replicable, however: recognizing where you are and starting there to organize around race and class.

Mike Prokosch is an organizer, carpenter, calligrapher, and popular economics educator who co-founded Dorchester People for Peace and the short-lived New Priorities Network to move money from the Pentagon to our communities.

PUTTING THE MOVEMENT BACK INTO THE LABOR MOVEMENT: THE CONVERGENCE OF LABOR, CIVIL RIGHTS, AND SOCIAL JUSTICE ORGANIZING

In recent decades, especially during the Cold War, organized labor has often seemed so tied to the Establishment that movement writers have failed to even discuss unions. The "movement" seems to have fallen out of the "labor movement." Many progressives see the labor movement as part of the problem rather than the solution.

And, as just discussed, labor has often deserved this discrediting. Early US labor leaders such as Samuel Gompers built a racist craft union model, a lily-white approach that sought to win white worker support by aligning them against workers of color. Racial division by unions helped to create a labor movement collaborating with business and tying workers to their employers rather than each other. Collective bargaining meant buying workers into the system at the price of people of color, women, and other groups more oppressed than the workers themselves.

The rise of the CIO (Congress of Industrial Organizations) and many grass-roots labor groups sprouting up during the Great Depression and the New Deal helped put the movement back into the labor movement. As already discussed in Chapter 3, industrial workers took power into their own hands, breaking from the craft system and conservative labor leaders. They engaged in thousands of sit-down and wildcat strikes and factory occupations. John L. Lewis led the formation of a more universalizing movement, organizing workers across industrial sectors and demanding not only worker rights, but broader social welfare benefits. Socialists and Communists played an important role in turning labor into part of an explosive larger struggle for social justice.

This rising social justice-driven labor movement was never revolutionary, but it created a universalizing force that lasted several decades, with up to 40% of workers unionized and supporting a New Deal social agenda benefiting diverse social groups. But the Cold War and the bureaucratization of the large unions eroded the universalizing. The rise of the Cold War, and then the rise of the 1970s New Right and 1980s Reagan Revolution, led to a corporate and political repression and reversal of the universalizing labor spirit. Reagan vowed to destroy unions altogether, and the labor movement went into decline, hunkering down in survival mode in its own siloes.

Nonetheless, the acceleration of both corporate globalization and domestic austerity created conditions that inevitably created new universalizing social justice organizing forces in the labor movement. The 1999 movement of "Teamsters and Turtles," converging labor, environment, and other social justice movements at the Battle of Seattle, was temporarily halted by the attacks of 9/11, and labor once again was forced back into silos like those of the Cold War, aided and abetted by the George W. Bush Administration's austerity and anti-labor policies as well as the "war on terrorism."

Nonetheless, after the 2008 economic meltdown, conditions once again emerged supporting the rise of a more militant and universalizing labor movement. Wages, jobs, and benefits, stagnating for several decades after the Reagan Revolution, led to new labor organizing, especially in the service sector, to attract the millions of workers falling into poverty as their jobs were outsourced and wages and benefits fell further.

Social and demographic changes helped to lay the groundwork for the resurrection of a social justice universalizing labor movement. A growing percentage of workers were females and people of color. This led service sector unions, including teachers' and nurses' unions, and manufacturing unions with a higher percentage of members of color, to become natural homes of a new universalizing social justice spirit.

Political changes intensified these shifts. In 2008, there was the victory of Obama and his "Hope and Change" message that would mobilize a new social justice spirit across the country. It would create an Administration more sympathetic to a "community organizer" commander-in-chief, who was Centrist politically, but elevated a sense that people could make a difference by organizing for their rights in their workplaces and communities.

Corporate attacks on labor sought to end this new prospect for labor universalizing. But it could not stop the rise of the tide of populism engulfing the working class, leading to the right-wing populism that Donald Trump embraced as his own movement, as well as the left-wing populism that led millions of workers and young people to support Bernie Sanders in the 2016 Presidential primaries. Hillary Clinton would be forced to move her rhetoric in the direction of Sanders' demands for empowering the working class and the labor movement to stop corporate trade agreements, outsourcing, and austerity measures, in favor of massive public investment and a newly mobilized populist labor movement.

After the 2016 Trump victory, many leaders of major unions recognized the need to put the "movement" back into the labor movement, speak more forcefully to the economic distress of their own members, and unite the white and Black members of their own unions, as well as come together with the civil rights and other social movements to stop Trump and create social justice for their own members. Leo Gerard, President of the United Steelworkers, acknowledged that Trump spoke more powerfully than many labor leaders to the pain of white workers, and in the process of highlighting outsourcing and trade agreements had stolen his union's own message.[15] Mary Kaye Henry, the head of the Service Employees International Union, said that in the Trump era, with unions under even greater attack, they would be able to defend workers only by uniting with women's, environmental, immigrant rights, and other grass-roots social movements.[16] For labor, universalizing has become essential for survival and this means that unions have to unite white and Black workers and link them both to universalizing social movements aimed simultaneously at economic justice and civil rights in the community and the political sphere.

This is becoming a new credo of the labor movement. Fred Redmond, International Vice President (Human Affairs) of the United Steelworkers, spends much of his official duties linking his union to other unions, to the civil rights movement, to environmental movements, and anti-racist movements. In essence, his position is that of official "universalizer" of his large and very influential union.

In 2015 and 2016, Redmond co-chaired the AFL-CIO Labor Commission on Race and Economic Justice with Marc Perrone, President of the United Food and Commercial Workers International Union. They conducted forums in cities across the United States of workers from diverse labor, racial backgrounds, and occupations to share experiences, anxieties, and solutions to the problems of racism and corporate and environmental injustice. In early 2016, they issued a report called "Race and Economic Justice for All," explaining how racism divides and weakens workers of all colors, including whites. In a subsequent national conference in Washington DC in 2016, they brought together thousands of union workers and civil rights activists, who discussed the need for all workers to stand together against the racial divisions that elites use to keep all workers down. Their only solution: stand together and organize together.

The conflict between right-wing and left-wing populism will persist in the general population and the working class in particular. But both forms of populism are anti-corporate and suggest the need for tying workers to more general social and political universalizing movements of both Right and Left. Unorganized workers were attracted to Trump's right-wing populism, but the nurses' and teachers' unions, among many others, threw their weight behind Sanders and a continuing "political revolution" pushing for a new democratic economic system—what Sanders called "democratic socialism." This new spirit will lay the foundation for a rising young generation of workers—in more militant, universalizing unions, more disposed to universalize their struggles in the workplace and put the "movement" back into the labor movement.

UNLIKELY PARTNERS: STANDING TOGETHER TO MOVE FORWARD

Fred Redmond

Like most progressives, I woke up on November 9, 2016, with a pit in my stomach. My mind was racing at times and completely numb at others. For several weeks following the jarring election, I tried to break down how the United States got to the point of choosing a man to serve as President who is openly racist and xenophobic, who brags about sexually assaulting women, who mocks the disabled, and who shows a clear disdain for the basic tenets of our democracy.

We must acknowledge that we were defeated in our own backyard in the industrial heartland of America. Perhaps these voters lost confidence that the Democratic Party would enact trade policies that work for them. Or maybe they lost hope that Congress would listen to workers as opposed to the lobbyists lining lawmakers' pockets. And possibly they lost respect for politicians who talk the talk, but rarely walk the walk.

We can speculate until we are blue in the face, but as a people, we spend too much time throwing analysis at the paralysis. The question that we must move on to now is simple yet challenging: where do we go from here?

My union prides itself on the morality of its core values and its mission of being a collective voice for the voiceless. We believe that no one working 40 hours a week should live in poverty. We believe everyone should be able to retire with dignity. We believe health care is a universal right. We believe in equal pay for equal work and we reject all discrimination based on race, gender, religion, age, national identity.

Clearly, the economic goals of the United Steelworkers (USW) are intertwined with social ones. It has been this way with the labor movement since the beginning. Think of the Bread and Roses strike a century ago. The women laboring long hours in the Massachusetts textile mills said that pay which bought only bread was inadequate. They needed dignity and respect, too. It remains so today.

That breadth of purpose means that the USW does not stand alone. It has natural partners and allies. We stand together with them to oppose any and all attempts to move this country back to dark days when some people lived their psychological lives in closets,

some were denied their constitutional right to vote, and many found it impossible to form unions to bargain for better wages and working conditions.

We have worked together with allies before and universalized our struggles before. The majority of economic and social justice achievements were not won by single-purpose activists fighting alone. They were won through solidarity and by reaching beyond walls instead of building them. Moving forward requires a united front composed of people and organizations marching in the streets hand-in-hand, even though they might not normally find themselves in the same room.

An example of this is the BlueGreen Alliance: unionists—the blues—and environmentalists—the greens. The stereotype is that the blues don't care what happens to the environment as long as there are good-paying jobs. But in 2006, the USW found common ground with the Sierra Club, the nation's largest grass-roots environmental group.

The USW's International President, Leo W. Gerard, and Carl Pope, then the Sierra Club's Executive Director, founded the BlueGreen Alliance (BGA) based on the conviction that it was possible to have both good jobs and a clean environment. Building and installing environmentally-friendly technologies such as wind turbines and solar cells could create good-paying jobs.

More than 10 years later, the alliance now comprises nine unions and five environmental organizations. It continues to focus on identifying ways that confronting environmental challenges can create and maintain quality manufacturing jobs, often for USW members, and build a stronger, fairer economy.

Leo Gerard is adamant about educating the country on this crucial relationship between combating climate change and jobs, saying in 2013 that, "Addressing climate change is critical— not only will bold action protect our environment and communities, it will also create good manufacturing jobs and economic growth across all sectors of our country." Carl Pope agrees, saying that, "Protecting workers' rights to organize is an essential part of building a clean energy economy that improves the environment and moves America toward energy independence."

The BlueGreen Alliance universalizes resistance by pounding the pavement and getting our hands dirty to get things clean and just. In California, the alliance worked with labor unions and environmental organizations to enact SB 1371, a bill that requires the California Public Utilities Commission (CPUC) to better account for the climate change impact of leaks in the state's natural gas distribution systems.

The fight, of course, does not stop at the domestic level. In 2010, the alliance pushed an agenda in Cancún, Mexico, to address the key issues related to a global climate agreement that will ensure the transition to clean energy which will benefit workers, revitalize the US economy, and launch a new model of global economic development. And in 2014 at the United Nations Framework Convention on Climate Change in Lima, Peru, the BlueGreen Alliance and its allies put the struggle for workers' rights front and center in the debate.

Recently, the alliance applauded the introduction of the National Infrastructure Development Bank Act, which would identify job-creating transportation, energy, and water infrastructure projects in need of funding, and match private sector or governmental investments with loans made by the bank. The BGA's Executive Director, Kim Glas, said, regarding the bank, that "This would not only keep our communities safer and healthier, it will also put Americans to work from coast-to-coast,

reduce pollution and greenhouse gas emissions from inefficient and broken systems, and strengthen our national economy."

We push for legislation like this on the state and federal levels to include provisions like Buy America, which invests in our workforce and ensures that significant infrastructure projects use domestically sourced, American-made products. This accomplishes the core mission of the alliance, which is to provide good-paying jobs for workers here in the United States while reducing environmental damage.

The labor movement also utilized this strategy of action through solidarity when the Trans-Pacific Partnership (TPP) trade deal was proposed. When Congress was set to vote on fast-tracking this agreement in 2015, USW President Gerard joined with many other labor activists, and spoke out boldly against the damage the trade deal would inflict on every facet of American life. He said:

> Workers in the 21st century deserve in-depth deliberation over trade proposals to ensure jobs, the environment, food safety and national sovereignty are protected. . . . Congress should perform its constitutionally required job and thoroughly investigate proposed trade deals, not rush them past the public to appease Wall Street and multinational corporations that want to ship even more factories overseas to low-wage countries with no labor or environmental protections.

Alongside hundreds of partner organizations, including environmentalists, religious groups, food-safety societies, clean water organizations, and social justice groups, our union and the labor movement as a whole fought back against this bad trade deal. Together, we relayed the message across the country to workers and non-workers alike that the deal would have been a disaster for everyone. Activists made thousands of phone calls to members of Congress and sent even more postcards in opposition to the deal. Benefit concerts held by punk-rock groups and poetry readings and student-led marches sprouted up all across America and the world, igniting a whole new generation of activists not previously involved in social justice or political issues.

In November 2016, after an entire summer of protests and successful actions, it was clear there was not enough support in Congress to pass the TPP, and the proposal was dropped. These are the types of wide-ranging and inclusive, universalizing movements that will be vital under Trump's Presidency. Fair trade is not a guarantee just because Trump likes to say the word "jobs." We have to be allied and ready to fight back against all attacks on workers, civil rights, the environment, and any vulnerable and marginalized community. Progressive causes of all contours, creeds, and colors will face more assaults that will threaten to drag us back in time instead of moving us forward.

And although at times we may feel overwhelmed, we must remember that when we fight together, we win.

Nowhere has this ideal been proven more effective than in North Carolina. In the dead heat of summer 2013, a movement led by Rev. William Barber, known as "Moral Mondays," burst onto the political scene. The goal was to show up to the streets and to the capital, week after week, to resist the state government's attacks on its most poor and defenseless citizens. Its rallying cry: "Forward together, not one step back!"

The inter-racial, inter-faith, and inter-generational movements use diversity to bring people together to create change. Activists from all backgrounds stood hand-in-hand, beginning in July 2013, to call out the state legislature's depraved assaults on its own people, including rewriting the tax code to benefit the rich, slashing unemployment benefits, denying Medicaid expansion, and attacking public education. They never let up, backed down, or fell silent.

And as time went on, the Republican stronghold in North Carolina began unraveling. In 2016, in an election dominated by the GOP in almost every state, progressives led by Rev. Barber and his fellow activists were able to oust Republican Governor Pat McCrory after 4 years of destruction, including the notorious HB2 "bathroom" law targeting transgender people.

I've been blessed to have known Rev. Barber for quite some time, and I share his belief that the movement in which we find ourselves belongs to everyone who seeks to build a society that reflects our most deeply held moral values. And it is indeed our moral responsibility to reject fascism, racism, discrimination, and degradation everywhere, because these depraved acts affect more than the single community they target.

Rev. Barber has been traveling around the country educating others on that truth. He made it known that the issue in North Carolina with HB2 isn't just about bathrooms. It represents absolute constitutional overreach and immorality, and the way to shut it down is through solidarity.

Rev. Barber developed the types of partnerships and universalizing resistance needed to combat the moral and ethical affronts we will encounter over the next few years. Expanding our platforms, including diversifying the labor movement and looking at the bigger picture, is essential. This is why I signed on as a co-chair of the AFL-CIO's Labor Commission on Racial and Economic Justice.

Established in 2015, the main goal of the Commission is to facilitate discussions among labor leaders around disparities facing American workers and how to make unions more welcoming, varied, and all-encompassing. Conversations about these issues are difficult, but they are crucial when it comes to strengthening labor and uniting people as a whole.

In the past, our movement has not been open to everyone. We have to acknowledge that reality regarding our history in order to move into a diverse and universalizing activist future. The 1% and the ruling class in Congress have created a culture of hate to pit workers against workers and split the country based on race, gender, religion, and other factors. And nothing scares authoritative rule and nothing threatens its fortress more than solidarity among those they attempt to dominate through division.

The labor movement has always said that an injustice to one is an injustice to all. We include it on our websites. We shout it at our rallies. We share it in our social media posts. But this election revealed that perhaps we have yet to make that motto a reality.

In order to truly do that, we must continue building coalitions like Moral Mondays and the BlueGreen Alliance. Whether it's combating Republicans' attempts to cut Medicare and Social Security or making sure that right-to-work-for-less legislation never passes in Congress, we must employ the same tactics we have in the past, and universalize in solidarity with other great movements toward achieving economic, social, racial, and environmental justice. It is a package deal, as one cannot be attained without the other.

We must reach across aisles to stand side by side with our brothers and sisters. When we make that commitment together, then our movement will have no bounds. Because if not us, then who?

Fred Redmond is Vice President of the United Steelworkers. Redmond was appointed to the AFL-CIO Executive Council in 2008. He is a board member of the Workers' Defense League, and the National Endowment for Democracy, and he also serves as chairman of the Board of Directors of the A. Philip Randolph Institute (APRI).

NEW PROSPECTS FOR UNIVERSALIZING AGAINST US MILITARISM: CAN THE PEACE MOVEMENT FIND COMMON CAUSE WITH BOTH LEFT AND RIGHT POPULISTS?

A surprising shift among white workers in the Republican populist base, led by Donald Trump and Ted Cruz, in 2016, is a partial opposition, as already noted above, to Establishment Republican military interventionism. Hyper-nationalist Trump opposed the wars in Iraq and US troops in Syria. Cruz critiqued the overthrow of Muammar Gaddafi in Libya. These positions pointed to a rift between the corporate, neoconservative Republican Establishment and right-wing populists. Even Charles Koch opposed, on libertarian grounds, the Iraq war and deeper Syrian involvement. White workers, while attracted to Trump's and other right-wing populists' hyper-nationalism and bombast, increasingly opposed traditional US corporate-backed interventionism for "democracy" and freedom. These workers supported Trump's arguments that the money now allocated to war should go to development in the United States, a point explicitly argued by Trump in one of the

2015 primary debates. So progressive universalizing may be able to attract Republican workers, as Ralph Nader has argued, in a movement converging anti-militarism with anti-crony capitalism, exploiting a surprising feature of the populist right-wing movement.

Nonetheless, it would be foolhardy to ignore the powerful convergence achieved by right-wing universalizing movements—that suggests a continuing militaristic focus, especially in the war on terrorism and drone warfare, which will keep white workers away from peace movements. The New Right developing in the 1970s, as discussed in Chapter 3, successfully united an unlikely coalition of Christian Evangelicals, Southern racists and anti-immigrants, large corporations, the Pentagon and military–industrial complex, small businesses, and white workers. While these different groups are strange bedfellows, the Left should study carefully how Right universalizers have achieved such potent convergence. It points to strategies and tactics that the Left needs to absorb in a hurry, as discussed in Chapter 12 on electoral politics.

One of the most important strategies involves the Far Right's willingness to combine grass-roots movements that are anti-systemic with a commitment to electoral politics and taking over one of the two mainstream political parties. Far more than the Left movements, the Right has worked at local, state, and national levels to run candidates, and take over town councils and state legislatures as well as the power centers of Washington DC through the Republican Party. The Right has shown that deep investment in electoral politics is a crucial universalizing strategy, and that political parties are by their nature aggregators of issues and identity groups.

The convergence of the Right escalated in a serious way with the election of Reagan, and reliance on uniting Southern Evangelists and conservative culture warriors with market libertarians and corporate elites. There were deep problems in these electoral universalizing coalitions, and they led to further electoral splits, with many populist conservatives forming the Tea Party, the Libertarian Party, and acting in and out of the Republican Party. The election of Donald Trump in 2016 represented the latest stage of right-wing universalizing convergence through electoral politics, a subject we dive into more deeply in Chapter 12, focusing intently on the relation between universalizing movements and electoral politics.

Peace movement alliances with the right-wing Trumpists are dicey at best. In the end, the peace movement will find its most powerful universalizing partners among progressives and the Left, both in the United States and abroad. One of the Left universalizing great pioneers is Medea Benjamin, who has led a campaign against US drone warfare and US militarism that brings together feminists, environmentalists, labor unions, and many other social justice movements. She has linked up with victims of American drone attacks around the world, brought them into the halls of Congress, and helped to dramatize the power of peace as a universalizing movement everywhere in the world. Benjamin is setting a model for universalizing progressive movements—against militarism, and for love and solidarity globally, that every activist can learn from. And she is special because she shows how to have fun and bring joy to universalizing resistance against such grim violent systems, embodying a life spirit that all activists and movements need to sustain their work.

BUILDING A MASS MOVEMENT TO STOP MASS KILLING

Medea Benjamin

The $600 billion annual cost of the US military budget eats up 54% of all federal discretionary funds. It's no wonder we don't have money to address the crisis of global warming, build effective public transportation systems, institute a Medicare-for-All health system, or provide the free college education that all our youth deserve.

You would think it would be easy to form a united front with activists from different movements who want to redirect our tax dollars. Students fighting for free education should understand that stopping just one weapons system, the expensive and unnecessary Lockheed Martin F-35 fighter jets, would fund the education of all college students for the next two decades. Nurses fighting for universal health care should understand that if we cut the bloated military budget, we'd have plenty of money for a national healthcare system like the Europeans have. Environmentalists paddling their kayaks to block oil-digging ships should understand that if we dramatically cut our military spending, we'd have hundreds of billions of dollars to propel us into the era of green, sustainable energy. Unions should recognize that the military is one of the worst creators of jobs in relationship to money spent.

It was easier to connect with other movements when the peace movement was strong while trying to stop George W. Bush's Iraq war. Students came to anti-war rallies calling for "Books not Bombs," nurses called for "Healthcare not Warfare," union leaders formed U.S. Labor Against the War. Globally, we universalized our protests, organizing a global day of action on February 15, 2003, a day that made the *Guinness World Records* as the largest demonstration in world history. So strong was our movement that *The New York Times* called global public opinion the "second superpower."

When Barack Obama was elected, the first casualty of his Presidency was the anti-war movement. People dropped out of the movement for a variety of reasons, but mainly because many people thought that Obama would end US military adventurism.

President Obama did achieve a few critical wins for diplomacy, but he invaded Libya, and he also championed a dangerous, new kind of remote-control killing: drone warfare.

Drones were designed as a way to kill enemies with great precision without putting American troops at risk. But they kill many innocent people—and they stir up anti-American sentiment that fuels an endless cycle of violence.

Drones allowed the US military and CIA to intervene militarily with ease, even in places where we were not at war. These institutions operated secretly, without Congressional approval, and they lied to the public about the accuracy and effectiveness of drone strikes. We were appalled when a 2012 poll revealed that a whopping 83% of Americans supported the killing of "terrorist suspects" with drones. How could so many Americans think we had the right to murder people thousands of miles away who were never charged, tried, or convicted of anything? Our first reaction was, "How are we going to change public opinion so that we can change policy?" We never thought we could build a mass movement against drone warfare as we had built a movement against the Iraq war, but we did think that a small group of committed activists could help move public opinion and then influence government policy.

CODEPINK, along with groups like Veterans for Peace and Voices for Creative Nonviolence, set about educating the public on the horrors of drone warfare. We organized two Global Drone Summits in Washington DC; we wrote books, articles, and op eds; we traveled around the country giving talks at universities, churches, and community centers. We protested at dozens of private and government entities connected with killer drones: the White House, the CIA, the Pentagon, Congress, factories and homes of drone manufacturers. We engaged the public by getting tens of thousands of people to sign petitions, and call the President and their Congressional representatives. We encouraged drone pilots to quit and become whistleblowers, and amplified the voices of those who did.

Civil disobedience was a key component of our campaign. We disrupted Congressional testimonies by drone czar John Brennan and Secretary of State John Kerry. We organized die-ins at the CIA. The most creative resistance happened at US military bases where drones were piloted. Hundreds of people were arrested at the bases. Some went to jail for just a day and others for as long as 6 months.

One way this campaign universalized resistance was by connecting with the families of drone victims. We took delegations to Yemen, Pakistan, and Afghanistan. In Yemen, among the family members we met was Mohammad Al-Qawli, whose innocent brother had been killed by a drone while driving his taxi, leaving behind a young wife and three children. Visibly angry, Al-Qawli told us the Americans refused even to explain why his brother was killed. "In our culture when someone commits a crime or a terrible mistake, they have to acknowledge what they did, apologize, and compensate the family," he said. "Could it be that my tribal culture is more evolved when it comes to justice than the USA?"

In Pakistan, we learned that drones had attacked weddings, funerals, markets, and schools, terrorizing entire communities. "To Americans, we are disposable people; our lives are worth nothing," an irate young man told us.

We were so moved by hearing directly from these families that we brought some of them to the United States to hold press conferences and speak before Congress. In 2013, the Rehman family—a father with his two children—traveled from the Pakistani tribal territory to the U.S. Capitol to tell the heart-wrenching story of the death of their 67-year-old grandmother. Listening to 9-year-old Nabila relate how her grandmother was blown to bits while picking okra softened the hearts of even the most hardened DC politicos. From the Congressmen to the translator to the media, tears flowed, and dozens of sympathetic stories appeared in the media.

With the globalization of the sale of drones, we also connected with groups in Europe, holding an international gathering that led to the formation of a European network to stop proliferation in their countries.

Our education campaigns, actions, and protests, while never constituting a mass movement and not successful in ending drone warfare, have had a major impact on both public opinion and policy. Public opinion in favor of drone warfare shifted from 83% in 2012 to 60% by 2014. President Obama was pressured to acknowledge and discuss the US drone program, promising that his Administration would reduce drone strikes and minimize civilian casualties. In Pakistan, strikes fell dramatically from a high of 128 in 2010 to 13 strikes in 2015.

In June 2016, the Administration released its first statistics on civilians killed by drones between 2009 and 2015 in areas "outside of active hostilities": Pakistan, Yemen, Somalia, and Libya. The figures of between 64 and 116 casualties were far below calculations of nearly 1,000 made by reputable organizations like the UK's Bureau of Investigative Journalism. Yet the fact that the Administration released any figures at all was the result of public pressure.

We were also successful in pushing for compensation for some of the families of innocent victims, which was especially critical for widows with no means to support their children.

As drones for other purposes proliferated at home, activists universalized resistance by making common cause with groups working on domestic issues. One connection was with people on the Left and Right concerned about privacy issues, as drones in the hands of anyone—from the FBI to neighbors to corporations—could be used to spy on people without their knowledge or consent. Another connection was with groups fighting the militarization of police forces, many of them activists related to the Black Lives Matter movement who worried about the police getting drones equipped with military-style weapons. In dozens of states, they formed coalitions that passed laws restricting the use of drones for surveillance and the weaponization of drones.

One other key connection emerged: people who went to prison for their anti-drone actions got a chance to see, firsthand, the similarities between the military–industrial complex and the prison–industrial complex, including how both profit from human suffering. On their release, many peace activists linked with groups fighting mass incarceration that supported former prisoners.

The peace movement has had many ebbs and flows since the 9/11 attacks. Resisting the Iraq war was so clear and urgent that it was possible to build universal resistance. Although we didn't stop the war, we did speed up public opposition, which helped to reduce military involvement and pave the way for the Iran nuclear deal.

At other times, as with Obama's secret drone killings, wars have been more covert, making it harder to build strong opposition. Yet making connections with other movements has been critical in counteracting the behemoth military–industrial complex. Moving forward, finding more effective ways of universalizing resistance to militarism across issues and continents, is key to building a more peaceful world.

Medea Benjamin is the co-founder of the peace group CODEPINK and the human rights organization Global Exchange. She is the author of a book about Saudi Arabia entitled Kingdom of the Unjust (OR Books, 2016) and of Drone Warfare: Killing by Remote Control (OR Books, 2013).

8

Democratize the World: Globalize and Localize

"There's two globalizations. There's the globalization of the elites, of the corporations, represented by the World Bank, the IMF, the World Trade Organization. That's the global state. It's a secret global government elite. There's another globalization that's grass roots globalization. The Fair Trade Networks, the Sister Cities, Sister Schools, Citizen Diplomacy, the work we do at Global Exchange, linking people up at the grass roots. That represents majority forces."

Kevin Danaher

"We are committed with our lives to building a different model and a different future for humanity, the Earth, and other species. We have envisaged a moral alternative to economic globalization and we will not rest until we see it realized."

Maude Barlow

"As a global protest movement rises and spreads within the US, expect surveillance tactics honed in the 'war on terror' to be used in the defense of wealth."

Sarah Jaffe

"Workers of the world unite!"

Karl Marx

Fourth New Rule: Link up with activists around the world! Build a worldwide movement of movements.

Big Questions: What are the best global strategies to build movements across nations? How can we best learn from and coordinate with sister movements in every nation?

Slogans: Think globally and act both globally and locally! There is no purely local solution and no purely global solution; act glocally!

What's New Here? If they operate in only one country, movements are non-universalizing. Today, solutions to systemic problems—most obviously climate change which threatens our very survival—can be achieved only by movements linking and unifying across nations. Universalizing creates movements spanning different nations that target global power elites and wage campaigns against the global universalizing system. Globalizing resistance is part of a new internationalism, built by universalizing global movements.

THE NEW GLOBAL SOLIDARITY: MOVEMENTS ACROSS BORDERS

Student, labor, and farmer activists in Wisconsin during 2014–2015 protests occupied the Wisconsin State House to protest Governor Scott Walker's assault on public sector unions and his fiscal austerity policy. Pizzas to nourish them came from Cairo, where Arab Spring activists (themselves uniting Egytian labor groups, students, and pro-democracy human rights organizations, and deeply involved in their own universalizing struggles against Hosni Mubarak) showed global solidarity through food-offerings and electronic communication with the Wisconsin activists. The Occupy Wall Street movement was also inspired by the example of Arab Spring activists, and maintained communication with them. In 2015, massive South African student protests in Cape Town and other South African universities against higher university fees, tied to broader neoliberal or austerity policies, triggered similar protests against fees and student debt around the world, from London to Quebec to Hong Kong to Boston. The climate change group, 350.org, has built a truly globalized resistance to the frightening global crisis of climate change. Democracy activists have come together with US progressive movements to fight Donald Trump's authoritarian, bigoted policies and the legitimacy of his Presidency.

These are clear examples of a universalizing global resistance conducted through virtual and rapid global connections that would have been impossible in earlier eras. Just as technology has facilitated globalization of the system, it enables new forms of global activism linking resistance movements across the world. In 2015, at the Paris global negotiations around climate change, environmental activists from scores of countries came together to press for more meaningful global curbs to carbon emissions. Before George W. Bush's invasion of Iraq in 2003, hundreds of thousands of peace activists in the United States, Europe, Latin America, the Middle East, and Asia rallied in unprecedented pre-emptive global solidarity against the war. Global labor movements protesting worldwide austerity policies link arms online to protest neoliberal trade policies. Globalization of the system is easier, but the same technologies enabling system universalizing make possible a new wave of global universalizing resistance that will help to define 21st-century transformational movements. Increasingly, we will be talking in terms of global wave eras, where rainbow (red, pink, orange, and other) transformational democracy movements in various nations spark each other and work together in a world-wide universalizing resistance. But, as we describe later in this chapter, globalization is triggering right-wing as well as progressive movements that are themselves universalizing, symbolized in the United States by the anti-trade and anti-immigrant politics of Donald Trump and by the anti-EU right-wing movements sprouting all over Europe.

Technology enables a 21st-century universalizing resistance (on both Left and Right) that is becoming more global in its core identity. Corporate globalizing helps Northern progressive resistance movements in the United States and Europe align with Southern resistance movements in Latin America, Asia, and Africa against corporate globalization, neoliberal trade agreements, neocolonial Western military interventions in the South, global racism and sexism, and extraction of profit and resources from the Global South to the Global North. Since the system is globalizing, anti-globalizing movements must move toward systemic alternatives: what Jeremy Brecher and Tim Costello have called "globalization from the bottom" rather than "globalization from the top."[1]

Universalizing resistance for global worker rights

© Christina Richards/Dreamstime.com

In the last several decades, major progressive universalizing movements across the planet, symbolized by the World Social Forum (WSF), a convening of resistance movements around the world, have directly targeted global capitalism and turned explicitly to the tasks of uniting global resistance to imagine and agitate for an alternative system: a "solidarity economy," a "sharing economy," a green economy, democratic socialism, anarcho-syndicalism, or other global systemic alternatives. The WSF is just one of the more visible forums of globalizing resistance that has erupted since the acceleration of corporate globalization itself, a potential harbinger of a new era of global labor, global environmental groups, global peace movements, and other popular movements unprecedented in the extent of their global communication and shared global identity. In the last few decades, progressive US resistance movements, such as the anti-globalization movement surfacing at the 1999 Battle of Seattle, began to grow and universalize, only to be subverted by 9/11 and the shift by movements to oppose the war on terrorism. In the aftermath of 9/11, as US movements faced increasing repression and demoralization, progressive American movements have turned to the Arab Spring activists, the Mexican Zapatistas, indigenous Canadian environmental movements, European peace movements, and other global catalysts as inspirations for their own universalizing activism. The globalization of resistance may help to spark the political imagination and fuel universalizing mass movements in the United States that face enormous domestic hurdles of repression, economic anxiety, and political despair and fatalism, as well as the rise of right-wing populist anti-globalization universalizing forces.

THE UNIVERSALIZER'S ALCHEMIST: THE WORLD SOCIAL FORUM

Suren Moodliar

On the eve of the momentous election that would send Donald Trump to office, Noam Chomsky, in a sober tone, concluded a speech with a terse declaration: "We cannot expect systems of concentrated power to address these crises unless they are compelled by constant, dedicated, popular mobilization and activism." Chomsky pointed his audience to both local activism and the need for organizing on a *global* scale.

Earlier, in 2003, Chomsky entered *Gigantinho* ("Little Giant") stadium at the World Social Forum (WSF) in Porto Alegre, Brazil. Greeting Chomsky, some 15,000 young people, reflective of the WSF's international composition, sang John Lennon's "Imagine," while performing "the wave" around the circular stadium as a giant Palestinian flag crowd-surfed its way over their heads. Then, Chomsky joined Arundhati Roy to climb the stage amidst a rock-star welcome and chants of "*Olé, Olé*." Referring to another, annual gathering of corporate and government elites in Davos, Switzerland, Chomsky declared, "the mood has darkened," but in Porto Alegre, the "mood is hopeful, vigorous and exciting. . . ." Indeed, from WSF 2003, an anti-war call-to-action resulted in more than 14 million people taking to the streets world-wide to pre-empt the US invasion of Iraq. Although that atrocity was not to be forestalled, the WSF-inspired mobilizers declared the existence of "another superpower"—world public opinion, in the words of *The New York Times*—restraining Pentagon aggression.

Since then, the World Social Forum has spread geographically and had important, diverse impacts. The times are now auspicious for a resurgence of WSF influence. There are at least three important reasons for activists concerned about increasing their power and universality to invest in the forum. In exploring these, one discovers just how the WSF differs from previous international gatherings. In its heyday, the WSF scaled to involve hundreds of thousands of individuals in a week-long series of events, exhibits, and festive activities. And serious work happened, perhaps none with more impact than those involving outcast communities.

1) From "Minorities" to Linked Actors on a World Stage

In Mumbai (2004), the WSF extended its presence in South Asia, but it also became a stage for the *Dalit* and *Adivasi* movements challenging Hindu domination and the caste system in a country that is home to a sixth of humanity. With the WSF, however, these movements were reaching out globally, making common cause with similarly oppressed and super-exploited peoples in Taiwan, Japan, Burma, Australia, and South Asia. Not only did WSF 2004 become a platform for these groups to ally and plan with one another, but it also became a space for engagement with other sectors of the Left that had failed to prioritize their claims. Such linkages not only added to the moral weight of these movements, but it also increased their numbers. Similarly, with WSF Belém (2009), when the process migrated northwards within Brazil, away from the whiter South, indigenous questions became the prism for the whole. Similar re-orientations came with the WSFs held in Dakar, Nairobi, and Tunis. Thus have successful framings, platforms, legal strategies, codes, and action repertoires been diffused and universalized across outcast and indigenous communities. These often have the by-product of inspiring sometimes despondent "majority" groups in their home countries. Witness the boost provided by the 2016 and 2017 Standing Rock movement in the United States where indigenous groups active in the social forum process played a leading role.

Activism by oppressed "minorities" has always had global dimensions: the protean 18th-century US abolitionist movement was deeply international in character, having African, French, British, and indigenous roots. In the 19th century, David Walker's "An Appeal to the Coloured Citizens *of the World*" (emphasis added) drew on international sources, including the Haitian Revolution, and birthed the militant abolitionism of the Garrison era. Similarly, anti-colonial movements routinely assumed an international character as exhibited by the Pan-African Congresses of the early 20th century. As global treaty processes in the post-Second World War era expanded, so too did parallel civil-society gatherings, often to challenge the dominant nation-state negotiating parties. Huge global youth gatherings also expanded over the decades of the Eastern Bloc's existence.

Where the WSF is different from previous experiences, however, is in its bringing together *grass-roots*-level activists requiring neither notable status nor elite endorsement. More importantly, unlike civil-society counter-summits at the treaty processes—e.g., the archetypal Rio Summit (1992) or the climate talks in Paris (2015)—the agendas of the WSF focus less on single issues and more on the multitude of concerns; less on what activists should oppose and more on what they must propose.

2) A Space to Imagine Alternatives

"Another world is possible!" It is the WSF's slogan and is a direct retort to Margaret Thatcher's diktat that "There Is No Alternative" to capitalism. By the third WSF, whole catalogs of micro- and macro-level alternatives to capitalism began to bubble up with publications and workshops. If one notes the chaotic assemblage of actors and causes present at *all* the WSFs, one cannot complain about the lack of alternatives. RIPESS—the Intercontinental Network for the Promotion of Social Solidarity Economy—is closely tied to the WSF process. Consequentially, alternative and regional currency systems, cooperative enterprises, sustainable and regenerative agriculture, grass-roots finance, participatory budgeting, and many other expressions of democratic economic models are now common intellectual property of insurgent projects the world over.

Equally, radical intellectuals who have been influenced by and who have shaped the WSF, including Thomas Ponniah, Julie Matthaei, Erik Olin Wright, and Boaventura de Sousa Santos, have produced an invaluable series of works that challenge capitalist logic and identify *macro*-level structural reforms—not only the micro- or enterprise-level innovations that solidarity economics normally recalls.

Policies for universal basic incomes, alternative pension systems, market regulation, and new forms of property and ownership are also now part of the Left's strategic armamentarium, just as privatization, deregulation, and austerity are part of the Right's.

Liberating the Left intellectuals and activists from national and local contexts provides the space for comparison, engagement, and the sharing of these ideas—overcoming a *deficit* created by the deft intellectual and political work that followed the Right's weaponizing of Milton Friedman and Friedrich Hayek via Augusto Pinochet, Margaret Thatcher, and Ronald Reagan. At the level of ideas, at least, the WSF has stripped Thatcher's diktat of its plausible patina.

Empty growth, under- and unemployment, yawning inequalities, environmental catastrophe, and resulting global dislocations and irrationalities—all rising from the global hegemony of the capitalist economic system—have rendered the ruling class incoherent . . . except in one important respect. Its financial and discursive dominance have allowed segments of it to engage in a shape-shifting maneuver. Where once they championed the ideology of the free market and reason, they now manufacture scapegoats, via nationalist appeals and unreason. Just as Pinochet and Thatcher prefigured Reagan, India's Narendra Modi and Italy's Silvio Berlusconi foreshadowed Trump.

If the WSF was a platform for the outcast and scapegoated, if it was a nursery for new ideas to emerge, can it also be a space for a counter-strategy?

3) A Platform for Strategy and Coordination

Many have seen the WSF as a jazz-like space for improvisation while still admiring its capacity to bring together activists for dramatic actions like 2003's Global Day of Action against the Iraq war, or for coordinating campaigns to challenge corporations. Another, more difficult question remains. Can it support global or regional strategies to build power, including in its political moment—winning elections? This is a legitimate question given the present electoral poverty of the Left. Evidence is not yet forthcoming. The spread of the WSF to the Middle East, motivated by 2011's Arab Spring, has little to show for it. Moreover, the Global North's first WSF (Montreal, 2016) failed to generate identifiable political initiatives.

But there is reason for hope. In the early 2000s, the spectacularly divided Greek Left, especially those parts outside the Communist Party, utilized the Greek Social Forum as a space to engage one another. One result was the consolidation of forces that eventually won national power as Syriza. If it could not usher in an alternative, it was *not* due to national deficits, but to the feebleness of its continental and global allies. Syriza's much hoped-for solidarity from other European movements failed to emerge.

Nonetheless, the present moment, with ascendant right-wing parties in Europe, the Global South, and the United States, provides an unparalleled global opportunity surpassing even that constituted by George W. Bush's Coalition of the Willing, *which inspired the Global Day of Action.* In the Right's moment of political triumph, the space for a global alternative has already been reserved by the WSF. Will the world's outcast and exploited, including an increasingly globalized labor force, wield *their* creation in response?

Perhaps. In the past, the champions of the oppressed have catapulted themselves onto the international stage in response to global crises. Even

in the bleak days after Africa's 1885 division among imperial powers, and with the rise of "scientific" racism, Edward Wilmot Blyden, the pioneering Pan-Africanist, refused to concede contemporary political weakness, emphasizing instead spiritual strength. In practical terms, even while constrained by conservative ideas, Blyden acted internationally, in the United States, in the West Indies, in Venezuela, in Europe, and in West Africa, and placed great stock on solidarity across borders. Similarly, of course, Karl Marx dedicated his activism to building the International Workingmen's Association, recognizing that as capitalism universalizes, workers have to universalize their resistance.

When the US Civil War cut off cotton supplies, therewith idling factories and depressing profits in England and France, both countries were tempted to intervene. Activists as diverse as Marx and Italy's Giuseppe Garibaldi mobilized in opposition to the US South; Marx rallied workers via his writing in both the English and German press, especially via Vienna's influential *Die Presse.* Garibaldi, through letters from a jail cell to his followers, mobilized workers in timely public demonstrations in France and England and also contributed to a battalion on behalf of the North. Rallied *in Europe* by US abolitionists like Sarah Parker Remond, anti-slavery activists demanded that the British and French governments neither recognize nor extend support to the Confederate secessionists. Such internationalism helped to recast the war as one *for freedom* and not merely national unity—making it "the cause of all nations."

The present moment combines the civilizational challenge of climate change, the rise in extreme capitalist inequality within and across nations, and the political urgency of ascendant international neo-fascism. With scant political and organizational resources, and energies refracted across a bewildering range of causes, the WSF is a singular platform and optic for refocusing the Left. With a sometimes paradoxical obsession with process, whipsawing from horizontalism to top-down decision making, inconsistent resources, and a huge carbon footprint, the WSF's shortcomings are well known, but susceptible to strategic reform. It remains a singular *methodology* and venue for disparate actors—whatever their national weaknesses—to come together, deliberate, and organize. Those who are denied economic and political capital are rich in moral capital. The forum may be that global majority's alchemist, transforming their claims into strategy. Similar hopes allowed Arundhati Roy to listen carefully in Porto Alegre, and to tell Noam Chomsky and 15,000 young people that "another world is not only possible, she is on her way. On a quiet day, I can hear her breathing."

Suren Moodliar *helped to organize the Boston Social Forum in 2004. He is the incoming editor of the journal* Socialism and Democracy *and a coordinator of encuentro 5, a shared movement-building space in Boston. With co-author Joseph Nevins, he is writing* A People's Guide to Greater Boston.

POPE FRANCIS AND THE GLOBALIZING OF RESISTANCE

Pope Francis's Encyclical on Climate and Inequality, issued in 2015, marked an important turning point in progressive global universalizing resistance. First, the Pope's call was for universalizing resistance against the intertwined issues of climate change, inequality/poverty and human trafficking, all of which he linked to a deadening culture and a violent global capitalist system. Response to the Pope's Encyclical was strong across the planet, creating massive activist and spiritual gatherings in support of the Pope in Latin America, the US, Europe, and other parts of the world.

The Pope spoke not for nation states but for humanity and "protection of our common home"—the title of his Encyclical. Francis thereby embodied and preached several aspects of universalizing resistance. First, he spoke as a global leader to a global citizenry, not in the name or service of any nation but the world as a whole. He represented the voice of a new 21st century internationalism. Second, he called for a universalizing resistance against global capitalism itself as it built a world system privileging the Global North over the Global South, and insisting on the need for a new global justice compact. Pope Francis wrote in his Encyclical: "We are faced not with two separate crises, one environmental and one social, but rather with one complex crisis which is both social and environmental. At stake is both global justice and global human survival, as well as the survival of all life forms on the planet."[2]

Strategies for a solution demand an integrated approach to combating poverty, restoring dignity to the excluded, and at the same time protecting nature and a human future. The Pope speaks like an intersectional sociologist, highlighting the systemic intertwining of the world's great new crises and the need for global convergence of economic, environmental, and human rights movements. He demanded the end of caste as well as class oppression, highlighting that the global system's greatest economic and environmental burdens were falling on the backs of long-oppressed people of color and women in the global South: "the deterioration of the environment and of society affects the most vulnerable people on the planet."[3] He continues "Both everyday experience and scientific research show that the gravest effects of all attacks on the environment are suffered by the poorest."[4] Fourth, he spoke movingly about the need to move away from the human-centric technocratic vision of Western capitalism, making clear that the natural world was not created to satisfy the cravings of humans for power or "lordship" over all peoples and the earth, but to provide a sustainable "common home" for all species of life, all deserving equal respect and protection.[5]

Finally, the Pope highlighted the nature of universalizing resistance as a global moral force, making clear that universalizing resistance to the system was the 21st century's great moral imperative. This was a call to people of all nations, religions, races, and ethnicities, potentially catalyzing the emergence of a new universalizing and globalized resistance movement that will long celebrate this Pope, even if its global activists' cadres include millions of atheists or agnostics. What greater global moral imperative can there be than saving humanity and all living species on the planet?

GLOCALISM: INTEGRATING LOCAL AND GLOBAL STRUGGLES

Anti-globalization and anti-corporate globalization in progressive circles helps build localizing movements on the Left that agitate for community economics and local production as a more democratic and sustainable model than globalized production. This raises the question of whether localizing movements can "universalize," since they often prioritize local organizing and community-building over global systems or alliances. Since strong "local economic" forces exist across the world, a universalizing movement of progressive localists may, however, become a leading form of universalized resistance. In this instance, universalizing localized movements could coalesce against a global system to promote a new localized system that is both more democratic and more ecologically sane and sustainable.

The very idea of "universalizing localists" sounds paradoxical: can localizers choose to ally with fellow anti-corporate globalist localists worldwide, and would they work toward a common goal? Since localists share a desire to stop corporate globalization and global warming, a universalizing localist movement may very well coalesce in anti-trade, anti-neoliberal, and anti-corporate movements, while also sharing visions about how to build localized alternatives. The ironic possibility is that universalizing against globalization may create a world of non-universal communities and economies, insistent on governing themselves by their own rules. And they may save humanity by building resilient communities that produce for themselves and massively reduce the carbon footprint of the global economy.

Corporate globalization may be one of the most important forces in history to help universalize progressive resistance movements—whether global or localist in their politics. Corporate globalization has rather different implications for right-wing universalizing, since it turns US and other Western right-wing movements into hot houses of anti-immigrant reactionary politics, breeding hatred and animosities in the US and European Right against immigration—and against the people and culture of the global South. Globalization creates a stark divide in the Right wing of developed nations such as the US, as global corporations, headquartered in the US and Europe, push the pedal to the metal to accelerate globalization while their right-wing base mobilizes against that very globalization—and the free-trade agreements, corporate welfare, and even the hard-line military interventionism that supports corporate globalization.

Anti-immigrant, America First populist right-wing movements, committed ideologically to hypernationalism and seeking to protect American jobs from global competition and global outsourcing are helping re-invigorate and universalize the US populist Right. Globalization has fueled the potent universalizing right-wing movement, led by Donald Trump, animated by hypernationalist anti-corporate globalist ideology, even as corporate America views globalization as its most important 21st century agenda. Globalization may thus polarize the corporate establishment and the populist base of the US Right, but it may also create links among the anti-immigrant right-wing populist movements emerging in developed nations across the world, particularly in the US and Europe. The British "Brexit" vote in 2016 to exit the European Union was a shot heard around the world, trigging potent global right-wing populist parties throughout Europe also militantly opposing immigration and corporate globalization, and also contributing to Trump's election. Globalization thus potentially fuels both left-wing and right-wing universalizing movements, which share anti-corporate globalization sentiments but have entirely different visions of the good society and the way to save humanity.

BEAUTIFUL RISING: A TOOLBOX FOR UNIVERSALIZING RESISTANCE

Juman Abujbara, Andrew Boyd,

Dave Mitchell, and Marcel Taminato

> "The design of the postcapitalist world, as with software, can be modular. Different people can work on it in different places, at different speeds, with relative autonomy from each other. It is not any longer a plan we need—but a modular project design."
>
> Paul Mason, *PostCapitalism: A Guide to Our Future*

We are at an unprecedented tipping point. The defining challenges of our era—growing levels of inequality, the rapid erosion of civil rights, and compounding disasters linked to climate change and war—cannot be adequately addressed by business-as-usual politics and top-down development policies. Only sustained, people-powered, social movements can bring about the changes needed. And indeed, today, from Rojava to Chiapas, from the schools of São Paulo to the streets of Oaxaca, grass-roots movements are responding to these challenges with astounding courage and creativity, even in the face of unspeakable violence. To win, these social movements must find ways to analyze, learn from, and share their experimentations and innovations—successful and not—with each other. We are part of a project that is seeking

to do precisely that by working with social movements across the globe, and particularly the Global South, to articulate a "universal grammar" of social change, and sharing the results through a modular toolbox we call *Beautiful Rising*.

Toward a Universal Grammar of Social Change

In his free time, Noam Chomsky writes blistering critiques of US imperialism, but by day, he's a linguistics professor who has revolutionized the discipline. Chomskyan linguistics is perhaps best known for the concept of "universal grammar"—the idea that all humans possess an innate capacity to learn language according to certain principles and parameters that span all cultures. Now, what if social change also operates by universal principles and parameters? Might the history and future of social change be approached as a shared, learnable, and evolving body of knowledge pulling societies toward greater freedom?

Like the *Beautiful Trouble* toolbox that preceded and informed *Beautiful Rising*, we have structured our work around the concept of a *pattern language*. Architect Christopher Alexander first introduced this concept in his 1977 book, *A Pattern Language: Towns, Buildings, Construction*, in which he sought to develop for the field of architecture "a network of patterns that call upon one another," each providing "a perennial solution to a recurring problem within a building context." He writes:

> Each pattern describes a problem which occurs over and over again in our environment, and then describes the core of the solution to that problem, in such a way that you can use this solution a million times over, without ever doing it the same way twice.

Pattern languages have since been developed for fields as varied as computer science, media studies, and group process work. We were inspired by Alexander's modular, interlocking format, its organically expandable structure, and the democratic nature of the form, which provides a variety of tools for people to adapt to their own unique circumstances, and encourages users to add their own patterns as they see fit.

As a pattern-language-inspired undertaking, the *Beautiful Rising* toolbox is, by design, continuously evolving. As new movements arise, new stories must be told, new insights gleaned, new tactics developed. The toolkit is designed to grow alongside the movements that use it, providing organizers with a nimble and responsive framework for thinking about their own activism alongside stories of success or failure shared by others around the world—stories such as that of the Ugandan students who smuggled two yellow-painted pigs into Parliament to protest corruption in 2014; or the Burmese students' long march against education reforms in 2015; or Lebanon's "Honk at Parliament" campaign that sought to drive from office politicians who clung to power long after their term had expired.

Lessons and Implications for Universalizing Resistance

The toolbox, and the larger network of organizations and activists that have coalesced around it, are now evolving into a horizontal and globally dispersed brain trust capable of analyzing common challenges and documenting innovative responses in order to spread these insights to a growing global network of social movements.

For example, one challenge that kept surfacing was the problem of *the NGO-ization of resistance*—the ways in which the rapid proliferation of non-governmental organizations (NGOs) under neoliberalism has inhibited struggles for democracy, freedom, and social change. Arundhati Roy has described how the NGO boom coincided with the requirements for structural adjustment and opening of markets to neoliberalism in the late 1980s and 1990s in India. As the neoliberal model slashed public funding for rural development, agriculture, energy, education, transport, and public health, NGOs stepped in to replace democratically accountable public services with charity-based band-aid solutions. This theoretical frame of NGO-ization resonated deeply with activists working in vastly different contexts across Asia, Africa, and the Americas. Naming it allowed them to recognize a key pattern across various struggles and challenges in which they were engaged, so as to more effectively target neoliberalism as a global repressive ideology and counter the NGOs that operate under its dictates.

A related challenge that activists across the Global South—a concept that

Vijay Prashad provocatively defines as "not a place," but "the name for the protests against neoliberal policies that produce an unequal world"— have been forced to navigate is the enduring dilemma of Western *"democracy promotion."* George Katsiaficas defines this as primarily US efforts to penetrate and control emergent civil societies in regimes deemed unfriendly and unstable by American policymakers. To counter this destructive force, he identifies the need for *solidarity, not aid*—both South–South solidarity and a rebalancing of the power dynamics of North–South solidarity.

If NGO-led development efforts have too often depoliticized social struggles and diverted energy from the grass-roots initiatives that are uniquely positioned to address the root causes of the problems they confront, a universal grammar for resistance needs to be rooted in and sustained by international solidarity and *intersectionality* among people power movements. Intersectionality, such as that exhibited by the Mexican students who organized the Zapatista Caravan to build public support for the indigenous uprising of 2001, can help to build a joint struggle across movements and foster a common understanding of global challenges that spans geographical boundaries and points of struggle.

The growing ferocity of state violence is another challenge faced by activists across the Global South. In response, activists have shared several principles that guided their work and helped ensure their safety, from *activating international human rights mechanisms*, to *seeking safety in support networks*, to *jail solidarity*.

While our work with activists has revealed many common global challenges, several also emerged that were

particular to a country or region—for example, the use of *"Baltajiah"* (thugs) by authoritarian regimes in the Middle East to repress rising movements. Though they're called different names in different countries (in Jordan and Palestine, *Sahijeh* or "clappers"; in Egypt, *Baltajiah* or "axes"; in Syria, *Shabiha* or "ghosts"), a common political formation shows up across the Arab World: an often marginalized grouping of individuals that support the state apparatus in the shadows, and coalesce momentarily to disrupt movements seeking change. The most famous example: the Battle of the Camel, in which camel riders attacked and killed protesters in Cairo's Tahrir square in 2011.

The toolbox and project are particularly focused on uncovering the innovative methods that movements are devising to creatively resist repression, address challenges like those named above, and route around the constraints they face. Sometimes we have noticed similar patterns of creative response, but with very different expressions from country to country. Take, for example, clandestine leafleting, which can be employed when it is too dangerous to be caught distributing subversive information. In Syria, activists sent a host of slogan-marked ping-pong balls bouncing through the streets, and in Myanmar (Burma), they wafted a fleet of leaflet-laden hot-air lanterns across the city. Though the creative solutions activists shared were sometimes intensely local and culturally specific, the challenges they addressed were often universal.

There is no single answer or magic bullet to the challenges facing humanity. However, the innovations and rapid prototyping that are unfolding in social movements around the world can and should be studied, replicated, celebrated, scaled up, and improved upon. Efforts to universalize resistance such as *Beautiful Rising* have a valuable role to play in the global struggle for freedom, peace, and justice.

Juman Abujbara *(not pictured on p.165) is a social change campaigner, human rights defender, and aspiring philosopher based in Amman, Jordan.*

Andrew Boyd *is co-founder of the Beautiful Trouble project, author of several odd books, and a long-time veteran of creative campaigns for social change. You can find him at http://andrewboyd.com.*

Dave Oswald Mitchell *is a writer, editor, organizer, and troublemaker, as well as a Saskatchewanian, bibliophile, and vagabond. He serves as the Editorial Director of* Beautiful Trouble.

Marcel Taminato *is an anthropologist, learning facilitator for non-violent resistance and movement building, co-founder of* Escola de Ativismo *(School of Activism) in Brazil and co-editor of the Portuguese edition of the book* Beautiful Trouble *(Bela Baderna: Ferramentas Para Revolução).*

9

Pachamama: Protect Mother Earth

"Now, a new anti-establishment movement has broken with Washington's embedded elites and has energized a new generation to stand in front of the bulldozers and coal trucks."

Scott Parkin of the Rainforest Action Network

"Resistance to high-risk extreme extraction is building a global, grass-roots, and broad-based network the likes of which the environmental movement has rarely seen. And perhaps this phenomenon shouldn't even be referred to as an environmental movement at all, since it is primarily driven by a desire for a deeper form of democracy, one that provides communities with real control over those resources most critical to collective survival . . ."

Naomi Klein

"Thursday (the publication of the Pope's Encyclical on climate) is launch day for Pope Francis's historic anticapitalist revolution, a multitargeted global revolution against out-of-control free-market capitalism driven by consumerism, against destruction of the planet's environment, climate and natural resources for personal profits and against the greediest science deniers . . . Yes, he's blunt, tough, he is a revolutionary. Pope Francis's call-to-arms will be broadcast loud, clear and worldwide. Not just to 1.2 billion Catholics, but heard by seven billion humans all across the planet. And, yes, many will oppose him, be enraged to hear the message, because it is a call-to-arms, like Paul Revere's ride, inspiring billions to join a people's revolution."

Paul Farrell, MarketWatch

Fifth New Rule: Protect not just people, but animals, plants, and all of nature! Create animal rights and broader rights of nature that will save all precious life on our planet!

Big Questions: How do we create a political vision protecting all species of life? What is that vision?

Slogans: Love nature as thyself! Our environment, ourselves—we live or die together!

What's New Here? Non-universalizing movements have historically been human-centric, focusing exclusively on humans. But one of the greatest changes in today's super-universalizing system is the deadly assault on the environment and all living species. As the system has universalized its violence beyond just humans to animals, plants, and the environmental "commons" that support life, universalizing resistance has to expand its fight for rights from humans to all of life and nature. Progressive universalizers recognize that the fight for social justice and human rights is inseparable from the fight to save the environment, and they redefine and expand the fight for human rights to broader "rights of nature."

THE RIGHTS OF NATURE

The most important and frightening consequence of system universalizing today is the degradation of the environment. Capitalism has long involved exploitation of the environment, with Marx and Engels writing a lot about the exploitation of soil and the environment. Marx wrote that:

> All progress in capitalist agriculture is not only a process in robbing the labourer but robbing the soil . . . the more a country develops its foundation of modern industry, the more rapid is this source of destruction . . . only by sapping the original sources of all wealth, the soil and the labourer.[1]

The system's universalization is now creating new and catastrophic environmental threats—most notably climate change—to the very survival of not only humans, but vast numbers of other animal and plant species. Every day, 150 animal species become extinct. Trump's Presidency, which seeks to undo all American policies to fight climate change and to dismantle international climate treaties such as the 2016 Paris Agreement, shows that universalizing to protect the climate is now essential to preventing extinction.

In the age of climate change, resistance must universalize to protect not just humans, but all life species and the environmental ecology that supports them. Protection of animal rights—and broader protection of plants, water, and the air—is hardly a new resistance agenda, but in the 21st century, it becomes an urgent priority, since the fate of humans as well as the

People's Climate March in New York City, 2014
© Patrimonio Designs Limited/Dreamstime.com

multitudes of other life species is on the line. This moves resistance toward a revolution not just in militarized capitalism's core institutions, but its epistemological foundations and its concept of rights.

We are now moving to link "human rights" to larger rights of nature itself. Bolivia has introduced into its legal system the Law of the Rights of Mother Earth, which creates rights for rivers and trees that can be litigated by a special cadre of environmental justice lawyers. "Earth is the mother of all," said Bolivian Vice President Alvaro García Linera. The Law of Mother Earth, he said, "establishes a new relationship between man and nature, the harmony of which must be preserved as a guarantee of its regeneration."[2] This is part of a broader "Rights to Nature" movement little known in the United States, but spread through Latin America and nations in many other regions.

It is easily accessible to Americans who read Wikipedia:

> Rights of Nature is a tradition of legal and political scholarship advocating legal standing for the natural environment. The rights approach is a break away from traditional environmental regulatory systems, which regard nature as property and legalize and manage degradation of the environment rather than prevent it. Since 2000 animals, plants and other organisms have their rights to dignity recognized by the Constitution in Switzerland (art. 120), but the implications of this disposition are still not very clear. With the enactment of its 2008 Constitution, Ecuador became the first country in the world to codify the

Rights of Nature and to inform a more clarified content to those rights. Articles 10 and 71–74 of the Ecuadorian Constitution recognize the inalienable rights of ecosystems to exist and flourish, [the Constitution] gives people the authority to petition on the behalf of ecosystems, and requires the government to remedy violations of these rights.[3]

Universalized resistance is a rights movement for all living species, rejecting militaristic capitalism's claim—and the horrifying position of Trump and most of the leadership of the Republican Party—that humans exercise rightful dominion over the earth and should yoke it to human, specifically profitable, interests.

PACHAMAMA: THE INSPIRATION OF INDIGENOUS MOVEMENTS AND THE CHALLENGE TO HUMAN-CENTRIC THINKING

Environmental movements around the world are looking to indigenous and other non-Western cultures to help transform our way of understanding humans and the natural world. Indigenous peoples are now taking a leading role in what Naomi Klein calls "Blockadia"—the massive popular movement to block the corporate extraction and pipeline flow of oil and fracked gas—and other universalizing resistance movements focused on protection of what Pope Francis calls "our common home."[4] The distinctive contribution of indigenous movements is highlighted by environmental movements and manifestos such the Canadian "Leap Manifesto" which declares:

> This leap must *begin by respecting the inherent rights and title of the original caretakers of this land. Indigenous communities* have been at the forefront of protecting rivers, coasts, forests and lands from out-of-control industrial activity. We can bolster this role, and reset our relationship, by *fully implementing the United Nations Declaration on the Rights of Indigenous Peoples.*[5]

The indigenous leading role in "Blockadia" arises from the worldview of many indigenous cultures that see nature as supreme and sacred, a sacredness which all humans are morally obligated to respect. This leads to the rejection of the idea that nature exists to serve human needs or is simply an instrument to fulfill profit and human gratification. As journalist John Vidal writes, the indigenous leadership arises partly from "a resurgent indigenous Andean spiritual world view which places the environment and the earth deity known as the Pachamama, at the centre of all life. Humans are considered equal to all other entities."[6]

Pachamama is one expression of what the radical lawyer, philosopher, and activist Boaventura de Sousa Santos, in his work, *The Epistemology of the South*, argues is a broader break from human-centric Western ways of thinking, to a nature-centered epistemology or way of knowing, in which humans

Protecting sacred water at Standing Rock Dakota Access Pipeline Resistance Camp, 2017

Photo credit: Janet MacGillivray Wallace

Rider for resistance at Standing Rock Dakota Access Pipeline Resistance Camp, 2017

Photo credit: Janet MacGillivray Wallace

are viewed as part of nature rather than its master. Santos writes that those in the South "believe that the transformation of the world may also occur in ways not foreseen by the global North," which the North, in fact, can never see fully because of its reification of science, and long history of colonialism and global exploitation, blinding it to other global ways of knowing. We are not just the masters of the universe as conceived in Northern epistemology, but "We are animals and plants, biodiversity and water, earth and Pachamama, ancestors and future generations . . ."[7]

Santos argues that there is an "ecology of knowledges," and that the knowledge of the North, while carrying much value, cannot gain insight into the ways of thinking that can integrate humans with nature and save the earth. Within this philosophy, also very strongly stressed by Pope Francis, a PhD chemist who has lived most of his life in the Global South, humans must live in harmony with other living species and nature itself, rather than dominate it for human interests. Coming from deep in the rainforests of Brazil, indigenous people have formed "The Pachamama Alliance" which pronounces its mission in a universalizing mode:

> Pachamama Alliance, empowered by our partnership with indigenous people, is dedicated to bringing forth an environmentally sustainable, spiritually fulfilling, socially just human presence on this planet. Our unique contribution is to generate and engage people everywhere in transformational conversations and experiences consistent with this purpose. We weave together indigenous and modern worldviews such that human beings are in touch with their dignity and are ennobled by the magnificence, mystery, and opportunity of what is possible for humanity at this time. We are here to inspire and galvanize the human family to generate a critical mass of conscious commitment to a thriving, just and sustainable way of life on Earth. This is a commitment to transforming human systems and structures that separate us, and to transforming our relationships with ourselves, with one another, and with the natural world.[8]

This perspective also finds partial resonance in Western universalizing resistance movements going back to Marx and Engels, with Engels writing prophetically: "Let us not however flatter ourselves over much on account of our human conquest over nature. For each conquest takes its revenge on us."[9] Universalizing resistance, whether deriving from Western critiques or indigenous culture, thus shifts resistance itself to a new epistemological and moral, as well as political, plane, in which humans create a form of solidarity and equality across species and all of nature. Twenty-first-century universalizing resistance means fighting not only human inequalities of caste and class, but inequalities across all life species that threaten any species'—human or non-human—survival and wellbeing.

With the rise of Trump, it is clear that this universalizing will require uniting with Democratic Party progressives and much of the public who, by large majorities, recognize that climate change is scientifically established and threatens human survival. The insanity of the Republican Party stance on climate is one of the world's most dangerous political realities, and climate movement activists see it as Trump threatens to undo President Obama's executive actions, and support building of the Keystone XL Pipeline and the Dakota Access Pipeline opposed by the historic movements led by Native American tribes, who are universalizing the tribes themselves as well as uniting with other climate activists, other movements, and many liberals in the Democratic Party. All this shows that universalizing climate activism is ultimately a political activism that requires taking down the Republican Party politicians who are on the payroll of the big oil, gas, and coal companies, and get hundreds of millions of dollars from climate-denial billionaires such as Charles and David Koch, who own one of the biggest oil and gas corporations.

STANDING ROCK: WHERE WATER LIT THE FIRE OF RESISTANCE

Janet MacGillivray Wallace

Fighting a fossil fuel pipeline, the Standing Rock resistance movement reunited indigenous peoples and catalyzed a historic moment at a time of our collective cultural and climate crises. Reclaiming sovereignty at the place of Sitting Bull's murder, on land protected by the 1851 Fort Laramie Treaty, the resistance became a keystone moment in the universalizing climate and indigenous movements. As Native American activist Leonard Peltier recently wrote from his prison cell, 40 years deep into a life sentence, "I am grateful to have survived to see the rebirth of the united and undefeated Sioux Nation in the resistance to the poisonous pipeline that threatens the life source of the Missouri and Mississippi Rivers."

Without the Standing Rock resistance, the Dakota Access Pipeline (DAP) would already snake 1,168 miles of fracked fossil fuel from North Dakota to oil refineries and export terminals in the blighted Gulf of Mexico region. Like other fossil fuel projects, this fracked Bakken oil pipeline results from entrenched systemic failures. Despite the name, there was no access granted; the Standing Rock Sioux Tribe's objections were repeatedly ignored and treaty rights trampled. Given that this pipeline had been automatically re-routed from primarily white Bismarck to Sioux territory, there was no cloaking racist intent.

Any nagging déjà vu response to the DAP makes sense, given ghostly recall of TransCanada's dormant Keystone XL Pipeline and the violent extraction of tar sands from indigenous territories in Canada's boreal forest. Although the Obama Administration nixed the Presidential permit needed for the international border-crossing section of Keystone, the rest of the pipeline system became fully operational. The Keystone tar sands pipeline drew attention to the reality that fossil fuel corridor projects benefit corporate bottom lines and recommit our planet to a doomsday trajectory.

Looking closer, the Obama Administration had schizophrenically rejected TransCanada's first application, but had expedited federal pipeline permitting. Construction of Keystone's dissected lower half was able to sail past opponents' frantic efforts, including those by an unexpected alliance of pro-oil Republican women bullied by TransCanada's abusive use of eminent domain and indigenous women at Canada's fossil fuel source. Later, Dakota Access Pipeline's builder, Energy Transfer Partners, would take a page out of TransCanada's book and break its project into micro-sections, allowing its pipeline to be fast-tracked under this same faulty federal permitting scheme that eliminates meaningful environmental review and public watchdogging.

But Keystone lessons and the alliances forged were not lost. On April 1, 2016, a handful of indigenous youth and a Keystone veteran set up Standing Rock Resistance Camp on homeland offered by Standing Rock Sioux tribal member LaDonna Brave Bull Allard. Youth catalyzed the resistance and their Runs for Peace drew national and international attention. Protestors, too, arrived from around the globe. One nation's flag became hundreds, symbolizing the unanticipated reunifying of all nations as the camp population swelled to 15,000 under a birthright collective purpose to protect "mni wiconi," the water of life.

While many environmental groups cautiously dip their toes into politically winnable battles, the gathering indigenous nations recognized these splintered fossil fuel pipelines as the Black Snake prophesied to bring destruction to people and planet. Prophecy also foretold that the Black Snake would be met by the rising Seventh Generation who would come to awaken the world at a perilous time. Peltier acknowledged the Standing Rock youth peacefully resisting the pipeline, saying, "It is an honor to have been alive to see this happen with you young people. You are nothing but awesome in my eyes." The Standing Rock resistance, perhaps the largest native gathering in world history, birthed the Seventh Generation and a new multi-nation tribe.

For these youth descendants of the original Treaty of Peace, the landscape of reservation life is bleak. They survive ancestral trauma to bury their peers and live in the shadow of their parents who know that cultural extinction has been the government's goal. Beyond Standing Rock, they are witnessing the refugee crisis sparked by oil wars and they see non-indigenous people facing too many Flint-like water crises, where an entire city's water supply is poisoned. This Seventh Generation understands: first, water is the precious energy for all living things; and second, humanity's ultimate genocide won't be racist. While corporations have moved to privatize water, government is lurking to privatize reservations and ensure a taking of the little that remains. Jasilyn Charger from Cheyenne River, who founded the International Indigenous Youth Council, says, "we are the voice of the future and the future needs to be heard because the future is coming fast."

Jasilyn and other women have been the frontline of the Standing Rock resistance. Indigenous women who are the protectors of water themselves face epidemic rates of sexual violence—yet have no legal right to sue. With dominance over the planet as a resource, the earth loses, communities lose, profiteers win, and the greed cycle spins on. Collectively, silenced women are reclaiming a voice for self and planet from a tone-deaf system. It's not a dismantling of patriarchy so much as the invitation of matriarchy that can cease perpetuating injustices.

Chief Arvol Looking Horse says, "It is time that all of us become Leaders to help protect the sacred upon Mother Earth—she is the source of life and not a resource." Despite determined efforts to demand a departure from carbon bombs from coal, oil, gas, and tar sands drilling, fracking, blasting, and leasing projects, we must recognize that Western legal systems simply regulate levels of permissible pollution on a commodified planet. What is legal is not justice. At the Standing Rock resistance to this fossil fuel pipeline, the water protectors demonstrated the pricelessness of water and de-commodified it as a resource.

Standing Rock cascaded a movement to decolonize. Indigenous people used their bodies to speak for what is essential to everyone. Non-indigenous peoples joined indigenous peoples to take back their outsourced environmentalism from a stymied environmental movement that hasn't yet slowed the momentum of the warming planet. Elders of other movements made a pilgrimage to the camp to honor today's living civil rights demonstration.

Corporate media bedfellows of industrial America refused to cover the story. In their willful silence at an historical moment, self-reporting witnesses intimately live-streamed unfiltered truth to millions. Watching the military spray mace at children, shoot rubber bullets at close range at unarmed women, and aim water cannons at winter vigils, was a real-time horrible enactment of "colonizers versus savages." This witnessing ripped the fabric of patriotic America: one does not want to identify with sub-human greed. Traditional media, the voice-box of corporate America, effectively lost control of the story because Standing Rock liberated citizens from reliance on a platform they would now reject.

Money was worthless in this shared economy, and Standing Rock became an alternative community that provided an aspirational option to outliers of the capitalist system. These united people instead value shared essential human needs. Perpetual elitist exclusion from the mainstream economy backfired and the appetite for apathy waned. Corporate goodies don't entice these citizens to mainlined distraction, isolation, and disempowerment when collective purposeful resistance can be experienced. The pipeline—a condemnation of climate—became the conduit of community.

In November 2016, beyond the pipeline, there was shock and awe felt by many who believed with unshakable knowledge that election day could not usher in a Trump Presidency. How disenfranchised must so many people feel such that we have the current President? Palpable betrayal was finally experienced by many. Standing Rock's undeniable images of reunited peoples and re-oriented priorities brought into focus a collective need to force the dial because the system is broken for virtually everyone. Welcome to the community of those who are outside the system. The dislocated welcome you as citizens united. As the Lakota say, "we are all related" ("Mitakuye Owasin").

On December 4, 2016, to fill the void of the commander-in-chief's silence after the North Dakota Governor announced Standing Rock's impending eviction, 2,500 unpaid US army veterans self-deployed to stand with the water protectors against the National Guard. On bent knee, Wesley Clark, Jr., son of the retired US Army general and former Supreme Allied Commander of NATO's military forces, tearfully sought forgiveness from indigenous Elders for the historical terror the government had waged. This image revealed that the colonized history fed to non-native children is a deceit we need to unlearn; collective shame cloaked as denial must be rejected.

If there is any doubt that Standing Rock fired up a movement, we look only to the reaction to the Obama Administration's December 5, 2016, announcement re-routing the DAP away from the Standing Rock Sioux Tribe's water. Late-arriving corporate media scrambled to stake ground on a story of success, but this historic resistance community knows that a pipeline re-routed elsewhere is no win. Standing Rock citizens reject exhuming fossilized energy and raiding the womb of Mother Earth as colonizing perpetuated.

And if there is any doubt that we need this lifeline movement to counter business as usual, Energy Transfer Partners immediately reiterated their plans to proceed, saying "Nothing this Administration has done today changes that in any way." Democratic Obama may have punted the Keystone XL and Dakota Access pipelines to Republican Trump, who has vowed their resuscitation—but the Standing Rock Resistance Camp is much more than a response to political musical chairs, or even a revolt against fossil fuels. It resuscitated resistance as an experiential movement, and this time the few have lost control of the many.

On January 12, 2017, the sacred fire at "the Horn," the spiritual center of Standing Rock, was allowed to burn down, its ashes and coals shared. Another original fire remains strong and sovereign while young Standing Rock leaders are dispersing in a network to protect all water, for all people, under their collective watch. Already in the south, the Two Rivers Resistance Camp is building resistance to the Trans-Pecos and Comanche Trail pipelines, two other Energy Transfer Partners-owned, Obama-approved pipelines. And the Sacred Water Camp and the Water is Life Camp stand guard before the threatening Sabal Trail Pipeline. The call to resist has sounded from the west to stop the Kinder Morgan Trans Mountain Pipeline, and from the east, the Split Rock Prayer Camp is an impasse to the Pilgrim Pipeline.

The reunited indigenous peoples who drew the line at Standing Rock shared with non-indigenous allies multi-generational stewardship and a form of decolonized justice. Resistance, often issue-based and geographically isolated, is spreading with the community that was convened, seeding the universal desire for the continuation of all life. With the rise of the indigenous voice, we together are re-envisioning the collective care principles for planet and people. Systemic betrayal has baptized a movement of resistance, and the pipeline has been the pathway.

Janet MacGillivray Wallace, JD, LLM, is an environmental attorney and climate change activist. She founded and directs the Seeding Sovereignty Project birthed at Standing Rock to amplify the role of indigenous knowledge for environmental justice; she is a former whistleblower, and has worked in legal and leadership positions at the EPA and national and international NGOs on the interconnected issues of water rights, land and food sovereignty, global trade, climate refugees, environmental health, and the rights of nature. Janet, of Muscogee (Creek) heritage, is a mother who dedicates her life work to the future of all children.

BEYOND CONSUMERISM: NEW LIFESTYLES AND NEW POLITICS

The urgency of new movements protecting animal rights and the broader environment, and the creation of the new philosophy underlying such movements, translates directly into universalizing movements challenging all aspects of the capitalist human lifestyle. The movements focused on food and agriculture are one example, and they have become so animated and central, particularly in the younger generation, that it is clear that this is not just idle talk, but a transformation in our way of living. As the system raises, slaughters, and sells enough meat to feed much of the world, all of the production processes related to animal production and meat-eating have become the source, by some estimates, of as much as 50% of all greenhouse gas emissions.

Shifting away from slaughtering and eating animals is just one example of the rise of a universalizing movement challenging meat consumption, the food industry, and poverty, as the great food critic, Michael Pollan, suggests:

> Many in the animal welfare movement, from PETA to Peter Singer, have come to see that a smaller-scale, more humane animal agriculture is a goal worth fighting for . . . activists for sustainable farming are starting to take seriously the problem of hunger and poverty. They're promoting schemes and policies to make fresh local food more accessible to the poor, through programs that give vouchers redeemable at farmers' markets to participants in the Special Supplemental Nutrition Program for Women, Infants, and Children (WIC) and food stamp recipients.[10]

But the universalizing of the food movement is emerging as part of a broader movement against all forms of current mass consumerism: from the purchase of big cars and big houses to stuffing our closets with throwaway clothes and other "stuff." Resistance to mass consumerism—and shifting our economy and personal lives from privatized production and consumption of "stuff" to creation and enjoyment of public goods—involves a profound universalizing of resistance, into the intimate fabric of our identity, lifestyle, and relationships. Challenging such intimate habits is extremely difficult, but its personal quality makes resistance and politics more viscerally meaningful and more likely to spread. The women's movement universalized when it embraced the idea that "the personal is political," bringing politics into the bedroom. The food movement now brings it into the kitchen.

This is a universalizing revolution so transformative of personal life that it may revitalize politics, catalyzing a new economy and lifestyle that throws out the "stuff." Lest this sound too utopian, millennials—who see the environmental movement as mainstream and part of their generational culture—are dissatisfied with elements of their own mass consumption. In a recent informal study of Boston-area college students, I asked them how they felt about American consumerism. As I have written in a 2013 Truthout opinion piece, almost all said they would prefer to be in a society that was less consumer-oriented, because consumer culture gives them these headaches:

- It creates fierce competitive pressure to have more and newer "stuff."
- It complicates their lives, always worrying about how to maintain, pay for, and use all the things they buy.
- It distracts from a quality life with their family and friends.
- It creates a "dirty" lifestyle that makes them and the planet sick.
- It leads to more inequality, with people seeking more at the expense of others.
- It distracts from political engagement—President Bush told them to go shopping as he was gearing up for war with Iraq after 9/11.
- It imprisons them in a life full of products and empty of meaning.[11]

This has implications for how they want to live their lives. They are already universalizing their resistance into new personal and intimate realms, moving away from suburban lifestyles, away from buying large houses and cars, away from accumulating massive suburban dwellings and all their big closets overflowing with "stuff," to living in the city, using public transportation or bicycles, using smaller closets for a shrinking supply of "stuff," and devoting more of their time in the "sharing" economy to enjoyment of public goods: among them the arts, leisure, play, and social interaction itself. Students are starting to grow food in gardens at their universities. Many adult Americans are living closer to work, so they can walk or bike to the job. Some are looking for companies offering the choice of shorter work hours, which liberates them from the work-and-spend treadmill. Some are joining the "share economy," where they share things—e.g., Zipcars and bikes—with others. Many are "downshifting" to a simpler life. But constraining consumerism requires far larger changes in US capitalism: severely limiting corporate power and rewriting corporate charters and international trade agreements to emphasize worker rights and environmental health. Quality must replace quantity as the measure of economic and cultural success. Government tax and regulatory policy must end extreme inequality and reduce production and consumption of dirty energy, unhealthy food, and luxury goods. Large investment in public transit, community-owned enterprises, national parks, and other public goods must substantially reduce private consumption. Such system-wide changes are politically difficult—and they may not limit consumerism fast enough to avert climate catastrophe or reverse dangerous inequality. But in the most optimistic scenario, if environmental justice movements universalize and align with anti-capitalist and labor movements, while continuing to build their mass base in the Democratic Party and the general public, they could put society on a new path toward a more sustainable, cooperative way of life.

FROM THE "UNIVERSAL" CONSUMER TO THE "UNIVERSAL" CONSUMER ACTIVIST

Juliet B. Schor

There are few things more universal than being a consumer. The orientation toward acquiring and spending became a mass phenomenon in the West during the early 20th century and is now spreading throughout the Global South. Automobiles, consumer electronics, processed food, commercialized culture—consumption is expanding rapidly. If there is any common culture around the world, it is surely consumer culture.

While consumer culture brings enormous benefits—refrigerators and washing machines reduce women's domestic burdens and cell phones connect people—it also comes with punishing downsides. Many cities in the Global South are practically unlivable because of air pollution and massive traffic jams. Junk food is fueling an obesity crisis among middle-class youth. Most ominously, the transformation of lifestyles is toward carbon-intensive goods and services. Autos are at the top of the list. But electronics, air conditioning, meat consumption, household appliances, and air travel are also large contributors to greenhouse gases. The modern consumer lifestyle is incompatible with climate security. While corporations are the world's main polluters, affluent and middle-class households are directly responsible for a good portion of emissions. If the world is to de-carbonize, dramatic changes in lifestyle practices will have to be a part of that transition.

This book has rightly focused on structural analyses. What does that imply for people's role as "consumers?" To answer the question, let's start with a bit of history to see how consumption has been understood in relation to political resistance. Only then can we envision a reformulation that unleashes the power of consumers *qua* consumers.

For the last 50 years, the Left has assumed that consumerism is in conflict with people's role as citizens and activists. Consumption has been seen as the ultimate individual, neoliberal activity. Even more, it's the most powerful force impeding resistance: pursuit of the consumer lifestyle distracts, pacifies, lulls, and seduces. The thousands waiting for days outside the Apple Store for the latest iPhone are victims of fashion, duped by marketers into false desires and blindness to social realities. By extension, this view holds that engaging in genuine political resistance means rejecting consumption.

It's not hard to see why this view took hold. In the West during the second half of the 20th century, consumer lifestyles *were* constructed as highly individualist. Suburban developments emphasized nuclear families, privacy, and an invidious consumer competition across households. Solidarity was eroded. But while consumers were created as individualist and apolitical, that doesn't mean these characteristics are intrinsic to consumption. They were features of the larger neoliberal order that was built during this era. Indeed, most social activities and institutions became less political, more individualistic, and more consensual. That was the nature of the times.

Once we recognize that consumption cultures, like everything else, are historically and socially constructed, we can see that they can take many forms. Consumption can be individualistic or solidaristic. It can pull people apart or bring them together. In a neoliberal time, consumption becomes neoliberal—like almost everything else.

With this perspective, a long history of consumer resistance comes into focus. Indeed, many of the historic mobilizations of resistance around the world have been "consumer" uprisings—food protests and riots. In early modern Europe, peasants frequently protested about the price of bread, as well as its quality. One of the earliest events in the French Revolution was the Women's March on Versailles, a mobilization over the price and availability of bread. The American Revolution was sparked by a consumption tax. In early 20th-century America, trade unions engaged in consumer boycotts, mobilizing the wives and mothers of their members. Gandhi's Indian independence movement was also oriented around consumer issues—salt taxes and opposition to imported cloth. More recently, the escalation of food prices at the beginning of the 21st century led to a wave of food riots around the world.

This is the context in which we should see the appearance of the 21st-century consumer movements. They are a part of the growing resistance to neoliberalism and corporate power. Contrary to those who still hold the old Left view that all consumer action is apolitical, mobilizations against sweatshops, movements for Fair Trade, and the shift toward "green" purchasing are yet another front in the fight for justice. And this front is attempting to create a socially conscious, climate-friendly consumer regime.

A movement called ethical consumption can now be found around the world. While this activity has been around for quite some time, it began to gain steam in the 1990s. As Nike, Disney, and other giant consumer companies expanded and outsourced to very poor countries, union and student activists took them on for the exploitative conditions in their suppliers' factories, using boycotts and other tactics against them. The Fair Trade movement emerged at this time, with Northern coffee consumers collaborating with producers' cooperatives in the Global South to guarantee a "Fair Trade" price. Over time, the Fair Trade movement has expanded to many other products—chocolate, bananas and other fruits, sugar, flowers, wine, and even apparel. Other consumer movements have targeted particular companies for bad environmental practices—palm oil producers for rainforest destruction; packaging, use of plastics, and toxics. Many of these consumer groups also encourage "buycotting"; that is, intentionally purchasing the products of more conscious companies. While people take these actions at an "individual" level, that perspective obscures the fact that much of this activity is organized by NGOs, be they labor, environmental, religious, or animal rights groups.

The conscious consumption movement has also expanded from concern about how products are produced to awareness that the overall volume of consumption is too high, especially for middle-class and affluent consumers. As the climate warms, the conscious consumption movement has argued for shifting and reducing consumption.

Doing without is better than buying a nifty "green" product.

This growth in consumer mobilization can be attributed to a number of factors. As the state has been increasingly captured by corporate and elite interests, it has been more difficult to get legislative or regulatory action to control corporate behavior. The market was seen as more hospitable territory. Furthermore, with large consumer companies that rely heavily on brand value, such as Nike or Disney, attacking the integrity of the brand has been seen as a potent strategy for gaining leverage over management.

Finally, because the consumer role has become such an important source of personal identity, activists reasoned that this would be a successful entry-point for getting people involved. In my research, I've found that political and consumer action are frequently linked. In contrast to the view that says consumption is a pacifying force, a significant number of the people I've surveyed begin with a boycott or buycott, and then move on to conventional political activism like pressuring legislators and going to demonstrations.

What does the emergence of these consumer movements mean in terms of other resistance movements and especially the fight for climate? I'll end with three answers. First, while there's a tendency to think of consumer actions as individual, consumer choices are already implicated in larger social and political meanings and struggles.

Second, actions to align consumption with values can be a source of empowerment and energy. People often find the contradiction between how they spend and what they believe to be frustrating and draining. Gaining more consistency in daily life helps people to feel more authentic and powerful. It also gives them more credibility as they speak out and become movement leaders.

Finally, while it is indisputable that personal actions like changing light bulbs or eating less meat will not solve or even significantly address climate change, structural transformations of lifestyles are absolutely necessary. Deep and rapid de-carbonization will entail major changes in consumerist patterns. Private automobility, meat-centric diets, frequent air travel, air conditioning, food waste, and lots of new products are not compatible with climate goals. We must shift away from these high-carbon activities toward a different way of life. This will require not just individual changes, but social transformation. We'll need fiscal support for public transportation, true-cost pricing of carbon-intensive goods, strict building codes, and relocalization of production. And we'll need concerted efforts to change the culture of consumption.

We are just beginning this journey. While the resistance movements discussed throughout this book are at the core, consumer activism and everyday personal choices also have a role to play. The innovative low-carbon consumption activities that people are modeling demonstrate what is possible, and they are sparking some of today's most popular lifestyle trends. Anti-consumerist movements that began in the West are being taken up in the Global South, where organic food, bicycling, small-scale technology, indigenous artisanal products, and new sharing initiatives are fast gaining in popularity. We can only hope that anti-consumerist lifestyles take hold as rapidly as consumerist lifestyles did. For then we'll see true and powerful consumer resistance, which universalizes resistance into the lifestyle choices of all people.

Juliet B. Schor is Professor of Sociology at Boston College, a board member of the Better Future Project and a co-founder of the Center for a New American Dream. She is the author of True Wealth (2011, Penguin Books).

10

Don't Just Say No:
Say Yes to Alternatives

"To create a world in which life can flourish and prosper we must replace the values and institutions of capitalism with values and institutions that honor life, serve life's needs and restore money to its proper role as servant."

David Korten

"If you look deeply, there are lots of elements that begin to form a mosaic, I think, potentially suggesting the direction of an America beyond capitalism . . . a decentralized democratic model that begins to give content to a different vision and practical experience to build towards it."

Gar Alperovitz

"[S]ocial inequalities are acceptable only if they are in the interests of all and in particular of the most disadvantaged social groups."

Thomas Piketty

"With the development of industrial capitalism, a new and unanticipated system of injustice, it is libertarian socialism that has preserved and extended the radical humanist message of the Enlightenment and the classical liberal ideals that were perverted into an ideology to preserve the social order."

Noam Chomsky

Sixth New Rule: Spell out alternatives to the system! Build a new economy and politics—in the United States and around the world—based on democracy, non-violence, and social justice!

Big Questions: How do universalizing movements converge to create a new systemic vision? What is that alternative vision? And how does it succeed in a society ideologically conditioned to hate "big government"—or any government—as a form of tyranny?

Slogans: Think beyond capitalism: create economic democracy! Build a green sustainable world free of racism, sexism, classism, and consumerism!

What's New Here: Non-universalizing movements do not seek total system change; they are ultimately reformers because they are fighting for changes in limited parts of a super-universalizing system. Universalizing movements pursue more revolutionary change, challenging TINA ("There Is No Alternative") and putting forth serious systemic alternatives to our militarized corporate capitalism. In earlier phases of capitalism, it was easier for activists to envisage systemic alternatives; ironically, as the system universalizes and becomes more pervasive, violent, and destructive, TINA has gained traction in many of today's movements. Universalizers put forward whole-system alternatives, recognizing that people will never change—even if they hate the current system—unless they see that there are better alternatives.

As highlighted at the very beginning of this book, universalizing resistance is not just resisting the policies of the existing order and elites. It is defined as well by a total commitment to a vision of a new society, and the taking of all steps necessary to build an economy and society based on social justice and democracy.

These alternatives must be both national and global. We need a new American economic model, but it will come about only in concert with a global movement for a new progressive internationalist global system. In this chapter, we focus mainly on alternatives in the United States, but turn briefly at the end to looking at what an alternative to neoliberal global capitalism looks like.

YOU CAN'T FIGHT THE SYSTEM WITHOUT A POSITIVE ALTERNATIVE

In the summer of 2015, Democratic Presidential candidate Senator Bernie Sanders, an avowed socialist, drew bigger crowds and attracted more individual small donors than any other candidate, including Donald Trump. Sanders also began closing the gap in a way few imagined possible on the heir-apparent Democratic favorite, Hillary Clinton. A popular, self-identified socialist candidate?

This is surprising news in the United States, but, as noted earlier (see Chapter 6), it reflects repeated polling over 5 years, at least, before Sanders' candidacy for President, indicating that almost half of US citizens, particularly the millennial generation, have a positive reaction to the word "socialism." Fifty percent also have a negative reaction to the word "capitalism." This suggests there may be unexpectedly fertile ground in the United States for universalizing resistance movements seeking to create a vision of an alternative system to US capitalism. While the dominant American ideology is "TINA" (There Is No Alternative), a view rooted heavily in the anti-government ideology of the Right that has been triumphant since the Reagan Revolution, visions of alternative models are beginning to sprout in recent movements, from Occupy, Fight for $15 (minimum wage) and other movements organizing against extreme inequality, to the climate movement, to the peace movement.

A coherent alternative has not taken root and unified all of these movements. In their Ear to the Ground study of activists, NTanya Lee and Steve Williams report that many activists themselves lament the failure of progressive and Left movements to create attractive alternatives:

> *33% said we lack a clear, inspiring vision of the world we are fighting for. We have a strong critique of the problems and long lists of policy ideas, but more than one-third of participants said we need clarity about our vision of the world we want to live in. Many decades of playing defense against the Right have hampered our ability to take the offensive in the battle of ideas. Our many sectors and movements each have compelling and even visionary ideas, but they have not cohered into a systemic vision that can unite our forces and build a "movement of movements."*[1]

THE NEW ECONOMY

Despite this failure to coalesce around a unifying alternative, universalizing movements are creating the seeds of many different and partly converging alternatives. These include:

1. a "cooperativist economy" based on worker, union, and community ownership and control (major coops are rising in cities such as Cleveland, Chicago, and Boston);
2. a "localist economy" based on community business rather than global corporations. These may be based on local currencies and bartering, a "sharing economy" where private ownership of goods and services is shared in a peer-to-peer system (think of Uber and Airbnb evolving toward barter or free usage);
3. a "solidarity economy" in which organizations and institutions build coalitions, especially among the poor and oppressed classes;
4. a "green economy" rooted in protection of the commons, clean energy, and living in harmony with nature;
5. "anarcho-syndicalism" based on workers' ownership and control of workplaces, and self-regulating communities;
6. "democratic socialism"—the term used by Bernie Sanders to discuss the democratizing of not just politics, but the economy and all other social sectors.

All these alternatives reject US corporate capitalism, and share a commitment to economic democracy, a core principle of the new society which universalizing movements champion. Putting democracy at the heart of the American system sounds radical, but also surprisingly American, since the United States has always enshrined democracy as its central value.

While some form of public ownership exists in most of these alternatives, they are not rooted in the "central command" authoritarian socialisms that have existed in earlier Communist or socialist movements. They reflect a decentralized vision of economic democracy, particularly resonant in the United States with a population ideologically turned against "big government." A small but influential number of political economists, such as Gar Alperovitz and Juliet B. Schor, are writing strikingly about "the new economy."[2] The new economy unifies many of these alternative visions—and the huge array of global movements supporting them—around the ideas of a democratic and sustainable political economy. It subverts the plutocratic billionaire Wall Street ruling class, replacing it with a cooperative, worker-owned, environmentally friendly, and deeply democratic system. It incorporates significant public ownership (but not an authoritarian "command" big government vision)—in which wealth is institutionally spread across the entire population, seeking to democratize wealth. And it creates the foundation of the new system which is at the heart of the universalizing resistance agenda.

IS THE ALTERNATIVE ECONOMY ALREADY UNDERWAY?

Socialist Bernie Sanders' enormous popularity among the young in the 2016 Presidential race suggests that popular opinion is becoming more open to alternatives to capitalism. Alperovitz argues that the alternative is already beginning to be built in the United States:

> [I]f there is to be a democratic alternative, what you look for is: Are there ways that democratic ownership can happen? Indeed, if you look closely, there are some 13 million people involved in one form or another of worker-owned companies, a form that changes who owns; there are 130 million people involved in credit unions and co-ops, another democratized form of ownership; there are 4,000 or 5,000 neighborhood corporations, devoted to neighborhood development; there are 2,000 utilities that are owned by cities.[3]

Beyond these "micro" workplace and community democratic transformations are alternatives of national and global system change involving public ownership—of banks, energy companies, and other huge global companies. Alperovitz recognizes their importance:

> More than 450 communities have also built partial or full public Internet systems, some after significant political battles. Roughly one-fifth of

all hospitals are also currently publicly owned. Many cities own hotels, including Dallas—where the project was championed by the former Republican mayor Tom Leppert. Some 30 states directly invest public funds in promising start-up companies.[4]

So the alternative *practice* may already be stronger or more widespread than the alternative *visions*. Much of the support for such economic democracy agendas comes from Left universalizing movements, including progressive labor unions, community organizers against poverty and inequality, anti-racist groups such as Black Lives Matter, democracy movements, and politically progressive organizations such as Democratic Socialists of America, MoveOn.org, and Our Revolution—activists who are organizing to expand the campaign of Bernie Sanders into a long-term movement for democratic socialism.

Support for redistribution of wealth and public ownership of capitalism arises not only among Left thinkers and activists (and some conservatives, as Alperovitz notes), but also among extremely influential liberal Keynesian economists, such as Thomas Piketty, who has made democratic distribution and control of wealth and capital the centerpiece of his policy agenda. While Piketty has garnered enormous attention (supported by Nobel Prize-winning economists Paul Krugman and Joseph Stiglitz), not enough attention has been paid to the fact that Piketty is reviving, in a different language, the socialist call for popular control over a democratized economy. Rather than advocating traditional socialism, he calls for "expanding the democratic control of capital" in a "social state."[5]

The social state requires a large role for government in the economy, and will, to some degree, reinvent private property and corporations. "More than ever," Piketty says, "new forms of organization and ownership remain to be invented."[6] When I asked Piketty whether he sees virtues to public ownership, the core of classic socialism, he said, "Yes, public ownership has proved to be the adequate form of organization in many sectors."[7] He sees virtue in many forms of ownership that are intermediate between public and private, and that involve "new forms of participatory governance, particularly in culture and the media."[8] He explained that he saw virtues to worker ownership as a way of further democratizing control of capital. Piketty's focus on promoting the spread of democratic ownership is a new variant of an alternative system that might move beyond European social democracy, an alternative moving closer to the Occupy Wall Street movement and the 1890s populist movement that called openly for public ownership of banks and energy companies.

Various forms of economic democracy and public ownership—especially of big banks, energy companies, and pharmaceuticals—are very important in almost all alternative system views—whether in the "solidarity economy," the "cooperativist economy," or other 21st-century universalizing alternatives. Many US thinkers are elaborating forms of participatory democracy, such as writer and activist Michael Albert, who has written provocative books on participatory economies that would restructure economic transactions through democratic councils rather than market exchanges. Marxist David Harvey elaborates 21st-century forms of socialism based on public ownership and control. Marxist sociologist Erik Olin Wright has studied "utopian" practices such as participatory budgeting in Porto Alegre, Brazil, and other global cities, that illustrate participatory economic democracy at work. Marxist John Bellamy Foster elaborates 21st-century forms of socialism based on public ownership and democratic control of national and global economies.

The emerging alternative—which embodies "new democracy" language— and models of what democratic socialists have long wanted to achieve are

Classic universalizing resistance slogan for democracy
© wow.subtropica/Shutterstock

gaining ground around the world, in parts of Latin America and Europe, including the Vatican. Universalizing movements urgently require, and are building, these alternative visions. While the current system creates sociopathic existential crises, people in power will successfully repress change until the populace rises in support of an alternative. All universalizing movements must create credible alternative visions of a better society; otherwise the existing system will persist, or could evolve to fascist or other authoritarian and racist models embraced by right-wing universalizing movements.

DEMOCRATIC OWNERSHIP AND THE PLURALIST COMMONWEALTH: THE CREATION OF AN IDEA WHOSE TIME HAS COME

Gar Alperovitz

On September 19, 1977—a day remembered locally as "Black Monday"—the corporate owners of the Campbell Works in Youngstown, Ohio, abruptly shuttered the giant steel mill's doors. Instantly, 5,000 workers lost their jobs, their livelihoods, and their futures. The mill's closing was national news, one of the first major blows in the era of de-industrialization, offshoring, and "free trade" that has since made mass layoffs commonplace.

What was not commonplace was the response of the steelworkers and the local community. "You feel the whole area is doomed somehow," Donna Slaven, the wife of a laid-off worker, told reporters at the time. "If this can happen to us, there is not a secure union job in the country." Rather than leave the fate of their community in the hands of corporate executives in New York, New Orleans, and Washington DC, the workers began to organize and resist. And they joined with a new coalition of priests, ministers, and rabbis—headed by a Catholic and an Episcopal bishop—to build support for a new way forward. I was called in to head up an economic team to help.

Working together, the steelworkers, the ecumenical coalition, and our team put forward a bold proposal to re-open the mill under worker–community ownership. With support from a creative Carter Administration official, a study was financed that demonstrated the feasibility of a plan to put the old mill back into operation with the latest modern technology. A worker–community-owned facility could operate efficiently, re-employ 4,000 people, and generate a profit.

Peace activist, civil rights advocate, and labor lawyer Staughton Lynd worked with me and the coalition to develop the transition effort. Lynd subsequently wrote:

> What was new in the Youngstown venture was the notion that workers and community residents could own and operate a *steel mill* . . . Employee–community ownership of the Campbell Works would have challenged the capitalist system on the terrain of the large-scale enterprises in basic industries . . . This was the ownership model the workers themselves chose.

The coalition knew that their only chance against big steel was to build a popular political base around the state of Ohio and even around the nation. They understood it was important to universalize the idea, to make it clear that the problem of Youngstown was a problem many communities would face. One of their themes was: "Save Youngstown, Save the Nation."

They also had to overcome the opposition of the national leadership of the United Steelworkers union which, in 1977, had no interest in the idea of workers owning a mill (or young activists getting ideas about organizing power!). A major victory of Youngstown's local, state, and national campaign was the 1978 decision by the Carter Administration to support the plan with millions of dollars in federal loan guarantees.

Perhaps not surprisingly—given how innovative the plan was in the 1970s—the coalition did not win the battle of Youngstown. After the mid-term elections of 1978, the Carter Administration withdrew its loan guarantees amidst pressure from industry lobbyists and antagonistic government officials. Without the loan guarantees, the effort collapsed.

The story, however, does not end there. The steelworkers and the ecumenical coalition knew they were up against some of the most powerful players in the country. They were fully aware they might well lose the battle. They also knew, however, that they were on to a very important idea, one whose time would come.

A centerpiece of the strategy was an all-out effort to help educate the public, the press, and the politicians in the state and around the country. And, in fact, the inspiring example of the Youngstown workers and ecumenical coalition has had ongoing and profound impact. There are now many worker-owned businesses in the state of Ohio, and the simple idea that workers can and should own their workplace is commonplace not only among workers, but also among businesspeople, many of whom (aided by certain tax benefits) now sell their successful businesses to former employees when they retire. Also in Ohio, the late John Logue, a Kent State professor inspired by the Youngstown effort, established the Ohio Employee Ownership Center at Kent State University, a support system for worker ownership in the state that is one of the best in the nation.

It is not just Ohio. The concept of worker ownership has become commonplace across the country and the world. A 2004 film, The Take, by Naomi Klein and Avi Lewis, documented the struggle of Argentinian workers to turn their factory into a worker cooperative, and it inspired many people to develop worker cooperatives. Also in 2004, the US Federation of Worker Cooperatives (USFWC) was established. Starting with just $7,000 in the bank, the USFWC has grown to represent and support more than 160 democratic workplaces and organizations, representing more than 4,000 workers, and has been instrumental in pushing state and local governments to support worker cooperatives as part of their economic development strategies.

In New York City, a coalition of grassroots community organizers and cooperative advocates—including the New York City Network of Worker Cooperatives, an affiliate of the USFWC, and The Working World (an organization founded by a young New Yorker who was motivated by The Take)—recently secured $1.2 million from the city's budget to support worker-owned businesses in low-income communities. One of the driving forces behind the New York City legislation is Cooperative Home Care Associates, the largest worker cooperative in the United States with more than 2,000 workers, most of whom are women of color, who enjoy above-average pay and benefits.

In Madison, Wisconsin, a measure has passed the city council earmarking $5 million over 5 years to support cooperative development. In Jackson, Mississippi, before his tragic death, Mayor Chokwe Lumumba was preparing an ambitious strategy to combat economic inequality in the heart of the Black Belt by building a "solidarity economy"—one that connected community and cooperative enterprises to municipal procurement and remains underway.

In 2008, the Evergreen Cooperative Initiative was launched in Cleveland, Ohio—where the population has fallen from more than 900,000 in 1950 to below 400,000 today. Here, a number of cooperatives are linked together with a community-building non-profit corporation and a revolving fund designed to create more such connected, community-building businesses. The Evergreen Cooperative Laundry operates out of a LEED [Leadership in Energy and Environmental Design] Gold-certified building, uses around one-fifth the amount of water that conventional laundries use, and has an advanced water heating system that saves energy. Evergreen Energy Solutions recently installed one of the larger urban solar fields in the country. And Green City Growers Cooperative—a 3.25-acre hydroponic greenhouse—can produce roughly 3 million heads of lettuce and 300,000 pounds of herbs per year.

An important new strategy in Cleveland uses anchor institutions—hospitals and universities in the area that purchase more than $3 billion a year in goods and services—to provide a long-term market for the worker-owned cooperatives. The United Steelworkers, whose national leadership once opposed the Youngstown effort, has also evolved. The union has adopted a major strategy to help build "union co-op" worker-owned companies around the nation. Efforts are underway, in particular, in Pittsburgh and Cincinnati.

This is not, however, simply a story about worker coops. It is much more about how change can happen—and about how an idea whose time has come actually "comes." The spirit of Youngstown lives on. At this time of writing, a major new initiative—"50 by 50"—aims to organize 50 million workers in worker-owned enterprises in the United States by 2050. And in many communities, other new initiatives have been building momentum. Philadelphia and Santa Fe, for instance, are actively considering new public banks to develop much more broadly democratized local economies. Activists in Boulder, Colorado, have won two major referenda to take over the local electric utility and convert it to less climate-destroying approaches.

Beyond this, the Bernie Sanders revolution gave millions of people a sense that things might move faster than the steadily developing worker coop revolution. So, too, Black Lives Matter activists have turned their attention to new community-building economic strategies. At another level, the Next System Project, backed by some of the nation's leading scholars and activists, along with 10,000 engaged citizens, is considering developmental trajectories that begin, like Youngstown, in the here and now, but look forward even to such major changes as turning the big Wall Street banks into public utilities, and nationalizing oil companies and other firms in the interests of dealing with climate change, on the one hand, and corporate power, on the other.

Slowly, like an image emerging in a photographer's darkroom, the basis of a different economy is beginning to appear, first in outline form, then perhaps with increasing pace over time, with more and more elements at all levels—community, region, nation. It might be called a "Pluralist Commonwealth" in its bringing together of different forms of democratic ownership, from neighborhood to community to region and beyond. At its core is a vision of community, one made real by the forms of economic life it nourishes.

The late Margaret Thatcher, conservative Prime Minister of the UK, famously declared that "There Is No Alternative" to capitalism, and the acronym "TINA" became a way to stifle new thought and action. What Youngstown, the myriad new experiments, the climate change and Black Lives Matter movements, and the Sanders revolution all suggest is precisely the opposite: there is an alternative—or rather, there is a powerful and fast-developing process underway that offers promise, though surely not inevitability, of a new way forward. And the Youngstown idea of linking both workers and community in a much broader universalizing model is fast developing, not only in Cleveland, but in cities like Rochester, New York State, and Richmond, Virginia.

Gar Alperovitz, author of America Beyond Capitalism *(2004, John Wiley & Sons)*, What Then Must We Do? *(2013, Chelsea Green Publishing)*, and *(with Jeff Faux)* Rebuilding America *(1984, Pantheon)* is co-chair of the Next System Project and co-founder of The Democracy Collaborative.

THIS IS HARD STUFF: OVERCOMING DANGERS, HURDLES, AND CLINGING TO WHAT WE KNOW

Creating alternative visions is essential to universalizing movements; the failure to do so helps to explain why universalizing movements in the past have not overthrown the system. Like abused children who cling to their parents when social workers try to remove them to safety, people hold on to the system they know, however harmful or destructive, unless they see an alternative which they believe is better and achievable.

Earlier universalizing movements did propose limited systemic alternatives (involving, for example, the nationalization of Wall Street banks by 1890 populists), but the visions of change were not framed in a way that captured the public imagination. Rather than a revolution, the 1930s New Deal sought to save capitalism from itself, while resistance movements that tried to challenge the system, such as the American Communist Party, self-destructed around slavish loyalty to the corrupt Stalinist model. The 1960s movements proposed more attractive ideals such as participatory democracy, but could not articulate the ideas in a clear vision of how such a society would be organized.

Alternative visions cannot and should not be detailed formalistic blueprints. They always emerge through experience and experimentation. Yet universalizers must formulate the basic principles of an alternative democratic society. They need to frame the vision in an electric, accessible way—using ideas, pictures, historical examples, utopias, spiritual messages, and stories based on human truths and complexities. Paulo Freire put this beautifully:

One of the basic questions that we need to look at is how to convert merely rebellious attitudes into revolutionary ones in the process of the radical transformation of society. Merely rebellious attitudes or actions are insufficient, though they are an indispensable response to legitimate anger. It is necessary to go beyond rebellious attitudes to a more radically critical and revolutionary position, which is in fact a position not simply of denouncing injustice but of announcing a new utopia. Transformation of the world implies a dialectic between the two actions: denouncing the process of dehumanization and announcing the dream of a new society. On the basis of this knowledge, namely, "to change things is difficult but possible," we can plan our political-pedagogical strategy.[9]

Too many movements create compelling critiques of the system, but fall on the sword of their own failure to create equally compelling alternatives. In many ways, this is the key task of universalizing movements: to create life-affirming systemic alternatives that they "live" in the structure of their own resistance. Universalizers need to walk their talk.

Alternatives proposed by universalizers must be more than just economic. The current system intertwines economy, politics, and culture—and it expresses itself through horrific violence and catastrophic environmental destruction as well as caste and class domination and the breakdown of loving communities. A post-capitalist society must be more than an economic alternative system eliminating the capitalist class structure. It must be a democratic social alternative that eliminates the "Kochamamie" political system, ends caste injustice in race and gender relations, stops military violence and environmental destruction, and undermines the system's death culture and threat to all life on the planet. It ultimately moves toward progressive internationalism, ensuring global survival and universal human rights, as discussed below.

The UR alternative is post-capitalist, but also post-caste, peaceful, and sustainable. It must be as holistic as the universalizing system itself and address all the sociopathy generated by the existing system. That is why all intersectional movements—economic, environmental, racial justice, anti-war, and feminist, among others—must contribute to and work together in creating the alternative. Historically, progressives have built alternatives that largely address their own core issue. But without a broader systemic approach, they can neither solve their own issue nor change the system.

Some global organizations, such as the World Social Forum (WSF), convene thousands of movements in scores of nations to share visions and strategies and build links across borders. In 2015, the WSF met in Tunis, assembling 50,000 activists from 120 countries. Rejecting TINA and uniting under the banner "Another World Is Possible," WSF has brought movements together each year for two decades to construct a holistic alternative. The meetings are dynamic and colorful, spawning global dialog among universalizing resisters. So far, they have created partially developed visions that have not captured the imagination of all the movements or the global public. Nonetheless, much has been accomplished in envisaging a consensual post-capitalist world, since the principles of equality, sustainability, community, cooperation, social welfare, public goods, non-violence, and democracy are at the root of virtually all their proposed alternatives. The values of the post-capitalist system are well-established and consensual in the movements; it is now a matter of fleshing out the *institutional arrangements* by which these values are secured. The movements should not run from their differences on issues, but work cooperatively on theory and practice to build greater consensus.

PROGRESSIVE INTERNATIONALISM

This chapter has focused on movements building an alternative system in the United States. But any credible US alternative has to be linked to movements building alternative economic models in other nations and for the global system as a whole. While this may seem daunting, prospects for American alternatives are strongly increased through solidarity with movements around the world seeking to create a new global order.

The reigning system, entrenched in the Reagan and Thatcher years, has been global neoliberal or corporate capitalism. It is structured as a capitalist "world system" based on corporate "free trade" agreements, globalized corporate power, and the neoliberal Bretton Woods agencies of the WTO, the IMF, and the World Bank.

The neoliberal global capitalist regime has had disastrous results, creating massive inequalities and poverty within and across both rich and poor countries. As a result, we are approaching a crisis in the neoliberal global regime, reflected in Latin American and Asian countries moving toward their own trading blocs and economic regimes, as well as intense opposition to corporate neoliberal globalization in the United States and Europe.

Right populist groups, including Trumpists, Brexiters, and other conservative populists in the United States and Europe, are mobilizing to create a new global order based on hyper-nationalism. As noted earlier, they are universalizing movements building alternative political economics hostile to corporate globalization, corporate trade agreements, and the global Bretton Woods neoliberal corporate global regime. Instead, they emphasize "America First," and other nationalist alternatives. They speak to a populist white working-class base that sees corporate globalization as stealing their jobs and enriching global corporate and financial elites. They replace that system with a version of racial nationalism that favors military and market job incentives at home, and blocking trade, outsourcing, immigration, and the global culture that they view as undermining the nation itself.

Left or progressive universalizing movements also oppose corporate and neoliberal globalization, but they champion very different alternatives from the hyper-nationalism of Trumpism and the Alt-Right. Instead, they have long advocated for a Democratic "Progressive Internationalism" based on economic democracy and worker solidarity across national boundaries. Some call it "Globalization from Below." National identity becomes subordinate to global identity, as in the original vision of the European Union, and the global economic system moves beyond corporate capitalism toward a global "solidarity," a cooperativist or democratic socialist system. Global capitalist power and hierarchy are replaced by global economic democracy.

THE ULTIMATE UNIVERSALIZING ALTERNATIVE: A WORLD BASED ON UNIVERSAL HUMAN RIGHTS

Visions of Progressive Internationalism have a long history in the United States, developing in modern form after the Second World War, as the United States helped to shape a world no longer ruled by European empires. American Left movements, including not only socialists and civil rights and feminist movements, but also progressive New Dealers such as Eleanor Roosevelt and Henry Wallace, fought for a world order based on human rights rather than profits. The vision of Progressive Internationalism was codified in the 1948 Universal Declaration of Human Rights and in the building of the United Nations itself as a world government supporting social needs and social democracy over international profits.

The Universal Declaration of Human Rights is a central element not only of Progressive Internationalism, but a foundation of the alternative order championed by universalizing movements. *To universalize resistance is to fight for the universal rights of all people everywhere on earth.* These are spelled out in clear and simple language in the 1948 Declaration, making it clear how universalizing resistance is ultimately a fight for the universal rights we all share by our shared humanity. These include the rights of everyone to food, a decent home, a living wage, health care, social security, and an equal economic and political voice in a democratic society.

The connection between universalizing resistance and building a world of universal human rights is clear: we universalize resistance because we are universally the same in our basic needs and rights as humans. Ultimately, universalizing resistance makes sense because the fundamental nature and needs we share as humans outweigh our differences and require that we come together to guarantee each other's shared humanity.

The 1948 Declaration has been officially embraced by most nations of the world. Europe has gone furthest in embracing these rights, reflecting the strength of 20th-century universalizing labor movements in most European nations. The Scandinavian nations, such as Sweden and Denmark, are most

Universalizing protest supporting universal health care
© Rrodrickbeiler/Dreamstime.com

fully organized around universal human rights, including universal social welfare, universal health care, universal child care, and other shared rights, reflecting the strength of their universalizing labor and social welfare movements. Despite the immigration crisis in Europe and the EU, most European nations embrace universal human rights as the constitutional bedrock of their own societies and of any civilized nation.

Even in the United States, which has been hesitant to embrace "positive rights" to food, shelter, medical care, and job security, the American founders, such as Thomas Jefferson and James Madison, Jr., wrote of inalienable human rights as central to American identity. Jefferson was a man of many contradictions, but he would not support the Constitution without the Bill of Rights that affirmed many crucial universal human rights such as free speech, privacy, freedom of religion, and other rights. These were mostly "negative" rights to be left alone, rather than "positive rights," but it highlighted the universality of rights. This suggests that universal human rights—the ultimate aspiration of universalizing movements—are not just utopian dreams, but aspirations shared by most nations—even in the United States—and are already rhetorically embraced in most national constitutions. Moreover, the majority of Americans already support positive universal rights such as Social Security, Medicare, a living minimal wage, and good public schools.

But, of course, history, led by Great Powers on colonial quests for hegemony, and neoliberal corporate globalization agendas would place great obstacles to the realization of these universalizing aspirations.

In the earliest phases of the 1944 Bretton Woods negotiations, where the shape of the new world system was hammered out, American negotiators were led by progressive New Dealers such as Harry Dexter White, a democratic socialist. The early American vision, supported by FDR himself, was of a social democratic global order that subordinated corporate profits to human rights and the meeting of social needs.

Such Progressive Internationalism was sabotaged by the Truman Administration which aligned itself with global capitalism and the Cold War. Corporate globalization took over and, by the 1970s, turned into a virulent neoliberal global capitalism, intensified during the Reagan Revolution.

But the financial meltdowns, economic inequalities, and massive wage stagnation and job losses of the neoliberal regime have led, since the 1999 Battle of Seattle in the United States, toward a universalizing opposition to the global neoliberal order and the building of global economic democracy. The anti-globalization and Progressive Internationalist movement in the United States, while set back by the 9/11 attacks and the war on terror, grew during the George W. Bush and Obama years into a major labor and environmental movement, universalizing resistance to the global neoliberal order.

This movement found its strongest political expression in the progressive economic populism of the Bernie Sanders campaign, which made opposition to neoliberal trade agreements and global financial capitalism its central concern. Progressive US movements—from labor to environment to feminism to anti-racism—have increasingly focused on building an alternative economic order, subordinating profits to worker and environmental rights. And they are increasingly linking with movements in Latin America, Africa, Europe, and Asia that share a growing commitment to creating a new solidaristic post-corporate global order, with features of localism as well as Progressive, UN-based, Internationalism.

The building of the global alternative—Progressive Internationalism—has become one of the most important aims of the global universalizing progressive and cooperativist or democratic socialist movement. Trumpist hyper-nationalism—as the identity politics of the Far Right and appealing to white workers—has increased the urgency of a progressive internationalist vision, based on universal human rights and uniting workers and unions around the world in a globalist and localist democratic system, in which corporate power is replaced by universalizing waves of cross-national worker and citizen movements seeking societies organized around universal human rights.

11

Create Media of, by, and for the People: Moving Beyond Propaganda

"From the streets of Cairo and the Arab Spring, to Occupy Wall Street . . . social media was not only sharing the news but driving it."

Dan Rather

"[Occupy] set up live stream channels for 24/7 video images, along with Facebook pages, Tumblrs, Twitter feeds, all manner of social linkages. The movement's live streaming was like 'reality TV on steroids' . . ."

Todd Gitlin

"Independent media can go to where the silence is and break the sound barrier, doing what the corporate networks refuse to do."

Amy Goodman

Seventh New Rule: Occupy indie and new social media to build our own media of resistance and change! Infiltrate both the new and old media to expose the system's propaganda, spread our universalizing message across communities and issues, and build the universalizing movement of movements!

Big Questions: How do you infiltrate and reach audiences of old media while spreading new resistance messages in indie and new media?

Slogans: The movement is the message! Twitter disruptive ideas! Occupy the news!

What's New Here? All movements—silo movements and universalizing ones—try to spread their messages in the mass media. What's new here (in the wake of corporate take-over of "old" media) is the explosion of new social media, a crucial technological and social breakthrough empowering universalizers. Universalizing movements have more difficulty getting heard in corporate mainstream media. They depend ever more on independent community-based alternative media and on new social media. Silo activists also increasingly depend on social media, but new social media are especially important for universalizers. Universalizers face more resistance from corporate media. They organize vast numbers of people across large geographical areas, across big issues, and against the system itself. Universalizers need media to aggregate and universalize activists and agendas *as big as saving the world*.

All mass media are universalizing spaces; multiple issues and communities are inevitably part of "the news." In corporate media, the discourse and messages are highly managed by elites, but can still serve important universalizing functions for movements. The new online media provide essential means of networking for activists; they are a new space for communication, messaging, recruiting, and coordinating universalizing activist campaigns. Just as there could be no new super-universalizing system without the Internet and online communication, it is hard to imagine universalizing movements without new social media.

All resistance movements know that they must spread the word, both to recruit new members and to convert the public. But the current ideological apparatus is remarkably adept at blocking or coopting movements' access to centralized media. Getting your message into mass media, especially new social media, is a crucial way to spread the universalizing vision and move beyond silo activism. Along with the educational system, the media represent one of the most important spaces where communities and movements can come together and build common messages and agendas. The new social media—indeed all media—are natural aggregators of issues. Universalizing movements absolutely must exploit these spaces for their universalizing aims.

CORPORATE MEDIA: PROBLEMS AND POSSIBILITIES

The old media—run by large corporations (even public radio and TV; PBS and NPR are increasingly dependent on corporate funding)—embrace the capitalist system, shrink the political discourse to reformism, and redefine the political spectrum in a way that defines the Left as liberalism and eliminates any discussion of alternatives to capitalism. As Chomsky argues, mainstream media promote corporate propaganda, but entertain just enough reforms and critical investigative stories to maintain public credibility as a "free press." Examples are MSNBC liberal journalists, such as Rachel Maddow and Lawrence O'Donnell, who have opened mainstream media further to the Left and invited spokespeople from universalizing movement groups such as MoveOn.org and Demos to be regular commentators on their shows. Trump's extremism and attacks on mainstream media may encourage more defiance of this kind, leading corporate media to become an unexpected new venue in which activists and movements may be able to get exposure to national and global audiences. Even CNN, under attack from Trump, has begun to bring on Left, or at least progressive, commentators from Van Jones to David Cay Johnston.

Universalizing movements often have resorted to violence or other spectacles to get their cause and message on the old media, which embraces TINA. This puts universalizers into a serious dilemma. Getting into the corporate media is possible, but usually only in ways that lead the system to stigmatize movements as violent (when it is the system itself that is violent), pure spectacle (when it is the system itself that is spectacle), or hedonistic and self-indulgent (when it is the system itself that is excessive). Very large protests can get old media attention, but the media focus is on the spectacle rather than the underlying issues.

Civil disobedience is a better approach to capture media interest without blanket condemnation. It has a better chance of getting media to focus on the issues that lead citizens to take such serious but non-violent action. Moreover, universalizing movements are developing ways of framing issues and attracting corporate media attention. One example is led by activist sociologist William Gamson, former President of the American Sociological Association, who runs an institute called Media Research and Action Project that helps movements to reach mass media.

As universalizing brings more people into movements, even the corporate media have to take note. Universalizers should target young journalists in old media, who are interested in their issues and have not been fully converted to system ideology; finding and cultivating these reporters is important to universalizing movements. Anti-system academics or public intellectuals who write op-ed essays in corporate media which explain the rationale for anti-system campaigns are also vital resources.

Another important action is "occupying" electoral politics. When candidates like self-identified socialist Bernie Sanders enter the fray, they draw center-stage attention to the virtues of democratic socialism, and they bring the idea of socialism itself into a new conversation on old media.

Universalizing activists, op-ed writers, and young journalists can help movements gain a new mass audience for anti-systemic ideas such as social democracy and socialism itself.

THE INDIE MEDIA: AMY GOODMAN POINTS THE WAY

Creating and growing independent media—or "indies"—are crucial to universalizing resistance. Most communities now have their own independent, local radio and community television stations that are important venues for building universalizing movements within the community. Such local indies are a crucial way of reaching a critical threshold of support within the community and creating narratives of universalizing at the local level.

The indies are powerful—indeed essential—media for national and global universalizing. Democracy Now!, hosted by Amy Goodman, is a nerve center for building a national audience for universalizing movements. Democracy Now! embodies the indie spirit that can help connect different movements to each other and to a large national and global audience. Goodman traveled to Paris for the 2015 Paris climate talks and provided a full week of coverage to global activists seeking to change extractive capitalism. We need to nurture many Amy Goodmans and many indie networks that will connect universalizing movements into a widespread public conversation devoted to universalizing analysis and politics.

THE NEW SOCIAL MEDIA

Social media is a new ball game, with virtues and liabilities. Much of it is "open source" and accessible to a much wider set of participants. Corporate filters operate with less blanket power, as hundreds of thousands—perhaps millions—of universalizers (and silo activists) can instantly send their messages to recruits and to the public on Facebook, Twitter, etc. Just as the Internet has transformed the corporate information system, social media has transformed system opposition. This is true for grass-roots movements outside electoral politics and for electoral campaigns run by populist insurgents such as Bernie Sanders. It is also true for right-wing populist universalizers as well as those on the Left: Donald Trump's incessant tweeting was his main way of reaching a huge audience, and demonstrated the power of new social media for universalizing movements of all political stripes.

The infrastructure of movements—increasingly favorable to universalizing—is now based not only on online messaging, but also through easy apps that allow everything from doodling to writing movement manifestos to arranging meetings within and across movements focused on different issues. Movement organizations and campaigns can organize, reach recruits, and build campaigns online on an unprecedented, popular scale and at warp speed.

The Arab Spring and Occupy Wall Street movements exploded out of nowhere from "anonymous" hackers and computer communities who were masters of the new media. As sociologist Todd Gitlin writes, "What took root in Zucotti Park (Occupy) and then sent out lateral shoots from there was, as

Anthony Barnett would write, 'the combination of high-tech networking and no-tech gathering'."[1] Gitlin continues, "individuals had faces and stories; there were electronic communiques in real time and electronic summons for emergencies."[2] Online communication, recruitment, messaging, and organizing of meetings and campaigns are as important for localized movements on a campus or in a community as for global movements, seeking to universalize resistance.

It is hard to imagine a serious universalizing (or non-universalizing) resistance without seeing resisters constantly on their laptops and on Facebook. New social media also facilitate universalizing in multiple ways:

1. building a mass base by enabling inexpensive mailings to millions of members or recruits (think MoveOn.org);
2. enabling the globalization of resistance as protestors in Cairo or Tunis communicate with Occupy activists in the United States;
3. facilitating convergence by enabling lively conversations among economic, climate, peace, and civil rights movements;
4. facilitating communication with old corporate media (Occupy sites created their own media centers and blasted mainstream media with newsworthy stories from tent cities);
5. transmitting movement events live with independent radio or television, such as the Pacifica network and major independent media shows with mass audiences, such as Democracy Now!

Online progressive and Left media and blog sites play a crucial role in the development of 21st-century movements. *We are witnessing the explosion of such sites as truthout.org, presente.org, alternet.org, commondreams.org, truthdig.org, Znet, counterpunch.org, and hundreds of others*. These have become key vehicles for building and universalizing movements today.

Such sites have hundreds of thousands of online readers, both activists and non-activists interested in digging into the stories that the mainstream corporate media do not cover. Many sites have their own investigative journalists on staff, who report on climate, inequality, war, and racism issues marginalized by mainstream media. They also offer space for op eds, blogs, and reviews that go beyond the "respectable discourse" or "necessary illusions" required by corporate media pieces. And such organizations also coordinate with other non-media movement groups to help build and coordinate major movement campaigns.

These online sites are powerful universalizing forces. While some focus on single issues or single-issue constituencies, many of these sites have embraced an anti-systemic, intersectional approach. They publish investigative articles, thought pieces, and campaigns uniting multiple identity groups and causes. They are a treasure for 21st-century movements because they require relatively small resources to help reach vast numbers of progressives, with the capacity to create online spaces and campaigns where intersectional thinking and activism can flourish.

It is difficult to exaggerate the importance of online news social media as new universalizing vehicles. And we have yet to see their full potential, since they have only taken root in the 21st-century computer age, and are still at the beginning of pioneering a new universalizing progressive online media. They have the potential to build a new 21st-century media that moves the national conversation in a radically progressive direction and educates new generations of young people who get their news and political ideas mainly online.

Yet new social media do not a movement make, despite their overwhelming importance. Face-to-face relations and community remain at the heart of all movements, which are ultimately based on trust, solidarity, and intimacy. People who do not know each other cannot sustain movements, and all major universalizing movements have depended on building real-life communities to sustain themselves and successfully reach others. Moreover, online petitions and other virtual activism can become the lazy activist's way of feeling one has done one's job. If the medium is the message, you can't take face-to-face relationships off the movement map, even though the powers of online media to facilitate all aspects of movement work are incalculable—a gift to the movements much as it has been to the system itself.

REMAKING MEDIA IN THE PURSUIT OF JUSTICE

Alana Yu-lan Price and Maya Schenwar

As editors of Truthout, an independent online news site, we believe that good journalism plays a role in the pursuit of justice.

The forms of injustice that we are up against—mass incarceration, white supremacy, widening economic inequality, and a militarized form of global capitalism that disproportionately affects people of color and women worldwide—all rely on silence and erasure.

Part of what journalists can do to counter these systems of injustice is to expose specific instances of injustice and tell stories of resistance, providing a platform for people who are experiencing and organizing against oppression to tell their stories. When we do this, we transform journalism into a form of *justice through storytelling*.

Rethinking journalism requires questioning pillars of conventional journalism, such as the idea that a journalist can be "objective." We question whether it is possible to construct a narrative without unconsciously shaping a story through one's "common sense" about whom to interview, what order to tell the story in, what context should be deemed necessary for inclusion and more. Fantasies of objectivity erode journalists' ability to think critically about how their own values, experiences, and social location shape their work.

Instead of prioritizing the principle of objectivity, we anchor our work in principles of accuracy, transparency, and independence from the influence of corporate and political forces. Within this frame, activists can write op eds about the struggles they are embedded in, so long as they are explicit about their relation to the material they're writing about. Reporters can structure their stories to spark action by reporting not only on instances of injustice, but also on how different groups are resisting.

In telling the stories of particular campaigns and acts of resistance, we aim to share the larger narratives of movements, not only helping to amplify activist efforts as they happen, but also building a critical historical record of movements from Occupy to Black Lives Matter, to Idle No More, to the fights against the Keystone XL and Dakota Access pipelines. By lifting up the voices of activists struggling against powerful forces—through both our articles and our active social media presence—we are both fueling current movements and providing key documentation upon which future movements will be able to draw.

We make no bones about the fact that our goal is to reveal systemic injustice and provide a platform for transformative ideas. In addition to amplifying and fueling activist movements, we seek to remove ourselves from the equation of injustice—an equation in which media groups have often

served as an arm of a violent power structure.

Just one example: until recently, the mass media rarely mentioned the sharp rise in incarceration between the 1970s and the present day. Moreover, by drawing on interviews with the police, rather than on interviews with incarcerated people and their families, mainstream reports on crime have often portrayed criminalized people as scary and evil, thus backing the establishment's justifications for locking people up.

This has occurred because getting friendly with the police and developing them as sources has long been one of mainstream reporters' jobs. And this has occurred because so many mainstream media outlets are run by people who have not personally experienced the violent effects of mass incarceration within their immediate communities.

So, it has mostly fallen to a small number of independent media outlets to tell the truth about prisons and track down the voices that aren't being heard. This means asking reporters to interview incarcerated people themselves and working with imprisoned people to write their own stories. Highlighting the voices, ideas, and analyses of people facing oppression serves as a central guideline in our work at Truthout.

Openly seeking justice, we don't call ourselves "fair and balanced." We know that "balanced" is a false goal, because society is not balanced. We don't have an interest in pitting injustice against justice. We want to strengthen all struggles for justice.

This frees us from having to represent the status quo and gives us the opportunity to start new transformative conversations.

We are creating methods along with creating content. Our orientation toward transformation informs our editorial practice at every level, affecting the stories that we deem "newsworthy," the guidance we give to authors, and even the style guide used by our copy-editor, which asks that Truthout's authors find new metaphors that do not equate society-damaging ignorance with blindness, deafness, or "insanity" (metaphors that further stigmatize people with disabilities and mental illness, whose devaluation arises from the same impulses at the heart of capitalism and white supremacy).

Although we do not generally articulate Truthout's orientation toward transformation through the specific discourse of "universalizing resistance" used in this book—in part due to a concern over the way in which calls for more "universal" struggles have sometimes been used by white men on the Left to de-legitimize efforts to fight racism and sexism alongside capitalist exploitation—we can see how many elements of our work are resonant with the universalizing framework as it is defined here.

Earlier in this book, Charles Derber writes that a core aspect of universalizing resistance is the insight that solving any inequality requires dealing with all of them.

We strive to put this insight into practice by commissioning stories that concretely show how different forms of oppression intersect, revealing the interconnections between struggles that are too often presented as existing in disconnected "silos." We hope that our media work will help expose connections between climate change, militarism, capitalism, white supremacy, colonial violence, and patriarchy globally.

For example, Truthout staff reporter, Dahr Jamail, has consistently revealed the intersection of US military policy and environmental destruction. Jamail has exposed plans by the US Navy to conduct vast war games over large stretches of public and private lands, including national parks. He has documented how the Navy has taken advantage of climate change to expand operations in the Gulf of Alaska and has simultaneously fueled climate change with its polluting, hazardous practices. These interconnections are critical to name and analyze.

In the wake of the United Kingdom's vote to leave the European Union, we commissioned a piece by Laleh Khalili titled "After Brexit: Reckoning with Britain's Racism and Xenophobia" that documented how class politics were articulated through a politics of race in the lead-up to the Brexit vote, showing the interlocking effects of austerity, privatization, and xenophobia.

And in Truthout's first print anthology, *Who Do You Serve, Who Do You Protect? Police Violence and Resistance in the United States*, we featured an article by Andrea Ritchie that discusses how centering women's and trans people's experiences will require movements against police violence to expand their analysis of state violence "to include sexual assault by the police, violence against pregnant and parenting women, policing of prostitution, deadly responses to domestic violence, and the routine violence and violation of police interactions with transgender and gender-nonconforming people."

By commissioning these sorts of articles—articles that explicitly focus on interlocking forms of oppression—we seek to connect the dots and show readers why solving any inequality requires dealing with all of them.

Meanwhile, as Derber also proposes, we don't discount the value of "single-issue" activism. We hope that when we present articles with a more single-issue focus, they will function like tiles in a mosaic, working in concert to present a larger picture of the many sources of injustice that exist, as well as the varied ways in which people are organizing against them.

The consciousness-awakening power of single-issue organizing is apparent in the inspiring stories that Alexis Bonogofsky has written for Truthout about the unusual coalitions that have emerged in local fights against extractive corporations. For example, Bonogofsky tells the story of how ranchers, members of the Northern Cheyenne Tribe, Amish farmers, environmentalists, and other residents of Southeast Montana organized to prevent Arch Coal from extracting billions of tons of coal from the area. She writes:

> In the beginning, there were a number of separate communities who all, for their own reasons, wanted to stop this project. . . . Six years of slow and steady relationship building created a powerful bloc of community members from all different backgrounds and political persuasions, united in opposition against the mine and railroad.

Reports like these are a compelling example of why so-called single-issue activism can be a powerful starting point. Even if the groups that come together around a particular issue don't have a shared analysis of intersecting oppressions going in, these sorts of campaigns can raise awareness of the intersecting issues and build relationships that lay the groundwork for future solidarity.

Moreover, placing articles on "single-issue" campaigns side by side can start to generate an awareness of transnational resonances and linkages, as well as the connective tissue between resistance movements. At Truthout, while Alexis Bonogofsky was reporting on how residents in Kunkletown, Pennsylvania, successfully organized to prevent Nestlé from bottling their community's water and selling it for a massive profit, Renata Bessi and Santiago Navarro F. were reporting on indigenous communities in Brazil who have alleged that, in an effort to make way for new development projects by transnational corporations (including Nestlé), the Brazilian government has been taking over their ancestral lands and hiring hit men to murder the indigenous residents of those lands.

Part of practicing transformative journalism—journalism in the service of justice—is recognizing that no one piece can stand alone as truly "universal." We hope that our continual efforts to lift up the work of resistance movements, highlighting both their intersections and their particularities, will bring these movements to a wider audience. We seek to interrupt the usual passivity of news consumption, provoking readers to think about their own complicity in systems of oppression—and awakening them to how they might engage with movements themselves.

We aim to be a force for the amplification of resistance, a spark for conversation and action, a bullhorn for revealing injustice, and a vessel for powerful new ideas, working alongside movements in the pursuit of a just world.

Alana Yu-lan Price is Truthout's Content Relations Editor and a co-editor of Who Do You Serve? Who Do You Protect? Police Violence and Resistance in the United States *(with Maya Schenwar and Joe Macare; 2016, Haymarket Books). She previously served as Managing Editor of Tikkun magazine. She brings a deep commitment to racial justice, economic justice, and queer and trans liberation to her journalistic work.*

Maya Schenwar is Truthout's Editor-in-Chief. She is also the author of Locked Down, Locked Out: Why Prison Doesn't Work and How We Can Do Better *(2014, Berrett-Koehler), and a co-editor of* Who Do You Serve, Who Do You Protect? Police Violence and Resistance in the United States *(with Alana Yu-lan Price and Joe Macare; 2016, Haymarket Books).*

12

Let's Get Political: Movements and Elections

"Friends, this campaign is not just about Bernie Sanders. It is about creating a movement of millions of Americans . . . in every community of our country. It is about fighting for a political revolution which transforms our country, and demands that government represents all of us, and not just a handful of billionaires."

Bernie Sanders

"What makes PDA unique as an organization is that we believe you have to work both inside to remind the Democratic Party of our progressive ideals as well as outside the party. Every great social movement whether it was the women's movement that began in Seneca Falls in 1848 and ended outside the White House with demonstrations that led to the 19th Amendment or the Civil Rights movement when Rosa Parks (in 1955) refused to move that resulted in the signing of the Civil Rights bill in 1964—every social movement has a uniting of the 'inside and the outside.' And that's what PDA is about—building a larger progressive social movement."

Joanne Boyer, Progressive Democrats of America

"Citizen advocates have no other choice but to close the democracy gap by direct political means . . . I have a personal distaste for the trappings of modern politics, in which incumbents and candidates daily extol their own inflated virtues, paint complex issues with trivial brush strokes, and propose plans quickly generated by campaign consultants. But, I can no longer stomach the systemic political decay that has weakened our democracy. I can no longer watch people dedicate themselves to improving their country while their government leaders turn their backs, or worse, actively block fair treatment for citizens. It is necessary *to launch a sustained effort to wrest control of our democracy from the corporate government and restore it to the political government under the control of citizens."*

Ralph Nader

Eighth New Rule: Use electoral politics to build and network our movements! Build electoral universalizing coalitions for radical reform, and go further: demand the impossible and fight to change the system and save the world. Avoid the election trap, but use elections to plant the seeds of transformation and prevent proto-fascist right-wing parties from gaining state power.

Big Questions: How do universalizing movements weave together disruptive resistance on the streets with electoral politics? How do we challenge the system through electoral parties committed to the system?

Slogans: Occupy politics! The movement is the party! This is what democracy looks like!

What's New Here? This rule of the road actually speaks to a dilemma that is not new and confronts both silo and non-silo movements. Social movements have long struggled with whether and how to get involved with electoral politics. More radical and universalizing activists have often just said no—seeing correctly that, as Naomi Klein puts it, "the future we want is not on the ballot."[1] While true, this is not an argument for either universalizers or non-universalizers to disengage from electoral politics. Occupying the electoral area is vitally important, though it remains important that we do not fall into "the election trap," an obsession with elections that is harmful.

THE BIG DEBATE: SHOULD MOVEMENTS GET INVOLVED WITH ELECTIONS?

Political parties and the electoral arena are vital spaces where issues and agendas get universalized. Parties function as a way in which multiple constituencies come together to build potent and universalizing political agendas linking major public issues and causes. These spaces are highly controlled in Western democracies, limiting the kinds of universalizing agendas that can be built. But if the progressive universalizing movements do not seek to influence that space, they will cede the ground to right-wing movements with the money and electoral passions to enact their own conservative or Far Right universalizing agendas. The election of President Donald Trump and the dominance, at this time of writing, of all aspects of government by a Far Right Republican Party has tragically shown the importance of this fundamental truth.

The relations of resisters—and especially UR activists—to electoral politics is a subject of great importance and great controversy. Many resisters of all stripes have rejected participation in electoral politics, viewing both Republicans and Democrats as centrally committed to preserving the system. To work for one party or the other is to reinforce the legitimacy of the system and to encourage public despair about achieving anything other than modest reforms.

Moreover, obsession with elections has true dangers. As visionary educator Paulo Freire noted, by engaging in mainstream politics, movements subject themselves to terrible manipulation: "the Left is almost always tempted by a 'quick return to power'."[2] Movements can forget the necessity of joining with the oppressed to forge an organization, and stray into an impossible "dialog" with the dominant elites. "Realism" takes over from resistance.

Many US movements recognize these dangers. When the Democratic Party issued a 2015 statement of support for Black Lives Matter, some spokespeople for the movement responded:

> We do not now, nor have we ever, endorsed or affiliated with the Democratic Party, or with any party. The Democratic Party, like the Republican and all political parties, have historically attempted to control or contain Black people's efforts to liberate ourselves.[3]

The statement continues: "True change requires real struggle, and that struggle will be in the streets and led by the people, not by a political party."[4]

Of course, millions of African Americans disagree with this rejection of electoral politics, including many in Black Lives Matter and other African-American resistance movements. Millions of resisters see electoral politics as a vital tool to strengthen their own movements and create a political environment more conducive to system change. Organizations such as the Progressive Democrats of America (PDA) and MoveOn.org do important work in connecting Left-leaning candidates with movements, fueling important conversations and connections between the Democratic Party populist base and justice movements.

WHY UNIVERSALIZERS MUST ENGAGE WITH ELECTIONS—EVEN WHEN THE SOLUTION IS NOT ON THE BALLOT

The communities of universalizers and non-universalizers are each divided about how and whether to participate. Since arguments on both sides have merits, one approach is to simply leave it up to particular organizations, movements, and activists, assuming that those who reject electoral politics and those who participate will each contribute something to social justice. Universalizing resistance, though, should and must spread resistance into the electoral system itself, occupying it for its own purposes. And these purposes turn out to be crucially important, even if sometimes limited.

To argue for engagement is not to argue for total immersion; resisters have too little time, money, and people to become election fanatics. In most eras, whether the President is Democratic or Republican does not significantly alter the prospects for universalizing movements. Universalizing movements should approach elections as an important context for their own core work, recognizing that devoting resources to electing and influencing politicians is highly significant, but not, in most historical eras, their primary mission. With the election of President Trump and total Republican dominance in Washington DC and many state legislatures, we are in a new era where electoral politics are of the utmost importance.

Naomi Klein is right that the solutions we need "are not on the ballot." But that does not mean universalizing movements should not engage with electoral politics or occupy the electoral arena. One core reason is to prevent the election of extremely dangerous demagogues such as Trump, which we return to shortly. It is a wake-up call to everyone who argued against any engagement with elections.

But there are other reasons to link movements with electoral politics. One core argument for engagement is because the President helps move the dial of discourse, with liberal leaders making liberalism itself legitimate in the mainstream, while right-wing Presidents make liberalism a dirty word, the "L" word.

Why does this matter for resisters, who seek something far beyond liberalism? Because as mainstream discourse moves toward the liberal side of the spectrum, it makes more transformative progressive or Left discourse less alien and scary to the public. Contrarily, when mainstream discourse moves further Right, as it has under Presidents Reagan and George W. Bush and now Trump, progressive universalizers become a fifth column with a totally alien discourse. The public is bombarded with the view that liberalism itself is unpatriotic—and the Left beyond the pale. Moreover, right-wing demagoguery, as under Trump, becomes "normalized," and is seen as integral to "respectable" civic and political discourse.

Presidents define the "center." This matters because the further to the Right the center becomes (and it has moved far in that direction today with Trump's bigotry and the Alt-Right), the harder it is for progressive system-changing discourse to find public traction. History supports this argument—liberal Presidents tend to open up space for wave eras and universalizing resistance, while right-wing Presidents such as Reagan have historically helped to shut down the space for progressive ideas and movements. Roosevelt opened up ideological space in the 1930s for universalizing labor and anti-capitalism movements (even though he was trying to save capitalism), and Lyndon B. Johnson opened up space for the major resistance movements—civil rights and anti-Vietnam—of the 1960s. The rationale for universalizers to support liberal rather than conservative Presidents is not because they will achieve movement goals or change the system, but because they open ideological space for the movements themselves, even as those movements challenge liberal leaders.

THE GRAVEST DANGER OF ELECTORAL DISENGAGEMENT: TURNING THE COUNTRY OVER TO THE FAR RIGHT

Another reason for both non-universalizers and universalizers to engage with electoral politics, as noted above in discussing Trump, is that to disengage cedes the terrain to right-wing ideas and movements, with dangerous consequences. Just as liberal Presidents open up space for labor, peace, and civil rights movements, conservative Presidents open up space for Far Right movements. The Reagan Revolution is a case in point. Reagan created opportunities for the New Right which has been one of the most powerful universalizing resistance movements in modern history. Likewise, George W. Bush opened up space for the Tea Party and Far Right movements, ranging from white supremacists to super-nationalists and jingoistic militarists to libertarians and austerians seeking to destroy the federal government (except for the military), with many of these groups now influential in a frighteningly reactionary Republican Party.

Donald Trump is the most important example at this time of writing. Just his candidacy, before the 2016 election, pulled Alt-Right white supremacists and neo-fascist movements into the open, giving these groups national visibility and credibility. Under President Trump, Far Right movements have gained immense new power, with leaders of the Alt-Right like Steve Bannon sitting in the West Wing talking to the President every day and shaping key national policy. Far Right movements, with deep grass-roots support across much of the nation, have the President's ear and can create a regime change toward a more overt authoritarian society, a new police state, or a neo-fascist America, all frightening trends in the age of Trump.

The more right-wing the President and Congress, the more repressive of progressive or Left resistance the state will become, literally denying public space to the movements and putting activists under surveillance or behind bars. As activism becomes more risky to the safety, jobs, and lives of activists, movements will find it harder to recruit new members, let alone sustain those they have. Since Trump's election, this fear is already palpable among many activists, partly explaining why they were out on the streets protesting even before he assumed office, trying to show that he could not intimidate or shut them down.

Fear has become a major problem for the movements today, particularly for young people who are afraid that protesting in a repressive era largely shaped by Reagan, George W, Bush, and Trump will hurt their job prospects and their physical safety. Too many of my own students who have been activists have told me, since Trump's election, that they feel anxiety about signing petitions online, going out to protest, or just speaking out. The fact that President Obama continued some of this repressive response is evidence that electoral regime changes such as the Reagan Revolution matter. Such regime changes pull liberal politicians to the Right, and end up preserving many of the anti-dissent policies of their conservative predecessors and making the work of resistance, always challenging, far more difficult. A key task of movements is to put the fear of God into politicians who don't listen to them. In historical eras when universalizers have little chance to take power, they can often ward off political drifts to the Right by raising the prospect that the costs in social disruption will be politically unacceptable to elected elites.

Indeed, many Left universalizers who reject electoral politics see this as an important role for their movements: planting the fear of disruption or revolt so deep in the minds of elites, that they will have nightmares about insurrection. President Nixon admitted that waking up every morning hearing the angry anti-war chants of protesters in Lafayette Park across from the White House affected him and might have restrained him in his endless Vietnam war-making.

LIBERAL LEADERS CAN HELP CREATE SPACE FOR RADICAL REFORMS

Yet another argument for electoral engagement is that liberal Presidents can be pushed more easily than conservative ones to make what French eco-Marxist theorist André Gorz called "radical reforms"; that is, reforms which are not system-changing, but are wedges that movements can use to create transformation. This is partly because liberal Presidents are more likely to protect the civil liberties of dissenters and thus give them a public platform denied by conservative Presidents. Moreover, the public platform becomes a vehicle for public advocacy of legislation that has system-changing potential, such as a campaign for universal public financing of campaigns, or universal health care, or ambitious plans for converting from fossil fuels to clean energy.

Historically, many other legal initiatives have been spurred by movements putting pressure on the electoral system and politicians: the Wagner Act of 1935 that legalized unions, the civil rights act of 1964 that ended many forms of segregation, the legalization of gay marriage. In fact, most non-universalizing movements almost always seek to petition, lobby, protest against, or otherwise influence politicians to make progress on their single-issue movements—and success is far more likely under liberal Presidents and Congresses than conservative ones, a clear argument for seeking to create a more liberal political class as an instrument for movement goals. In wave eras, major converging and universalizing movements, such as the 1960s' civil rights and anti-war movements, also gain more traction when they have liberal rather than conservative politicians in power, also evidence of the utility of electing and pressing liberal political elites rather than conservative ones. Liberals do not fulfill the aims of system-changing movements, but they make their work easier.

THE UNIVERSALIZING VIRTUES OF PROGRESSIVE POLITICAL PARTIES

Another argument for engagement with electoral politics, applying in the United States mainly to Third Parties, but sometimes also to the Democratic and Republican parties, is that political parties themselves can become resistance movements with system-changing agendas. Think of the 1892 People's Party created by the agrarian populists; they embraced a transformative program, as noted in Chapter 3, that would nationalize the big Wall Street banks and move the entire economy toward a cooperative, egalitarian system. Or consider Eugene Debs, the Socialist Party candidate for President in 1916 who ran against war, racial injustice, and capitalism, surely part of a universalizing politics. Or reflect on the Green Party in the United States today, which links environmentalism to racial justice, peace, transformative economics leading toward the end of inequality in income and wealth, the end of corporate personhood and Citizens United, universal single-payer health care, immigrant rights, women's rights, the end of neoliberalism, bringing down the corporate plutocracy, and other social justice issues, all part of a broad pro-democracy universalizing movement.

In 2016, we saw both the Democratic and Republican parties showing the potential of mainstream parties to begin melding with resistance movements. Bernie Sanders was a "movement" candidate, who pushed the Democratic Party toward left-wing "political revolution," as he called it. Donald Trump also called himself a "movement" candidate, aligned himself with the right-wing universalizing populists against the Establishment, and rode their power and his own charisma to control of the country as President.

Political parties are, by their nature, aggregators of issues (if not of movements). Radical parties must offer voters—or the constituencies they aim to influence—a rainbow of anti-systemic convergent ideals around which universalizing movements can coalesce. Even within the Democratic Party in the United States, candidates ranging from Shirley Chisholm (a Democratic Presidential candidate in 1972) to Bernie Sanders (in 2016) offer up universalizing agendas, one of the rationales for groups such as the Progressive Democrats of America (PDA) which help to orchestrate an important dance between left-wing electoral politics and universalizing movements.

Of course, within the Democratic Party, there will never be a full anti-systemic politics, and Bernie Sanders fell well short of universalizing movements seeking to end militarized capitalism in his positions on everything from war and foreign policy to capitalism itself. Nonetheless, Sanders contributed to universalizing simply by introducing socialism as a "mainstream" idea that drew the interest of millions of Americans. After the first Democratic Party primary debate, when CNN moderator, Anderson Cooper, encouraged a conversation between Sanders and Hillary Clinton about socialism and capitalism, the most widely-searched word on social media right after the debate was "socialism." Moreover, a majority of Americans, as noted in Chapter 6, now say they could vote for a socialist Presidential candidate. Throughout the 2016 primary season, Sanders was polling ahead of all Republican candidates, beating them by larger margins than Hillary Clinton. Sanders, at a minimum, was thus beginning a universalizing conversation almost unheard of in contemporary American mainstream politics, about anti-systemic politics and alternatives to capitalism.

CAN ELECTORAL POLITICS CONTRIBUTE TO UNIVERSALIZING RESISTANCE?

Bill Fletcher, Jr.

Photo credit: Arlene Holt-Baker

The US Left is torn by ambivalence over electoral politics, and for good reason. The United States has one of the most undemocratic electoral systems on this planet, yet calls itself a democracy. The "winner-take-all" system predisposes the electorate toward the acceptance of only two parties. Minor parties are regularly ignored. And "politics" is generally reserved for those moments when a voter enters the voting booth to choose a candidate for higher office.

The US electoral system discourages voter engagement. Voter registration—and voting itself—is often complicated and is increasingly under threat from voter suppression by the Republican Party. Moreover, the two parties are actually more akin to electoral coalitions. Left theorist Carl Davidson has suggested that the Democratic Party is actually the amalgam of six "parties," each with a distinct base and platform, though none of them self-identifying as parties or even factions.

These electoral coalitions that go by the name of Democratic and Republican parties are dominated by political forces which seek the preservation of capitalism. They have different and sometimes similar visions on how to do that, but neither party challenges the system in its fundamentals.

So we are stuck in the realm of ideology rather than entering the sphere of politics; that is, the steps necessary in order to gain and secure power. For, while it is true that this is an undemocratic system where the decks are stacked against the oppressed, it is also true that elections have, can, and will make a real-world difference to regular people, as suggested by the election of President Donald Trump. A "joke" often cited by some on the Left is that if elections were truly important, they would be illegal; one could just as easily flip that and offer that if elections were of no importance, why would the rich always vote? Why would the right to vote for women, African Americans, and Chicanos have been so intensely obstructed—*and not just in the past?*

The fury on the Left over electoral politics reflects a failure to appreciate the strategic need to build a *popular-democratic bloc of social forces* aligned in a progressive direction. Such a bloc is not an abstraction. It is a majoritarian sentiment in which masses of people see themselves in and through this bloc. The Popular Front period in US political history—roughly 1934–1946—was such an era. The "Second Reconstruction" era was a similar such period.

A popular-democratic bloc is not simply to influence the ruling elite, but to win power for the oppressed and dispossessed. "Winning power" is not a reference to the entry of a period of fundamental social transformation; that is, the winning of socialism, but rather a period that involves the dramatic expansion of democracy—the battle for consistent democracy. It is a more immediate and no less important struggle than the struggle for socialism.

A popular-democratic bloc does not consist of one issue or campaign. Great united fronts and causes are, indeed, built along those lines. A popular-democratic bloc represents a congealing of various social movements and causes that overlap and yet coexist in contradiction. The bloc is *not* an organization with decision making. In a peculiar way one could describe it

as a sense of direction, or a *common sense*.

Electoral engagement is part of the process of materializing this popular-democratic bloc. But it is far from the only method. Social movements, such as Occupy, the movements for Black Lives, environmental justice, new labor, immigrant rights, and gender freedom/anti-patriarchy, all contribute toward such a bloc. When individuals and groups in vastly different social movements start seeing themselves in other social movements and causes, we are then on our way toward the construction of a popular-democratic bloc.

Electoral engagement, then, is not about popularity contests. It acts as a barometer to ascertain where masses situate themselves. This includes factoring in the non-voter, as we in the United States regularly see during the low-participation midterm elections.

Left engagement in elections is also not primarily, at least at this moment, about running independent political parties (and candidacies) in order to distance ourselves from the rottenness of the two capitalist parties. The 2016 Bernie Sanders candidacy for President demonstrates the potential of running within the Democratic Party, including the level of media coverage one gets in contrast to independent campaigns.

Left electoral engagement today needs to be envisioned as Left-led electoral work—work that is far broader than the Left in isolation, but where the Left is playing a major, if not leading role. The role of much of the Left in the 1988 candidacy of the Rev. Jesse Jackson is a great example of very constructive Left work that helped to advance the Jackson campaign as well as the Left, despite the disappointing decline of the National Rainbow Coalition after 1988.

Yet a Left electoral engagement is also much more than supporting one candidacy. This was a lesson learned from the demise of the National Rainbow Coalition, and it can also be learned from other candidacies; for example, the 2004 Dennis Kucinich campaign. People engage in electoral politics for reasons that are often different from the reasons of those who join organizations. Electoral campaigns have a time-limited duration. Mass organizations, on the other hand, have a longer-term purpose. The sorts of organizations and efforts that the Left needs to lead in advancing are those that help the popular-democratic bloc to gel and move toward power. Some of the energy for such formation may arise from specific electoral candidacies, such as that of Sanders, but one should never assume that a candidacy will fold into an ongoing and unified movement, let alone organization.

What are some of the conclusions one can draw? As I have regularly argued, one is that there is a desperate need for a national, progressive electoral strategy. In the electoral realm, this will represent the efforts at building the popular-democratic bloc and simultaneously obstructing the neoliberal and, indeed, neo-Confederate, directions of the State under President Trump and the Republican Party. Today, these twin efforts are essential in this moment. While there are many ways of resisting the political Right (whether the corporate Right or right-wing populist movements largely melded in the Trump Administration), depriving them of governmental power—or weakening the exercise of that power—is essential to our arsenal.

Left engagement in the electoral realm must be a state-based undertaking. While nation-wide organizational efforts can certainly help, the efforts at bloc-building must be locally based and factor in the concrete conditions of each state. Efforts such as the New Virginia Majority and the New Florida Majority, to name just two, are examples of such work. Neither of these has set itself up as an independent party,

nor should they. The Vermont Rainbow Coalition was, in many ways, a thematic precursor of such efforts, as was the Alabama-based New South Coalition. The essence was the elaboration of *independent politics* through the form of a non-party coalition; that is, a formation that was not legally constituted as a political party, but had an independent raison d'être.

Such efforts need to begin quietly and involve an assessment of the social forces in each state. This means gaining a proper understanding of the various social movements and campaigns; the nature of the bases of these efforts; existing organizations and the character of their leaderships; as well as gaining a proper understanding of our political opponents, including those who claim to be Democrats and/or progressives.

Learning from the practice of the political Right, one must engage on three levels simultaneously: electoral/legislative; legal; and mass movements. The electoral work that has largely been the focus of this Interlude supplements but never replaces the other arenas. This means that there is no one particular organizational form that can host all such activities. Mass movements are not subordinate to electoral/legislative work nor to the legal effort; the Democratic Party will never be a sufficient venue for resistance, even though joining some campaigns with Bernie Sanders and other Progressive Democratic Senators such as Elizabeth Warren is one vital part of a broader universalizing to Democratic Party progressive activism. Universalizing movements must plunge into a huge number of local, state, and federal primary elections supporting Left Democratic candidates, something akin to the vast electoral efforts initiated by the Tea Party in Republican primaries to build their right-wing universalizing populism. We already have organizations such as the Progressive Democrats of America that are seeking to build a vast Left electoral agenda at every level, all across the country, for new candidates tied to the movements and supporting the non-electoral organizing they are doing. We are already seeing fresh faces at the local level, including many anti-racist, anti-militarist "democratic socialists" elected to city councils from Seattle to Cleveland to Baltimore, who are working with Left local and national movements.

We have historical modes of movements—such as Jesse Jackson's National Rainbow Coalition—working inside and outside the Democratic Party, and now we have important current models, including the Working Families Party, and the New Virginia Majority and New Florida Majority mentioned above. All carry some of the force of right-wing models, such as the Tea Party, that synergize the energies arising from universalizing movements with a mainstream political party, harnessing the power of an "inside–outside" strategy.

As universalizing movements work in tandem with progressive candidates in elections and elected progressive officials, they must recognize that there will be contradictions— sometimes quite significant—between each. Those will have to be managed, but cannot be ignored or suppressed. In the age of Trump, it is essential to build these universalizing partnerships and weather the contradictions sufficiently to beat back the horrific national threat posed by the Trump regime and the Trumpist movements that will follow him.

Finally, the Left needs to take the lead in theorizing the nature of governmental power under democratic capitalism. What does it mean to win under the conditions of democratic capitalism? It is this prospect that scares many on the Left for fear that winning will lead to a morass of managing capitalism. Yet if the Left fails to seek governmental power, it will forever be condemned to the role of commentator and critic of the capitalist parties—and, as in the Trump election, relegated potentially to an unprecedented era of popular repression—rather than as an agent of direct change and a vehicle for the eventual emancipation of the oppressed.

The excitement associated with any one campaign or social movement can never replace the efforts needed to bring about the materialization of a popular-democratic bloc. This is the challenge for and fate of the Left, clearly urgent in the Trump era, but always the case. To borrow from Frantz Fanon, this is a challenge and fate we can either accept or abdicate. The choice is ours, but avoiding the choice is actually not an option.

Bill Fletcher, Jr., is a long-time Left activist and writer. He is also a talk-show host and syndicated columnist. Follow him on Twitter, Facebook, and at www.billfletcherjr.com

MELDING PROGRESSIVE MOVEMENTS AND ELECTORAL CAMPAIGNS: THE CASE OF BERNIE SANDERS

In the foreground and aftermath of his Presidential campaign, Sanders illustrated the way that politics itself can be universalizing—and how electoral politics and movements are intimately and explosively connected. As journalist Harold Meyerson has shown, Occupy Wall Street activists, as early as 2013 and 2014, were calling for political campaigns to be launched to turn Occupy and broader Left movement demands into electoral campaigns and an agenda for a Presidential race. They started with Senator Elizabeth Warren and then turned to Senator Sanders, being among the very first groups to speak for and coalesce around a Sanders socialist Presidential race with a focus on the 1% and Wall Street. Meyerson shows that grass-roots movements such as Occupy made the Sanders campaign possible and were essential in conceiving and launching it.

Sanders recognized his dependency on the movements and acknowledged that his candidacy could succeed and fulfill its platform only by mobilizing grass-roots movements and activists in communities all over the country. The Sanders campaign began to erase the distinction between a Presidential campaign and a social movement. Sanders understood that his campaign was really a convergence of social movements with electoral politics. If elected President, he could create system change only by joining forces with universalizing grass-roots movements seeking a "political revolution." These included, of course, Occupy, MoveOn.org, and other universalizing movements that helped launch his campaign.

The key insight from Sanders is about the crucial interdependency of movements and progressive electoral politics in the universalizing process. Progressive politics is itself a potential key instrument for aggregating and converging issues and movements that can save the world. Progressive politicians' role is to mobilize and help to empower universalizing movements; and the movements' roles are to mobilize the entire population for true system change that no elected President can achieve on his or her own. Movements desperately need the most progressive possible Presidents—and those elected leaders' main role is to empower and legitimate universalizing movements.

Sanders created major mojo for the movements. Those movements, after his loss in the primaries to Hillary Clinton, were the real fruit of his campaign. As Trump became President, Sanders' followers have organized themselves in connection to other movements, to fuel a new wave of movements and millennial activists who will continue his "political revolution," both by swelling the power of universalizing movements and helping them to change public consciousness and change the discourse in elections and legislative bodies. The Sanders campaign was the beginning, not the end, of universalizing and melding politics with movements. A new generation of activists, after the elections, has begun to dive into movements and begin their own electoral campaigns at local, state, and federal levels. They will continue the transformation of electoral politics into a partnership with universalizing movements—the labor, climate, peace, and civil rights movements—that Sanders himself had understood were always the agents of the real change he wanted.

After Trump's election, in an interview on December 22, 2016, with National Public Radio host Tom Ashbrook, Sanders made it very clear that universalizing resistance across movements and into the political arena was the only way forward. "On virtually every issue, we've gotta be in vigorous opposition," Sanders said. "We have got to mobilize people and use the resources that we have in the Congress to stop those ugly attacks against immigrants, Muslims. We cannot compromise one inch in terms of bigotry."[5]

Sanders continued:

> On every major important issue, the American people are on our side . . . We can defeat Trump, we can stop his ugly initiatives, we can push forward some progressive initiatives, if we are effective at organizing and mobilizing millions of people . . . The only way that we are effective and stop bad things are when people mobilize and fight back. If we stand together, I think we can effectively take on his ugly ideas and continue the fight for a progressive vision for this country.[6]

The melding of movements and parties will never be complete—at least not for a long time. Mainstream parties in capitalist nations will never become fully transformative, limited by the constraints of money and capitalist ideology in capitalist states. The movements will always be the force pushing for the full systemic change we need—and they can never simply dissolve into political parties. The movements, while building close relations with progressive politicians such as Sanders, must always maintain their autonomy to prevent cooptation and to mobilize themselves for true revolutionary change. As Bill Fletcher, Jr., has noted in his Interlude earlier in this chapter,

Universalizing feminism, immigrant rights, and human rights at anti-Trump protest

© Czuber / Dreamstime.com

contradictions will always exist between parties and movements, but they must be managed rather than simply permitted to dissolve the important work that parties and movements can do together.

At this time of writing, radical parties in Europe, such as Podemos in Spain, Syriza in Greece (and its offshoots to its Left), a transformed Labour Party in the UK led by socialist Jeremy Corbyn, and many other political parties opposing US hegemony and agitating for a new economic and political system in their nations and the world economy, show that electoral politics is today emerging as a player in progressive universalizing social movements. After the 2016 UK Brexit vote, Far Right parties in Austria, Hungary, France, and other European countries demonstrated that the same electoral dynamics are playing a major role in building right-wing and neo-fascist universal movements. These parties, whether on the Left or Right, help to build a larger mass base than the movements themselves can achieve, and create another force for convergence of issues across the rainbow spectrum.

AFTER SANDERS: ELECTORAL POLITICS AND UNIVERSALIZING MOVEMENTS

Mark Solomon

A well-known aphorism from the Italian Marxist Antonio Gramsci goes: "The crisis consists precisely in the fact that the old is dying and the new cannot be born; in this interregnum a great variety of morbid symptoms appear."

The unexpected election to the Presidency of fascist-tinged racist and misogynist Donald Trump is perhaps the most egregious of those "morbid symptoms." The ascendancy of a narcissist, bereft of core beliefs, promising to return the country to a lost mythical greatness and to regenerate employment out of dying industries appealed, in part at least, to workers who felt betrayed and forgotten by government and "elites."

The movement of voters to Trump, especially working-class voters, was a complex phenomenon. Filtering through the economic pain of working people was the latent presence of white supremacy cloaked in "dog whistles" promising to return the country to its (white) "greatness," to reverse the demographic onslaught of a diverse society built on multiculturalism. Racism and misogyny pulsated through Trump's campaign, consuming with varying levels of passion many followers, while others were principally motivated by deep economic grievance and responded to Trump's hyper-nationalist and right-wing populist ravings with acquiescence to its racist message, but with less enthusiasm.

Progressives cannot concede those aggrieved communities to Trump. With modesty and candor, without pretense and with clarity of language and argument, progressives can win those working people to the principles and programs fully consonant with their own interests.

Many currents are breaking through the "morbid symptoms" and cumulatively represent an influential counterforce against Trump's ascendancy to the White House. The Occupy Movement has challenged capitalist inequality. Black Lives Matter became a pivotal force in awakening protest and resistance to the long train of police violence against Black men and women—challenging a criminal justice system steeped in racism. Abysmally low wages were confronted by a movement (Fight for $15) from a rising multi-racial generation, largely of younger workers. New forms of labor organization, like community-based workers' centers, supplemented resurgent union combativeness, symbolized by the successful 2016 Verizon strike.

A growing, militant environmental movement—commensurate with the urgency of the planetary crisis—has challenged and at times defeated the fossil fuel industry. Movements to defend LGBTQ and women's reproductive choice rights, movements to overturn Citizens United and combat voter suppression, movements to fight student debt, movements for universal health care and economic justice all fed Bernie Sanders' remarkable Presidential campaign.

The unexpected success of the Sanders campaign was movement-driven. Its clarion call to end "big money" corporate influence in politics became the heart of the "revolution," affirming the importance of electoral battle joined to mass movements.

Crucially, the campaign established an undeniable Left pole in the country's political life. After a century of disregard, it brought socialism back into public discourse. Its 13 million votes, its 22 primary and caucus victories, its huge rallies, its large grassroots operation, and its ability to raise

tens of millions of dollars in small contributions—all confounded and undermined the corporate two-party duopoly, opening the door to unanticipated prospects for the Left in electoral struggle.

The Sanders campaign confirmed that the Democratic Party can become contested terrain, shaking the Party's corporate-influenced Establishment, striking a deeply responsive chord among young people, unlocking powerful energy in the millennial generation that has, as Sanders proclaimed, "won the future."

In the wake of the ill-fated election, the Sanders organization founded Our Revolution—an independent vehicle dedicated to continuing the movement to cleanse politics of corrupting corporate money, and to forcing open the doors of the Democratic Party to grass-roots participation. A promising mass movement fueled by millennial energy needs a strategic direction to bring that promise to fruition.

That strategy is more urgent than ever with Trump's election and its ugly validation of repression, racism, and misogyny. Forging a progressive majority powerful enough to challenge and throttle the proto-fascist current embodied by Trump must be the prime strategic objective of Sanders' movement and all progressive forces.

Energetic as the Sanders revolution proved to be, it has much more to do to achieve the numbers required to defeat the Right and advance its program of braking ecological disaster, curbing Wall Street, reforming the broken criminal justice system, advancing tuition-free education, as well as achieving universal health care and economic security for all working people.

A crucial starting point in building an indispensable progressive majority is the need to draw into coalition with the Left the liberal and Centrist organizations and individuals that supported Hillary Clinton. A distinction must be drawn between neoliberal corporate Centrism, represented by Hillary Clinton with her Wall Street supporters, and the Centrism of many Clinton voters who support progressive policies, but have fallen prey to skepticism about transformative change that has been in the country's marrow for centuries.

A crucial strategic objective in building a Left-Center majority is the linkage of Left groups with the powerful Centrist unions and national organizations that largely supported Hillary Clinton. The magnitude of the dangers inherent in a Trump Administration should facilitate Left-Center resistance along with a proactive fight to advance the Sanders program that corresponds to labor's own interests. The AFL-CIO, the American Federation of Teachers, the NEA [National Education Association], UAW [United Automobile Workers], SEIU, AFSCME [American Federation of State, County and Municipal Employees], and some others possess the resources, organization, and cohesion to play a role in helping the millennial "next Left" to adopt a strong, permanent presence. Large national organizations, like Planned Parenthood, the NAACP, liberal and progressive churches, and single-issue groups can be called upon to ally with the newly insurgent movements—Sanders youth, the Movement for Black Lives, Fight for $15, etc.—to support and strengthen intergenerational unity.

Bernie Sanders has called upon activists to contest for office from local school committees and municipal councils to Congress. That objective cannot be brought to fruition without vigorous organizing, linking movements to electoral strategies and candidates.

The debate lingers in progressive circles over whether Trump's unanticipated victory was due to deeply wounding inequality and voters' feelings of betrayal by those in power, or whether it was due to relentless racism and misogyny. The two elements are mutually reinforcing and inseparable. While one or the other of those currents varied in intensity among individuals, economic grievance yoked to deliberately misdirected racial and sexist resentment were staples of Trump's political arsenal. Given the inseparability of those elements, it is impossible to engage one without engaging the other.

Exit polling has confirmed that the bulk of support for Trump did not come from the lowest rungs on the economic ladder, but from typically Republican higher-income levels that surpassed Clinton's base in financial resources. But the support for Trump given by white men and women without college exposure was indisputable. Progressives have had little contact with that crucial constituency.

There was a time when the Left moved forcefully, resolutely, and at times successfully, to cement Black and white unity among working people. While that history is not fully analogous to the present, it nevertheless contains important insights for progressives seeking to build cooperation between whites and historically oppressed nationalities.

In the 1930s, organizers on the Left never hectored white workers about their "privileges." Rather, they spoke to the material conditions of all workers; they punctured the pablum of white supremacy, exposing it as a monumental hoax designed to drag down the living standards of both whites and Blacks. They hammered at the fact that the most economically, socially, and educationally depressed regions of the country were afflicted with the most severe forms of segregation and racist oppression. Leftists did not make appeals to either race based on sentimentality or moralism. They rooted their calls for bi-racial solidarity in concrete efforts to foment change—bringing Black and white together within the framework of specific campaigns for mutual survival and better conditions for all. For example, the call went out on March 6, 1930, for mass demonstrations across the country for "Work or Wages," demanding social insurance for the unemployed. That date marked the convergence of large numbers of impoverished whites and Blacks onto common ground in a struggle for survival. Today, with respectful dialog (especially exposing Trump's lies about "draining the swamp" of elite power and privilege), with efforts to advance the fight for $15 an hour, for the right of unions to organize, for resolutely combating growing inequality and advancing the interests of all races—the regressive front of white supremacy can be undermined and ultimately defeated.

A Left-Center alliance to defeat the Right wing holds within it the potential to extend the influence of the Left as the collaboration deepens and grows. The Left can influence the Center by virtue of its ideas and commitment to overcome the present crisis and usher in a revolution of expanded democracy and wealth redistribution. The strategy of a Left-Center alliance would include:

- linking issues and building multi-issue cooperation;
- confronting and overcoming an interventionist foreign and military policy;
- establishing a seamless relationship between electoral work and issue-oriented movement;
- seeking a non-contradictory relationship between those contesting in the Democratic Party and those working to build an independent party or movement;
- building a multi-racial unity and talking respectfully with white workers about the costs to them of institutional racism.

The country is entering a period of historic political realignment. Both parties are confronting internal strains, the consequences of which are as yet unforeseen. A striking analogy is the decade before the Civil War, when a large segment of the abolitionist movement understood that the successful emergence of a new anti-slavery party required the cultivation of anti-slavery forces in both major parties, the creation of an independent new party as a vessel for those leaving the old parties, and a breadth of vision that embraced the aspiration of liberation.

Let's hope that the newly energized progressive forces today grasp the vision and spiritual generosity of the 19th-century abolitionists. With so much at stake, the emergent progressive majority must prevail to secure peace, democracy, and justice.

Mark Solomon is Professor of History, Emeritus, at Simmons College and is an associate at the Hutchins Center for African & African American Research at Harvard University. He is author of The Cry Was Unity: Communists and African Americans *(1998, University Press of Mississippi).*

RIGHT-WING MOVEMENTS AND ELECTORAL POLITICS

Right-wing universalizing movements have been more committed and effective than Left universalizers in using electoral political means to advance their ends, leading in 2016 to the election of President Trump. The Far Right has long worked fervently to combine grass-roots populist and authoritarian movements that are anti-systemic with a commitment to electoral politics and, in the United States, taking over one of two mainstream political parties. Far more than the Left movements, the Right—forming the Tea Party as its main electoral organization—has worked at local, state, and national levels to run candidates, and take over town councils and state legislatures as well as the power centers of Washington DC through the Republican Party. As we show below, the Tea Party universalizing strategy to capture the Republican Party was so successful that it inspired progressives after Trump's election to create their own "Tea Party" strategy aimed at discrediting Republicans and transforming the Democratic Party.

The Right has shown that deep investment in electoral politics is a crucial universalizing strategy, and that political parties are by their nature aggregators of issues and identity groups.

The most powerful historical example of right-wing electoral universalizing is Weimar Germany in the 1920s, when the failure of liberal parties and electoral disengagement of Left movements opened the door to Far Right nationalist movements such as the Nazis. The analogy is not far-fetched in the United States today, in the age of Trump.

The political convergence of the Right escalated in a serious way with the election of Reagan, and reliance on uniting Southern Evangelists and conservative culture warriors with market libertarians and corporate elites. There were deep problems in these electoral universalizing coalitions, and they led to further electoral splits, with many populist conservatives forming the Tea Party, the Libertarian Party, and acting in and out of the Republican Party. The election of Donald Trump represented the latest and most triumphant stage of right-wing universalizing movement convergence through electoral politics. Even after Trump leaves office, Trumpism will remain a potent universalizing force on the Right, threating to turn American electoral politics into a breeding ground for an authoritarian extra-constitutional state in the name of constitutionalism.

The potency of political parties, even mainstream ones, as instruments for universalizing movements is a global phenomenon. In Europe, right-wing movements are sprouting up and universalizing through mass Far Right anti-immigrant parties from France to Germany to Hungary, exploding to a new level of mass organization after the 2016 UK Brexit vote. In the United States, the Republican Party is becoming so closely tied to right-wing populist movements that they are hard to disentangle. The Grand Old Party is, in many respects, itself a quasi-movement advancing the grass-roots transformational agenda of the religious Right, libertarian revolutionaries, white supremacists, and authoritarian militarists. It is capturing power in a state and local revolutionary electoral movement that is unprecedented, with governorships, and state and local governments falling like dominoes into the hands of the Tea Party and other Far Right groups. If Left universalizing does not make its own strong forays into electoral politics, it may find itself facing an electoral Far Right "soft coup," where what the political scientist Bertram Gross calls "friendly fascism" takes over, a product of right-wing universalizing movements understanding the connection between movement power and electoral strategies.

But there is another opening in electoral politics that has been highlighted by Ralph Nader. The right-wing populists, rooted in culturally conservative white workers, share many ideological elements with the Left. They are anti-"crony capitalism"—vehemently opposing Wall Street and big bank bailouts, corporate welfare, free trade agreements, big money in politics, as well as military interventions such as the 2003 war in Iraq and US troops on the ground in Syria. As discussed earlier (see Chapter 7), Donald Trump, Ted Cruz, and other leaders in the populist segment of the GOP that oppose the Republican Establishment have taken aim—at least rhetorically—at elements of crony capitalism and military spending—essentially taking "Left" positions from the Far Right (with the Right arising from racism, anti-immigration, and a more isolationist hyper-nationalism and "America First"-ism). Nader argues that this surprising alignment of Right and Left populism could transform American electoral politics. This could be a crucial dimension of the forays of progressive universalizing movements, looking to build the kind of populist grass-roots electoral coalitions around the Right–Left coalitions that Nader identifies. This is a challenging political coalition to create, but potentially part of a crucial universalizing to whites discussed throughout this book.

Nader has drawn another key lesson from the Right and the Tea Party. Small numbers of populist Tea Party members have had extraordinary success in organizing at the local level to take over local Congressional seats, state and local legislatures, school committees, and other key parts of the base of America's political system. This has been a remarkably effective coup, with small numbers of right-wing populists building from the ground up. Congressional district by Congressional district, they have changed the face of American politics, leading to the Republican Party total dominance achieved after the Trump election in 2016.

As Nader argues in his Interlude below, the Right has set a model for universalizing progressive and Left movements to follow. Small groups of activists—maybe just you and ten of your neighbors—in every Congressional district can gain remarkable power by going to the Congressional representative offices in their towns and putting unceasing pressure on them on everything from saving Medicare, to increasing the minimum wage, to eliminating Citizens United. And there is already movement of the kind Nader is proposing. Former President Obama has made such local mobilization his central goal in his own post-Presidential career. And Bernie Sanders' Our

Revolution has, likewise, made such mobilization of citizens in the local grass roots, in every Congressional district of the nation, a central priority. Another grass-roots organization, Indivisible (whose name itself suggests universalizing), has emerged as a progressive version of the Tea Party, working, along with Our Revolution, in seeking to take back Congress by supporting progressives and socialists to run for office at every level of politics. The goal is not just lobbying on issues, but electing progressives and Leftists to city halls, state legislatures, and Congress all over the country. This may prove to be one of the most potent ways in which our movements will universalize into the political arena in coming years.

UNIVERSAL MOBILIZATION: EASIER THAN GOING IT ALONE, ISSUE BY ISSUE

Ralph Nader

The great abolitionist, Frederick Douglass, declared: "Power concedes nothing without a demand; never has and never will." Logical follow-ups to this memorable exhortation are: "What, and strategically to whom, is the demand?", "What is necessary to turn the demand into change?"

There is a dampening quality to most progressive exposés, analyses, and advocacy. While we live in a golden age of muck-raking (books, articles, and documentaries pouring out daily), there are fewer positive results today than decades ago, when such output was a fraction of today's. One explanation is that exposés themselves often leave readers and viewers with nothing concrete to do. Witness Michael Moore's popular documentary, *Sicko*. After riling up the audience with outrageous stories, the last scene ends anticlimactically with Michael taking his dirty laundry up the Capitol steps. Investigative books are no better. Look at the last page or two of most muck-raking books and see how they tail off with some vague exhortation to get active, if that. It's as if getting concrete and programmatically strategic would take away from the artistry of the work.

Unfortunately, the progressive intelligentsia hardly read each other's works. They rarely come together to jointly strategize beyond their specific agenda; or about any of the larger-scale urgencies as we saw during past populist, labor, and civil rights movements. Progressive leaders often admit, when asked, that they don't even know what other progressives are doing, the Internet notwithstanding. There are, to be sure, exceptions to these generalizations about the self-limiting silo syndrome. "Can-do" neighborhood or community groups and some well-networked environmental groups are examples.

By and large, however, the continual deterioration of our democratic society, the relentless concentration of corporate power—economically, politically, culturally, psychologically, militarily, technologically—and the maturing corporate lock on the government, whose elected officials they fund, are racing far ahead of any self-restraint, accountability, or control under the rule of law. Power increasingly rules over law. Global corporations are power-concentrating machines. Opposing consumer, environmental, and labor groups are outnumbered, overpowered, and mostly on defense. Playing defense means almost never playing offense. This is a license for the corporate supremacists to rule over the unorganized populace driven to ever-lower expectations (or demands). Monetized elections are operated in their own zone of charade by a two-party tyranny that lunges to see who will service their corporate paymasters and weaken democracy. Notice how the entire civic community and its groups—the fountainhead, historically, of our striving for justice—are deemed by these parties and their "horse race"-obsessed media to be irrelevant and are regularly excluded from media coverage of elections.

Why, then, do I go around the country telling people that "it's easier than you think" to make serious changes in our country? Abraham Lincoln often said that "public sentiment" is everything, which today is described as public opinion. As my book, *Unstoppable: The Emerging Left–Right Alliance to Dismantle the Corporate State* argues, there has long been a broad convergence of agreement between Left and Right on many issues, especially when you deal with where people live, work, spend, and raise their families.

Binary politics thrives from the few real divisions between people. The drumbeats about "our polarized society" serve the agendas of the Republican and Democratic parties as well as the plutocracy. Divide-and-rule has been the tactic of ruling groups for thousands of years. Consider instead some areas of concurrence by the Left and Right that enjoy widespread public support, some as high as 70% or more—often a decisive eyebrow raiser for members of Congress. They include opposition to crony capitalism or corporate welfare, support for excision of anti-civil liberties portions of the Patriot Act, criminal justice reform, cracking down on corporate crime against consumers, clean elections, programs such as Medicare and Medicaid, worker rights and privacy, break-up of the big New York banks that are too big to fail, a higher minimum wage, not being the world's policeman, ridding the Defense budget of its enormous waste, revision of trade agreements, access to the courts, a Wall Street speculation tax directed to investments in public works and upgrades in communities throughout the country, shareholder power, clean air and water, stopping commercialization of childhood that undermines parental authority, and many more. In the past, despite strong corporate opposition with campaign cash, Congress handily passed the auto safety law (1966), the Freedom of Information Act amendments of 1974, the False Claims Act of 1986 and the Whistleblower Protection Act of 2013. Why? Left–Right support from back home.

Except for the Congressionally-generated GI Bill of Rights of 1945, almost every major stride for justice never required more than 1% active citizenry, a small number of full-time organizers, strategists, thinkers, and lawyers plus a swelling of majority opinion. These included advancing the right of women to vote, economic protections for farmers and workers, political reform, increased civil rights, environmental protection, disability rights, and consumer protections. The 1% estimate even includes the larger number of people who occasionally marched, demonstrated, or were engaged in non-violent, civil disobedience. A modest amount of money, often from unions or rich benefactors, helped pay the bills for this advocacy. The long decline and bureaucratization of unions have been devastating to the civic culture.

The point I'm making is that on issue after issue, the question that must be asked and answered is: what combination of energies is required to prevail? Not just brilliant exposés, diagnoses, and prescriptions. What is required is action on the ground and human and financial resources, all part of the process I call Subordination and Displacement.

Bringing overdue advances on behalf of a sovereign people under our Constitution requires subordinating corporate sovereignty to the sovereignty of the people, thereby stripping the artificial corporate entity of its personhood and equivalent constitutional rights that real persons, including those in corporations, have been accorded. *Subordination* is a key unifying reform for all these justice movements affected by corporatism. The second fundamental unifying direction is *Displacement*—or *what happens* as local economies receive tens of billions of consumer dollars for credit unions, local renewable and efficient energy firms, cooperatives, farmer-to-market vendors, community health clinics emphasizing prevention, and all sorts of small-scale, locally based, and accountable businesses. They diminish the sales of big corporations.

Control of Congress over time is the giant kick-starter of the processes of *Subordination* and *Displacement*. That means using Congress for what it is—the most generic and powerful of the three branches of our government with its powers to tax, appropriate, declare war, conduct oversight and investigative hearings, confirm nominees for the courts and government agencies, and pass citizen-empowering legislation. *Is there any decisional tool of a just democracy that is remotely comparable?* As Congress comes to operate under the influence of an organized people in each electoral district, mutually reinforcing specific redirections and reforms can be

enacted veto-proof, with great alacrity. Even modest public pressure back home led the Congresses of 1964 to 1974 to enact our generation's major civil rights, consumer, environmental, and worker protection laws and the crucial Freedom of Information Act amendments. Remember, information is the currency of democracy. I witnessed this productive output first-hand, day after day, in Washington DC. I noticed the impact a fraction of 1% of the people, backed by public opinion and a few full-time advocates, could have in passing laws that protect people and strengthen our democracy.

So let's ask the key question that allows our imagination to envision real possibilities. *What if* about 100 seasoned leaders and 100 promising young successors came together to determine what resources and level of organization are needed to take control of Congress for electoral reforms, long-overdue necessities for the people (many of which were already in operation in Europe soon after the Second World War), and to plan, foresee, and forestall perils rapidly approaching or on the horizon of a perceptive, deliberative, democratic society?

On a time frame of 36 months, spanning one election, they could reasonably conclude that a $200 million budget would be needed to start the requisite Congress advocacy groups in each Congressional district, backed by 2,000 serious people (totaling less than 1 million people), each pledging 200 hours of volunteer time, and donating or raising $200 each per year to open two offices in each district with four full-time "public citizens" directing action and coordinating these volunteers throughout their districts (each district has a population of about 700,000 persons).

Demonstrations and marches at key locations, including the local

Congressional offices, are important to spark the élan, raise visibility, and attract new recruits. However, the thrust of the pressure must be on laser-like, *in-person lobbying*. The most powerful lobbies do not engage in mass rallies and marches. They are acutely concentrated on *in personam* lobbying. They work to know everything they can about the Senators and Representatives—personal, impersonal, friends, relatives, how they spend their leisure, their tastes and dislikes, their staff, their physician, dentist, clergy, lawyer, donors, cronies back home, ambitions, weaknesses, skeletons in the closet, voting record, public statements at committee hearings and on the floor, etc. So it is not surprising that the NRA [National Rifle Association], AIPAC [American Israel Public Affairs Committee], the military weapons companies, and many commercial interests eschew public demonstrations that only energize the ether and bring unwelcome attention to their power. All these successful lobbyists provide large campaign contributions to obliging members of Congress. But lurking in the background, if these legislators stray, is the stick—namely, withdrawal of campaign money and a possible primary or general election challenger. These lobbies can shift some votes, but they cannot compare with the new Congress advocacy groups backed by majority public opinion, spreading their Left or Right roots all over the district. This is especially the case in the first 36-month session. Members of Congress fear new civic energies coming out of their constituency that they find unconducive to their gaming tactics and routines. Note the sudden emergence in 2009 of the tiny Tea Party in Congress.

This conference of 100 leaders and 100 successors will have to add up the assets they could assemble to get started as they convey their dramatic escalation of combined impacts to tap further energies within local communities. However, the pre-eminent hurdle they must overcome is whether they can invoke the crucial wisdom that "the whole is greater than the sum of its parts." Can they work together as a top priority, or will their silo-ridden, "hold the fort" routines make that impossible and require new organizations?

Our experience suggests that getting together existing capable groups to build a movement of far greater consequences and power is improbable. Being mostly on the defensive, their time cup is filled, their worries about meeting next year's budget are omnipresent. Sometimes they feel competitive with one another for funding or public attention, or access to friendly legislators. However, their long-time backers and their frustrations can move them to at least help to jump-start mobilizations toward the democratic civic transformations over corporatism and militarized Empire.

It comes down to, alas, money. Where can enough timely, agenda-supported funds come from? From social media, as with the remarkable Bernie Sanders campaign? A national political campaign with an organized civic foundation? A dutiful search for several enlightened billionaires unwilling to leave their country in such perilous decline for their descendants? All of the above? Clearly, some skilled extroverts of progressive bent need to be called to duty. Savvy people, who are persuasive in face-to-face meetings with pre-selected super-rich individuals. Two hundred million dollars can be compared with many similar or greater donations by individuals to universities or with Ted Turner's $1 billion to the United Nations. The examples are there for other very large donations.

By this time, readers may wonder why not much has been said about elections. Two explanations. First, when the people mobilize to recover the power they have given to Congress, incumbents begin changing their votes. Note the lessons of progressive history from needed regulation to social safety nets to the most recent turnaround on LGBT rights.

Who gave any of *them* a chance against the entrenched powers-that-be before Lincoln's "public sentiment" provided the cutting edge?

Second, the much-lamented gridlock in Congress due to divided government has revealed a serious fault line among progressives and others that can't be ignored. *They've largely given up on Congress passing their legislation.* "That's not where the action is," summarizes the astonishing responses I received from the offices of Al Gore, George Soros, and Tom Steyer, after sending them an outline for a powerful new citizens' lobby on climate change, saturating Congress daily and connected to groups back home.

Somehow the corporate world doesn't agree. With bi-partisan fervor, they attend to Congress, smothering that institution with lobbyists, getting their people installed in key staff positions, and pouring campaign money into the lawmakers' coffers.

A universal mobilization to recapture our national legislature, our most powerful instrument for justice, is the key to the future of a just country. We can start by organizing the required presence in each Congressional district and presenting a formal summons to each Senator and Representative to attend our town meetings around our diverse agendas. The active Sanders organizers and networkers should help to lead the way on this, not only attracting the large Sanders constituencies, but attracting Left and Right support into an unstoppable dynamic on Capitol Hill for democracy and justice.

We begin by announcing the emergence of the sovereignty of the people so revered in our Constitution's preamble! The election of civic champions will follow the rise of sustained civic power. It's easier than you think.

Ralph Nader *is the famed consumer advocate, former Presidential candidate, and author of many books, including* Unstoppable: The Emerging Left–Right Alliance to Dismantle the Corporate State *(2014, The Nation Institute). His latest is* Breaking Through Power: It's Easier Than We Think *(2016, City Lights Books).*

13

Think, Learn, and Teach: Education as Activism

"No oppressive order could permit the oppressed . . . to question: Why?"
Paulo Freire

"For the ancient Greeks, the ultimate test of the educational system was the moral and political quality of the students that it produced."
Henry Giroux

"To be changed by ideas was pure pleasure. But to learn ideas that ran counter to values and beliefs learned at home was to place oneself at risk, to enter the danger zone. Home was the place where I was forced to conform to someone else's image of who and what I should be. School was the place where I could forget that self and, through ideas, reinvent myself."
bell hooks

"American education has a long history of infatuation with fads and ill-considered ideas. The current obsession with making our schools work like a business may be the worst of them, for it threatens the survival of public education. Who will stand up to the tycoons and politicians and tell them so?"
Diane Ravitch

Ninth New Rule: Fight the corporatization of education! Stop endless testing and start endless critical thinking. Forever end the separation between learning and action!

Big Questions: How do we bring critical thinking and social movements into the schoolyard and on to the campuses? How do we help teachers help students to be their own thinkers and teachers? How do we make the classroom and the campus seedbeds, not only for service but activism?

Slogans: Stop the corporatization of education! Educate the educators! Learn through action and activism! Join the student movements on your campus and get an education that can change the world!

What's New Here: Young people have always sparked new movements, animated by their thirst for knowledge and their receptivity to new thinking and change. But in today's universalizing system, the schools and universities are being corporatized, creating a form of test-based, technical education designed to create acceptance of the system's authority rather than to question it. Critical thinking is the true mission of education—and in a super-universalized system, it is the only way to stop the transformation of education into indoctrination. Education is the ultimate foundation for universalizing movements, because critical thinking leads to asking the big questions and connecting the dots—fostering a way of thinking that is as universalizing as the system it must challenge and subvert. Education should always be the greatest aggregator of critical thinking and citizen activism. But as the corporate system takes over the schools and universities,

Student march against fees universalizing with worker resistance, London
© Elena Rostunova/Dreamstime.com

universalizing movements are beginning to emerge on campuses, challenging not only the corporatization of the university, but engaging with all the large social justice issues that are raging in the larger society. Universalizers always seek to build the home that they deserve in the schools and universities, whose mission, after all, is to cultivate thinking that is the foundation for universalizing resistance.

WHY UNIVERSALIZERS MUST OCCUPY THE SCHOOLS

The education system is a contradiction. It is part of the ideological apparatus of the system, inculcating capitalist values and thinking, and teaching conformity and acceptance of authority. Yet it is often the most liberal part of the ideological apparatus, sometimes encouraging creative and critical thinking, conducive to resistance. This reflects contradictions in the larger capitalist system, which requires obedience and loyalty to the system among the young, but in the high-tech "STEM" (Science, Technology, Engineering, and Mathematics) economy also needs schools to encourage scientific questioning and critical thinking.

This economic and cultural contradiction of capitalism opens the door to universalizing movements to influence what and how students learn. It is one of the most promising universalizing imperatives. Universalizers must occupy the school system and encourage teachers and designers of curricula to teach critical thinking in a participatory and dialogic style. In brief, we must teach a form of pedagogy of the oppressed that analyzes power in the system, the death culture of class and caste domination, the existential crises that can end the human experiment, and strategies of emancipation and saving the world.

Education is a key foundation for universalizing, as it can facilitate all other new rules of the road: it can build the foundations for a majoritarian new consciousness in the younger generation. It can help young people to analyze the system and teach anti-system ideas and system alternatives, especially in social science curricula. It can help "connect the dots" and fuel convergence by analyzing the "matrix of dominations" and the need for intersectional resistance. And it can help nurture the younger generation to move beyond passive citizenship into engaged social change. As bell hooks writes:

> The academy is not paradise. But learning is a place where paradise can be created. The classroom with all its limitations remains a location of possibility. In that field of possibility we have the opportunity to labour for freedom, to demand of ourselves and our comrades, an openness of mind and heart that allows us to face reality even as we collectively imagine ways to move beyond boundaries, to transgress. This is education as the practice of freedom.[1]

Sociologist and public intellectual, Henry Giroux, writes in the same spirit:

> Universities should be about more than developing work skills. They must also be about producing civic-minded and critically engaged citizens—citizens who can engage in debate, dialogue and bear witness to a different and critical sense of remembering, agency ethics and collective resistance.[2]

This concept of education is in danger of disappearing, which would be a disaster. We need the critical education that puts the system and its institutionalized injustice and racism and apocalyptic dangers into the full view of the younger generation, which already senses the dangers in its bones. In our current era of systemically-fueled injustice and existential crises, the most important civic function of education is to nourish the critical thinking and activism that can help the younger generation to analyze the super-universalizing apocalyptic system, and empower them to change it before it is too late.

CHALLENGING THE CORPORATIZATION OF EDUCATION

To live up to Giroux's vision, universalizing movements must combat the industrial–education complex where large corporations—and well-organized right-wing movements—are themselves moving rapidly and forcefully into education and fighting to shape the curricula and teachers according to their own worldview. This turns education into a mill for technical skills rather than a cultivation of critical thinking. These movements are trying to break teachers' unions even as they create a new class of adjuncts and underpaid teachers in charter and private schools. The right-wing aim is to create different curricula and stratified schools for the poor and the rich, and a strong focus on discipline, authority, and test-taking, ultimately challenging the public education system itself and seeking to privatize it.

Progressive and Left-leaning universalizers must battle to save the public school system, seeking to end its stratification by class and caste, and its authoritarian culture. They must enlist teachers in the mission that attracts many of them: to encourage creative learning and critical thinking in youth, and especially in those most impoverished and most in need of a pedagogy of the oppressed. This will require social justice movements to encourage empowerment of students; strengthen teachers' unions fighting for the freedom of educators to teach critical thinking; support parents and community organizations, especially in poor and working-class neighborhoods fighting to save their kids' creative imagination and activism; as well as participate in the reshaping of a curriculum. The fight around textbooks, which the Right wing has taken on, with massive funding, seeks to crush dissent among the young. This culture war in schools is the frontline of the larger culture wars about the system, and progressive universalizers must fully engage.

CREATING CRITICAL THINKING: PEDAGOGY OF
THE OPPRESSED FOR UNIVERSALIZERS

Pedagogy of the oppressed, the revolutionary vision of learning and schools proposed by the Brazilian educator and visionary, Paulo Freire, is an inspirational guide for universalizing movements. It recognizes that education is inherently political. In a world long divided into colonizers and the colonized, education must challenge the colonizers and their worldview, while encouraging students to affirm their own humanity and creativity as they educate themselves, in dialog with teachers and with their peers, how to live an emancipated life and make a democratic revolution.

The revolutionary work of Karl Marx and Frantz Fanon strongly shaped Freire's thinking, and it has influenced millions of educators, schools, and students around the world. Pedagogy of the oppressed can be viewed as a way in which resisters occupy the classroom and reconstruct it as a learning environment for critical thinking and system change. Education becomes melded with social change, and learning becomes a tool of disruptive resistance. Such resistance can be to the school itself, and as it universalizes, to the larger society. Pedagogy of the oppressed is associated with educational currents in elementary and high schools, but it is equally crucial for higher education, where the universalizing system is corporatizing the university. Students who are facing mounting debt in a lousy job market, and faculty facing adjunct positions that pay poverty wages and offer no security, are prime candidates for learning and teaching a pedagogy of the oppressed.

EDUCATION AS ACTIVISM

A small but influential sector of faculty, educated by professors who were radicalized in the 1960s, are critical thinkers who see their academic mission as creating a pedagogy of critical thinking that translates into resistance and transformation, targeting the corporatized university and society. Along with their students, they are engaging in universalizing resistance, whether it involves campaigns for the university to divest from fossil fuel companies, or building solidarity with poor communities in service and educational projects, or getting Wall Street and participating government and university agencies to forgive student debt. Black students on campuses are helping to lead movements against racism, seeing themselves as part of a new civil rights movement connected with Black Lives Matter. In 2015, after protests erupted against university racism at the University of Missouri, backed by Black student athletes, like-minded protests spread around the nation, evocative of the student movement in the 1960s. This challenges the most pathological element of our educational system which seeks to separate education from action or activism, as if true learning is corrupted when tied to social advocacy or transformation.

It is true that education should not turn into brainwashing or indoctrination of the sort that the state and media themselves seek to promote; it must encourage, above, all, critical thinking that teaches students to think for themselves. But, as Freire writes about schools, as well as all personal and social life, "washing one's hands of the conflict between the powerful and the powerless means to side with the powerful, not to be neutral."[3] Education that teaches students to separate what they learn from how they live, a tragic condition I have seen in far too many institutions of higher education, is ultimately sterile. But when education nourishes critical thinking and activism, which is the heart of the pedagogy of the oppressed, universalizing resistance can spread like wildfire through the younger generation and in the larger society, as it did in Bernie Sanders' 2016 campaign.

The pedagogy of the oppressed makes it clear that part of the challenge is not what—but how—to teach. The question is how to create a school and classroom experience that reflects the values of critical thinking, participatory democracy, and resistance or activism at the heart of progressive universalizing. The medium reflects the message, so teaching critical or system-challenging ideas may have little impact unless the classroom and the relation between teacher and students is anti-authoritarian, dialogic, and a reflection of the participatory democracy and system-change ideas that universalizing movements prize for the society. As Paulo Freire writes, "Education must begin with the solution of the student–teacher contribution by reconciling the poles of the contradiction such that both are simultaneously teachers and students."[4]

The system has created an educational system largely oriented toward discipline rather than resistance, toward passing tests rather than honing critical thinking, toward passive reception of facts rather than the creative empowerment and agency of students. As Henry Giroux writes:

> Today, in the age of standardized testing, thinking and acting, reason and judgment have been thrown out the window just as teachers are increasingly being deskilled and forced to act as semi-robotic technicians good for little more than teaching for the test . . .[5]

Ironically, the schools for more wealthy kids are more likely to encourage a degree of critical thinking (since many of these students will need the creative skills demanded by high-tech and creative jobs), and focus less on discipline and punishment than schools filled with poor kids and minorities, who are destined for dead-end, boring jobs. Bringing the pedagogy of the oppressed to schools in poor communities is thus a high priority for UR, to be realized by working in solidarity with socially committed teachers eager to teach the oppressed, and supported by teacher unions which are the target of intense hostility and punishment from right-wing movements.

Universalizing and occupying education thus require building alliances between community activists, teacher unions, and student rebels and organizers who create a new educational system prefiguring the ideals of a society based on critical thinking, empowerment, and resistance. Works by critical sociologists such as Giroux and Stanley Aronowitz, inspired by Freire, as well as best-selling educational critics such as Diane Ravitch, make compelling arguments for transformational education, showing how the system creates a deadening of the imagination, but a universalized "critical education" movement flowing into the schools can create a new generation of universalizing resisters.

PUBLIC HEALTH AND SOCIAL JUSTICE: TEACHING COURSE-BASED ACTIVIST SKILLS

Shelley White

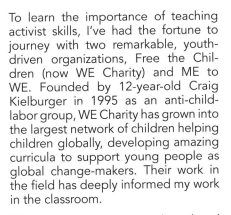

Teaching young people about social change, from elementary age through to adulthood, I have learned an important lesson: it's not enough to tell people who are moved by a sense of injustice to get out there and change the world. If we want them to be successful, we have to embrace our responsibility to teach a skill set for social change. Just as computer science or nursing students learn skill sets, students learning about social problems need to learn skills to address the systemic inequalities shaping our world.

As a scholar-activist teaching in Public Health, Sociology, and Social Justice programs, I have always valued introducing my students to the power of social movements to address the intersectional issues we are studying. This is particularly important when studying the history and contemporary context of inequalities; otherwise students can be left with the depressing and misguided notion that change is impossible!

To learn the importance of teaching activist skills, I've had the fortune to journey with two remarkable, youth-driven organizations, Free the Children (now WE Charity) and ME to WE. Founded by 12-year-old Craig Kielburger in 1995 as an anti-child-labor group, WE Charity has grown into the largest network of children helping children globally, developing amazing curricula to support young people as global change-makers. Their work in the field has deeply informed my work in the classroom.

With these lessons in mind, I piloted a new interdisciplinary course in 2015 titled "Public Health and Social Justice." It was developed for the Health Sciences Department and cross-listed in Sociology, Global Studies, Women's Studies, and Honors at Worcester State University. Many of my students faced systemic obstacles and oppressions themselves—as first-generation college students, immigrants and non-native English speakers, GLBTQ students, economically disadvantaged students, and students of color. Our study of local and global injustices was personal to many.

By design, I wanted this to be an "in action" course experience, challenging students not only to learn about social injustices, but to *do something* about them. The course had three major components:

1. We surveyed a variety of social justice issues, such as entrenched health disparities, food sovereignty and sustainability, water rights and privatization, institutionalized racism and sexism, and economic inequality. Inspired by Freire's *Pedagogy of the Oppressed*, we typically reserved 1 hour of our weekly seminar to engage in student-led dialog about social justice topics.
2. We reserved time each week to learn and practice organizing skills, including: public speaking, event planning, campaign design, publicity, engaging with mainstream media, leadership and teamwork, coalition building, power mapping, and more. Most importantly, students were guided through a careful action-planning curriculum I had helped to introduce to Free the Children years earlier.
3. Students engaged in action teams throughout the semester to design, carry out, and evaluate a campaign for social change. Each was supported by weekly reflective writing assignments where students analyzed content, processed skills modules, interrogated their own positionality, and created and evolved personal and team goals and plans. Students also engaged in peer review and problem solving, where action teams would present their ideas, plans, struggles, and strategies, and receive input from the full class community.

The team action projects were the driving force of the course experience—and they far exceeded our collective expectations! One team launched a new student organization, the Social Justice Coalition, establishing a membership of more than 80 students in one semester, and emerging as the most visible social justice student organization on the campus within a year. Another team organized the campus' first Fair Trade Fair, partnering with ten local vendors and organizations, and attracting 650 attendees for educational talks, chocolate, coffee, ice cream, and nut butter tastings—along with a petition campaign eventually gathering more than 1,000 Fair Trade request cards targeting the campus' food services.

Yet another team connected our food consumption with global warming and campaigned, successfully, for the campus to initiate Meatless Mondays in the main cafeteria's food line. One team examined the corporatization of water, gathering more than 100 pledges to kick the use of bottled water and collecting a similar number of petition signatures for Corporate Accountability International's campaign to stop water privatization in Lagos. Some students took on activist research projects in partnership with the Worcester Division of Public Health. One team examined community–police tensions post-Ferguson, completing a media content analysis, attending listening sessions, and organizing an expert panel to discuss a federal Department of Justice review of Worcester's policing practices.

Across each of these (and other) team projects, students learned important lessons:

1. Students learned that social justice issues are deeply interconnected—indeed, we engaged a universalizing framework to understand how racism is connected to

corporatization and militarism, how climate change is connected to health inequalities, how gender justice is connected to food justice, etc. We used an ecological model to understand the "upstream" nature of determinants shaping health and other inequities, and we emphasized the importance of tackling structural forces and oppressions.

2. Students also learned that social change requires a skill set—and they left having taken a giant leap forward in practicing those skills. Students' enthusiasm led to a unanimous decision to keep their core text, *Take More Action* (an ME to WE publication), an unusual decision for this largely financially-challenged student group. They said they expected to return to this skill-based book many times in planning their future social justice campaigns.

3. Students learned that action planning for social change is an iterative process that requires long-term commitment. Each team had great success, but each team also struggled and needed to problem solve, resolve conflict, and adjust their plans along the way.

4. Finally, students learned the importance of building a community around social justice organizing, one which transects silos of interest and identity. Through the course, students were introduced to some incredible mentors who modeled this ethic, and much more. Some were action-planning experts who taught skills, some were former course students serving as Student Teaching Assistants, and some were community organizers visiting to share their lessons from working on pressing challenges locally and globally. These experiences helped us to make universalizing connections, to see beyond our classroom and our campus, to connect across various social issues, to meet some inspirational individuals involved in justice movements, and to imagine the possibilities of broad, systemic change.

This course was a great success on many levels:

1. I received my favorite kinds of final course evaluations, where students reported that they worked much harder than in other courses, but valued this course experience deeply. In fact, the final evaluations were among my highest in my teaching career.

2. Students created tangible, long-term social change on our campus, and contributed to successful campaigns off campus. Even after I moved to a new university, the Social Justice Coalition continues to thrive, carrying forward our initial campaigns, innovating new projects, and mentoring a new generation of students. The potential for sustained social action is exciting!

3. Many graduated students have initiated careers or engaged in ongoing activism targeting inequalities. Indeed, those with jobs already found that their leadership on campus translated nicely into job-ready skills. These students continue to tackle local and global justice issues, such as HIV/AIDS, corporate power, climate justice, and other intersectional challenges. They are seeking true universalization.

Shelley White teaches Sociology and Public Health at Simmons College, where she serves as Director of the Master of Public Health in Health Equity program. Her scholarship focuses on global and domestic health inequalities, the politics and political economy of health and health policy, and social movements and social justice; she participates in global movements for trade justice, food sovereignty, children's rights, and health equity.

FROM SERVICE TO ACTIVISM

The system has channeled the natural impulses of young people to create a better and sustainable world into a culture of service rather than activism. Universalizing resistance in education has to address this taming of millennials, by recognizing the seeds of activism in service projects, and helping students to find their own path from service to resistance. This is a natural progression because service projects expose students to poverty, violence, hunger, and other suffering that leads to the question: why does a wealthy society create so many poor people at home and abroad? Students returning from service projects want to understand the roots of the suffering of the people they have just served.

Many "graduates" of community service look for courses concerned with political economy and social justice. They seek to understand the systemic roots of society's problems and how to make a difference. I teach many of these students. After getting their hands dirty building houses or dishing out food to the homeless and hungry, students returning from service projects often want to tie their learning to action. They enroll in classes that analyze the system and teach strategies of resistance and transformation, with some teachers and professors helping them dirty their hands and shoes by working in the communities surrounding their campus and cities where public suffering under the weight of the system is most agonizing.

The corporatized university resists the melding of learning and action, seeking to separate what students learn from how they live. The sociopathic compartmentalization is endemic to higher education and the whole society; universalizing resistance's aim, then, is to occupy education, and, in the face of deep institutional opposition by top administrators on campuses, demonstrate that students learn from activism—and that skilled resistance to the system is a strong indicator of students' knowledge and critical thinking skills. Grading is degrading, but students' academic merits and rewards should include an A for activism that flows naturally from the subjects they have been studying. In 2015, a new wave of student activism—led by African-American students against racism on campus, but joined by students of all races protesting against student debt, for free speech, for divestment of fossil fuel stocks held in the university portfolio, supporting unionization of adjunct faculty, and opposing the corporatization of the university—has promise of a new generation of students eager to universalize resistance and help to save the world.

Student activism in the United States and abroad may be enhanced by the rising acceptance of different races, nationalities, and sexual and gender orientations among younger generations that are increasingly educated and globalized. My own students tell me that they may not be as activist as the students of the 1960s, but they are creating a new culture of tolerance and

Women's March sign protesting Trump's border policy in Denver, January 21, 2017

Photo credit: Dean Birkenkamp

diversity. This has been catalyzed partly by their education, as well as their unprecedented global travel, and by social media connecting them across continents.

In their view, this new millennial culture has important implications for their own politics. They believe that they will resist the historical racism, sexism, and hyper-nationalism of past generations, and will embrace a new internationalism. Such internationalism may well turn into a universalizing movement for international human rights, peace, global worker solidarity, and the overarching fight against global climate change.

Much rests on whether my students are correct. Ultimately, it is their generation that will shape the future of movements universalized enough to save the planet. The mass outpouring of students on campuses opposing Trump's election—and some of the largest protests ever rallying against his inauguration in Washington DC—may well be a harbinger of the generational politics my students believe is possible. Threatening all the core millennial values of diversity, tolerance, environmental sustainability, and economic justice, Trump may be a core catalyst for a new student universalizing movement seeking a new society based on social justice and democracy.

Universalizing millennials, raised in a new culture of diversity and global consciousness—and uniting resistance to Trump—may create a global politics of universal human rights. The vision of such rights was expressed in the 1948 Universal Declaration of Human Rights, adopted by the United Nations.

Protest for immigrant rights and support of Dreamers
© Juan Camilo Bernal/Dreamstime.com

A universalizing global politics of student movements in scores of nations, all oriented toward ensuring a new global system of internationalism and universal rights, is one of the most promising prospects of the millennial generation, which has the potential to turn universal resistance into a universalizing movement for universal rights.

GENERATION *Y NOT*: MILLENNIAL ACTIVISM FOR MULTI-ISSUE STRUCTURAL CHANGE

Jonathan White

Robert Kennedy, paraphrasing George Bernard Shaw, once said "Some men see things the way they are and ask 'Why?' I dream of things that never were and ask 'Why not?'" We have in front of us today the most attuned and action-ready generation since the 1960s: Generation Y (A.K.A. the millennials). This appears to be a generation of young people increasingly disillusioned with the powers that be, and they are seeking ways to use their skills to force change. More than in prior generations, millennials seem to have a deeper grasp of the interconnectedness of issues, and thus, that it is essential to universalize, as embodied, for instance, in the Occupy Movement, the Bernie Sanders campaign, and the WE Movement.

I am consistently impressed with how much more this new generation is looking to ask "Why not?" about a different world system, and how much more sophisticated they are in seeing intersectionalities of issues and the need to universalize their activism. The *American Freshman: National Norms* survey (2015) backs this up, reporting that the percentage of incoming students who indicate that there is a "very good chance" that they would participate in student protests is at the highest level since 1967.

In my previous teaching position at Bridgewater State University in Massachusetts, I worked with a group of students who formed the Social Justice League. They developed an impressive movement on a campus that, until then, had little social justice activism. This group educated the campus on a wide range of domestic and global issues, and effectively challenged the administration with thoughtful and strategic confrontation. Moreover, they intentionally created universalized bridges on and off campus with multicultural and GLBTQ student groups, environmental clubs, etc., and with off-campus groups such as the local Unitarian Universalist congregation, Free the Children, Witness for Peace, Fair Trade Campaigns, and Occupy Boston. The justice issues they tackled ranged from homelessness to refugees, from racism to war, from hate crimes to genocide, from domestic labor abuses to global labor abuses, from GLBTQ rights to disability rights.

Each fall, they slept out in the middle of campus for a week in a makeshift "Tent City," raising awareness about homelessness, bringing speakers, garnering media attention from *The*

Boston Globe and other media, and helping to activate the administration to create new campus programs addressing homelessness.

This student movement—strategic, skillful, and confrontational when needed—scored many successes. The campus bookstore sold "sweat-free" products, the university took measures to become a Fair Trade University, cafeteria workers received better wages and benefits, a hate crime against a gay student was confronted with a powerful march and activist rally, the campus integrated social justice into its mission (and practice) in meaningful ways, and several other student activist groups were created.

Likewise, students in high schools and colleges across the nation are realizing their activist power, bringing attention to social justice issues, and demanding action for structural change. Today's students are not rallied around a singular issue, but instead are tackling myriad domestic and global issues in parallel. Nationally, most notable are issues of racism, policing, GLBTQ rights, climate change, fair and living wages, healthy and fair food systems, and the wealth gap. Some, amongst many recent examples, include:

- Seventy-five higher education institutions faced demands from student activists on a variety of racism issues, demanding policy change (91%), increased resources (88%), better/further anti-racism training (71%), and deepened curriculum (68%).
- In the state of Washington, a group of 12–16 year olds calling themselves The Climate Kids are rallying for the Department of Ecology to create stricter regulations on carbon emissions.
- On commencement eve, the University of Chicago's Student President and 33 other students took over the university President's

office, demanding living wages for campus workers, greater account-ability from university police, and divestment from fossil fuels.

- At CalArts, 200 students walked out of classes, with some briefly taking over the administration office, to protest the school's han-dling of a rape case. They used the protest to develop a set of changes, much of which the school later agreed to.
- A student at Columbia University carried the mattress upon which she was sexually assaulted around campus to protest the universi-ty's inaction against her assailant, bringing broad attention on cam-pus and nationally. Hundreds of her classmates, as well as students from 130 colleges, joined her. Protests against the seemingly universal sweep-under-the-carpet approach of universities are forc-ing them to develop new systems to more effectively handle college rape and sexual assault, and have led the U.S. Department of Educa-tion to investigate 94 universities for possible Title IX violations.
- Colgate University students staged a 5-day occupation of the Admis-sions Office, forcing many conces-sions around issues of racism and diversity, based on their 21-point action plan.
- Syracuse University students over-took the administration building for 18 days, winning concessions on their demands, such as more scholarships for non-white stu-dents and the hiring of more men-tal health professionals.
- Duke University students occupied the President's office for a week, demanding employee rights and a $15 per hour wage.
- Over 600 Tufts University students protested the death of Michael Brown in Ferguson by lying down in the middle of traffic in the cold of December for 4.5 hours, the same amount of time that Brown's body was left in the street after being shot.

As student debt has increased from an average of just over $16,000 per student in 2000 to just over $26,000 in 2016, and as young people see this rise as stemming from an unfair sys-tem, it has also opened students' eyes to wider economic, systemic forces that are harming the middle and lower classes. This is a major reason why Bernie Sanders, who advocated "dem-ocratic socialism" and "political revo-lution," had a 55% favorability rating amongst millennials.

There remains the misperception that this generation is somehow apathetic and uninvolved. In fact, they are more active than most prior generations, though they are spread out over a wider array of issues. This is why I believe the universalization of their issues into an intersectional movement is absolutely crucial, in order to lend power to each other, to increase the visibility of aggregated unrest, and to parlay this into a broader movement that challenges systems of political, economic, social, and cultural injustice.

My students at Bridgewater were the most effective students I've ever worked with. The key to their success was their intentionality in creating a universalized movement on campus, eliminating issue silos, so that various student activist groups could count on each other for support. *Generation Y Not* is asking *why not* create a world with justice along racial, gender, sex, age, and ability lines; *why not* create a world with justice for laborers and cooperativism rather than corporatiza-tion; and *why not* create a world with a planet that has a future? For those of us in older generations, it is important to recognize this moment of increased student activism, and to lend our skills and experience to the movement they are creating.

Is this the generation we've been waiting for? If they have the right support, I would have to ask Y Not?

Jonathan White, Associate Professor of Sociology at Bentley University and Director of the Bentley Service-Learning and Civic Engagement Center, has co-authored books including The Engaged Sociologist *(with Kathleen Odell Korgen; 5th edition, 2015, Sage),* Sociologists in Action: Sociology, Social Change and Social Justice *(with Kathleen Odell Korgen and Shelley K. White; 2nd edition, 2014, Sage), and* Sociologists in Action on Inequalities: Race, Class, Gender, and Sexuality *(with Kathleen Odell Korgen and Shelley K. White; 2014, Sage). He sits on the Board of Directors for several global social movement organizations and is chair of the US Board for Free the Children/WE.*

14

Choose Life and Love:
The Culture of Activism

"We cannot in all good conscience obey your unjust laws, because noncooperation with evil is as much a moral obligation as is cooperation with good. Throw us in jail, and we shall still love you. Bomb our homes and threaten our children, and we shall still love you. Send your hooded perpetrators of violence into our community at the midnight hour and beat us and leave us half dead, and we shall still love you. But be ye assured that we will wear you down by our capacity to suffer. One day we shall win freedom, but not only for ourselves. We shall so appeal to your heart and conscience that we shall win you in the process, and our victory will be a double victory."

Martin Luther King (letter from Birmingham jail)

"Because love is an act of courage, not of fear, love is a commitment to others. No matter where the oppressed are found, the act of love is commitment to their cause—the cause of liberation."

Paulo Freire

"If I can't dance, I don't want to be part of your revolution."

Emma Goldman

"Be the change you want to see"

Gandhi

Tenth New Rule: Build activist universalizing movements of love and solidarity! Disrupt the system with every non-violent strategy and tactic that build the universalizing thinking and spirit of the movement! Connect with other movements to challenge the system with humor, invitations, non-cooperation, and inclusive diversity!

Big Questions: How do you engage in disruptive universalizing resistance that builds public support and does not alienate large sectors of the public—and attracts other movement organizations? How do you avoid the mistakes of earlier Left movements? How do you overcome organizational hurdles that prevent you from connecting and working closely with other organizations and movements? How can the movements embody the life culture rather than the death culture? How can the life culture create the big change among a mass base that can save the world?

Slogans: Love your comrades! Love also your enemy! Walk your talk! Disarm with humor! Connect all the issues! Non-violence forever!

What's New Here? As the universalizing system spreads greed and apocalyptic violence—fomenting a death culture spreading throughout the world—universalizing movements succeed by walking their talk of an alternative system based on non-violence, community, and love. Silo movements and earlier anti-systemic movements often have aspired to the same values. But it is especially important now, as more people succumb to despair, isolation, and the weakening of the will. Universalizing movements must be the incubators of another way of loving and living, showing in their own culture and actions that people working for change together can find a purpose and pleasure in life. When movements achieve that non-violence, solidarity, and joy, they will attract vastly more supporters, connect far more readily with other activist organizations, and carry out winning campaigns for system change. Joining movements—and a movement of movements—will be the way for millions to find a reason for living and loving, most of all to save the world itself.

WALKING THE TALK: MOVEMENTS MUST LIVE THEIR OWN VALUES OR BURN OUT

The forms of resistance movements and their strategies must be guided by non-violence, democracy, solidarity, and other life-affirming values. The system is eroding the will to live of millions of people globally. Universalizing resistance's most important task is to build a movement of movements that revives among participants and the general public the love of life. Ultimately, movements can build a mass following and create transformation only if they build within the movement solidarity, meaning, and affirmation of life.

While non-violence and love define the struggle, that does not mean holding back from militant non-cooperation that shuts parts of the system down. Quite the contrary! Resistance can be symbolic, but at its core it must also be empowering and even shocking, in the sense of awakening the people to the evils of the system and the terrifying end-result if we allow business as usual to continue. Resistance is rage at injustice and at the insanity of institutions that kill and exploit for money and power. Melding that rage with love is the art of activism.

THE DYSFUNCTIONAL CULTURES OF MOVEMENTS: HOW EASY IT IS TO REPRODUCE THE VERY SYSTEM ONE IS FIGHTING

Since the resistance movements are themselves part of a sociopathic society, they are shaped by it even as they resist it. Too often, movements have reproduced the sociopathic competitiveness, ego-tripping, isolation, dogmatic thinking, and hostility that define the larger system. The power of the universalizing system to infiltrate resisters and resistance organizations renders difficult the creation of life-affirming movements that are not marked by their own death culture.

In the Ear to the Ground study, many activists reported disillusionment, negativity, and a sense of despair in their movement experience. They persevered, not because of what they experienced in the movements, but because of their strong personal commitment to the cause. NTanya Lee and Steve Williams summarize it as one of the greatest problems:

> *30 percent of participants said that the culture of the social justice movement is too negative, and reproduces destructive practices we've learned from the broader society. Participants were particularly passionate about this subject, sharing frustrations with aspects of movement culture that "sometimes make us our own worst enemies," including: "ego-driven" work not in the movement's best interests; organizational competitiveness and divisiveness; harshly judgmental and disrespectful interpersonal behavior; overwork, martyrdom and self-marginalization; and a culture that often communicates more anger than hope.[1]*

BUT MOVEMENTS CAN SAVE YOUR LIFE WHILE THEY SAVE SOCIETY AND ALL LIFE

Although activists describe such negative movement experience with disappointing frequency, many activists also offer far more uplifting reports. In Vivian Gornick's memoir of the 1930s Communist Party in the United States, *The Romance of American Communism*, she documents how the movement created an intimate community of "beloved" comrades who married each other, studied and learned together, created their own culture and music, and a purposeful life working for social transformation, an altogether life-affirming society despite the pathologies of doctrinal Stalinist ideology that ultimately destroyed the movement. Indeed, challenging the system may be the most powerful way to affirm life, a reality that should draw millions of people to movements to revive their own sense of purpose and will to love and live.

Movements today are still more than capable of infusing the lives of many contemporary activists with meaning and hope. One activist from Atlanta in the Ear to the Ground study said:

> I was really angry for a long time. I was lucky that as a teenager, I was mentored by people who recognized my anger and channeled it. They started sending me to all these trainings, very pre-organizing, but it flipped the script for me. I had to take responsibility. I'm either going to die from the rage or transform it . . . **Honestly, I feel like organizing saved my life.**[2]

Another activist interviewed in the same study, a student from Chicago, reported a similar uplifting:

> I didn't grow up understanding what racism, classism or sexism were— although of course they impacted me. I just felt like something was wrong with me and my family. I just internalized oppression, struggled with mental health issues. There was no counter-message. But then I got politicized in college and I began to understand my life. I found activists and organizers. I spent spring break with an indigenous resistance movement, and I came alive for the first time. So many things burst open in me. It gave meaning to studying, to being on the planet. I was able to channel my rage in a targeted, strategic way, to move through it, and move past it with a sense of energy and purpose.[3]

The forms of the movement—its structure and culture—will help determine whether the movements themselves can provide an alternative to the system's death culture. What does this mean for the organization of the movements? They must incubate in their own organizations and actions the structures and values they seek to spread in the larger culture. Historically, universalizing movements have contributed to their own destruction by reproducing the larger system's hierarchies of power, dogma, violence, and even the will to die (redefined by many revolutionary activists in history as meaningful sacrifice in the service of revolution).

THE STRUCTURE AND CULTURE OF LIFE-AFFIRMING MOVEMENTS: LOVE IS THE ANSWER

Avoiding this trap requires embracing anti-systemic, new, and experimental structures and values: organizational and movement democracy; "leaderful" organizations in which leadership roles are rotated among all the members; a high proportion of empowered minority and female participants; an organizational culture rejecting the dogma, egoism, and status-striving dominant in the larger system; and a movement embrace of cooperation, solidarity, love, and community.

The Occupy Movement became both famous and infamous because of its commitment to leaderlessness, horizontality, rituals of collectively repeating each person's words in a "General Assembly," and equal participation for everyone. The mass media ridiculed many of these as meaningless rituals and utopian anarchism, and even some Occupy activists got fed up with the endless talking and rituals of participation. Yet the right to speak, especially in public space, and the commitment to democratic models affirming community and the self-worth of each person in public democratic assembly is hardly trivial. It signaled mass resistance to the closing of public space and free speech by a system increasingly repressive of dissent, and helped activists to enact a way of being that was different from the way they had been raised.

Because activists are raised in the system they are fighting, they must fight sociopathic principles of competition, greed, and egoism. Building a universalizing movement means rebuilding the core of our own identity and owning up to sociopathic impulses that we must fight in ourselves. Such internal intra-personal movement "work" is essential to authenticity and success for universalizing activists.

A LOVE SUPREME

Matt Nelson

"The concepts of love and power have usually been contrasted as opposites, polar opposites, so that love is identified with a resignation of power, and power with a denial of love . . . What is needed is a realization that power without love is reckless and abusive, and that love without power is sentimental and anemic. Power at its best is love implementing the demands of justice, and justice at its best is love correcting everything that stands against love."

Martin Luther King ("Where Do We Go from Here?", 1967)

Mothers are among the 34,000 immigrants required to be detained on any given day, per Congressional mandate in the Department of Homeland Security's Appropriations Act. In 2009, the Women's Refugee Commission reported that women represented 10% of those in detention. That was prior to the "border crisis", which saw thousands of Central American women come to the United States seeking asylum.

"These mothers—our mothers and our families—deserve love, not imprisonment." This was the rallying call from thousands of loving, compassionate Presente.org activists and our partners who asked the nation a question: how would you feel if your mother were locked up just because she did everything she could to make a better life for herself and her family?

As one can imagine, Mother's Day can be a difficult time for those who are not able to be with loved ones. So, on Mother's Day 2016, Presente. org hoped to inspire the much-needed persistence, compassion, and resilience necessary to end mass incarceration and the horrible private prison industry that separates families, through a powerful show of love for mothers.

Presente.org partnered with Forward Together, CultureStrike, Northwest Detention Center (NWDC) Resistance, and other organizations. Activists and artists across the country collab-orated to create cards of hope, love, solidarity, and resistance through the "Strong Families Mama's Day" e-card campaign.

The result was an amazing action in which activists delivered hard copies of more than 5,000 cards to mothers into more than a dozen detention centers across the country, including the Berks Family Residential Center in Berks County, Pennsylvania—an ICE [Immi-gration and Customs Enforcement] detention center that lost its operat-ing license in February 2016 due to its unlawful practice of imprisoning immigrant families, including children. At the time of this writing, many of the mothers in this facility are on hunger strike protesting their detention and the conditions at the detention facility.

We leveraged Mother's Day to support the growing numbers detained, and to shine a light on the devastation caused by private detention centers. Presente. org and our partners were able to har-ness the universal, supreme love for mothers into a campaign against the inhumane practice of detaining moth-ers and separating families.

The Mother's Day action, equal parts organizing and love offering, high-lighted a critical dichotomy: the poli-cies of those in power are driven by a racist culture and the profit imperatives of the larger militarized capitalist sys-tem, without regard to the humanity of that policy's victims. In other words, the policies of those in power lack love. By contrast, those protesting are replete with love, but often lack the power to implement policies reflective of that love. One side has all the power and none of the love, while the other side has love to spare, but little power.

In a real, tangible, and fundamental way, our work must put some power behind our love in order to put some love inside of power.

Movement building and culture shifts—that have real power—are driven by love, which is too often deprioritized and given the back seat to talking points and short-term tac-tics. Although sometimes fueled by rage, which is often another form of love, strong feelings and emotional connections inspire deeper action, which can lead to transformative work.

Our work should reach people's hearts and spark their imagination, not just their short-term, logical minds. And to build a powerful, lasting, and growing movement, we cannot just be fighting against something. We also need to be moving forward values-based orga-nizing, leading people to say "Yes!" to a better world. We need to elevate the stories of people who are otherwise forgotten in order to inspire more of us to participate in making the world a beloved community.

This values-based organizing approach is felt throughout all of our campaign-ing. Presente.org is the nation's larg-est online Latinx (of Latino extraction) organizing group, advancing social justice through technology, media, and culture. Our campaigns program exists to build Latinx political power and deeply engage the dynamic, multi-racial, multi-gender, and multi-generational Latinx diaspora in the practice of liberation and the undoing of oppression.

Even as a national digitally-native orga-nization, we understand the power of connection and sharing stories across bars and borders online and offline.

With dual goals of building a powerful organization and making concrete improvements in the lives of Latinx, we work with our members, partners, and allies to create bold, winning campaigns that amplify Latinx voices. We fight for the dignity of all peoples, recognizing that the Latinx community can only empower itself as part of a larger struggle against racism, sexism, and militarized capitalism.

We see our action as a form of universalized resistance—in the spirit of liberating all those unjustly incarcerated. We see it as an act of love and solidarity with the millions of people, from all communities, who are brutally locked up, with their families torn apart.

Love shows up in the way we support our allies from the Movement for Black Lives, worker rights movements, and those who have been incarcerated and their families. Love shows up in how we organize with you. It shows up in how we talk about policy and how we reach people through art and culture, knowing that when our people are connected to each other—hearts and minds—we go beyond transactional campaigning and into the realm of transformational change. Culture-shift guided by love and human compassion can be an inspiring and universalizing force of resistance, uniting many different communities and causes. And to create lasting change is to know that our movements are bigger than any one person, group, state, or country.

The huge response to our call for Mother's Day cards attests to how powerfully this cultural movement-building strategy resonated with our members for several reasons.

First, culture is an appealing way for people to engage. People often fail to prioritize culture and culture-based strategies, but culture creates a participatory influence. Artists build trust.

There are multiple ways to tell a story, with art as an effective organizing and movement-building tool that evokes an emotional response. To build empathy, we create ways for folks to feel.

Also, when we asked people to write a card, we created a human way to connect and form a participatory bond with another person you may never meet, which requires imagination. When you sign on to something, you affirm your agreement; when you participate and use your imagination, however, you invoke an emotional response that is more powerful than knowledge. Logic alone is not enough to create behavior change, which requires emotion. Good technology, good imagery, good user design—and, of course, compelling cultural content—are the elements to create a successful campaign with strong, deep participation.

When our activists make the emotional connection, they take deeper action in our crimmigration (criminal justice plus immigration) campaigns. They understand that these oppressive systems work in tandem and embolden our oppressors, our abusers, and our de-humanizers—while undermining our fundamental right to safety and dignity. WE ARE HUMAN! For many immigrant mothers, the primary motivation behind leaving their home countries is for a better life for their families. The real crime is that these acts of love and sacrifice are even considered criminal, and that these families are made invisible by the dominant culture and racist bias. With so many families celebrating their first Mother's Day in the United States in prison, we must move from solitary to solidarity.

Love, courage, dignity, and full humanity can be universalizing forces. If strong enough, these powerful feelings offer new momentum that can counter the current universalizing forces of corporate capitalist exploitation, militarism and violence, patriarchy, and racism. The near-term result will be much-needed relief for those on the frontlines of this fight—and policies that better support us and our families across the country.

The politics of love, with thousands and thousands of activists acting in solidarity against current leadership, can tip the scales, and not only liberate our mothers, but transform our entire culture and political system.

And at the end of a brutal election season, we find ourselves living in a moment when anti-immigrant rhetoric, racism, and xenophobia are reaching a fever pitch in the United States. Trump represents the convergence of white supremacy and corporate domination, or "power with a denial of love," fueled by racist culture and by the profit imperatives of our larger militarized capitalist system.

In the Trump era, private detention centers are primed to become immensely profitable, a "growth industry" much like private prisons. Under the Trump Administration, corporations will increasingly make profit from further criminalizing our communities and accelerating mass incarceration,

unless we stop them. Our actions universalize across race and economic power systems. We combat hatred of immigrants with struggle against corporations profiting off racism, and our anti-corporate action is driven by love for immigrants and all others subjected to corporate abuse.

In the face of a government that will force deportations, engage in ruthless privatization and rabid sexism, cultivate overt appeals to white nationalism and enforce brutal crackdowns on protesters, we have a duty and responsibility to act, to build, and to resist hate, fear, and violence. His agenda must be opposed at every turn with thoughtful, effective strategy and powerful, loving, unprecedented organizing.

Matt Nelson is the Executive Director of Presente.org—the nation's largest online Latinx organizing group, advancing social justice with technology, media, and culture. Before his work at Presente.org, Matt was the Organizing Director at Color Of Change, and has co-founded several cooperative enterprises in multiple Midwestern cities; he was also featured in the first major book on the Ferguson Uprising, entitled Ferguson Is America: Roots of Rebellion *(Jamala Rogers, 2015).*

ONLY NON-VIOLENT MOVEMENTS CAN FIGHT SYSTEMIC VIOLENCE

Universalizing movements have to sort through complex issues of strategies and tactics. In the spirit of affirming the life impulse, six principles seem particularly important:

1. *Total Commitment to Non-Violence.* Since violence is a defining feature of the system, any movement violence involves an embrace of the system's core logic and its death culture. A long tradition of non-violence, illustrated by Gandhi and Martin Luther King, and articulated in the classic work of non-violence theorist, Gene Sharp, has shown that non-violence is the moral imperative, and the most effective way to elicit non-cooperation with the system in the population and build support for the movement. As Sharp cautions, "By placing confidence in violent means, one has chosen the very type of struggle with which the oppressors nearly always have superiority."[4]

Non-violence is increasingly important as militarism of all forms pervades the American system, driven to new heights by fear-mongering about jihadi attacks. Violence is moving to the white-hot center of the American regime. Non-violence, then, becomes the essential means of authentically negating the system itself. Embrace of violence dooms universalizing movements by essentially reproducing the most sociopathic quality of the system they are fighting.

This commitment to non-violence helps to distinguish right-wing and left-wing universalizing movements. The history of both Right and Left movements globally is written in blood, with Jacobins and Stalinists and Maoists as murderous as Hitler.

In the United States, non-violence is a core value of progressive universalizing movements and when Left movements become violent, they degrade the humanity and liberation of their resistance. In the 1960s, some white Leftist students in SDS (Students for a Democratic Society) formed the "Weathermen" and turned to violence, romanticizing the violence of the Black Panthers, with disastrous effects. The bulk of the US Left, however, both in the 1960s and throughout American history, has tended to reject violence and see non-violence as both the only moral form of resistance and the most effective.

Right-wing movements, on the other hand, often use violent rhetoric, with some viewing violence as their most important strategy. This is true especially of extremist racist groups such as the Ku Klux Klan (KKK) and anti-government militias who blow up government buildings. The landscape of the US Right is littered with violence, in the form of lynchings, shootings of civil rights workers, and attacks on minorities, immigrants, and Left activists protesting peacefully on the streets—or even just seeking to vote.

The rhetoric of violence has entered a new phase with the nomination and election of Donald Trump—and the rise of Trumpism. Trump gained attention by threatening to "punch out" protesters at his rallies in the 2016 Presidential primaries and refusing to condemn supporters who punched, pushed, or even yelled death threats to anti-Trump activists. Trump's embrace of violent rhetoric signaled a new stage of mainstream right-wing strategy that found its way into the center of 21st-century Republican Party politics. No wonder so many saw Trump as the rise of an American fascism.

2. *A Passion for Truth and Justice.* This commitment to truth must be uncompromising, no matter how "extreme" or brazenly disruptive it seems in the light of the ideology propagated by the system itself. Non-violence, in the context of universalizing, is anything but moderate. Non-violent universalizers will achieve their ends only if driven by utterly principled convictions

that are heresy in the mainstream. Like the "crazy" people locked up in the asylums in the film, *Shoot the Moon*, universalizers are the incarcerated people who are the beacon of sanity in the larger world. Sublime madness is both moral—and likely the most efficient strategy and state of mind of universalizing movements in their early stages. Such "madness" leads to civil disobedience, flash mobs, die-ins, blocking traffic, blocking coal mountaintop removal and oil and gas pipelines, sit-ins, street theatre, lockouts, wildcat strikes, tax resistance, general strikes, and other disruptive practices.

The challenge is to carry out truly disruptive actions that prevent the system from operating normally, frightening the elites, while drawing in large parts of the population who dislike the "disorder" that disruptive resistance can easily appear to promote. This is one of the strategic paradoxes of universalizing movements, because the urgency of the system crises requires repeatedly showing that the system and its elites can and must be obstructed, shamed, and stopped by relentless disruption, even while inviting in popular majorities. This seems paradoxical, but French unions have sometimes shut down public transit in ways that deeply inconvenience commuters and ordinary French citizens, while maintaining citizen support. They have built a reputation of not just fighting for their own union members, but for the most essential needs of the entire population.

This is an incredibly important lesson to be absorbed by the protesters rising up against Trump and the Republican Party. After Trump's election, millions took to the streets with righteous outrage about his Mexican wall, Muslim ban, attacks on women's rights, and many other bigoted policies. Other protestors flocked to town hall meetings to express rage at the terrifyingly regressive budgetary, environmental, and social policies of the Republican Party and their own Congressperson. The anger and disruption has been healthy and necessary, a sign of rational rage against a sociopathic power elite in Washington DC. But the rage has to be combined with an invitational spirit that draws in millions of more citizens to join the protests. The paradox is to meld the rage with love, to combine anger with humor, to block the system while beginning to build a new one that will provide benefits and life itself for virtually the entire population, including many who voted for Trump.

This is the key to the Trump era of dissent. Create militant disruption while manifesting a love and solidarity that draw more and more people—even those inconvenienced by the protests. A universalizing movement can win only by melding rage and disruption with a loving spirit that draws strong support from the majority not on the streets.

3. *Go for the Gut.* Universalizers must personalize issues that seem remote or abstract to many Americans, whether war or climate change. The system

is cancerous. Universalizing movements must show that the cancer is spreading and that survival and wellbeing—and the survival of all humanity—depend on fighting the system with the same intensity and concentration that they would fight a cancer within themselves. Universalizers should learn from feminism that movements must always create a politics that is personal.

4. *Confront and Invite.* Universalizing movements must present the face of invitation as well as that of confrontation, a key strategic and tactical means to "aim for the majority" and build a mass base. Invitation is any tactic that disarms opponents with humor, art, music, and self-deprecation (see the book, *Beautiful Trouble*, for a brilliant exposition of such tactics, core to the arsenal of 21st-century resistance). Humor is powerful because it is hard to be hateful when you're laughing. When you're moved by visual images or songs, defensive armor is replaced with emotional opening. When you're modest and vulnerable, you elicit compassion, empathy, and collaboration.

5. *Build Surprising Allies.* Universalizers should not pre-emptively refuse collaboration with strange bedfellows, whether the rich or the Right. Billionaires may provide resources and legitimacy for universalizing resistance.

Universalizing peace activism through the arts

© Kunal Mehta/Shutterstock

Everybody in the 1% is a human being who might be sympathetic, if only because they have discovered that being rich does not make them happy. Ralph Nader has pointed out that there are surprising areas of convergent resistance between the populist Right and the populist Left, who share opposition to corporate welfare and corporate bail-outs, and other sociopathic elements of the system. I have argued throughout this book that despite the extreme dangers of Trumpism and Trump himself, he has used populist rhetoric—about predatory corporations that outsource, a rigged system, the need to "drain the swamp in DC," the injustice of stagnant wages, the need to dismantle corporate trade agreements, and the need for an assault on corporate globalization—that could help Left populist universalizing movements reach a large public, including some Trump voters who now see him for what he is.

6. *Be a Practical Revolutionary.* Activists need to confront the practical hurdles to universalizing in their own thinking and activism. This can start with an intensive new educational process in organizations about how to universalize their thinking and activism. Universalizers can propose books and articles to read; open regular conversations and workshops about how the problems they organize around are fueled by the larger system; how they are connected or disconnected with other movement organizations focused on the same or different issues; and how they can unite with other movement groups to build new universalizing visions and networks robust enough to change the system and save the world.

Such universalizing education needs to focus on redefining the social problems they are challenging as systemic issues, inherently linked to other issues. Climate change is an economic justice issue as well as an environmental crisis. Militarism is an environmental problem as well as a peace issue. Inequality is not just a labor problem, but a problem that can also be defined as a military and environmental issue. How do you connect the dots in thinking and organizational structures to follow up on the implications?

Universalizers also need to look closely at the mission, structure, funding, and culture of their own organizations. Is the mission defined broadly enough to permit the shift from silo to universalizing? What are the organizational hurdles to universalizing? Does the funding of the organization play a big role in maintaining a silo activism? Do donors require commitment to a single issue or campaign? Are there ways to change the culture of the organization to encourage a new universalizing of thinking and acting?

Universalizing resistance can now transcend traditional ideological and partisan boundaries. The systemic sociopathy of money and power is corrupting both mainstream US political parties and is creating a deep realignment, redefining the political landscape and carving out a niche for universalizing resisters across the traditional political spectrum. Universalizers need to reach everyone. The underlying humanity of their causes, as well as the existential perils threatening everyone, mean that everyone's survival and humanity are at stake. Universalizers should invite everyone to their resistance party. They need to keep inviting, even when it seems that few want to join. Perseverance in the righteousness and necessity of the party is the only antidote to the hopelessness and fatalism that can overcome all activists when the going gets tough and seems impossible.

At the same time, the rise of Trump and the Republican Party as a Far Right universalizing movement, points to the extreme importance of using every possible strategy to combat Trumpism and other right-wing populist groups championing authoritarianism and bigotry. The main long-term progressive agenda remains the transformation of militarized capitalism, but the short-term imperative is to prevent Trumpism and Far Right Republicanism from taking over the country and crushing progressive movements and institutions. Yes, as I have emphasized here, there may be areas of surprising convergence between Left and Right populists against the system. But make no mistake that the authoritarian dangers of Trumpism and Far Right populism cannot be overstated. The militarized capitalist system itself is intersecting more and more with Trumpism and Far Right populism, so the agenda for the progressive universalizers is to discredit Trumpists, Far Rightists, and other authoritarians whose aim is to eliminate progressives, dissent, and democracy itself. At the same time, they can reach many white workers drawn to Trump by championing their economic interests more meaningfully than Trump and by highlighting some of their shared cultural values, including the honor of labor and hard work, the importance of community, and the commitment to government not for the crony capitalists, but for the ordinary people.

TACTICS OF UNIVERSALIZING IN THE CLIMATE JUSTICE MOVEMENT

Corrie Grosse

Youth today have only lived in a high-carbon world. We have grown up while communities are losing their homes to rising seas and species are going extinct at unprecedented rates. I say "we," because I too (age 26), have a personal, political, and scholarly stake in the future.

Alongside the climate crisis, people's *resistance*—the Arab Spring, Occupy Wall Street, the People's Climate March, and #BlackLivesMatter—is shaping our lives. The climate justice forces are building an inclusive movement composed of women, people of color, labor, and youth from everywhere.

Young people are "universalizers" of resistance. They are making the connections between climate, environment, and social injustices, highlighting the shared roots of these struggles and the need for intersectional organizing. This includes participation of diverse people, and practices that recognize and work to address injustice at the root of many different issues.

In Santa Barbara County, California, young activists organize in and around universities. They work in a county that pioneered offshore oil drilling and infused energy into the environmental movement following the infamous 1969 oil spill. Recently, young people mobilized to ban extreme oil extraction through a county ballot initiative, to divest cities and universities (University of California, Santa Barbara [UCSB] and Santa Barbara City College [SBCC]) from fossil fuels, and to build coalitions focused on racial inequality and economic justice. I interviewed 28 of these activists, having organized alongside many of them since 2013.

By prioritizing coalition building, youth activists have taught me the importance of "calling each other in" across lines of difference. In the historically white, privileged US environmental movement, calling attention to oppressive behavior is necessary for dismantling power structures—for realizing climate justice. It is a constructive way to recognize privilege and power. Activists can use "calling in" to alert white men dominating conversation in a meeting of the need to make space for other voices. The practice asks activists to open themselves to the tensions and learning involved in inclusive organizing. Writer Ngọc Loan Trần (2013) explains calling in as:

> a practice of loving each other enough to allow each other to make mistakes; a practice of loving ourselves enough to know that what we're trying to do here is a radical unlearning of everything we have been configured to believe is normal.

The practices and values that youth employ to nourish relationships of trust—to facilitate calling in—are valuable for realizing a diverse, inclusive, and justice-oriented climate movement.

Youth activists are dedicated to horizontal organizational structure. 350 Santa Barbara has no formal leadership and uses consensus decision making. The Environmental Affairs Board (EAB) of UCSB has co-chairs and 19 leadership positions. Recently these posts were held by a majority of women and students of color. Members in both groups sometimes introduce themselves with names and preferred gender pronouns as a way to practice gender inclusivity.

Connecting social and environmental justice is a priority and a way for youth to broaden the base. Some activists challenge capitalism as the root of all injustices, while others challenge its most damaging qualities; for example, profit without conscience, and externalities, in the case of the divestment movement. Others, like Kori Lay, a former leader in the California Student Sustainability Coalition (CSSC), organized the group's biannual Convergence to have two-thirds of the panels and workshops engaging with interconnections of environmental and social problems. She invited a keynote speaker who told attendees: "Right now we are meeting on Native American lands that we took away from them." Kori recounted, "I wanted people to hear and talk and be uncomfortable . . . I wanted people to have hard conversations."

In 2014, CSSC members showcased their commitment to fostering intersectionality by writing a statement in solidarity with Ferguson and #BlackLivesMatter:

> [W]e recognize and affirm that our struggle and liberation is indelibly

bound to the liberation of others. We cannot have climate justice or a sustainable planet without racial justice. . . . If we want freedom from the fossil fuel industry, if we want freedom from tuition hikes, then we must also have freedom from oppression and racial injustice.

CSSC must stand with Ferguson in order to—together—resist these injustices and to—together—build the future we want and need to see. We also recognize that we are part of a larger community that holds a LOT of privilege. . . . Our struggles may or may not be the same but we are bound nonetheless.

Activists recognize that there is much to do to realize the goals articulated in CSSC's vision. That youth are so conscious of the shared roots of struggle for all kinds of justice gives me hope. To begin walking the walk of this talk, activists consider how their own identities and privilege inform their work and relational organizing.

Emily Williams, former Campaign Director for CSSC, explains that *relational organizing* is rooted

> in having these really intentional one-on-one conversations that are not about campaign strategies, it's not talking about the campaign at all . . . it's focusing on getting to know someone, what's driving them, where they are coming from, and using a whole series of them [conversations] to build up this trust between two people. And so when they organize together, there's that relationship built.

Theo Lequesne, a core organizer in UCSB Fossil Free, realized the importance of relational organizing after engaging in two divestment campaigns. One was at the University of Warwick in the UK, where the divestment group was a tight group of friends who persuaded 75% of the students to vote for a divestment referendum. The other, at UCSB, struggled to retain members. Now, after spending the 2015/2016 school year building relationships, UCSB Fossil Free has ten core organizers and is increasing outreach. Activists are able to learn each other's strengths, the gaps in their knowledge of their campaign and strategy, and create a community that laughs, learns, and strategizes together.

More broadly, relational organizing is valuable for coalition building. It entices people to show up to each other's events. Rob Holland, former leader in the California Public Interest Research Group, explained, "The leaders of the big environmental groups on campus are good friends with the leaders of the cultural groups so they know that it's stuff that they should support." These friendships facilitated support of each other's campaigns.

Common values guide these activists' practices. Many, like "meeting people where they're at" are important first steps in the relational organizing process. For Kai Wilmsen, former leader in the EAB and Students Against Fracking, the most important thing in facilitating environmental justice conversations

> is to not hit people over the head with it . . . Try to *meet people where they're at* first and . . . then have a conversation as individuals and be like "hey, I hear what you are saying, but what about this?"

Kiyomi, former leader in Students Against Fracking, advised: "[T]ry to befriend as many perceived enemies as possible [laughs] and actually become friends and hang out . . . you have to be gentle, and be patient."

Activists stressed the importance of learning in celebratory community events, good listening, and working to expand their social networks. Colin Loustalot, co-founder of 350 Santa Barbara, recounted how, during a Keystone XL Pipeline protest, an angry man yelled at him. Rather than arguing, Colin now wishes he had invited him to coffee.

> I think those are opportunities where, instead of fighting . . . if you can somehow turn conversations into something more, or you can find the common ground. . . . That's behind the scenes type work, and it happens on a social level, so when people just have empathy and give a shit about each other, then they start to listen.

A final concern is the importance of appealing to people's values. Theo, who wrote a Master's thesis on the topic, advocates attention to how activists communicate the threat of climate change and alternative futures. He argues that this can be accomplished without saying "climate change." Instead, one can talk about the drought in the Midwest, or extractive industries poisoning water and food.

In Idaho, another site where I have engaged in resistance to extreme energy extraction and interviewed 62 activists, appealing to core values and avoiding discussions about climate change prove critical. Idaho, in contrast to Santa Barbara, is a new frontier for the fossil fuel industry. Since 2009, natural gas companies have drilled 17 wells. Citizens Allied for Integrity and Accountability (CAIA) is a grass-roots group resisting this development. Among the unlikely alliances advocating renewable energy—the Cowboy Indian Alliance and Green Tea Coalition—

CAIA brings people together across dividing lines. On its board, the group has had former leaders of a local Tea Party group, conservatives, Independents, Democrats, environmentalists, and climate change skeptics.

Talking across lines is the practice that enables this group to mobilize, attract broad support, and stall gas companies' expansion. Board member Jim Plucinski explains that talking across lines is about

> taking a piece of paper and folding it in half, [there's] the left side and the right side and the line in the middle is the center, list all the things that different political affiliations would land on. . . . Then try to find things down the center that both people, both mindsets, would see a common interest [in].

By checking party affiliation and beliefs about climate change at the door, and focusing on core issues (land, water, soil) and the accountability and integrity of government and industry, CAIA can organize resistance to fracking in one of the reddest regions of the United States.

Though they are operating in a vastly different context from youth organizers in Santa Barbara, CAIA members also focus on core values to enable talking across lines. It parallels youth's focus on meeting people where they're at to build relationships. Activists in both settings call people in to their movements and recognize the common roots of the injustice they face.

Coming together through these practices enables people to "see your face and your passion" (Rob Holland) and begin to enjoy the community that activists are building. Though they fight against what is wrong, activists are not negative people. Former Black Student Union and EAB leader Nia

Mitchell explains: "activists are some of the most positive people I've ever met, cuz it means we think we can change something." Activists I have talked with share her assessment, and through their work, help others realize that a different world is possible. The first step is having a conversation and cultivating relationships of trust.

Corrie Grosse is a doctoral candidate in the Department of Sociology at the University of California, Santa Barbara. Climate justice is her research, teaching, and activist passion.

PART

FROM VISION TO PRACTICE

15

Grand Strategy: Answering the Big Questions

I conclude this book more with questions than answers: questions that are essential to the universalizing project. There are, first, great questions about social change and grand strategy that I have not delved into deeply enough—or in some cases, even raised. And there are vital questions about the practical steps that we must all take to enact the universalizing project; I take these up in this chapter and the next to help add some "how to" steps for universalizers seeking a handbook for big change.

Universalizing is a grand strategy for creating system change, but I have only touched on some of the key issues at the heart of social change. These involve big questions of social theory, but I want to address them here as briefly and as concretely as possible, focusing on how they are crucial for activists thinking about how to create transformational change. I want to discuss briefly five grand strategic questions that have great importance for universalizing activists. These are questions that nobody in or out of the movements have answered definitively, but must be explored to succeed in the universalizing project. Then, I'll turn, in Chapter 16, to "how to" measures.

1. *What kinds of systemic conditions, balance of forces, and changes tend to open up opportunities for transformational change?*
    Theorists have debated this question for centuries—and we still don't have definitive answers. The broad answer that I have put forward here is that the universalizing of the system is now a catalyzing force for universalizing resistance that can change the system. New stages of capitalism

have often led to new forms of resistance—and that is the case today as super-universalizing capitalism takes control.

Common sense suggests that when the system becomes more oppressive and destructive to more people—which is what super-universalizing capitalism is doing—the legitimacy of the system will erode. People will begin to look for alternatives when they are desperate, as was the case in the Great Depression. But great waves of resistance, as in the 1960s, also developed during periods when the system was universalizing under more favorable conditions and a new majority experienced unexpected affluence. The "success" of the mainstream system did not meet people's deepest human needs and led to new anti-systemic challenges, often by the most privileged young people.

So transformational change can emerge in periods of systemic universalizing leading to socio-economic decline or to renewal, with decline the more likely 21st-century condition that universalizing movements will now confront. One of the organizing challenges, then, is to reach and organize "losers" in today's super-universalized capitalism who are fearful and angry, leading them to demonize other victims. They may be attracted to demagogues who encourage such "blaming the victim"—and the challenge of progressive movements is to universalize their message to downwardly mobile groups before they succumb to the appeal of Far Right movements, including, of course, Trumpism and Far Right authoritarian populists who have become the base of the Republican Party and, after Trump's election in 2016, dominate government at all levels.

We are entering a new extreme stage of super-universalizing capitalism, one in which the balance of power is changing dramatically and for the worse, concentrating wealth and political control in a smaller group of huge global financial institutions and other corporations. As markets globalize and grow larger, corporations—and especially financial institutions such as the biggest Wall Street banks and hedge funds—grow far larger in order to ensure profits from these universalizing markets. Workers, unions, and communities cannot move with the same speed and efficiency to secure their position and organize themselves globally. Countervailing power declines as market scale grows, shifting the global balance of power from workers to corporations.

Universalizing resistance must find ways to build popular power when systemic changes are not in their favor. Fortunately, opportunities for mass opposition exist. Loss of power and erosion of popular democracy—and the existential dangers bred by elites pursuing profit over the survival of life itself—create anger against the Establishment, exposing a raw contradiction between the system's democratic ideals and the realities of corporate sovereignty.

The balance of power has not tilted so far in the direction of the 1% and the big corporations since the Gilded Age of the 1880s and

1890s. The huge power and wealth gap in the Gilded era catalyzed a universalizing populist movement against Wall Street and the Robber Barons, led to the organization of a new "People's Party," and created new universalizing struggles against predatory capitalism. This history shows that new stages of systemic universalizing can fuel new stages of universalizing resistance fighting corpocracy and promoting democracy.

At the same time, as emphasized throughout this book, the structural conditions giving rise to progressive and Left universalizing movements are also fueling Far Right and authoritarian universalizers. The battle between Left and Right populist movements will define US politics for a long period to come, with the Establishment seeking to maintain its power by allying with Trumpists and other Republican and Far Right populist movements.

2. *What are the most importance systemic issues of the 21st century that we need to confront? And what are the most important groups or communities that face the great exploitation and are most crucial and most conducive for universalizing movements—and have already begun to move the universalizing project forward?*

In the 21st century, this question seems to answer itself. Universalizing capitalism is creating existential threats that could end human civilization, notably climate change and nuclear war. Climate change and nuclear war are now imminent existential threats and, since they are driven by the new super-universalizing stage of capitalism, they make universalizing change more urgent than ever before. Extinction is the greatest crisis we have ever faced—and all the other issues discussed below must be viewed in the context of this unprecedented apocalyptic threat.

The issue of class is central. It is hardly new, but it is creating new universalizing oppression and misery. Overcoming the class system itself—focusing especially on the progressive winning over of the poor and working population, including those who voted for Trump and became disenchanted with him—is clearly a huge part of the universalizing agenda. Creating more equality of income and wealth, consistent with the aims of creating a democratic economy and government that shares the wealth and offers material wellbeing and equal rights for the 99%—is obviously already an overwhelmingly central cause, championed by Bernie Sanders in 2016 and also exploited by Donald Trump. Class politics is cultural as well as economic, since it focuses on the core value of work—dignified, meaningful, and well-paid for all people, and helping to unite workers across race, and across rural "traditional" and urban "cosmopolitan" cultures.

And, then, there are the ancient crises of caste—especially those of racism and sexism. These are tied to crises of immigration and ethnic conflict, as well as to discrimination and hatred in the United States that elites use to divide and conquer. Since racism and sexism are used by system elites to sustain control—and are ever more intimately intertwined with class divisions as the system universalizes and seeks to legitimate itself under difficult conditions, they also must be a central focus of universalizing movements.

Finally, there are the great overarching questions of democracy. In a universalized system, where wealth and political power are so concentrated, we need a universalizing political movement that separates money from politics and replaces plutocracy and authoritarianism—the greatest threat posed by the Trump Presidency—with real democracy in politics, the economy, the schools, and all other major institutions.

All universalizing movements are "democracy movements" because it is only when the public reclaims power that any of the fundamental rights of all our communities can be realized. And the great existential issues of economic justice, climate change, and militarism—threatening human survival—can only be won when the public has taken back power from the 1% and created popular governance of, by, and for the people.

Democracy is thus the great universalizing issue—it unites all the issues and all the movements. And the super-universalized stage of capitalism—which is undermining democracy in the authoritarian era of Trump, and threatening the very existence of humanity—is the "mother of all issues."

But the universalizing perspective suggests that the question of which issues or communities matter most is misleading—and inhibits the rise of the resistance and change we need. Its premise seems to be that the issues are different and separate—and we must choose among them as we fight for a better world. The thrust of this book has been to highlight not only that these issues are inextricably intertwined, but they should not be defined as separate issues. They are all part of the same problem and actually should be understood as the same issue.

Militarism is an integral part of capitalism; so is climate change. Militarism is violence against the environment, and climate change fuels militarism. Racism and class warfare are inseparable; the same is true of sexism and class warfare.

After the election of 2016, a major debate broke out in the Democratic Party and in the Left movements about the virtues of class politics and identity politics. In this book, I have consistently argued that class, race, and gender are intimately connected—and that we need to universalize class politics in identity movements and universalize identity movements that take full account of class.

Classism, racism, and sexism are constituent essential features of the same super-universalizing capitalism. We need to unite identity politics with class politics, not throw away one at the expense of the other. And all the other issues discussed above—climate change and militarism especially—threaten to end human civilization.

It is time to stop defining our issues in the old way. It is part of our problem. We need to see all the key issues above as simply different expressions of the same systemic pathology.

Once we've redefined what we are fighting, the movements that we need can launch at full throttle!

3. *What are the social and economic communities or groups most likely in this century to be activist and lead progressive universalizing change? Which have already begun to do so?*

Marx answered this question in a way that guided much of progressivism and the Left in the 20th century. He believed that because the capitalist system was based on the exploitation of the working class by the capitalist class, workers and labor movements would lead the struggle for social justice.

Marx was not entirely wrong. Workers and worker organizations have been important in struggles for justice almost everywhere. This will have to be true in universalizing 21st-century resistance too. The epitaph on Marx's tombstone—"Workers of the World Unite"—may well be ascendant in 21st-century universalizing struggles.

But there are at least three problems with Marx's answer today, particularly in the United States. First, universalizing system elites have crushed the labor movement, with only about 6% of private sector workers organized into unions. Second, white workers—especially those that are downwardly mobile and feeling the full weight of universalizing capitalist exploitation—have moved in a conservative direction and are increasingly likely to vote Republican; most, including those who voted for Trump, seem hardly the vanguard of a new Left movement against militarized capitalism. Third, class movements, such as labor, even at their strongest moments, have not, at least in the United States, been leaders of universalizing struggles. They have largely focused on benefits for their own members. They have not fought against the capitalist system itself. In the New Deal and beyond, they have been important actors in the social justice struggle, but most—with some important exceptions—have not been transformative leaders.

That role seems to have fallen more to the civil rights community, which has raised the most catalytic and inspiring movements, not only against racism, but against the militarism and violence of the system itself. African-American movement leaders, such as Martin Luther King, have been pioneers in universalizing struggle. And it is important to remember that African Americans, Hispanics, and other people of color are on the way to becoming the majority in the United States, highlighting the possibility that their leadership may become ever more important in universal resistance.

Race-based movements appear poised at this time of writing to lead a new universalizing struggle. Not only are organizations such as Black Lives Matter uniting African Americans in a vital new civil rights struggle, focusing on color-blind and institutional racism that connects with gender and sexual orientation movements. But the new civil struggle movement is also emerging as a new struggle against poverty, the injustice of capitalism, and the terrible violence of militarism abroad—all of which threaten global annihilation in the age of weapons of mass destruction (WMD) and militarized police at home.

Historically, the most enlightened phases of the feminist movements have also played this role. Think of the "intersectoral" feminists, who have seen the oppression of women as part of the larger system of catastrophic violence and injustice—and the movement for women's rights as part of a larger struggle for human rights. This has been especially true of Black feminists and socialist feminists—who may be in the ascendancy in 21st-century universalizing struggles.

Once again, though, the universalizing perspective suggests that the identity question itself may be misleading for several reasons. First, the "different" communities are not entirely different; as the system universalizes, they are increasingly intertwined in their identity, the existential challenges they face, and the social spaces they occupy. We recognize now that race and gender are only partly biological; they are also "social constructions." There are millions of bi-racial or multi-racial people, blurring the identity of separate racial groups. Transgender identity, along with changing gender norms, blur the once iron-clad differences between male and female.

Second, all races and genders are increasingly intermingling in the workforce. In the United States, the working class is increasingly a melding of Black, brown, and other people of color. Castes (or race and gender groups) are increasingly economic classes and economic classes are increasingly castes.

Moreover, we are increasingly seeing labor struggles as a new civil rights movement of the 21st century in the United States—and in the world as a whole.

All this points to the need to move, in super-universalizing capitalism, beyond ideas of separate groups with separate struggles. The universalizing perspective highlights the ways in which identity groups and economic classes increasingly share a common identity as targets of exploitation and violence within the new stage of capitalism.

As such, no one group can be singled out as a vanguard, since the groups are not truly distinct and are increasingly melded into a common struggle against the same universalizing system. The working class is increasingly female and people of color, so class struggles require bringing together working-class white males with their fellow workers— women and people of color; coming together on the workplace floor and with guidance from unions, this will mobilize a struggle that is both class-based and identity-based.

At the same time, the election of Trump on a right-wing populist agenda—and the attraction of Sanders' left-wing populism—suggest the need for a rebalancing of class and identity politics in the Democratic Party and Left movements. Class politics has been, to a large degree, discarded in the Democratic Party since its "corporatization" under President Bill Clinton's "Third Way" Democratic Centrism. The Democratic Party became a collection of oppressed identity groups, tied to professionals who service them as well as to corporate elites. Likewise, the essential focus on class and resistance to global capitalism has become less central to universalizing progressive movements, which have become more centrally focused on identity politics.

Trump's election has catalyzed a much-needed debate about rebalancing, and a new focus on class politics. This does not mean de-emphasizing identity issues, as besieged and frightened identity groups will need even more protection and rights than ever in the Trump era, but reframing them with a greater sensitivity to the intertwining of class and identity politics, ensuring that identity politics strengthens rather than weakens class unity and class politics.

4. *What are the "spaces" or settings where we can begin to see the rise and spread of universalizing progressive activism?*
Marx also had a clear answer to this question. The workplace was the "hot spot" for organizing. Marx believed that resistance could only grow in physical spaces where workers came together and developed a sense of community and solidarity. In early industrial capitalism, the factory floor was that place.

But times have changed. As the system universalizes, workers change jobs frequently. Many people work at home or off-site, sometimes meaning that there is no shared workplace. The workplace is often divided now into isolating cubicles where workers can't meet and interact. Or workers are glued to their computers, interacting only with their electronic screens. The universalizing system has hammered unions, doing everything possible to eliminate them.

This hardly makes the workplace an irrelevant site for organizing. It will remain vitally important in the 21st century, as people work longer and labor issues remain ever more central in people's lives in universalizing capitalism. Unions remain a vital universalizing force of countervailing power. In fact, unions are more necessary than ever because the workplaces are the most important sites where working people can find common bonds and struggle in union halls and campaigns.

This role for unions has become more important in universalizing resistance than perhaps ever before. Workplaces are increasingly sites where Blacks and whites, women and men, actually meet and rub shoulders, and become friends. Unions play a key role in building this cross-race and cross-gender community and political resistance, offering a different political narrative from Trumpism and other right-wing populism which seeks racial and gender division. Moreover, it is in the workplace that a universalizing culture valuing "hard work" and good jobs can be built among all workers.

But as the system universalizes, the sites for organizing also universalize beyond the workplace alone, despite its ever growing importance.

One site already gaining prominence is the community or neighborhood. The system has universalized oppression and violence into the neighborhood, as corporations, the militarized police, the surveillance state, and environmental pipelines and poisons harm and transform the local community. Like the workplace, community and neighborhoods may be weakening in America, but they are still one of the major sites where ordinary people are experiencing the heavy hammer of universalizing exploitation, and can come together and interact and build solidarity.

Organizing strategies, thus, increasingly are focusing on the community as well as the workplace. People of color are taking a lead, developing thousands of different community-based organizations to deal with problems of affordable housing, hunger, police violence, and gang violence. Poor urban communities, often disproportionately made up of people of color, are now feeling the system's universalizing violence most intensely in their communities.

These trends have led in recent decades to a strategy of "base-building" focused in the neighborhood and community. While currently prominent among people of color, it also has a history in white poor and working communities, operating according to the "Alinsky" organizing school.

The Occupy Wall Street movement points to a third core site for organizing: the streets and public space. As the universalizing system spreads its tentacles and privatizes more and more public space, the fundamental right to assemble and petition is in jeopardy. In fact, public space itself is disappearing, occupied and policed by corporations, malls, private retail stores, apartment buildings, private estates, condo and apartment buildings, universities, and many levels of government with restricted access.

The universalizing system's conquest of private space is one of its unique and distinctive features. It represents the final enclosure of the commons. Of course, it is not complete. We still have public streets, sidewalks, parks, and other public spaces. But increasingly, the right to congregate, socialize, and protest in these spaces is being restricted through time-consuming rules to get permits and due to violent repression of dissent. Occupy Wall Street was a reassertion of the popular right to create and take back public space for the people.

Since Occupy, the idea that we must reclaim public space is growing. Claiming space is part of the universalizing strategy. The remnants of public space are still important environments in which people congregate, socialize, and develop a sense of collective identity as citizens with free speech, assembly, and protest rights. In this sense, all 21st-century universalizing movements will be Occupy movements, because universalizing movements are about reclaiming the commons we all share and asserting our inalienable rights to congregate and socialize in "our public space" as public citizens.

Popular power and movements always bring people into the streets—and the streets and other public spaces are themselves key "sites" of organizing. This is especially true for universalizing movements, where different activists in different movements come together in conversation, planning, and common action.

Public space is a physical symbol of our universalized identity as public citizens. It is also the natural watering hole for all people—whatever their race, gender, work, community, or cause—to gather, organize, and build universalizing resistance.

5. *How much time do we have left to build a universalizing movement? And how do we win when time is scarce?*
This is the scariest question. The universalizing system has created a new doomsday clock for activists, showing that we are running out of time.

In all prior movements, the assumption has been that history is on our side. We can embrace the "long march" through institutions and gradually build—over decades and centuries if necessary—the movements to persuade the mass public of the need for transformation.

The universalizing system has changed all this. Its new existential threats—climate change and nuclear war—can destroy civilization and end history. This can happen in a blink of the eye in the case of nuclear war, and possibly in just a few decades in the case of climate change, disasters that Trump's policies are accelerating.

The new time constraints change everything about grand strategy. They add urgency and may fire up the intensity and militancy of movements. But they also attack hope and prospects for organizing that depend on centuries for fulfillment.

What kind of grand strategy can operate under these terrifying constraints of time? The truth is that we don't know. We all feel the urgency, and at some deep level, know that we may be too late. But this is not a recipe for surrender. Rather, it should concentrate our minds and lead us to as much concentrated intelligence, commitment, and universality as we can achieve—as quickly as possible.

Universalizing is, in some sense, both the cause of our time crisis and the solution. As the system has universalized, it has changed our timescale, and has created the most urgent and immediate catastrophic possibilities that we have ever faced. But it will also make clear that piece-meal reform and silo activism don't have endless time to coalesce. We need to move as quickly as possible toward transformative change, because if we don't universalize our resistance in this sense now, we may never have the time to do it.

The time crisis is the strongest argument for the universalizing project. It recognizes the compression of space and time in the universalizing system. It thus sets forward universalizing resistance as the only strategy that has even the possibility of working. Universalizing is our best approach as time grows scarily short, because it calls for unifying virtually everyone for urgent systemic change to preserve all life. Only by working with all communities and all the issues can we ever imagine a solution to the crisis of time and collective survival that no movements have faced before.

16

Walking the Talk: Nuts and Bolts

In this final chapter, I want to highlight three concrete organizing tasks for universalizing change—and raise questions about how best to achieve them. I raise them mainly as questions, since they will be answered only in practice, by universalizers in the movements themselves. My hope is that this book will help to catalyze the conversation among activists and their supporters that will lead to practical steps which are realistic and can help overcome very substantial hurdles within movements themselves.

First, how and where do universalizing movements educate themselves, their supporters, and the general public about the new apocalyptic stage of capitalism, the completely intertwined nature of the issues, and the kind of universalized resistance and social change that we urgently need to prosper and survive?

Education is the name of the universalizing resistance game—or at least the most important first step. In my view, education and activism are always intertwined. Activists are always educating themselves—by reading, interacting, talking to the public, and constantly thinking through their goals, aims, and tactics. My experience tells me that most activists are intellectuals of the streets—and many are gifted thinkers and writers.

I believe, then, that most activists will jump at the chance to build new and exciting educational agendas and programs.

The educational aim is to understand super-universalized capitalism more deeply, to grasp as fully as possible the injustice and threats to human survival that it breeds, and to create the grand universalizing strategy and tactics to transform it.

Movements are already major institutions of popular education. I have heard so many activists say that they have learned the most about the world through their activism.

What are the practical steps movements can take to educate themselves for universalized resistance? Here are a few suggestions—and key questions you need to put at the top of your agenda:

1. Select a set of books, articles, and blogs each year that bear on universalizing, intersectionality, and the movement of movements. Pick a time each month to discuss them.
2. Think of this as your organization's "book club" or "salon." Take it very seriously.
3. Have a series of major discussions or workshops in your organization about whether you are carrying out silo activism. If yes, how do you feel about that? Do you see a way to change it?
4. In those same discussions, talk about whether you want to become a universalizing organization. If yes, why? What are the most important ways to get there? What are the pros and cons of universalizing as you see it?
5. Focus on emotions as well as ideas. What are your feelings about being in a silo organization focusing on an issue you feel passionate about? What are your feelings about moving to campaigns based on more universalizing visions and campaigns?
6. Invite speakers knowledgeable about political economy and social change to come to your organization and discuss grand strategy and tactics.
7. Invite activists from other organizations to come and talk about universalizing and their own educational programs.
8. Ask that leaders of major campaigns in your organization discuss the books, articles, and ideas that point to how the campaign can be universalized.
9. Ask your funders or contributors whether they like the idea of universalizing campaigns, and whether they would support educational campaigns to assist them.

Second, how do we construct the conversations, spaces, and campaigns that can bring together our current silo movements and overcome the many organizational, financial, cultural, and personal hurdles that stand in the way of the convergence and universalization necessary to save the world?

Interviews with activists suggest that many social justice advocates may be ready to move beyond silo activism. My sense is that the motivation is widespread, but doing it is daunting.

This reflects partly many serious hurdles. Movements are still largely organized around single issues such as inequality, climate, or militarism. Other identity movements most often focus on a particular racial group or gender. This means that the entire movement is still structured largely as a system of silo activism.

This creates many practical obstacles, including:

- Activists join because they are passionate about their own causes and campaigns.
- Their organization's mission statement focuses on one identity group or cause.
- Their financing or donations come from foundations or other organizations or constituents committed to the one issue or group.
- Their public support is based among those dedicated to their single issue or identity.
- Dealing with the greatest issues of global injustice and the survival of all life on earth is simply too psychologically overwhelming to focus on.

These are formidable problems. And even resistance movements resist changing themselves.

Nonetheless, we have long heard discussions of moving in a new direction. Naomi Klein's idea of a "movement of movements" has long been one of the most popular slogans in the activist world. On campuses, the idea of intersectionality is commonplace among activists and among many other students and faculty. Some important organizations, such as Greenpeace, demonstrate their commitment to universality in their name.

So a new conversation has already begun. We need to pose and deal with several further issues and questions about the space for and nature of such conversations to move beyond silo activism and advance universalizing resistance.

First, we need to bring activists from different movements to meet and talk. This means finding space and time to socialize and strategize. How do we create that space and time?

Second, we need to institutionalize such spaces. Should we have annual conferences bringing together leaders of movements in different issue or identity silos? Should each organization's budget provide some money for this? Should donors or public supporters be asked to contribute? What would the agenda of such conferences look like? And who would set that agenda? Would it produce more competition than cooperation?

Third, we need networks made up of multiple movement organizations that offer a foundation for ongoing conversation and strategizing across issue and identity movements. We already have networks linking organizations fighting for the same issue, such as peace. There are a growing number of networks that bring together organizations focusing on different issues, such as those linking jobs and climate change. How do we build a lot more of them?

One approach may be to work with donors such as foundations or groups of individual donors to help create such networks. Program officers in foundations funding progressive causes or community causes are well positioned to bring their recipient organizations together to talk and strategize on a regular basis. Is this realistic? How can we do it?

Finally, we need to build demonstrations, rallies, and campaigns that unite silo movements and build working arrangements among them. What experience can we build on? What are the most promising areas in which to build such campaigns and create enduring relations across the silos? And what are the most militant and effective actions that can help?

A universalizing movement must ultimately come together and target the system of militarized capitalism. What do anti-systemic agendas and actions look like in practice? Can we move beyond demands for radical reform to demands to transform the entire system?

The World Social Forum is quite explicit about such demands. Occupy didn't have demands, but implicitly called for building a new system. How do we build the infrastructure for such explicitly anti-systemic demands and campaigns?

What about radical reforms? Which are the most effective in building support for more explicitly anti-systemic movements? How do we distinguish radical reforms that should, and do, animate many of our movements and campaigns from reformist reforms?

Third, how do we build the kinds of campaigns and movements and political agendas that can reach and mobilize the larger public for the urgent systemic change necessary to save the world? What is the role of electoral politics, mainstream parties, and their candidates? What about Third and Fourth Parties?

Thus far, we have focused on building the vision and infrastructure of universalizing resistance among activists and their organizations. But ultimately this depends on building support for the universalizing project in the public. And this depends not just on the internal culture and infrastructure of the movements, but on shifts in public consciousness.

The universalizing project requires an understanding of the universalizing system in the public and a new politics to support it.

Politics—including mainstream electoral and party politics—is incredibly important for universalizing movements. It is the arena where public consciousness and public issues get named, framed, and shamed. You can't have a public committed to universalizing ideas without those ideas penetrating elections and political conversations in the media, political parties, and among their candidates.

This returns us to the essential dance between universalizing movements and electoral politics. Universalizing movements have to universalize into the electoral arena, including the parties, the elections themselves, the media that cover them, and the think tanks and "experts" brought into the public eye to help shape the conversation.

The election of Trump and the rise of Trumpism and a more authoritarian and dangerous Republican Party make clear the extreme importance of progressive movements universalizing into electoral politics. As long as a militarized, corporatized, and "Trumpized" authoritarian Republican Party dominates national politics, progressive universalizers' top priority has to be mobilizing the mass population to stop authoritarianism and its expressions in Trumpism and Far Right populism, as well as in the structural hierarchies of corporate power and the military state.

Progressive universalizing into mainstream elections and politics is challenging, but not impossible—and is now critically important as the Republican Establishment melds with Trumpism and a more authoritarian corporate and militarized system. In fact, the explosion of groups of the kind discussed in Chapter 12, such as Indivisible, Our Revolution, and Swing Left—all made up of masses of the angry Democratic Party base swarming to challenge Republican Congresspeople in their town halls, and to run progressive Democratic Party activists for local state and federal office, show that Trumpism has catalyzed a new era of movement-based electoral politics. Thousands of outraged liberals, Leftists, and ordinary citizens are throwing their hat into the electoral party ring, determined to stop Trump, push the Democratic Party far to the Left, and meld Left movements with a new revolutionary progressive electoral politics, not unlike the Tea Party strategy after 2009 carried out by right-wing universalizing movements.

Let us return once again to the example of Bernie Sanders, whose work will help guide all these new electoral activists. Sanders ran as a socialist in the Democratic Party against both Trump and Hillary Clinton. This immediately changed the discourse in the party, the media, and the public. We should discuss it again because even if the Sanders phenomenon is temporary, it illustrates how the crucial dance between grass-roots movements and electoral politics is ultimately essential, to stop Trump, the larger Republican Party, and the corporatized and military-friendly Democratic Party Establishment.

Recall that Sanders changed public conversation by making "socialism" a respectable topic of American political discourse. Millions of Americans

Googled the word "socialism." Political commentators on mainstream media had to talk about socialism and offer their own notions of what it meant. Pollsters showed that the public was remarkably favorable to the word "socialism"—especially young people and Democrats themselves. This created the beginnings of a new phase of political conversation in America, and helped movements gain credibility as they expanded on what socialism meant to them.

Sanders' rival, Hillary Clinton, had to move out of the old mainstream and run a more progressive campaign. She embraced the system, of course, but she was forced to highlight extreme inequality, low wages, the decline of the middle class, vast racial and gender income and wealth gaps, the unacceptability of gun violence and police violence. These shifts changed the tone of her campaign in a way that made it easier for movements to raise these issues in a more meaningful way. They helped to make the case for a need to consider changing the system itself.

As Sanders gained enthusiastic support by his focus on capitalist inequality and Wall Street sociopathy, the limits of Clinton's version of feminism and siloed identity politics became evident. Too many females, especially young women and women of color, resonated to Sanders' systemic and universalizing critiques. He headlined an economic populist agenda that many white workers could vote for, bridging Black and white workers, and also linking class politics with a politics of race and gender.

Sanders helped to push a politician as mainstream as Hillary Clinton toward a more progressive and universalizing discourse. But her class politics—like those of the Democratic Party—were too weak and detached, failing to express with the desperate and visceral urgency the economic crisis that fueled both Sanders and Trump.

What were the larger implications for movements and systemic change? Clinton's loss showed the bankruptcy of a Democratic Party as a collection of identity groups abstracted from class and economic transformation. Trump's victory showed the power of a right-wing universalizing movement linking class resentment to right-wing identity politics. Clinton's loss and the mobilizing power of Sanders showed that the Left universalizing movements had to find a melding of Left class struggle and identity politics that could counter Trumpism (even while exploiting some of its populist economic rhetoric), and gain traction in the national conversation and in Washington DC, as well as in communities and on the streets around the nation.

How can movements best exploit that political space that Trump broke into and took over, while also catalyzing the new anti-Trump electoral activists in Indivisible, Our Revolution, and other new Leftist Tea-Party-style activists? This leads to key strategic questions about how universalizing movements can use elections and mainstream politics—and join with Indivisible,

Our Revolution, and the other new universalizing electoral activists. Several issues and questions come to mind.

First, movement organizations reaching the mass public, such as MoveOn. org, could help mobilize millions of the new Indivisible, Our Revolution, and all the other raging Democratic, liberal, and Left electorally-oriented activists at the local, state, and national levels, to think and act in the spirit of Sanders, socialism, and all the labor, environmental, peace, civil rights, and feminist movements in a new way. They could help connect these new masses of citizen activists to the movements that Sanders had begun to make respectable. This would begin to mainstream an anti-systemic agenda and connect the support for Sanders to a much larger base of support for the movements, especially among the diverse working and middle classes who are newly politicized. How can such work be expanded and empowered?

This leads to the second question, as to how universalizing online organizations such as MoveOn.org, Color of Change, Truthout.org or Presente. org—all of which aggregate issues and help influence a mass public—can connect more effectively to the movements. They are enormously powerful and essential tools for universalizing movements. How can we build sustainable and effective relations between such organizations and the universalizing resistance movements on the ground, including all the new electoral activists, some of whom have never been active in movements before?

Third, this points to the importance of movement organizations, such as the Progressive Democrats of America (PDA), whose mission is to help universalize movement messages into the electoral and political arena. How can the movements work with PDA and related groups to help organize, coordinate, expand, and universalize the incredible energy and numbers of new electoral activists who want to push the Democratic Party far to the Left in the spirit of Sanders—and essentially become part of the universalizing movements that we have described throughout this book? How can the movements contribute to the success of PDA in moving candidates to the Left and closer to movement ideas? What kind of relations should be built between organizations such as PDA and other movements that may or may not get involved in electoral politics, but can benefit from their success?

Fourth, what is the role for Third Parties? They clearly are natural vehicles—like all political parties—for aggregating and universalizing the ideas and agendas of the movements. The American Green Party has promoted a universalizing agenda integrating many key movement demands. Should the movements be embracing the Green Party or other such movement-oriented political parties more fully? What can be done, and how—and is it the right strategy?

Fifth, it's past time for universalizing movements to think through and develop a mass political strategy. Can we bring different leading movement organizations to discuss this issue—to find out whether we can find a consensus? Can the movements coalesce around shared agendas that they bring into the political process? Can they universalize both a content and strategy in the electoral arena?

Sixth, should universalizing movements be shifting toward the creation of their own party? Would this be a good way of universalizing their message to the public and building a mass base? Is it a wise use of movement time and money?

This leads to a concluding Grand Strategy question of great importance to the universalizing project. Is the ultimate aim the conquest of state power? This question focuses the mind, but universalizing movements have yet to offer clear and persuasive answers. There are great differences on this question among the movements, including universalizing ones.

Traditional Marxists saw conquest of state power as essential to build a new system while preventing military and corporate elites from implementing their own universalizing agenda. From this point of view, if we don't embrace the goal—as long-term as it might be—of gaining state power, we will cede the terrain to the system and the Far Right.

Anarchists and other movements opposing all concentration of power have long argued, against traditional Marxists and socialists, that state power would destroy their movements. The movements would become the new oppressors simply by occupying and controlling the state, which inevitably concentrates and militarizes great power.

This old debate may seem academic in the United States, since conditions are not ripe any time soon for gaining state control. But it remains an underlying question that universalizing movements must consider.

For, in the end, super-sized capitalism depends on control of the state for its own purposes. At a minimum, a universalizing Grand Strategy must accomplish three goals.

First, it must create enough non-violent disruption and mass non-cooperation with the super-sized capitalist state to de-legitimate it, and render it incapable of pursuing its agenda which puts all of humanity and all living species at risk.

Second, it must organize full throttle against President Trump (even while using some of his populist economic rhetoric) and the rise of an authoritarian Republican Party that will ultimately meld with the Establishment and erode the niches of democracy, human rights, and prospects for human survival built into the system by decades of progressive activist struggle.

Third, it must build up the new alternative democratic governments—at the local, regional, national, and global level—that collectively move the world toward sanity, sustainability, and self-governance.

To succeed would be the Greatest Transformation of all time. To fail will ultimately guarantee the end of the human experiment.

We must universally embrace this universalizing project—which would unify us all in the most important hope and action of all time: saving the world and creating democracy and justice for all.

Notes

Introduction: A Call to Action

1 Stephen Colbert, quote posted on www.betterworld.net/quotes/CitizensUnited-quotes.htm
2 Michelle Alexander, "Breaking My Silence," *The Nation*, September 4, 2013.

1 The System and Its Discontents: The Militarized Matrix versus Us

1 Warren Buffett, "Stop Coddling the Rich," *The New York Times*, August 14, 2011, www.nytimes.com/2011/08/15/opinion/stop-coddling-the-super-rich.html?_r=0
2 Paul Hawken, *Blessed Unrest*. New York: Penguin, 2008.
3 Camille Paglia, www.brainyquote.com/quotes/quotes/c/camillepag411514.html
4 Karl Marx and Friedrich Engels, *The Communist Manifesto*. London: International Publishers, 2014 (originally published 1848).
5 Pope Francis, "Laudato Si: On Care for Our Common Home," *Our Sunday Visitor*, July 18, 2015.
6 Patricia Hill Collins, *Black Feminist Thought*. New York: Routledge, 2013.
7 Shiri Eisner, www.goodreads.com/quotes/1189210-it-means-understanding-that-different-kinds-of-oppression-are-interlinked
8 Mychal Denzel Smith, "A Q&A with Alicia Garza, Co-Founder of #BlackLivesMatter," *The Nation*, March 24, 2015, www.thenation.com/article/qa-alicia-garza-co-founder-blacklivesmatter/
9 Ibid.
10 Audre Lorde, Quotes—Goodreads, www.goodreads.com/author/quotes/18486.Audre_Lorde
11 NTanya Lee and Steve Williams, "More than We Imagined: Activists' Assessments on the Moment and the Way Forward," Ear to the Ground report, May 2013, http://eartothegroundproject.org
12 Randy Lowens, "How Do You Practice Intersectionalism? An Interview with bell hooks," June 2009, http://nefac.net/bellhooks
13 Cornel West, "Toward a Socialist Theory of Racism," Chicago DSA reissue of pamphlet published by the Democratic Socialists of America, 1985, www.chicagodsa.org/CornelWest.html
14 Sheryl Sandberg, *Leaning In*. New York: Knopf, 2013.
15 Bill Fletcher, Jr., *Solidarity Divided*. Berkeley, CA: University of California Press, 2009.
16 Rob Kall, "Chomsky Talks about Psychopaths and Sociopaths," Op Ed News, February 15, 2014, www.opednews.com/articles/Chomsky-Talks-about-Psych-by-Rob-Kall-Corporations_Health-Mental-Sociopath-Narcissism_Narcissism_Psychopath-140215-378.html

17 Pope Francis, cited in Tom Huddleston, Jr., "5 Times Pope Francis Talked about Money," *Fortune*, September 14, 2015, http://fortune.com/2015/09/14/pope-francis-capitalism-inequality/

18 John Maynard Keynes, cited at http://ifinallyfoundwaldo.tumblr.com/post/104060784681/capitalism-is-the-astounding-belief-that-the-most

19 Karl Marx and Friedrich Engels, *The Communist Manifesto*, cited in Charles Derber, *Marx's Ghost*. New York: Routledge, 2011, p. 8.

20 C. Wright Mills, *The Sociological Imagination*. New York: Oxford University Press, 1957.

21 Thomas Piketty, *Capital in the Twenty-First Century*. Cambridge, MA: Harvard University Press, 2014.

22 Emma Goldman, *Anarchism and Other Essays*. Createspace Independent Publishing Platform, 2013.

23 Noam Chomsky, *Necessary Illusions: Thought Control in Democratic Societies*, 2nd edition. Toronto, ON: House of Anansi Press, 2013.

24 George Orwell, *Nineteen Eighty-Four*. New York: Signet Classic, 1961.

25 Karl Marx and Friedrich Engels, *A Contribution to the Critique of Political Economy*. New York: International Publishers, 1979.

26 Paulo Freire, *Pedagogy of the Oppressed*, 30th anniversary edition. London: Bloomsbury Academic, 2000.

27 Pope Francis, "Laudato Si: On Care for Our Common Home." Op. cit.

2 The PAC-MAN System: Universalizing and Extinction

1 Emily Peck, "These 8 Men Have as Much Money as Half the World," *The Huffington Post*, January 15, 2017, www.huffingtonpost.com/entry/income-inequality-oxfam_us_58792e6ee4b0b3c7a7b13616

2 Thomas Piketty, *Capital in the Twenty-First Century*. Cambridge, MA: Harvard University Press, 2014.

3 Karl Marx and Friedrich Engels, *The Communist Manifesto*. London: International Publishers, 2014.

4 Percy Barnevik, www.quotescodex.com/i-would-define-globalization-as-freedom-for-my-group-companies-to-invest-where-it-wants-when-it-wants-to-produce-what-it-wants-to-buy-sell-where-it-percy-barnevik-79739/

5 Thomas Friedman, *The Lexus and the Olive Tree*, 2nd edition. New York: Picador, 2012.

6 Noam Chomsky, quoted in https://chomsky.info/197305_

7 Stephen Colbert, cited by Medea Benjamin, "Drone Warfare: Killing by Remote Control", Flag in Distress, Sept 25, 2012, http://flagindistress.com/2012/09/drone-warfare-killing-by-remote-control/

8 Helen Caldicott, *The New Nuclear Danger*. New York: New Press, 2002.

9 Glenn Greenwald, *No Place to Hide: Edward Snowden, the NSA, and the U.S. Surveillance State*. New York: Metropolitan Books, 2014.

10 Edward Snowden, cited in David Michaelis, "Edward Snowden and Daniel Ellsberg, Two of a Kind," aNewDomain, http://anewdomain.net/2015/11/11/profiles-courage-two-kind-rebels-nsa-barred-court/

11 Daniel Ellsberg, cited in Arundhati Roy, "Edward Snowden Meets Arundhati Roy and John Cusack: 'He was small and lithe like a house cat'," *The Guardian*,

November 28, 2015, www.theguardian.com/lifeandstyle/2015/nov/28/conversation-edward-snowden-arundhati-roy-john-cusack-interview

12 Michelle Alexander, *The New Jim Crow*. New York: New Press, 2012.

13 Thomas Friedman, *The Lexus and the Olive Tree*. Op. cit.

14 Noam Chomsky, http://noam-chomsky.tumblr.com/post/33229691921/citizens-of-the-democratic-societies-should

15 Boaventura de Sousa Santos, *Epistemologies of the South*. New York: Routledge, 2014.

16 Ibid.

17 Center for Biological Diversity, "The Extinction Crisis," www.biologicaldiversity.org/programs/biodiversity/elements_of_biodiversity/extinction_crisis/

18 Ibid.

19 Bernie Sanders, quoted in www.brainyquote.com/quotes/quotes/b/berniesand504827.html

20 Bill Moyers, "We Are this Close to Losing Our Democracy to the Mercenary Class," Alternet, January 19, 2015, www.alternet.org/tea-party-and-right/bill-moyers-we-are-close-losing-our-democracy-mercenary-class-0

21 Pope Francis, "Laudato Si: On Care for Our Common Home," *Our Sunday Visitor*, July 18, 2015 (emphasis in original).

22 Inga Muscio, cited in Goodreads, www.goodreads.com/quotes/152231-what-happens-to-people-living-in-a-society-where-everyone?page=2

3 Irresistible Resistance: The Big Waves of Social Change

1 André Gorz, *Ecology as Politics*. London: Pluto Press, 1983.

2 Eugene Debs, *The Railway Times*, 1897.

3 Martin Luther King, cited in Avia Shen, "4 Ways Martin Luther King Was More Radical Than You Thought," ThinkProgress, January 20, 2014, https://thinkprogress.org/4-ways-martin-luther-king-was-more-radical-than-you-thought-44347fff44ab#.oqodl1365

4 Martin Luther King, "Beyond Vietnam," http://kingencyclopedia.stanford.edu/encyclopedia/documentsentry/doc_beyond_vietnam/

5 Mary Lease, cited in Harvey Wasserman, *Harvey Wasserman's History of the United States*. Harveywasserman.com (publisher), 1st edition, 2004.

6 Ibid.

7 Lawrence Goodwyn, *The Populist Moment*. New York: Oxford University Press, 1978.

8 Tom Watson, cited in Harvey Wasserman, *Harvey Wasserman's History of the United States*. Op. cit.

9 Terence Powderly, cited in Harvey Wasserman, *Harvey Wasserman's History of the United States*. Op. cit.

10 Eugene Debs, *The Railway Times*, 1897.

11 James Oppenheim and Caroline Kohlsaat, "Bread and Roses," 1912, http://lyricsplayground.com/alpha/songs/b/breadandroses.shtml

12 Nate Shaw, quoted in Howard Zinn, *A People's History of the United States*. New York: Harper Perennial, 2005.

13 Tom Hayden, *The Port Huron Statement*. Students for a Democratic Society, 1962.

14 Mario Savio, Speech before the FSM Sit-In, December 3, https://en.wikipedia.org/wiki/Mario_Savio
15 Todd Gitlin, *Occupy Nation*. New York: It Press, 2012.
16 Ibid.

5 Fight the Power, A.K.A. the System: Choose Democracy Over Authoritarianism

1 Niebuhr, cited by Chris Hedges, "A Time for Sublime Madness," January 20, 2013, Truthdig, www.truthdig.com/report/item/a_time_for_sublime_madness_20130120
2 Chris Hedges, *Wages of Rebellion*. New York: Nation Books, 2016.
3 NTanya Lee and Steve Williams, "More than We Imagined: Activists' Assessments on the Moment and the Way Forward," Ear to the Ground report, May 2013, http://eartothegroundproject.org (emphasis added).
4 Noam Chomsky (edited by Carlos Otero), *Language and Politics*. Chico, CA: AK Press, 2004 (emphasis added).
5 "GREENPEACE," presentation by Zuha Ather, January 13, 2014, https://prezi.com/vhwoyorgqlfv/greenpeace/
6 NTanya Lee and Steve Williams, "More than We Imagined." Op. cit.
7 Amazon reviewer of Todd Gitlin, *The Twilight of Our Common Dreams: Why America is Wracked by Culture Wars*. New York: Holt reprint editions, 1996, www.amazon.com/Twilight-Common-Dreams-America-Wracked/dp/0805040919
8 André Gorz, *Ecology as Politics*. London: Pluto Press, 1983.

6 Win the Majority: It's Easier than You Think

1 Richard Flacks, *Making History*. New York: Columbia University Press, 1988.
2 Paulo Freire, *Pedagogy of the Oppressed*, 30th anniversary edition. London: Bloomsbury Academic, 2000.
3 Paul Hawken, *Blessed Unrest*. New York: Penguin, 2008.
4 NTanya Lee and Steve Williams, "More than We Imagined: Activists' Assessments on the Moment and the Way Forward," Ear to the Ground report, May 2013, http://eartothegroundproject.org
5 Howard Zinn, *A People's History of the United States*. New York: Harper Perennial, 2005.
6 Ibid.
7 Charles Derber, "Capitalism: Big Surprises in Recent Polls," *Common Dreams*, May 18, 2010, www.commondreams.org/views/2010/05/18/capitalism-big-surprises-recent-polls
8 Ibid.
9 Ibid.
10 Max Ehrenfreund, "A Majority of Millennials Now Reject Capitalism," *The Washington Post*, April 26, 2016, www.washingtonpost.com/news/wonk/wp/2016/04/26/a-majority-of-millennials-now-reject-capitalism-poll-shows/
11 Cited in Jonathan Freedland, "Welcome to the Age of Trump," *The Guardian*, May 19, 2016, www.theguardian.com/us-news/2016/may/19/welcome-to-the-age-of-trump
12 Stanley Feldman, cited in Jonathan Freedland, "Welcome to the Age of Trump." Op. cit.
13 Ibid.

14 Thomas Frank, *What's the Matter with Kansas?* New York: Henry Holt and Co., 2005. Arlie Russell Hochschild, *Strangers in Their Own Land*. New York: New Press, 2016.

15 Guy Molyneux, "Mapping the White Working Class," *The American Prospect*, Winter 2017, pp. 11–14.

16 Ibid.

7 Converge! Get Out of Your Silo

1 NTanya Lee and Steve Williams, "More than We Imagined: Activists' Assessments on the Moment and the Way Forward," Ear to the Ground report, May 2013, http://eartothegroundproject.org

2 Naomi Klein, "Reclaiming the Commons," *New Left Review* 9, May–June 2001, https://newleftreview.org/II/9/naomi-klein-reclaiming-the-commons

3 Occupy slogans cited in Todd Gitlin, *Occupy Nation*. New York: It Press, 2012.

4 Michelle Alexander, "Breaking My Silence," *The Nation*, September 4, 2013.

5 Ibid.

6 Ibid.

7 Ibid.

8 Paul Hawken, *Blessed Unrest*. New York: Penguin, 2008.

9 Richard Flacks, *Making History*. New York: Columbia University Press, 1988.

10 "Dr. King's—Bill of Economic and Social Rights," readable, www.allreadable.com/e7705MX1

11 "King Quotes on War and Peace," The Martin Luther King, Jr., Research and Education Institute, https://kinginstitute.stanford.edu/liberation-curriculum/classroom-resources/king-quotes-war-and-peace

12 Mychal Denzel Smith, "A Q&A with Alicia Garza, Co-Founder of #BlackLivesMatter," *The Nation*, March 24, 2015, www.thenation.com/article/qa-alicia-garza-co-founder-blacklivesmatter/

13 Fred Small, "Global Warming Is a Justice Issue," www.rateaquote.com/q/global-warming-is-justice-issue-its-justice-issue-because-global-warming-is-theft-theft-from-our-own-children-grand-children-their-right-to-fred-small-138764/ (emphasis added).

14 Naomi Klein, *This Changes Everything*. New York: Simon and Schuster, 2014. See also Suzanne Goldberg, "Naomi Klein: We Tried It Your Way and We Don't Have Another Decade to Waste," *The Guardian*, September 14, 2014, www.theguardian.com/books/2014/sep/14/naomi-klein-interview-capitalism-vs-the-climate

15 Steven Greenhouse, "What Unions Got Wrong," *The New York Times Sunday Review*, November 27, 2016, p. 2.

16 Ibid.

8 Democratize the World: Globalize and Localize

1 Jeremy Brecher and Tim Costello, *Global Village or Global Pillage*. Boston, MA: South End Press, 1999.

2 Pope Francis, Laudato Si. On Care for Our Common Home. Op.cit.

3 Ibid.

4 Ibid.

5 Ibid.

9 Pachamama: Protect Mother Earth

1 Karl Marx, cited in Jasmine Ali, "Marx's Ecology," Solidarity.net.au, December 3, 2009, www.solidarity.net.au/climate-change/marxs-ecology/

2 John Vidal, "Bolivia Enshrines Natural World's Rights with Equal Status for Mother Earth," *The Guardian*, April 10, 2011, www.theguardian.com/environment/2011/apr/10/bolivia-enshrines-natural-worlds-rights

3 Wikipedia, "Rights of Nature," https://en.wikipedia.org/wiki/Rights_of_Nature

4 Pope Francis, "Laudato Si: On Care for Our Common Home," *Our Sunday Visitor*, July 18, 2015.

5 "The Leap Manifesto: A Call for Canada Based on Caring for Nature and for One Another," https://leapmanifesto.org/en/the-leap-manifesto/ (emphasis in original).

6 John Vidal, "Bolivia Enshrines Natural World's Rights." Op. cit.

7 Boaventura de Sousa Santos, *Epistemologies of the South*. New York: Routledge, 2014.

8 "Mission & Vision," The Pachamama Alliance, www.pachamama.org/about/mission

9 Friedrich Engels, "Engels' Dialectics of Nature," Marxists Internet Archive, www.marxists.org/archive/marx/works/1883/don/ch09.htm

10 Michael Pollan, "The Food Movement, Rising," *The New York Review of Books*, May 20, 2010, http://michaelpollan.com/articles-archive/the-food-movement-rising/

11 Charles Derber, "Consumerism and Its Discontents," May 27, 2013, www.truth-out.org/opinion/item/16582-consumerism-and-its-discontents

10 Don't Just Say No: Say Yes to Alternatives

1 NTanya Lee and Steve Williams, "More than We Imagined: Activists' Assessments on the Moment and the Way Forward," Ear to the Ground report, May 2013, http://eartothegroundproject.org (emphasis added).

2 Gar Alperovitz, *What Then Must We Do?* White River Junction, VT: Chelsea Green Publishing, 2013. Juliet B. Schor, *True Wealth*. New York: Penguin Books, 2011.

3 Gar Alperovitz, cited in David Barsamian, "A New Economic Paradigm: An Interview with Gar Alperovitz," Truthout, May 15, 2012, www.truth-out.org/news/item/9144-a-new-economic-paradigm-an-interview-with-gar-alperowitz

4 Ibid.

5 Thomas Piketty, *Capital in the Twenty-First Century*. Cambridge, MA: Harvard University Press, 2014.

6 Ibid.

7 Piketty, quoted in Charles Derber, *The Disinherited Majority*. New York: Routledge, 2015.

8 Ibid.

9 Paulo Freire, *Pedagogy of Freedom*. Lanham, MD: Rowman & Littlefield, 2000.

11 Create Media of, by, and for the People: Moving Beyond Propaganda

1 Todd Gitlin, *Occupy Nation*. New York: It Press, 2012.

2 Ibid.

12 Let's Get Political: Movements and Elections

1 Naomi Klein, cited by Joshua Ostroff, "Leap Manifesto: 'The Future We Want Isn't On the Ballot'," Ecocide, http://ecocidealert.com/?p=14190
2 Paulo Freire, *Pedagogy of the Oppressed*, 30th anniversary edition. London: Bloomsbury Academic, 2000.
3 Black Lives Matter, "Statement on Political Affiliations," August 30, 2015, http://blacklivesmatter.com/blacklivesmatter-statement-on-political-affiliations/
4 Ibid.
5 "Sen. Bernie Sanders: 'We Need to Organize and Mobilize'," On Point, wbur, www.wbur.org/onpoint/2016/12/22/sen-bernie-sanders-organize
6 Ibid.

13 Think, Learn, and Teach: Education as Activism

1 bell hooks cited in Barry Burke, "bell hooks on Education," infed, http://infed.org/mobi/bell-hooks-on-education/
2 Henry Giroux, "Angela Davis, Education and the Meaning of Freedom," *The Huffington Post*, The Blog, April 10, 2013, www.huffingtonpost.com/henry-a-giroux/angela-davis_b_3055913.html
3 Paulo Freire, *Pedagogy of the Oppressed*, 30th anniversary edition. London: Bloomsbury Academic, 2000.
4 Ibid.
5 Henry Giroux, *Youth in a Suspect Society*. New York: Palgrave Macmillan, 2010.

14 Choose Life and Love: The Culture of Activism

1 NTanya Lee and Steve Williams, "More than We Imagined: Activists' Assessments on the Moment and the Way Forward," Ear to the Ground report, May 2013, http://eartothegroundproject.org (emphasis added).
2 Ibid. (emphasis added).
3 Ibid. (emphasis added).
4 Gene Sharp, "Quotes," www.goodreads.com/quotes/602475-by-placing-confidence-in-violent-means-one-has-chosen-the

Index

Note: Page numbers for illustrations appear in italics.

Welcome to
the Revolution

When the Women's March gathered millions just one day after Donald Trump's inauguration, a new era of progressive action was born. Organizing on the Far Right led to Trump's election, bringing authoritarianism and the specter of neo-fascism, and intensifying corporate capitalism's growing crises of inequality and injustices. Yet now we see a new universalizing resistance, growing out of prior decades of struggle against a militarized corporate state, among progressive and Left movements for truth, dignity, and a world based on democracy, equality, and sustainability.

Derber offers the first comprehensive guide to this new era and an original vision and strategy for movement success. He convincingly shows how only a new universalizing wave, a progressive and revolutionary "movement of movements," can counter the world-universalizing economic and cultural forces of intensifying corporate and Far Right power.

Derber explores the crises and eroding legitimacy of the globalized capitalist system and the right-wing movements that helped to create the Trump era. He shows how Left universalizing movements can—and must—converge to propel a mass base that can prevent societal, economic, or ecological collapse, stop a resurgent Right, and build a democratic social alternative. He describes tactics and strategies for this new progressive movement. Brief guest "interludes" by Medea Benjamin, Noam Chomsky, Ralph Nader, Bill Fletcher, Jr., Juliet B. Schor, Gar Alperovitz, Chuck Collins, Matt Nelson, Janet MacGillivray Wallace, and other prominent figures tell how to coalesce and universalize activism into a more powerful movement wave—at local, community, national, and international levels.

Vivid and highly accessible, this book is for activists, students, and all citizens concerned about the erosion of justice and democracy. It thoroughly illuminates the rationale, theory, practice, humanism, love, and joy of the social transformation that we urgently need.

This book, generously funded by the Wallace Action Fund, brings together nationally prominent activists to advise and to contribute ideas toward furthering a national movement.

A life-long activist and public speaker, **Charles Derber** is the author of 20 books and is Professor of Sociology at Boston College. He writes for and has been reviewed in *The New York Times*, *The Washington Post*, *The Boston Globe*, *Time*, *Newsweek*, *Newsday*, Truthout, and *The Christian Science Monitor*. He has made hundreds of radio and television appearances. His books have been translated into Chinese, Korean, Tamil, German, Portuguese, and Polish—and he is a best-selling author in South Korea; he has done extended book tours in German bookstores and blues coffee houses, and has lectured often in Italy. Derber is a public intellectual—shortlisted in 2006 by IPPY (Independent Publisher Book Awards) for best book in current affairs—who believes that serious ideas should be written in an accessible and entertaining style. His most recent books include *Bully Nation* (with Y. R. Magrass; 2016, University Press of Kansas); *Sociopathic Society: A People's Sociology of the United States* (2013, Routledge); and *The Disinherited Majority: Capital Questions—Piketty and Beyond* (2015, Routledge).